A GRAMMAR

OF

THE TAMIL LANGUAGE

A GRAMMAR

OF

THE TAMIL LANGUAGE

BY

C. T. E. RHENIUS

GYAN

Published by

Gyan Publishing House
5, Ansari Road
Daryaganj, New Delhi-110002
Phone: 011-47034999, 9811692060
E-mail: books@gyanbooks.com

Distribution Network
gyanbooks.com
India, USA, Canada, UK, Australia

ISBN: 978-81-212-2346-1 (PB)
First Published, 1836

2nd Impression 2024

Printed at: Gyan Press, Delhi.

A GRAMMAR OF THE TAMIL LANGUAGE
AUTHOR: C. T. E. RHENIUS

A GRAMMAR

OF

THE TAMIL LANGUAGE,

WITH

An Appendix.

BY

C. T. E. RHENIUS,

MISSIONARY, TINNEVELLY.

MADRAS:

PRINTED AT THE CHURCH MISSION PRESS.

1836.

CONTENTS.

Orthography.

Etymology.

Syntax.

Appendix.

Miscellania.

INTRODUCTION.

THE following Grammar of the Tamil language was composed several years ago. I had found the grammatical works, previously published, defective in various respects, especially in regard to Syntax; and originally purposed to publish only a Treatise on Tamil composition; but having been advised by various friends, to whom I submitted the manuscript, to add the other parts of Grammar, and thus form at once a complete work, I yielded to their advice.

In constructing the chapters on Orthography and Etymology, I have followed more the order of the native Grammars, than that of European languages, because I judged it expedient to introduce the student at once to the native manner of treating the subject; and to facilitate the study of the native Grammars themselves. I have, however, every where noticed the difference between the Tamil and the European languages, and in the Appendix given a translation of the English particles into Tamil, noticing various other differences between the English and Tamil idioms.

It is not the object of the above observation to detract any thing from the valuable works of Ziegenbalg, Beschius, and others. They did in their days what they could in Tamil literature, and we are greatly indebted to them for the degree of knowledge they have given us of the Tamil language. But they all have failed in giving us pure

Tamil; they have mixed vulgarisms with grammatical nicities, and left us in want of a regularly digested Syntax.

The present work will, I trust, supply these deficiencies. It is not a Grammar of the high, or rather the poetical, Tamil language; in order to study this, the learned Beschius' second work will still be necessary; but it is a grammar of the vernacular Tamil, as it is spoken and written by well bred Tamulians, yet so as to avoid the errors against grammar which are found among them. It steers between the high and vulgar Tamil, avoids the intricacies of the former, and the barbarism of the latter. The student will, however, find notices of both interspersed in the work for his information, which will be useful to him when he either reads the poetical works or hears the common talk of the illiterate.

The Tamulians have many classical books, and these are all in poetry. They are of two kinds; one is called இலக்கணநூல், which comprizes the Grammars, such as தொல்காப்பியம், நன்னூல், &c., and the other is called இலக்கியநூல், which comprizes books written according to the former, such as the Poems of திருவள்ளுவர், நாலடியார், &c.

Besides these two, there are other written books, both in prose and poetry, such as the விக்கிரமாதித்தன்புத்துமை; சிவவாக்கியர்பாட்டு, அகத்தியர்பாடல், &c., the authors of which are not known. And, lastly, there are translations into Tamil from the Sanscrit Puranas and other stories, such as திருவிளையாடற்புராணம், இராமாயணம், காந்தப்புராணம், பஞ்சதந்திரம், போசஇராசன்கதை, &c.

From the poetical writings, Tamil style and diction, as used in common life, cannot be learned; because they contain so many old Tamil words, which are not at all in use now, and so many terminations, and modes different from those in common conversation, that it is not at all intelligible, except after hearing the explanation of learned men; and even they cannot understand at once any poem written in that manner, without much difficulty. Those poetical writings contain indeed explanations in prose; and from them something more of Tamil style and diction may be attained; but they also differ much from the style used in civil life, and not unfrequently require another explanation to make them intelligible.

The poems of சிவவாக்கியர், அகத்தியர்பாடல், &c., are much of the same cast as the former; they contain also vulgar expressions; not at all approved by the learned, simply to fill up the metre.

As for the translations of stories from the Sanscrit, the idiom may certainly be learned from them to a considerable degree; but as the translators seem, mostly, to have been Bramins, they have left many Sanscrit words in them, and even followed in various instances the Sanscrit idiom; not to mention many Tamil vulgarisms, which they have embodied in their works.

In all the Tamil books there are other errors of various kinds, owing to the circumstance of their being all in manuscript. No two copies agree together.

The prose works of the learned Beschius have much of the same character. The Tamil idiom may, on the whole, be learned from them; but they contain vulgarisms. We can, on the whole, understand what he means, but in many instances it will be impossible to analyse the sentence without meeting with difficulties. The copyists, however, may perhaps be charged with a great part of these errors.

After what I have said, it will be asked, " How then shall we acquire the proper Tamil idiom ?" I answer, that it can only be acquired by the assistance of a learned Native, who knows the native grammars well, has had no practice in English and foreign compositions, possesses a clear and logically thinking intellect, and is no flatterer. With persons of this character I was early brought into connexion; and to this providential circumstance must be attributed whatever degree of critical knowledge I have obtained.

It will not be uninteresting to the reader to obtain some information about the history of the Tamil grammatical works, of which the நன்னூல் is the chief.

The Madura Province, including Tinnevelly, is confessedly the seat of the purest Tamil. Towards Madras it becomes mixed with the Teloogoo and other dialects. About 500 years ago when Pandiya Rajah was reigning at Madura, Agastier, the famous Muni of the Hindoos, lived; who, upon the desire of the king, wrote the first Grammar of the Tamil language; which was called அகத்தியநூல். He had twelve disciples whom he instructed in the language, one of them was Tolkapiyer, who appeared to be the most clever in acquiring it: Soon after, Tolkapiyer prepared another Grammatical work, of which the அகத்தியநூல் was the basis; and which was called தொல்காப்பியநூல். The former gradually sunk into oblivion, and is now lost, excepting the fragments contained in Tolkapiyer's work.

Some time after, when Sïyagangen Rajah reigned in Madura பவணந்திவித்துவான் (Pävänändi Vittuvän) a learned man of the Jaina Sect, abridged the Tolkapiya Nul; and called it நன்னூல். Of the 5 parts in which the Tolkapiyam was divided, (viz., எழுத்ததிகாரம், *i. e.*, the chapter of letters or Orthography; சொல்லதிகாரம், *i. e.*, the chapter of words, or Etymology; பொருளதிகாரம், *i. e.*, the chapter of matter; இயாப்பு (or செய்யுள்) *i. e.*, the chapter of Poetry; and அலங்கார அதிகாரம், *i. e.*, the chapter on Beauty, (or Rhetoric), and in which Pavanandi also divided his work, only the two first chapters have been preserved; the rest are lost; though they were afterwards supplied by other persons.

After him was a learned man of the சமணர், *i. e.*, the Jaina Sect, who wrote an explanation of the நன்னூல்.

About the same time arose a learned Sivapattikaren, named வயித்தியநாதபண்டாரம், and pretending to find errors in the text of the நன்னூல், wrote a grammatical work called இலக்கணவிளக்கம், *i. e.*, the light of rules, in which he changed some parts of the நன்னூல், and added others at his discretion, but retained the before-mentioned division in 5 parts.

About the year 1770, there was a poet in Tinnevelly, named சங்கரநமச்சிவாயப்புலவர். Upon the request of the Ootamallei Poligar (மருதப்பத்தேவன்) he wrote the நன்னூலுரை *i. e.*, an explanation of the text of the நன்னூலுரை made by Pavanandi.

This Sankaranama Sivaya Pullaver's master சாமிநாததம்பிரான் (Saminadatambiran) wrote a grammatical work, which he called இலக்கணக்கொத்து, *i. e.*, a collection of rules; wherein he treats especially on the Tamil declensions and conjugations.

About the same time, சிவஞானத்தம்பிரான், a learned Sanniyasi, wrote a work, in which he exposes the errors of the இலக்கணவிளக்கம், made by the above mentioned Vayittiyanada Pandaram. This work he called இலக்கணவிளக்கசூறாவளி, *i. e.*, the Blast or Strong Wind on the Light of Rules, with which he intended to extinquish the Light of Rules. He wrote also the சூத்திரவிருத்தி, in which he explains the Tolkapiyam; moreover, he undertook to examine and compare the former three works, viz., இலக்கணக்கொத்து, இலக்கணவிளக்கசூறாவளி, and சூத்திரவிருத்தி; made the needful extracts, and embodied them in the நன்னூல், prepared by Sankaranama Sivayam. The thus enriched நன்னூல் is now in use among the Tamulians, and held in high estimation as the best classical work. It is called நன்னூலுரை, *i. e.*, an exposition of the Nannul.

முத்துக்குமாரசுவாமியோதுவார், who studied with Saminada Tambiran, died in Tinnevelly in 1809. His chief disciple அம்பலவாணக்கவிராயர், is still living in the same place, with whom, among others, திருப்பாற்கடல்நாதன்கவிராசர், studied, who has since 14 years been a most valuable assistant to me.

To give the student an idea of Tamil style as exhibited in the Nannul, I shall at the end of the Appendix give a specimen of it, with an analysis, and a translations of it in plain Tamil and in English; which I recommend to his study after he is well acquainted with the other parts of the Grammar.

To God, the eternal and almighty Jehovah, and author of speech, be glory for ever and ever!

PALAMCOTTAH, Oct. 1834. } C. T. E. RHENIUS.

A

TAMIL GRAMMAR.

CHAPTER I.

ORTHOGRAPHY.

§ I.

Tamil Orthography treats of the form, names, sound, number, and division of letters; also of their transmutation, omission, and augmentation.

§ II.

1. The Tamil language has 30 simple letters; as follows:—

5 short vowels.	அ,	a,	as in America.
	இ,	i,	as in still.
	உ,	u,	as in full.
	எ,	e,	as in self, &c.
	ஒ,	o,	as in long.
7 long vowels.	ஆ,	a,	as in ah !
	ஈ or ஈ,	i, or ee,	as in reel.
	ஊ,	u,	as in rule.
	ஏ,	e,	as in they
	ஓ,	o,	as in sole.
	ஐ,	ey,	as in eye.
	ஔ,	ou,	as in foul.

18 mute consonants.

க்,	k,	as in king.
ங்,	ng,	as in long.
ச்,	s,	as in so.
ஞ்,	gn,	as in impugn.
ட்,	d,	pronounced hard.
ண்,	n,	do. do.
த்,	t,	as in duty.
ந்,	n,	as in no.
ப்,	b, and p.	
ம்,	m,	as in my.
ய்,	y,	as in yarn.
ர்,	r,	as in round.
ல்,	l,	as in lap.
வ்,	v,	as in vain.
ழ்,	a kind of rl.	
ள்,	l, pronounced hard.	
ற்,	r,	as in cry.
ன்,	n,	as in on.

There is a letter, ஃ or ஃ, called aitham, vulgarly, *akkuna,* nearly corresponding to the German *ch,* as in licht; but it seldom occurs in common language.

2. The vowels, when subjoined to consonants, lose their initial form; thus:

The short vowel அ, a

is inherent in every consonant, and is always understood, except where the mark ° shows that the consonant is to be pronounced mute,* thus க is ka, ச, sa, ஞ, gna, ட da, ண, na, &c. &c.

The long ஆ, a, is changed into ா and affixed thus: கா, ka, சா, sa, ஞா, gna, டா, da, &c., except ணா, and

---

* This mark however is seldom found in native writings.

ன, which receive the following form, ணா, nā, றா, rā, னா, nā.

The short இ, i, is changed into ி thus: கி, ki, சி, si, டி, di, ணி, ni, தி, ti, நி, ni, பி, bi, மி, mi, யி, yi, லி, li, வி, vi, ழி, rli, ளி, li, றி, ri, னி, ni.

The long ஈ, i or ee, is changed into ீ thus: கீ, kee, சீ, see, டீ, dee, ணீ, nee, தீ, tee, &c.

The short உ, ŭ, is changed into ு or ு, or ு, thus: கு, kŭ, சு, sŭ, டு, dŭ, ணு, nŭ, து, tŭ, நு, nŭ, பு, bŭ, மு, mŭ, யு, yŭ, ரு, rŭ, லு, lŭ, வு, vŭ, ழு, rlŭ, ளு, lŭ, று, rŭ, னு, nŭ.

The long ஊ, ū, or oo, is variously changed, mostly into ூ, or ூ, as: கூ, koo, சூ, soo, டூ, doo, ணூ, noo, தூ, too, நூ, noo, பூ, boo, மூ, moo, யூ, yoo, ரூ, roo, லூ, loo, வூ, voo, ழூ, rloo, ளூ, loo, றூ, roo, னூ, noo.

The short எ ĕ is changed into ெ, and prefixed to the consonant after which it is pronounced; as, கெ, kĕ, செ, sĕ, டெ, dĕ, ணெ, nĕ, தெ, tĕ, &c.

The long ஏ ē, is changed into ே, and is prefixed as the former; thus: கே, kē, சே, sē, டே dē, ணே, nē, தே, tē, &c.

The short ஒ ŏ, is changed into ெ-ா, the consonant being placed between them; as, கொ, kŏ, சொ, sŏ, டொ, dŏ, தொ, tŏ, &c. In ண, ற, and ன, the form is thus: ணொ, nŏ, றொ, rŏ, and னொ, nŏ.

The long ஓ ō, is changed into ே-ா, with the same exceptions as the former, thus, கோ, kō, சோ, sō, டோ, dō, தோ, tō, &c. ணோ, nō, றோ, rō, and னோ, nō.

The long vowel ஐ, ey, is changed into ை, and is likewise prefixed; as, கை, key, சை, sey, டை, dey, தை, tey, &c. except ண, ல, ள, and ன, with which

ன is united ; thus, னை, ney, லை, ley, ளை, ley, and ணை, ney.

The long vowel ஔ, is changed into ௌ, and the consonant put between ; as: கௌ, kou, சௌ, sou, டௌ, dou, &c., but it is usually written thus, கவு, kăvoo, *i. e.* kou, சவு, săvoo, *i. e.*, sou, &c. *

Hence the Tamil alphabet may be said to consist of 247 letters ; though the combined letters are more properly syllables than letters.

Besides these letters, three letters are sometimes borrowed from the Grantham or Samscrit, viz., ஷ sh, ஸ். s, and ஹ, h.— ஸ், is always mute. ஷ is used only with some vowels, as, ஷ sha, ஷா, sha ஷி shi. ஹ is not yet much in use ; but it is highly desirable that it should be more extensively adopted. The learned do not properly admit the use of these letters, and in words, borrowed from the Samscrit, change the ஷ and ஸ, when not mute, into ட ; and, when mute, into the same consonant with which they are connected ; thus for புருஷன், they write புருடன் *pŭrŭdĕn*, a man ; for வருஷம், வருடம் *vărŭdăm*, the year ; for கஷ்டம், கட்டம் *kăttăm*, distress, for நஷ்டம், நட்டம் *năd:ăm*, loss. The ஹ is expressed by க, as for வாஹனம் they write வாகனம் *vāgănăm*, a vehicle. But, in common language it is better to retain the Samscrit letter, to avoid ambiguity.

It is also to be observed that the ஸ is never used with a vowel, but is always mute except in the

---

* In the poetical Tamil and other native books, the distinction here observed between short *and* long vowels, is usually not marked ; both are written alike, as எ short and ஏ long ; கெ short and கே long ; ஒ short and ஓ long ; கொ short and கோ long, &c. ; likewise the small stroke at the foot of the ர r, is not observed, but written the same as the characteristic of long ஆ, viz. ா.

word இங்ஙனம் *ingngănăm*, this place ; and ஞ is used only with அ, ஆ, எ, and ஒ.

Here is a list of all the Letters.

அ	ஆ	இ	ஈ	உ	ஊ	எ	ஏ	ஐ	ஒ	ஓ	ஔ
க	கா	கி	கீ	கு	கூ	கெ	கே	கை	கொ	கோ	கௌ
ங											
ச	சா	சி	சீ	சு	சூ	செ	சே	சை	சொ	சோ	சௌ
ஞ	ஞா					ஞெ			ஞொ		
ட	டா	டி	டீ	டு	டூ	டெ	டே	டை	டொ	டோ	டௌ
ண	ணா	ணி	ணீ	ணு	ணூ	ணெ	ணே	ணை	ணொ	ணோ	ணௌ
த	தா	தி	தீ	து	தூ	தெ	தே	தை	தொ	தோ	தௌ
ந	நா	நி	நீ	நு	நூ	நெ	நே	நை	நொ	நோ	நௌ
ப	பா	பி	பீ	பு	பூ	பெ	பே	பை	பொ	போ	பௌ
ம	மா	மி	மீ	மு	மூ	மெ	மே	மை	மொ	மோ	மௌ
ய	யா	யி	யீ	யு	யூ	யெ	யே	யை	யொ	யோ	யௌ
ர	ரா	ரி	ரீ	ரு	ரூ	ரெ	ரே	ரை	ரொ	ரோ	ரௌ
ல	லா	லி	லீ	லு	லூ	லெ	லே	லை	லொ	லோ	லௌ
வ	வா	வி	வீ	வு	வூ	வெ	வே	வை	வொ	வோ	வௌ
ழ	ழா	ழி	ழீ	ழு	ழூ	ழெ	ழே	ழை	ழொ	ழோ	ழௌ
ள	ளா	ளி	ளீ	ளு	ளூ	ளெ	ளே	ளை	ளொ	ளோ	ளௌ
ற	றா	றி	றீ	று	றூ	றெ	றே	றை	றொ	றோ	றௌ
ன	னா	னி	னீ	னு	னூ	னெ	னே	னை	னொ	னோ	னௌ

§ III.

Besides the division into vowels, mute consonants, and combined vowel-consonants, the Tamil grammarians have divided the 18 consonants into six hard, six soft, and six middle letters.

The six hard sounding letters are called வல்லின எழுத்து, *i. e. vällinä ërlüttù;* they are க, ச, ட, த, ப, ற.

The six soft sounding letters are called மெல்லின எழுத்து, *i. e., mëllinä ërlüttü;* they are ங, ஞ, ண, ந, ம, ன.

The middle letters are called இடையினவெழுத்து, *i. e., ideyinä ërlüttü;* they are, ய, ர, ல, வ, ழ, ள.*

§ IV.

1. To express the names of the letters *nă* is added to every short letter, and *vĕnă* or *yĕnă* to the long; thus:

அ,	a,	is called ānă,	க,	kānă,	ச,	sāna,
இ,	i,	...... eenă,	கி,	keenă,	சி,	seena,
உ,	u,	...... oonă	கு,	koonă,	சு,	soona,
எ,	e,	...... ēnă,	கெ,	kēnă,	செ,	sēnă,
ஒ,	o,	...... ōnă,	கொ,	kōnă,	சொ,	sōnă,
ஆ,	ā,	...... āvĕnă,	கா,	kāvĕnă, &c.		
ஈ,	ee,	...... eeyĕnă,	கீ,	keeyĕnă, &c.		
ஊ,	oo,	...... oovĕnă,	கூ,	koovĕna, &c.		
ஏ,	ē,	...... ēyĕnă,	கே,	kēyĕnă, &c.		
ஐ,	ei,	...... eiyĕnă,	கை,	keiyĕna, &c.		
ஓ,	ō,	...... ōvĕnă,	கோ,	kōvĕna, &c.		
ஔ,	ou,	...... ouvĕnă,	கௌ,	kouvĕna, &c.		

* These artificial divisions are only of use when studying the native grammars; in which, to avoid repetition, they are frequently referred to.

But among the learned கரம் *gărăm* is usually added to every short letter, and காரம், *i. e., gārăm* to every long letter ; thus :

அ, ă, is called அகரம், *i. e.* ăgărăm.
க, kă, ... ககரம், *i. e.* kăgărăm.
இ, i, ... இகரம், *i. e.* igărăm.
கி, ki, ... கிகரம், *i. e.* kigărăm.
உ, ŭ, ... உகரம், *i. e.* ŭgărăm.
கு, kŭ, ... குகரம், *i. e.* kŭgărăm. &c., and
ஆ, ā, ... ஆகாரம், *i. e.* āgārăm.
கா, kā, ... காகாரம், *i. e.* kāgārăm.
ஈ, ee, ... ஈகாரம், *i. e.* eegārăm.
கீ, kee, ... கீகாரம், *i. e.* keegārăm. &c., and,

2. Again, a letter is called எழுத்து, *i. e., ěrlŭttŭ ;* a vowel is called உயிரெழுத்து, *i. e., ŭyirěrlŭttŭ,* which means the *letter of life,* because it gives, as it were, life to the consonant ; a consonant is called மெய்யெழுத்து, *i. e., meyěrlŭttŭ,* which means the *letter of the body ;* because the consonant is considered as the body of the vowel ; they call it also ஒற்றெழுத்து, *i. e., ŏttěrlŭttŭ,* which has the same meaning, and the vowel consonant is called உயிர்மெய்யெழுத்து, *i. e. ŭyirmeyyěrlŭttŭ,* which means *letter of body and life,* because it consists both of a vowel and a consonant. A short vowel is called குற்றுயிரெழுத்து or குறிலுயிரெழுத்து ; and a long vowel, நெட்டுயிரெழுத்து.

3. I would here observe, that the Tamulians in writing do not leave any space between the words, but connect all the words even of a whole discourse ; thus : மனிதர்கள்நல்லவர்களல்ல, *i. e., mănithěrgěl,* (men) *năllăvěrgěl,* (good) *ăllă,* (not.

This is difficult, particularly to beginners ; but exercise and acquaintance with the terminations of the several parts of speech make it more easy;—still it is highly desirable to introduce spaces, or some marks of separation between words.

§ V.

The pronunciation of the letters has been already pointed out in the table § II.

A few farther particulars remain to be noticed,

1. The short vowel அ, ă, before ர, ல, ள, and ன, at the end of polysyllabic words, is not exactly pronounced like ă mentioned in the alphabet, but somewhat like ĕ, as in men; thus:

அவர் *ăvĕr* they, not (avar.)
சொல்லல் *sŏllĕl*, a saying, not (sollal.)
மரங்கள் *mărăngĕl*, trees, not (marangal.)
அவன் *ăvĕn*, he, not (avan.)

2. The vowels இ, i, and எ, ĕ, receive a somewhat deeper sound than they have ordinarily, before ட, ண, ழ, ள, and ற, so that the இ, is sounded somewhat like the French u; or like the (ü) in the German word "Mühle;"—and the எ, like the French (eu), or like the (œ) in the German word "bœse;" thus:

வீடு, (a house,) pronounce *vüdŭ;* but வீதி, (street,) veethi.
பெண், (a woman,) pronounce *poen*, but பேசு, (speak,) *pēsŭ*.
கீழ், (under,) pronounce *kürl*.
தேள், (a scorpion,) pronounce *toel*.
பிறக்க, (to be born,) pronounce *pürăkkă*.

3. The vowel ஐ, ei, is in monosyllabic words pronounced like the diphthong ai, or ei; as:

கை, *kai*, the hand.
மை, *mai*, ink.

4. The letters, க, k, த, t, and ப, p, are at the beginning of a word pronounced hard, as in the table; but in the middle, when single, they are pronounced soft; viz., க, is sounded like the German *ch*, or like *g*, in God, with an aspirate, த like *th*, and ப like *b*, as:

கண், *the eye*, pronounce *kăn*; but பகல், the day, pronounce *păchĕl* or *păghĕl*.

தலை, *the head*, pronounce *tăley*, but பாதம், the foot, *pāthăm*.

பகை, *hatred*, pronounce, *păghei*; but அபாத்திரம், unworthiness, *ăbātthirăm*.

But if they occur double in the middle of a word, both are pronounced hard, as:

பக்கம், *the side*, pronounce *păkkăm*.

பத்திரம், *firmness*, pronounce *păttirăm*.

இருப்பு, *being*, pronounce *irŭppŭ*.

5. The letter ச, in the middle of a word, when single, is pronounced the same as in the beginning, viz. like s; but when double, it is pronounced like j, or rather dj; or as g, in rage; thus:

சபை, *congregation*, pronounce *săbey*.

பிரவேசம், *entrance*, pronounce *pirăvĕsăm*.

but இராச்சியம், *kingdom*, pronounce *irājiyăm*.

Again, சச, after ழ or ர, is pronounced harder than j, nearly like the *ch*, in breach, as:

புகழ்ச்சி, *praise*, pronounce *pŭghărchi*.

தொடர்ச்சி, *succession*, pronounce *tŏdărchi*.

The same hard sound is given also to ச after ட், or ற், as:

மாட்சிமை, *excellence*, pronounce *mātchimey*.

முயற்சி, *exercise*, pronounce *mŭyărtchi*.

6. The difference of sound between, ங, ஞ, ண, ந, and ன, is so nice, that it can only be learned from the mouth of a native. Observe, that when they

are mute, the following letters follow them, as being most congenial to their sound, viz.

ங, is followed by க.
ஞ, ... ச.
ண, ... ட.
ந, ... த.
ன, ... ற.
also ம, ... ப.

Thus : சங்கம், *assembly*, pronounce *săngăm*.
மஞ்சள், *yellow*, ,, *mănjĕl*.
கண்டம், *a part*, ,, *kăndăm*.
சாந்தம், *meekness*, ,, *sānthăm*.
ஒன்று, *one*, ,, *ŏnrŭ*.
அம்பு, *an arrow*, ,, *ămbŭ*.

7. The difference of pronunciation between ர், ழ், and ற். and between ல், and ள், must likewise be learned from the mouth of a Tamulian. For ழ், we have no proper sound in English or any other European language; it is a mixture of *r* and *l*, and imperceptibly coalescing by turning the tongue upward to the roof of the month. Many of the common people, and nearly all in the southern parts of India, pronounce it erroneously like, ள், l. But the difference between the two is material, and ought to be strictly observed; for அழி, means *destroy*, but அளி, *give*.—ர I would call a soft or single *r*; but ற், a hard, or double one; so also ல், is pronounced softly, but, ள், strongly : *f. i.*

பேர், name, pronounce pēr.
பேறு, birth, ,, poerŭ.
வேலை, work, ,, vēley.
வேளை, time, ,, vœllei.

8. A double ற்ற, is not pronounced like *rr*, but like tr; though the r is sounded rather softly and quickly; thus:

குற்றம், *guilt*, pronounce *kŭtrăm*.
பெற்று, *received* „ *pœtrŭ*, &c.

But the common people usually pronounce it like tt, as, *kŭttăm*, *pœttŭ*.

9. ன்ற, is pronounced *dra*, as,
என்றான், *he said*, pronounce *ĕndrān*.

But many pronounce it *nda*, viz., *ĕndān*. Thus also, சென்று, proceeding, *sĕndrŭ*, vulgarly; *sĕndŭ*.

10. Double ட்ட, is pronounced like *tt*, as,
கேட்டேன், *I heard*, pronounce *kōĕttēn*.

11. A mute ய், either at the end or in the middle of a word, is pronounced like *ĭ* or *y*, as,

மெய், *truth*, pronounce *mei*, or *mey*.
செய்தாள், *she did*, pronounce *sĕithāl*, or *seythāl*.

12. The pronunciation of a long vowel or double consonant, requires twice the time necessary for a short vowel or single consonant. The natives call the length of time for the pronounciation of a short vowel, or of a single consonant, மாத்திரை, *māttĥĭrei*, *i. e.*, a measure, which they define by a single twinkling of the eye, or a snap of the fingers; accordingly, a long vowel or a double consonant requires two such measures. A strict observance of this rule is of importance, as a neglect of it will produce misunderstanding; thus,

பதம், *păthăm*, means *a word*; but,
பாதம், *pāthăm* —— *a foot*.

13. Every long vowel, or every compound syllable, by which I mean a syllable composed of two consonants and a vowel, has naturally a particular emphasis or accent. Thus in காது, *kāthŭ*, the ear; the syllable கா has the stress; in சொல்லுகிறேன்,

sŏllŭgirēn, I say, the syllables சொல் and றேன் have the stress.

Besides this natural emphasis, Tamil syllables have no accent. In words consisting of two or more short syllables, every such syllable is pronounced alike.

Samscrit words of three syllables are often written in Tamil with four syllables; *e. g.*, அவச்யம், is written அவசியம்; in this case the emphasis of the Samscrit is retained; thus, pronounce, *ăvăsĭyăm.*

§ VI.

The transmutation of letters takes place when two words are joined together, and affects the last letter of the preceding word and the first letter of the following word. The transmutation of letters is called திரிதல், *tirithĕl.* It is done in the following cases.

1. When the preceeding word ends in a mute consonant, and the next begins with a vowel, that vowel is dropped, and its characteristic mark is joined to the mute consonant; thus:

அவன் இல்லை, is written அவனில்லை, *he is not.*
கோபம் உள்ள, ——— கோபமுள்ள, *angry.*

2. When ம் is followed by க, the ம் is changed into ங்.
ச் .... ஞ்,
த் .... ந்,

as, செயம்கொண்டான் is written செயங்கொண்டான், *he conquered.*

பாவம்செய்தான், is written பாவஞ்செய்தான், *he sinned.*

புத்தகம்தந்தான், is written புத்தகந்தந்தான், *he gave a book.*

3. When ல் is followed by க, ச, or ப, the ல், is changed into ற்.*

Thus: பால்கல், *gravel stone,* is written பாற்கல்.

பதில்சொல், *a word in return,* is written பதிற் சொல்.

முழங்கால்படியிட்டான், *he kneeled down,* முழங் காற்படியிட்டான்.

But when ல் is followed by த், both are changed into ற், as:

பதில்தந்தான், *he made a return,* பதிற்றந்தான்.

கடல்திரை, *the sea shore,* கடற்றிரை.

And if the word ending in ல் is a monosyllable, the ல் before த் is changed into ஃ, and the த் into ற், as:

கல்தீது, *the stone is bad;* கஃறீது.

அல்திணை, *the neuter gender,* அஃறிணை.

Again, if a monosyllable ending in ல், is followed by ம், the former is changed into ன், as: கல்மலை, *a rock,* கன்மலை. And if it be followed by ந், then ந் also is changed into ன், as:

கல்நெஞ்சு, *a heart of stone,* கன்னெஞ்சு.

4. When ள் is followed by க, ச, or ப, the ள is changed into ட், as:

ஒருநாள்பிரயாணம், *a day's journey,* ஒருநாட்பிர யாணம்.

திருநாள்கடன், *the duty of a holy day,* திருநாட் கடன்.

உள்புறம், *the inside,* உட்புறம்.

பலநாள்செய்தி, *the news of several days,* பலநாட் செய்தி.

---

* The custom of not changing ல் into ற், but doubling the following letters க, ச, த, ப, is not authorized by the native grammars, *e. g.,* பால்க்கல், பதில்ச்சொல், &c., and ought to be abandoned, as there is no particular difficulty in adhering to the proper rule, excepting perhaps when ல் is followed by த்.

When ள் is followed by த, both are changed into double or single ட், as:

> கள்தந்தான், *he gave tody*, கட்டந்தான்.
> நாள்தோறும், *daily*, நாடோறும்.
> அவள்தாய், *her mother*, அவடாய்.
> தாள்தாமரை, *a lotos-like foot*, தாட்டாமரை.

But if the word ending in ள் be a monosyllable, the ள், is changed before த் into ஃ and த் into ட், as:

> முள்தீது *the thorn is bad*, முஃடீது.

Again, if ள் is followed by ம், that is changed into ண், as:

> முள்முடி *a crown of thorns*, முண்முடி,
> முள்முறிந்தது, *the thorn is broken*, முண்முறிந்தது.

And if it be followed by ந், the ந் also is changed into ண, as: முள்நிலம், *a thorny ground*, முண்ணிலம்.

5 When ண் is followed by க, ச, or ப, the ண் is changed into ட், as:

> பயிரின்கண்கிள்ளை, *the parrot of the field*, பயிரின்கட்கிள்ளை.
> இளமைக்கண்செல்வம், *prosperity in youth*, இளமைக்கட்செல்வம்.
> மண்பாத்திரம், *an earthen vessel*, மட்பாத்திரம்.

And when it is followed by த், the latter is changed into ட், as:

> கண்திறந்தான், *he opened the eyes*, கண்டிறந்தான்.
> மண்தலம், *the earth*, மண்டலம்.

But if the word ending in ண் be in the oblique case, then both the ண் and த் are changed into ட், as:

> கடலின்கண்திரை, *the sea shore*, கடலின்கட்டிரை.

Again, when ண், in monosyllabic words, is followed by ந், the ந் is changed into ண், as:

> கண்நெடிது, *the eye is long*, கண்ணெடிது.

கண்நீர், tears, கண்ணீர்.
கண்நோவு, eye pain, கண்ணோவு.

6. When ன் is followed by க, ச, or ப, the ன் is changed into, ற், as:

பொன்கம்பி, a golden wire, பொற்கம்பி.
பொன்சிலை, a golden image, பொற்சிலை.
பொன்பாத்திரம், a golden vessel, பொற்பாத்திரம்.

And if it be followed by த, the latter is changed into ற, as:

பலன்தந்தான், he gave reward, பலன்றந்தான்.

But if the word ending in ன் be in the oblique case, then both the ன் and the த are changed into ற, as:

பொன்தகடு, a golden plate, பொற்றகடு.

Again, if a monosyllabic word ending in ன், is followed by ந, the ந changes into ன், as:

மின்நெடிது, the lightening is long or extended, மின்னெடிது.
முன்நிலை, something that stands before, முன்னிலை.

7. Certain words ending in உ, when they are united with some other words, as adjectives, change the உ into ஐ, and in some cases change the preceding soft into a hard letter also, as:

ஆண்டு, a year, மூவாண்டைநெல்லு, rice three years old.
பண்டு, ancient, பண்டைச்செய்தி, old news.
அன்று, former time, அன்றைப்பாடு, former trouble.
அன்று, former time, அற்றைக்கூலி, former wages.
இன்று, present day, இன்றைத்தினம், this day.
இன்று, present day, இற்றைநாள், this day.
மற்று, other, மற்றைக்காலம், another time.

The same change takes place, when personal nouns are formed of them, as:

From ஆண்டு, *year,* ஈராட்டையான், *a boy two years old.*

மற்று, *other,* மற்றையவர், *other persons.*

§ VII.

The omission of letters is called கெடுதல், and takes place in the following cases.

1. With the exception of words containing two shorts syllables, such as எகு, பசு, நடு, &c., which kind of words the Tamil Grammarians call தனிக் குறில்முற்றியலுகரம், all other words, ending in உ, drop this vowel when another vowel follows, and take the vowel of the following word, thus:

காடு அலர்ந்தது, is written காடலர்ந்தது, *the desert flourished.*

வண்டு இமிர்ந்தது, is written வண்டிமிர்ந்தது, *the wasp made a noise.*

தெளிவு அரிது, is written தெளிவரிது, *clearness is difficult.*

வந்து இருக்கிறான், is written வந்திருக்கிறான், *he is come.*

காது உள்ளவன், is written காதுள்ளவன், *one that has ears.*

போதிப்பு இனிமை, is written போதிப்பினிமை, *instruction is sweet.*

மாடு ஓடிற்று, is written மாடோடிற்று, *the ox ran off.*

ஆடு ஐந்து, is written ஆடைந்து, *five sheep.*

2. When a polysyllabic word, ending in ண், or ன், or a long monosyllabic word ending in the same

letters, is followed by ந, the ந, is dropped, or rather is absorbed in the ண் or ன், thus:

கவண்நெடிது, is written கவணெடிது, *the sling is long.*

கலன் நெடிது, is written கலனெடிது, *the boat is long.*

மாண் நெறி, is written மாணெறி, *the excellent way.*

கான் நெறி, is written கானெறி, *the desert road.*

3. When a polysyllabic word, or a long monosyllabic word ending in ல், is followed by ந், or any other of the letters called மெல்லினம், the ல is changed into ன, as before stated, and the ந is dropped, as:

விரல்நீளம், *the length of a finger,* விரனீளம்.

நூல்நுனி, *the end of a thread,* நூனுனி.

விரல்நீண்டது, *the finger is lengthened* விரனீண்டது.

4. When words of the same description, ending in ள், are followed by ந், &c., the ள் is changed into ண், and the ந் is dropped, as:

இருள்நிலம், *a dark place,* இருணிலம்.

இருள்நீண்டது, *the darkness has extended,* இருணீண்டது.

5. When a word ending in ம் is followed by another beginning with ம் or ந, the ம of the former word is dropped, as:

காரியம்நடந்தது, *the business proceeded,* காரியநடந்தது.

மிருகமும்மாண்டது, *the beast also perished,* மிருகமுமாண்டது.

§ VIII.

The augmentation of letters, called மிகல், takes place in the following cases:

1. If the preceding word end in அ, ஆ, உ, ஊ, ஒ,

ஓ, or ஔ, and be followed by a word beginning with any vowel, the letter வ is inserted between both; with the exception of such words ending in உ, as have been mentioned in the former § No. 1, thus:

அல்லஎன்றான், *he said no*, is written அல்லவென்றான்.

குல்லாஇனுடைய, *of the cap*, குல்லாவினுடைய

கடுஉண்டான், *he took poison*, கடுவுண்டான்,

நடுஇலே, *in the midst*, is written நடுவிலே.

பூஎடுத்தான், *he took a flower*, is written, பூவெடுத்தான்.

However, அது, *that*, and இது, *this*, may follow either this rule or the rule § VII. No. 1, as:

அதுஎன்ன, *what is that?* may be written அதுவென்ன or அதென்ன.

These words are written also with an ஃ, thus: அஃது, இஃது, &c., and then the connecting letter வ is not required.

2. When the preceding word ending in இ, ஈ, எ, ஏ, or ஐ, is followed by another word beginning with a vowel, ய is inserted. This ய and the preceding வ, are called புணரெழுத்து, *i. e.*, connective letter, thus:

மணிஅது, is written மணியது, *of the pearl*,

தீஆடிற்று, is written தீயாடிற்று, *the fire blazed*.

சொல்லேஅல்லது, is written சொல்லேயல்லது, *either a word*.

கைஇல், is written கையில், *in the hand*.*

3. When monosyllabic words, ending in ஐ or ய், are followed by words beginning with ம், or any other மெல்லினம், the latter may be doubled, thus:

கை மாறினது, may be written, கைம்மாறினது, *that which has been exchanged*.

---

* In a very few cases வ follows எ or ஏ, instead of ய, as, வே-அ is வேவ, *to burn*.

கைநீண்டது, is written கைந்நீண்டது, *the hand was long.*

மெய்மறைந்தது, is written மெய்ம்மறைந்தது, *the truth was hid.*

மெய்நிலை, is written மெய்ந்நிலை, *true firmness.*

They may also be written without doubling the ம, which indeed is more common.

4. When a short monosyllabic word, ending in a consonant, ர, and ழ excepted, is followed by a vowel, the consonant is doubled, as:

கண்ஆசை, is written கண்ணாசை, *the lust of the eye.*

என்ஆசை, is written என்னாசை, *my desire.*

மெய்ஆசை, is written மெய்யாசை, *true desire.*

கல்அழகு, is written கல்லழகு, *the stone is beautiful.*

மண் உடைய is written மண்ணுடைய, *of the earth.*

5. The four letters க, ச, த, ப, at the beginning of the following words, are very frequently doubled. Many of the cases, however, in which their augmentation is required, depend so much upon custom, that it is impossible to define them all by rules. The principle cases are these:

i. When the preceding word ends in அ, in the following instances, namely, after the infinitive mode, after the indeclinable pronouns, அந்த, *that,* இந்த, *this,* எந்த, *which?* after போல, *like,* மற்ற, *other,* அல்ல *no,* and after some nouns which have dropped the last letter ம, and end therefore in அ, the duplication takes place, as:

வரக்கட்டளையிட்டார், *he commanded to come.*

போகச்சொன்னான், *he told to go.*

சொல்லப்போனான், *he went to tell.*

அந்தக்கனி, *that fruit.*
இந்தத்தலை, *this head.*
எந்தப்புத்தகம், *what book?*
என்னைப்போலக்கொடுத்தான், *he gave like me.*
மற்றச்சனங்கள், *other people.*
அப்படியல்லக்கொடு, *not so, give!*
நியாயத்தீர்ப்பு, *equitable judgment.*
மரக்கொம்பு, *the branch of a tree.*
பயப்படல், *fearing, &c.*

ii. After any long vowel, க, ச, த, ப are doubled, as:

நாக்கிழிந்தது, *the tongue split.*
மிடாத்தகர்ந்தது, *the pot broke.*
ஈச்செத்தது, *the fly died.*
தீப்பற்றிற்று, *the fire kindled.*
பூப்பூத்தது, *the flower blossomed.*

Exceptions are நீ thou, the 3d person plural neuter of the negative verb, and some words derived from the Samscrit, thus:

நீசொன்னாய், *thou hast said.*
அவைவாராபின்பு, *they (the things) will not come; afterwards.*
மகாசந்தோஷம், *great joy, &c.*

iii. After words ending in இ; namely, after the verbal participle terminating in இ, after இனி, தனி, இப்படி, அப்படி, எப்படி, and after many nouns ending in இ, and standing in the oblique case, க, ச, த, ப, are doubled, as:

சொல்லிக்காண்பித்தான், *saying, he showed.*
போற்றிச்சொன்னான், *praising, he said.*
நாளன்றிப்போனான், *he went another day.*
இனிச்செய்வேன், *I shall do hereafter.*

> தனிப்பிரயாணம், *a solitary journey.*
> இப்படித்தந்தான், *he gave thus.*
> அப்படிப்போனான், *he went so, or that way.*
> எப்படிச்சொல்லுகிறாய், *how doest thou say?*
> கிளிக்கால், *the foot of a parrot.*
> புலித்தோல், *the skin of a tiger.*
> அத்திப்பழம், *a fig.*

Exceptions are nouns ending in இ, which denote men, and a few other nouns, as:

> தம்பிகை, *the hand of the younger brother.*
> தபசிசரீரம், *the body of a devotee.*
> கத்திதேய்த்தான், *he whetted the knife.*
> புத்திசொன்னான், *he exhorted.*
> செட்டிபோனான், *the merchant went.*

iv. After words ending in உ, namely, after such as have the last consonant double, which includes many verbal participles, and the dative case; after words of two short syllables, excepting the pronouns அது, இது, and எது, and the numbers ஒரு, இரு; after words ending in ட்பு, ட்கு, ற்கு, and after nouns ending in உ, standing in the oblique case, க, ச, த, ப, are doubled, as:

> கடுப்புக்கடிது, *the pain is acute.*
> அச்சுப்பெரிது, *the axletree is large.*
> வயிற்றுக்கடுப்பு, *pain in the stomach,*
> ஆட்டுக்குட்டி, *a lamb.*
> முகத்துச்சாயல், *likeness of the face.*
> மருந்துப்பை, *a bag of medicines.*
> அழைத்துத்தந்தான், *he called and gave.*
> பெற்றுக்கொண்டான், *he received.*
> எனக்குக்கொடுத்தான், *he gave to me.*
> மலைக்குப்போ, *go to the mountain.*
> புதுச்சுவாமி, *a new god.*

பொதுச்சொல், a common word.
மறுத்தொடைத்தான், he wiped off the spot.*
குருப்படிப்பித்தார், the priest taught.
திருப்பாதம், the sacred foot.
நட்புக்கொண்டான், he became friendly.
பட்டினத்திற்குப்போனான், he went to the city.
குரங்குத்தலை, the head of a monkey.
வண்டுச்சிறகு, the wing of a wasp.
பாம்புப்படம், the head of a cobra.

v. After words ending in ஐ, namely, after the second or accusative case; after இல்லை; after some nouns, ending in ஐ, standing in the oblique case; and after some nouns which unite with verbs to form other verbs; க, ச, த, ப are doubled, as:

அதைக்கண்டேன், I saw it.
அவனைப்போல, like him.
இல்லைக்கொடு, no! give!
முருங்கைக்காய், a certain vegetable.
இலந்தைக்காய், a certain vegetable.
மலைப்பக்கம், the side of the mountain.
ஆசைப்பட்டார்கள், they desired.
மகிமைப்படுத்தினர், he glorified.

Exceptions are எல்லை and மட்டை; after which those letters are not doubled, thus:

எல்லைகடந்தான் he passed the boundary.
மட்டைசீவினன், he scraped the branch.

vi. After the verbal participles போய் and ஆய், and after nouns ending in ய், ர, or, ழ, standing adjectively, க, ச, த, ப are doubled, as:

---

* But when மறு means மற்ற, *another*, the duplication does not take place, as:
மறுகறிகொண்டுவா, *bring another curry.*
மறுபிழைப்பில்லை, *there is no other livelihood.*

போய்ச்சொன்ஞன், *he went and said.*
சத்தியமாய்ப்பேசிஞன், *he spoke truly.*
பொய்ச்செல்வம், *false riches.*
கார்ப்பருவம், *ripeness of the field in August and September.*
பாழுக்கொல்லை, *a garden lying waste.*

A few words ending in ய், ர், or, ழ், when in the oblique case, have the following க, ச, த, ப doubled or before க், ங் inserted, as:

வெய்க்குறை, *diminution or fault of the bamboo.*
வேர்க்குறை, *diminution of the root.*
காழ்க்குறை, *diminution of the hardness of the inside of a tree.*
வெய்ங்குழல், *a flute of bamboo.*
ஆர்ங்கோடு, *the branch of the Aar-tree.*
பாழ்ங்கிணறு, *an empty well.*

§ IX.

Some words are variously changed, of which are,

1. சில *some*, and பல *many, several:*—When they are written twice to denote variety, they may be joined together without any change; or the first letter of the second word may be doubled; or the last vowel of the first word, viz., அ, may be dropt, and the remaining ல be changed into ற், as:

சிலசில, *some*, பலபல *several.*
சிலச்சில, *some*, பலப்பல *several.*
சிற்சில, *some*, பற்பல, *several.*

Again, when சில, or பல, unites with another word, the terminating vowel அ, may either remain or be dropped, and then the regular changes must be made in either case, as:

பலகலை, *many rules*, சிலகலை, *some rules.*

பற்கலை, *many rules,* சிற்கலை, *some rules.*
பலநாள், *many days,* சிலநாள், *some days.*
பன்னாள், *many days,* சின்னாள், *some days.*
பலமணி, *many grains,* சிலமணி, *some grains.*
பன்மணி, *many grains* சின்மணி, *some grains.*
பலவணி, *many rows,* சிலவணி, *some rows.*
பல்லணி, *many rows,* சில்லணி, *some rows.*
பலதொடை, *many concatenations,* சிலதொடை, *some concatenations.*
பஃறொடை, *many concatenations,* சிஃறொடை, *some concatenations.*

2. The word தமிழ், *Tamil,* may be used either with the mute ழ், or with an additional அ, when it is joined to words beginning with letters of the வல்லினம் class, as:

தமிழ்ச்சொல் or தமிழச்சொல், *a Tamil word.*
தமிழ்க்கூத்து, or தமிழக்கூத்து, *a Tamil play.*

3. The word தேன், *honey,* may be united with other words without any change, as:

தேன்கடிது, *the honey is thick,*

or the following various changes may be made with it, as:

தேன்குடம், is written தேக்குடம், or தேங்குடம், *a honey vessel.*
தேன்கடிது, is written தேக்கடிது, or தேங்கடிது, *the honey is thick.*
தேன்மொழி, is written தேமொழி, *a sweet word.*
தேன்மாண்டது, is written தேமாண்டது, *the honey is spoiled.*

4. The words தன், *his,* and என், *my,* may be united to words beginning with a letter of the வல்லினம்

class, without any change, or the ன் may be changed into ற், as:

> தன்பகை, or தற்பகை, *his own hatred*, namely, *self-hatred.*
> தன்பொருள், or தற்பொருள், *self-interest.*
> என்பகை, or எற்பகை, *my hatred.*

5. The words ஊன், *marrow*, and குயின் *a cloud*, never suffer a change in the last letter, though the first letter of the following word may, as:

> ஊன்கடுமை, *the hardness of the marrow.*
> ஊன்றீமை, *the badness of the marrow.*
> குயின்குழாம், *a collection of clouds.*
> குயின்றிரள், *a collection of clouds.*

6. Besides the above, the Tamil Grammarians enumerate nine kinds of changes which some words undergo, not by rule, but by custom. They are these, as:

i. A மெல்லினம் letter is sometimes changed into a வல்லினம் letter which they call வலித்தல், *i. e., hardening*, as:

> வாய்ந்தது, becomes, வாய்த்தது, *it is fair or good.*

ii. A வல்லினம் letter is changed into a மெல்லினம் letter; which they call, மெலித்தல், *i. e., softening*, as:

> தட்டை *a bamboo stick* தண்டையினக்கிளிகடிவாள் *she drives the various parrots with a bomboo stick.*

iii. A short vowel becomes long, which they call நீட்டல், *i. e., lengthening*, as:

> நிழல், *shadow, becomes* நீழல்.

iv. A long vowel is made short, which they call குறுக்கல், *i. e., shortening*, as:

for பாதம் *a foot*, பதம்.

v. A syllable is contracted, which they call தொகுத்தல், that is, *contracting*, as:

for வேண்டாதார், *they say*, வேண்டார், *persons who have no desire.*

vi. A syllable is extended, which they call விரித்தல், that is, *extending*, as:

for தண்டுறை, they say, தண்ணந்துறை, *i. e.*, குளிர்ச்சிபொருந்திய அழகானகரை, *a cool beautiful shore.*

vii. The first syllable of a word is omitted, which they call முதற்குறைத்தல், or தலைக்குறைத்தல், *i. e., shortening the first*, as:

for தாமரை, they say மரை, a *tumarey* or *lotus flower.*

viii. The last syllable of a word is omitted, which is called கடைக்குறைத்தல், *i. e., shortening the last*, as:

for நீலம், *blue colour*, நீல்.

ix. The middle syllable is omitted, which they call இடைக்குறைத்தல், *i. e., shortening the middle*, as:

for யாவர், *who?* யார்.

7 When two Samscrit words are united, they are often used in Tamil with the same changes that they undergo in Samscrit.

i. If a final அ, be followed by a word commencing with an அ, or ஆ, the two vowels coalesce into ஆ.

வேதஆகமம், is written வேதாகமம், *a book of the Ved.*

பஞ்ச அங்கம், is written பஞ்சாங்கம், *the calendar.*
பாத அரவிந்தம், is written பாதாரவிந்தம், *the lotus-flower-like foot.*
குள ஆம்பல், is written குளாம்பல், *a water flower.*
விக்கிரக ஆராதனை, is written விக்கிரகாராதனை, *idolatry.*

ii. If the following word commences with இ or ஈ, the vowels coalesce into ஏ; if with உ, into ஓ, as:

சுர இந்திரன், is written சுரேந்திரன், *the Indiren of the Gods.*
சீத இந்து, is written சீதேந்து, *the cold moon.*
கமல உற்பவி, is written கமலோற்பவி, *one born of the Tamarey, i. e., Sarasvadi.*
மகா உதரம், is written மகோதரம், *the palsy.*
சக உதரம், is written சகோதரம், *brothership.*
சுத்த உதகம், is written சுத்தோதகம், *clear water.*
சூரிய உதயம், is written சூரியோதயம், *the rising of the sun.*
மகா உன்னதம், is written மகோன்னதம், *very great.*

iii. To express multitude or great variety some nouns are written twice; in which case the last consonant of the first word is dropped, the remaining vowel changed into ஆ; and the வல்லினம் letter of the following word united without doubling it, as:

காலாகாலம், *many* or *various times.*
தேசாதேசம், *many* or *various countries.*
குலாகுலம், *many* or *various castes.*
கோடாகோடி, *many millions.*

Observe, however, that these three kinds of changes are not authorized by Tamil Grammarians; the words should be written according to the rules formerly laid down, thus:

Instead of வேதாகமம், it should be வேதவாகமம்; and for பஞ்சாங்கம், it should be பஞ்சவங்கம், &c.

And instead of doubling the words to denote multitude, as in iii. பலபல or தோறும் should be used, as;

for காலாகாலம், should be பலகாலம், or பலபல காலம், or காலங்கள்தோறும்;
for தேசாதேசம், should be பலதேசம், or தேசங்கள்தோறும், &c.

8. Besides the regular changes of letters, the Tamil Poets have indulged themselves in changing, adding, or omitting letters and even transposing syllables, to suit their purpose. It will be sufficient to notice a few instances, simply for the information of the student, as:

For இன்முன் *the fore part of a house*, some have written முன்றில்.
— பின், *after*, பின்றை.
— கோவில், *temple*, கோயில்.
— பொதுவில், *a common house*, பொதியில்.
— அருமருந்தன்னான், *one like the nectar of the Gods*, அருமந்தான்.
— கிழங்கன்னபழஞ்சோறு, *old rice which is left*, கிழங்கம்பழஞ்சோறு.
— சோழநாடு, *the Sola country*, சோணாடு, the same as சோரமண்டலம், *Coromandal*.
— பாண்டியநாடு, *the Pandia country*, பாண்டிநாடு.
— மலையமாநாடு, *the Malayala country*, மலாடு.

For தஞ்சாவூர், *Tanshour*, தஞ்சை.
— பனையூர், *Paneiyoor*, பனசை.
— சேந்தன்மங்கலம், *Sendamangalam*, சேந்தை.
— ஆற்றூர், *Attoor*, ஆறை.
— ஆதன்றந்தை, *the father of Aden*, ஆந்தை.
— பூதன்றந்தை, do. *Pooden*, பூந்தை.
— வடுகன்றந்தை, do. *Vadugen*, வடுகந்தை.
— என்றந்தை, *my father*, எந்தை.
— நுந்தந்தை, *thy father*, நுந்தை.

§ X.

In conclusion I add a list of the changes of letters, to present them to the student at one view; the first letter being the last of the preceding word, and the second letter the first of the following word, viz.

*	ம்க	is changed into	ங்க.
*	ம்ச	....	ஞ்ச.
*	ம்த	....	ந்த.
	ம்ம	....	ம.
	ம்ந	....	ந.
*	ல்க	....	ற்க.
*	ல்ச	....	ற்ச.
*	ல்ப	....	ற்ப.
	ல்த	....	ற்ற, or ஃற.
	ல்ம	....	ன்ம.
	ல்ந	....	ன்ன, or ன.
	ள்க	....	ட்க.
	ள்ச	....	ட்ச
	ள்ப	....	ட்ப.
	ள்த	....	ட்ட, or ட or ஃட.
	ள்ம	....	ண்ம.
	ள்ந	....	ண்ண, or ண.
	ண்க	....	ட்க.

ண்ச	is changed into	ட்ச.
ண்ப	....	ட்ப.
ண்த	....	ண்ட, or ட்ட.
ண்ந	....	ண்ண, or ண.
ன்க	....	ற்க.
ன்ச	....	ற்ச.
ன்ப	....	ற்ப.
ன்த	....	ன்ற or ற்ற.
ன்ந	....	ன்ன, or ன.

Note. It is evident that these changes form a part of that system of artifices, by which the ancient Hindoo literati excluded the common people from understanding their writings, making them too perplexing to be studied by every one; hence it is, that they are not strictly observed in the common intercourse of life; and it is to be wished that they were altogether banished from the language. Until that take place, it should be always a rule in prose writings, to admit only such changes as are easy, and such as do not obscure the meaning of words or phrases. With this view I have observed in this work only those which in the above table are marked with an*; those according to which க, ச, த, and ப must be doubled; and such particular words as are usually changed even in common writings; such as,

தண்ணீர்	from	தண்-நீர், *cold water.*
வெந்நீர்	——	வெம்நீர், *hot water.*
கண்ணீர்	——	கண்நீர், *tears, the water of the eye.*
நன்னூல்	——	நல்நூல், *good rule.*
பன்மை	——	பல்மை, *plurality.*
வெண்மை	——	வெள்மை, *whiteness.*
நாடோறும்	——	நாள்தோறும், *daily*, &c.

ETYMOLOGY.

§ XI.

The Tamil Grammarians divide all the words of their language into four principal parts, viz., Nouns, Verbs, Particles, and Adjectives. They have no Article; the Pronoun is included in the Noun; the Preposition, Conjunction, and Interjection in the Particle. and the Adverb in the Adjective.

§ XII.

THE PARTICLES.

I commence with this part of speech, because it is much used in the formation of the other parts. A previous knowledge of it will, therefore, facilitate the study of the language.

1. What I have called "the Particle" is in Tamil called இடைச்சொல், that is, *middle word;* namely, words or letters which are used to connect other words. Apart from this connexion they have no individual signification.

They are subdivided into eight classes;

2. *The first class* contains the particles which form the cases of the Nouns. These are called வேற்றுமையுருபுகள், *i. e., forms of declension.* As they will necessarily be stated in the chapter of the Nouns, I omit them here.

3. *The second class* contains particles which form the modes and tenses of the Verbs, and are called வினையுருபுகள், *i. e., forms of the Verb.* They will likewise be stated in the chapter of the verbs.

4. *The third class* are the particles that are used to connect the forms of declension and conjugations with the roots, and are called சாரியை. They are seventeen in number, viz;—

அன், ஆன், இன், அல், அற்று, இற்று, அத்து, அம், தம், நம், நும், ஏ, அ, உ, ஐ, கு, and ன.

They are without meaning even when connected.—The mode of connexion will be mentioned wherever it occurs in the sequel.

5. *The fourth class*, contains particles of similarity or comparison, and are therefore called உவமைச்சொற்கள்; they are these:

> போல, ஒப்ப, நேர, நிகர, படி, புரைய, இயைய, கடுப்ப, மான, எய்ப்ப, அன்ன, and இன்ன.

They all signify in connexion, "*as, like as, equal to, according to*, and so on, and do not under go any change when used; but the nouns with which they are connected may be either in the nominative or accusative case, thus:

> அதுபோல (ஒப்ப, நேர, நிகர,) *as* or *like, near that*.
> அதைப்போல (ஒப்ப, நேர, நிகர,) *like, near that*.

But, படி takes இன் one of the third class particles before it, as அதின்படி, *according to that*, or as *that*. The rest are not used in common language.

Again, ஒப்ப, நேர, and நிகர, receive in common life the adverbial form in ஆய், as:

> ஒப்பாய், நேராய், நிகராய், *like* or *near*, and then require the dative case, as:
> அதற்கொப்பாய், *like that*.
> அதற்குநேராய், *strait to that, in the same direction*.
> அதற்குநிகராய், *equal to that*.

6. *The fifth class*, consists of particles which in different connexions have different meanings, and are therefore called, தத்தம்பொருளைக்காட்டிய இடைச்சொற்கள்; they are these:

> ஏ, ஓ, உம், என, என்று, முன், பின், கீழ், மேல், மட்டு, மற்று, இனி, ஆங்கு, ஆ, அ, இ, எ, உ,

என்று, என்னு, ஒடு, தில், மன், கொல், அந்தில், அம்ம, மா, ந, ஆ, அ, அந்தோ, ஐயோ, அன்றே, தொறும், தோறும், எனும், ஆனும், &c.

Many of these are used only in poetical Tamil. Those used in common life are the following.

ஏ, ஓ and ஆ, are interrogative, emphatic, and disjunctive particles, answering to our sign of interrogation, or to, *indeed*, *yea*, &c. For their use, see § LXXXIII., LXXXIV., LXXXV.

உம், is mostly conjunctive, answering to our *and*, *also*, but sometimes also disjunctive meaning *even*, *than*, see § LXXXVI.

என, என்று, are likewise conjnnctions, answering to *that*; but sometimes also meaning *similarity*, see § LXXXVII.

முன், or முன்பு, or முன்னமே, means *before.*—It is also used absolutely as a conjunction of time, in which case it means *formerly*, see § LXXXIX.

பின், or பின்பு, or பின்னர், means *after*, see § LXXXIX.

கீழ், means *under*, *beneath*. } see § LXXXIX.
மேல் means *above*, *over*. . } see § LXXXIX.

மட்டு, or மட்டும், means *until*, *as far as*, see § XC.

மற்று, means *other*, and with உம், viz., மற்றும், *otherwise*, is used adverbially, see § XCI.

மற்ற, means likewise *other*, and is used adjectively, see § XCI.

இனி or இனிமேல், means *hereafter*, used absolutely, see § XCII.

தோறும் and தொறும், mean *every one*, *without exception*, see § CXI.

அந்தோ and ஐயோ, are interjections of *woe* or *pity*, and answer to our *oh! alas!* see § XCIII.

எனும் and ஆனும், mean *even if, at least, although, either, or*, &c., see § CIV.

7. Besides these there are many words, which, though they belong to other parts of speech, are used as our prepositions, or conjunctions: I therefore subjoin them here:—

i. Infinitives of verbs.

கூட, means *together*, from கூடுகிறது, *to join.*

கிட்ட, means *near*, from கிட்டுகிறது, *to approach.*

தவிர, means *except*, from தவிருகிறது, *to separate, remove.*

ஒழிய, means also *except*, from ஒழிகிறது, *to cease.*

ஏறக்குறைய, means *about, nearly, more or less*, from ஏறுகிறது, *to ascend, increase*, and குறைகிறது, *to lessen.*

அற, means *off, from, without*, from அறுகிறது, *to cease, to be cut off.*

சூழ, *round about*, from சூழுகிறது, *to surround.*

ii. Verbal participles.

குறித்து, with the accusative, means *concerning, about*, from குறிக்கிறது, *to define, point out.*

இல்லாமல் and இன்றி, with the nominative, mean *without*, from the irregular negative verb இல்.

அல்லாமல் and அன்றி with any case, mean *besides, except*, from the irregular negative verb அல்.

சூழ்ந்து, from சூழுகிறது.
சுற்றி, from சுற்றுகிறது. } *around* with the accusative case.

விட்டு, *from*, with the Accusative case, from the verb விடுகிறது, *to leave*.

iii. Subjunctive moods.

இல்லாவிட்டால், means *if not*, *unless*, from இல் and விடுகிறது.

ஆனால், *if*, from ஆகிறது, *to become*.

ஆகிலும். } mean, *even if*, *although*, *yet*, *at least*,
ஆனாலும். } from ஆகிறது.

iv. Nouns:

பரியந்தம், added to a nominative case, means *until*.

வரையில், the ablative of வரை, and வரைக்கும், the dative of the same, mean *until*.

அளவு, means *until*, composed of அளவு, *a measure*, and உம், the conjunction.

மாத்திரம், *a measure*, means *only*.

மருங்கு, *the side*, *the hip*, added to a genitive, means, *near*.

பொழுது, *time*, added to participles, means *when*.

அப்பொழுது or அப்போது, from பொழுது, *time*, and அ the demonstrative pronominal letter, means *that time*, *then*.

இப்பொழுது, means *this time*, *then*.

பொருட்டு, means *for the purpose of*, *that*.

படிக்கு, the dative of படி, *manner*, *measure*, means *in order to that*.

நிமித்தம், *a sign*, *omen*, means *for the sake of*.

உடன், உடனே, means *immediately*.

ஆகையால், the ablative of the verbal noun ஆகை, *being*; literally, *by being*, means *therefore*, *wherefore*.

8. *The sixth class* contains particles that are merely emphatic, to lengthen the sound; and are therefore called இசைநிறைக்கிற இடைச்சொற்கள். They are but two, தெய்ய and ஒடு, and are used only in poetical Tamil.

9. *The seventh class* of particles are likewise only emphatic or expletive, and are called அசைநிறைக்கிற இடைச்சொற்கள். Ten of them are used only in poetry with the second person. They are these:

மியா, இகம், மோ, மதி, அத்தை, இத்தை, வாழிய, மாள, ஈ, யாழ.

The rest are:

யா, கா, பிற, பிறக்கு, அரோ, பொ, மாது, இகும், சின், குரை, ஓரும், போலும், இருந்து, இட்டு, அன்று, ஆம், தாம், தான், கின்று, நின்று.

Of these, இருந்து, இட்டு, ஆம், தாம், தான் and நின்று only are used in common language, see § XVI. 5. § LVI. 7. a. f. § CX. § LXVI. 2.

I would also notice, as belonging to this class, ஆனவன், என்பவன், ஆனது, ஆவது, which are affixed to nouns, and என்பது which is affixed to nouns and sentences, see § LXIV. 4, § LXVI. 4, 5.

10. *The eighth class* contains particles which stand for marks of certain sounds, such as of thundering, clapping with the hands, &c.; they are therefore called குறிப்பிடைச்சொல், *such are* ஒல், கல், &c. &c., such words may be formed indefinitely to express any sound.

NOUNS.

§ XIII.

The Noun is called in Tamil பேர்ச்சொல். It is

divided by the Native Grammarians into many classes; which belong rather to Logic than to Grammar. The principal of those divisions is into சிறப்புப்பேர், *i. e., proper nouns;* and பொதுப்பேர், *i. e., common nouns.*

1. The சிறப்புப்பேர், or proper nouns, imply every specific name, not only of men, but of all other beings, as: சாத்தன், *Sattan*, மாமரம், *the mango tree*, புலி, *a tiger*, வயிரம், *a diamond*, &c.

2. The பொதுப்பேர், or common nouns, include all the rest, as: மனிதன், *a man*, மரம், *a tree*, மிருகம், *a beast*, கல், *a stone*, &c.

§ XIV.

They further divide all nouns, whether proper or common, into two principal classes, which express their sex or caste, nearly the same as our gender.—The one is உயர்திணை, *i. e., high caste*, and the other is அஃறிணை (அல்திணை,) *i. e., no caste.*

1. The உயர்திணை, or *high caste*, implies all words that signify men, gods, and infernal spirits, whether male or female, as: தகப்பன், *father*, பிதா, *father*, அவன், *he*, பெண், *woman*, அவள், *she*, தேவன், *god*, பசாசு, *devil*, &c.,

2. The அஃறிணை, or *no caste*, are all the nouns that are not included in the former class, whether things animate or inanimate, male or female, as: அது, *it*, ஒளி *light*, கல்வி, *science*, ஆத்துமா, *soul*, மனசு, *mind*, மச்சம், *fish*, பறவை, *fowl*, குதிரை, *horse*, யானை, *elephant*, &c. &c.

§ XV.

Again, these two principal classes, are subdivided into five smaller, which they call பால் *i. e., part;* which include our genders and numbers; they are : ஆண்பால், *i. e., masculine high caste ;* பெண்பால், *i. e., feminine high caste ;* பலர்பால், *i. e., common high caste ;* ஒன்றன்பால் *i. e., singular of no caste ;* பலவின்பால், *i. e., the plural of no caste.*

1. The ஆண்பால் or *masculine of high caste nouns,* includes all nouns of the male sex of the class உயர்திணை, in the singular number, as : அவன், *he,* மகன், *a son,* புருடன், *a man,* தேவன், *god,* &c.

2. The பெண்பால், *i. e., feminine,* comprehends all nouns of the female sex of the உயர்திணை, in the singular number, as: அவள், *she,* மகள், *daughter,* ஸ்திரி, *woman,* தேவி *goddess,* &c.

3. பலர்பால், *i. e., common high caste,* includes three kinds of plurals ;—i. The plural of the masculine nouns, such as புருடர், *husbands.* ii. The plural of the feminine nouns, such as பெண்கள், *women* ; and iii., the plural common to both masculine and feminine, *e. g.*

அவர்கள், *they,* (male or female.)
மனிதர்கள், *persons,* do. (the human species.)
தேவர்கள், *gods,* do.

4. ஒன்றன்பால், *i. e., the singular of no caste nouns,* includes all the words of அஃறிணை in the singular number, as, வீடு, *house,* இறகு, *feather,* கத்தி, *knife,* நாய், *dog,* குருவி, *bird,* &c.

5 பலவின்பால், *i. e., the plural of no caste nouns,* comprehends all nouns of அஃறிணை in the plural number, as : வீடுகள், *houses,* கத்திகள், *knives,* பாம்புகள், *snakes,* &c.

Note. 1. To distinguish the nouns in regard to this division, we must chiefly observe their meaning and not their termination ; for though அன் usually denotes the masculine, and அள் the feminine, yet there are nouns with other terminations, which still belong to the masculine or feminine class, as :

பிதா, *father,* ஸ்திரி and பெண், *a woman,* குரு, *teacher,* &c.

And on the contrary, there are nouns with the masculine termination that are neuter, as:

கறையான், *an insect,* கடற்காளான், *the sea sponge,* இகலன், *a jackal.*

Note. 2. The formation of the plural number of any பால் or திணை, is by adding the syllable கள் to the singular, with due observation of the rules of the changes and augmentation of letters, thus:

of பிதா, *father,* the plural is பிதாக்கள், *fathers.*
பெண், *woman,* the plural is பெண்கள், *women.*
மரம், *tree,* the plural is மரங்கள் *trees.*
கழுதை, *an ass,* the plural is கழுதைகள், *asses.*
வீடு, *a house,* the plural is வீடுகள், *houses.*
கல், *a stone,* the plural is கற்கள், *stones.*
நாள், *a day,* the plural is நாட்கள், *days.*
குரு, *a priest,* the plural is குருக்கள், *priests.*

If the singular ends in ன், and the noun is of the உயர்திணை class, ன் is changed into ர், to which கள் may be added, as:

புருடன், *husband,* புருடர் or புருடர்கள், *husbands.*
மனிதன், *a man,* மனிதர் or மனிதர்கள், *men.*
குமாரன், *a son,* குமாரர் or குமாரர்கள், *sons.*
அவன், *he,* அவர் or அவர்கள், *they.*

But மகன், *a son,* has மகார், *sons;* which plural, however, is used chiefly in poetry. In common life they use குமாரர்.

Again, some nouns of the உயர்திணை take மார் between the singular and the plural terminations, as:

தகப்பன், *father,* தகப்பன்மார்கள், *fathers.*
போதகன், *teacher,* போதகன்மார்கள், *teachers.*
அண்ணன், *elder brother, the chief,* அண்ணன்மார்கள், *elder brothers, superiors.*
தோழன், *a companion,* தோழன்மார்கள், *companions,* so also பிள்ளைமார், *the caste called Pilley;* துரைமார், *gentlemen,* &c.

In some words of this sort, மார் is fixed after the கள், as:

குருக்கள்மார், or with the change of letters குருக்கண்மார், *priests.*

The formation of the plural of pronouns deviates from the general rule, and will be noticed in § XX.

§ XVI.

In declining Nouns, the Tamulians have eight cases, which they call வேற்றுமையுருபுகள், *i. e., forms of changes.*

1. *The first case*, is our nominative, and is called in Tamil, எழுவாய், or கருத்தா, *i. e., the beginning*, or *the first, the principal*. The noun itself is always in this case without any addition; as, மனிதன், *a man*, கல்வி, *science*, நோவு, *pain*, வில், *a bow*.

2. *The second case* is our accusative, and is formed by adding ஐ to the nominative; whence it is called ஐவேற்றுமை, as: மனிதனை, *the man*, கல்வியை, *the science*, நோவை, *the pain*, வில்லை, *the bow*.

3. *The third case*, is our ablative, and has two forms, the one is ஆல், denoting the instrument or the cause, as: மனிதனால், *by the man*; கல்வியால், *by the science*; நோவால், *by the pain*; வில்லால், *by the bow*; the second is, ஒடு, ஓடு, or உடனே, denoting connexion, as மனிதனோடு, or மனிதனொடு, or மனிதனுடனே, *with the man*, &c.

4. *The fourth case* is our dative, and is formed by adding கு to the nominative, as, மனிதனுக்கு, *to the man*; கல்விக்கு, நோவுக்கு, வில்லுக்கு, &c. The inserted உ in மனிதனுக்கு, and in similar nouns, is a சாரியை, see § XII. 4, used to connect the கு to the mute consonant; and the duplication of க் is made according to the rules of augmentation.

Some nouns receive ஐ also, one of the சாரியை, before the termination கு, as:

நாள், *a day*, நாளுக்கு and நாளைக்கு.
இன்று, *this day*, இன்றுக்கு and இன்றைக்கு.
அன்று, *that day*, அன்றுக்கு and அன்றைக்கு.
என்று, *what day?* என்றுக்கு and என்றைக்கு.

5. *The fifth case* may be called the ablative of separation or motion; and is formed by adding இல் or இன் to the nominative, as: மனிதனில், *from*

a man ; கல்வியில், *from science ;* நோவில், *from pain ;* வில்வில், *from the bow,* &c. Very frequently also, the particle இருந்து or நின்று is added to this case, as: மனிதனிலிருந்து or மனிதனினின்று ; கல்வியிலிருந்து or கல்வியினின்று, &c. ; the meaning is the same.

6. *The sixth case* is our genitive, and is formed by adding அது, or உடைய to the nominative, as: மனிதனுடைய or மனிதனது, *of a man,* but the former is more common than the latter.* Neuter nouns, particularly such as end in a vowel, take இன் (a சாரியை) before this termination, thus ; கல்வியினுடைய, கல்வியினது, *of the science ;* நோவினுடைய, நோவினது, *of the pain ;* வில்லினுடைய, வில்லினது, *of the bow,* &c. The termination is sometimes dropped, as: கல்வியின், நோவின், பிதாவின், &c.

7. *The seventh case,* is an ablative of place, and is expressed in poetical Tamil by no less than 28 terminations, viz :—

> கண், கால், கடை, இடை, தலை, வாய், திசை, வயின், முன், சார், வலம், இடம், மேல், கீழ், புடை, முதல், பின், பாடு, அளை, தேம், உழை, வழி, உளி, உழி, உள், அகம், புறம், இல்.

All these words severally are equivalent to *at* or *in,* when used as forms of this case ; however, only இல், and இடம், and this declined இடத்தில், are in common use ; which also may receive the சாரியை, இன், thus: மனிதனில், மனிதனிடத்தில், or மனிதன்கண், &c., *at or in the man ;* கல்வியில், கல்வியினிடத்தில், கல்வியின்கண், *at or in the science,* &c.

---

* Some have used also உட for the genitive case, as: மனிதனுட, &c., but it is obviously a corruption of உடைய, and not authorized by the rules of grammar.

8. *The eighth case* is our vocative, and is called in Tamil விளிவேற்றுமை, *i. e., mode of calling.* The most common form is that of adding the particle ஏ to the nominative, as: மனிதனே, *O man!* கல்வியே, *O science!* மரணமே, *O death!* &c.

Besides this, there are various other forms partly in common use, partly peculiar to Poetical Tamil, viz:—

i. The nominative of any noun may be used as a vocative. This however is ambiguous.

ii. If a noun end in இ, this short vowel may be changed into the long one, as: நம்பி-நம்பீ, *O Lord!* சாத்தி-சாத்தீ, *O Satee,* தும்பி-தும்பீ, *O wasp!*

iii. Words ending in ஐ, change this vowel into ஆய் or ஆ, as: அன்னை-அன்னாய், or அன்னா, *O mother!* தந்தை-தந்தாய், *O father!* விடலை-விடலாய், *O king!* மடந்தை-மடந்தாய், *O woman!* நாரை-நாராய், *O heron!*

iv. Words ending in ன், form the vocative variously, (1) by dropping the ன், as: இறைவன்-இறைவ, *O king!* நாதன்-நாத, *O lord!* சிநேகிதன்-சிநேகித. (2.) by lengthening the last vowel, as: பெருமன்-பெருமான், *O thou great one!* நம்பன். நம்பான், *O Siven!* (3.) by dropping அன், and adding ஆ, as: இறைவன்-இறைவா *O king!* தோழன்-தோழா, *O companion!* (4.) by dropping அன் and adding ஆவோ, as: அய்யன்-அய்யாவோ, *O sir!* அப்பன்-அப்பாவோ, *O father!* (5.) by dropping ன், and adding ஓ, as: திரையன்-திரையவோ, *O Tireiyen!* பெருமான்-பெருமவோ, *O thou great one!* (6.) by changing ன் into ய், as: மலையான்-மலையாய், *O mountaineer!* பூணன்-பூணாய், *O Pōonān!* (7.) by changing the last syllable ஆன் into ஓயே, as: வாயிலான்-வாயிலோயே, *O possessor of a gate!*

(8.) by changing அன் into ஏ, as: முருகன்-முருகே, *O Soopramanian! ஐயன்-ஐயே, O father! O sir!*

9. The சாரியை-இன், and also அன், may be inserted before the termination of any case, the vocative excepted; particularly in words that do not end in ன்; *e. g.*, கல்வி; 2d case கல்வியினை, கல்வியினால், கல்வியினோடு, &c.—The dative case may then be either இனுக்கு or இற்கு, contracted, according to the rules of changes of letters, from இன்கு, thus: கல்வியிற்கு, மனிதனிற்கு, &c.

10. In forming the cases the common rules of changes and augmentation of letters are observed, as before exemplified in கல்வி, which inserts ய, according to rule, § VIII. 2, நோவு, which drops உ, according to rule, § VII. 1, வில், which doubles the mute consonant according to rule, § VIII. 4.

11. The same forms of the cases are used also in the plural number, as will be seen from the following

PARADIGM

Of the Tamil Declension.

	Singular.	*Plural.*
1st, Nom.	மனிதன். *a man.*	மனிதர் or மனிதர்கள் *men.*
2d, Acc.	மனிதனை, *a man.*	மனிதரை or மனிதர்களை, *men.*
3d, Abl. instr.	மனிதனால் *by a man.*	மனிதரால் or மனிதர்களால், *by men.*
Abl. Soc.	மனிதனோடு *with a man.*	மனிதரோடு or மனிதர்களோடு, *with men.*
4th, Dat.	மனிதனுக்கு *to a man.*	மனிதருக்கு or மனிதர்க்கு or மனிதர்களுக்கு or மனிதர்கட்கு. } *to men.*
5th, Abl. mot.	மனிதனில். or மனிதனின். or மனிதனிலிருந்து or மனிதனினின்று. } *from a man*	மனிதரில் or மனிதர்களில், மனிதர்களின், மனிதர்களிலிருந்து மனிதர்களினின்று. } *from men.*

	Singular		Plural	
6th, Genitive,	மனிதனுடைய, or மனிதனது.	*of a man.*	மனிதருடைய or மனிதர்களுடைய, மனிதர்களினுடைய, மனிதர்களினது.	*of men.*
7th Abl. loc.	மனிதனிடத்தில் or மனிதன்கண் or மனிதனில்.	*at or in, a man.*	மனிதரிடத்தில் or மனிதர்களிடத்தில், மனிதர்களின்கண், மனிதர்களில்.	*at or in men.*
8th, Voc.	மனிதனே,	*O man!*	மனிதரே or மனிதர்களே,	*O men!*

Note.—According to the Latin form, it will be thus:

		Singular.	*Plural.*
Nom.	1st,	மனிதன.	மனிதர்கள.
Gen.	6th,	மனிதனுடைய	மனிதர்களுடைய.
		மனிதனது.	மனிதர்களினது.
Dat.	4th,	மனிதனுக்கு.	மனிதர்களுக்கு.
Acc.	2d,	மனிதனை.	மனிதர்களை.
Voc.	8th,	மனிதனே.	மனிதர்களே.
Abl.	5th,	மனிதனால்,	மனிதர்களில்.
		மனிதனின்,	மனிதர்களின்.
		மனிதனிலிருந்து	மனிதர்களிலிருந்து.
		மனிதனினின்று.	மனிதர்களினின்று.
—loc.	7th,	மனிதனிடத்தில்.	மனிதர்களிடத்தில்.
		மனிதனில்.	மனிதர்களில்.
		மனிதன்கண்.	மனிதர்களின்கண்.
—instr.	3d,	மனிதனால்.	மனிதர்களால்.
—Soc.	3d,	மனிதனோடே.	மனிதர்களோடே.

12. All nouns are declined as மனிதன், with the following exceptions:—

i. Nouns ending in அம் drop this syllable in the singular and add the சாரியை, (அத்து) before the terminations; excepting the vocative, as:

	Singular.	*Plural.*
1st,	மரம், *a tree.*	மரங்கள் *trees.*
2d,	மரத்தை or மரத்தினை, *of a tree*	மரங்களை ———
3d,	மரத்தால் or மரத்தினால், *by a tree, &c.*	
	மரத்தோடு or மரத்தினோடு, *with a tree.*	

4th, மரத்துக்கு or மரத்திற்கு, *to a tree.*
5th, மரத்தில் or மரத்தினில், *from a tree.*
6th, மரத்தினுடைய *of a tree.*
7th, மரத்தினிடத்தில், *at a tree.*
8th, மரமே, *O tree!*

The Plural is மரங்கள், &c.

ii. Nouns ending in டு and று, preceded only by one syllable with a long vowel, or preceded by more than one with short vowels, have the ட் and ற் doubled before the addition of the terminations, excepting the vocative case, and the plural number, as:

> வீடு, *a house*, வீட்டை or வீட்டினை, வீட்டால் or வீட்டினால், &c.
> ஆறு, *a river*, ஆற்றை or ஆற்றினை, ஆற்றால் or ஆற்றினால், &c.
> தகடு, *a flat metal plate*, தகட்டை or தகட்டினை, தகட்டால் or தகட்டினால், &c.
> வயிறு, *the abdomen*, வயிற்றை, வயிற்றினை, வயிற்றால் or வயிற்றினால், &c.
> But the plural is வீடுகள், வீடுகளை, &c., ஆறுகள். ஆறுகளை, &c.

13. There is a general oblique case, formed without the regular terminations; and used either as the 6th or as the 7th case.—One form is by adding only the சாரியை இன், as:

> வாக்கியத்தின்பொருள், *the substance* or *sense of a verse.*
> புல்லின் வண்ணம், *the colour of the grass.*

Another form takes place in nouns ending with ம், by changing it into the சாரியை, அத்து, and in nouns ending with டு and று (mentioned above), by doubling the consonant of those final letters, as:

> முகத்துச்சாயல், *the likness of the face.*
> காட்டுவழி, *the way of,* or *through a jungle.*
> வயிற்றுவலி, *pain of,* or *in the abdomen.*

Again, other nouns in ம only drop the last letter, as:

> மனநோவு, *distress of mind,* or *mental distress.*
> தேவகட்டளை, *the command of God,* or *the divine command.*

Again, nouns ending in a vowel receive no alteration, as:

> தலைநோவு, *head-ache.*
> தம்பிகை, *the hand of the younger brother.*
> எழுத்ததிகாரம், *the chapter of letters.*

Some of these forms are often used thus:

> அறவாழி, *the sea of virtue,* composed of அறம் and ஆழி.
> பாற்கடல், *the sea of milk,* of பால் and கடல்.
> சமாதானசவுக்கியம், *the happiness of peace,* or *peaceful happiness.*

PRONOUNS.

§ XVII.

What we call Pronouns the Tamil Grammarian classes with the nouns. They are divided into தன்மைப்பேர்ச்சொல், *i. e., nouns referring to ourselves,*—

முன்னிலைப்பேர்ச்சொல், *i. e., nouns referring to persons standing before us;*—படர்க்கைப்பேர்ச்சொல், *i. e., nouns referring to persons or things at a distance;* வினைப்பேர்ச்சொல், *i. e., nouns of interrogation;* and எண்ணின்பேர்ச்சொல், *i. e., nouns of number.*—What we denominate "person," the Tamulians call இடம், *i. e., place;* and thus:

> *The first person is called* தன்மையிடம்.
> *The second person is called* முன்னிலையிடம்; and
> *The third person is called* படர்க்கையிடம்.

These three together they call மூவிடம்; *i. e., the three places.*

§ XVIII.

The தன்மையிடத்துப்பேர்ச்சொல்; *i. e., words of the first person,* are நான் or யான், I, in the singular; and நாம் or யாம், and நாங்கள், we, in the plural. They are thus declined:

	Singular.		*Plural.*	
1st,	நான்,	*I.*	நாம், or நாங்கள்,	*we.*
2d,	என்னை,	*me.*	நம்மை or எங்களை,	*us.*
3d,	என்னால்,	*by me.*	நம்மால் or எங்களால்,	*by us.*
	என்னோடு,	*with me.*	நம்மோடு or எங்களோடு,	*with us.*
4th,	எனக்கு,	*to me.*	நமக்கு or எங்களுக்கு,	*to us.*
5th,	என்னில், or என்னிலிருந்து, என்னினின்று.	*from me.*	நம்மில் or எங்களில், நம்மிலிருந்து or எங்களிலிருந்து, நம்மினின்று or எஙகளினின்று	*from us.*
6th,	என் or எனது, or என்னுடைய,	*of me.*	நம் or எங்கள். நமது or எங்களது, நம்முடைய or எங்களுடைய,	*of us.*
7th,	எனனிடத்தில், or என்னில், or என்கண்.	*in, or at me.*	நம்மிடத்தில் or எங்களிடத்தில், நம்மில் or எங்களில், நம்மின்கண் or எங்களின்கண்,	*in, or at us*

Observe the difference between நாம் and நாங்கள். நாம் implies yourself and the person or persons to whom you speak, but நாங்கள் excludes the latter. —The Tamulians in Ceylon seem not to observe this difference, otherwise it is adopted throughout the Tamil and Teloogoo countries; though the native Grammars do not mention it.—In Government proceedings நாம் always means *we, i. e., the person who writes the order.*

§ XIX.

1. The முன்னிலையிடத்துப்பேர்ச்சொல், *i. e.*, words of the second person are நீ, *thou*, in the singular, and நீங்கள் *you*, in the plural.—They are thus declined:

	Singular.		*Plural.*	
1st,	நீ	*thou.*	நீங்கள்,	*you.*
2d,	உன்னை,	*thee.*	உங்களை,	*you.*
3d,	உன்னால்,	*by thee.*	உங்களால்,	*by you.*
	உன்னோடு,	*with thee.*	உங்களோடு,	*with you.*
4th,	உனக்கு,	*to thee.*	உங்களுக்கு,	*to you.*
5th,	உன்னில் or உன்னிலிருந்து, உன்னினின்று,	*from thee.*	உங்களில், உங்களிலிருந்து, உங்களினின்று.	*from you.*
6th,	உன், உனது, உன்னுடைய,	*of thee.*	உங்கள், உங்களது, உங்களுடைய.	*of you.*
7th,	உன்னிடத்தில், உன்னில், உன்கண்,	*in,* or *at thee.*	உங்களிடத்தில், உங்களில், உங்களின்கண்.	*in,* or *at you.*

2. நீங்கள், besides being used simply as a plural, is also applied to a single person, as an honorific by inferiors to superiors. When equals address

each other politely they use நீர், which is thus declined:

1st,	நீர்,	*thou* or *you.*
2d,	உம்மை,	*thee* or *you.*
3d,	உம்மால்,	*by thee* or *you.*
	உம்மோடு,	*with thee* or *you.*
4th,	உமக்கு,	*to thee* or *you.*
5th,	உம்மில் உம்மிலிருந்து, உம்மினின்று.	*from thee* or *you.*
6th,	உமது, உம்முடைய,	*of thee* or *you.*
7th,	உம்மிடத்தில், உம்மில்	*in,* or *at thee,* or *you.*

§ XX.

1. The படர்க்கைப்பேர்ச்சொல், *i. e., nouns referring to the persons* or *things of which we speak, are masculine, feminine and neuter.*—They are the same as the demonstrative Pronouns, called in Tamil சுட்டுப்பேர்;—and are of two sorts, the one pointing out the remote person or thing, and the other that which is near or before us. They are formed of the demonstrative letters அ and இ with the terminations அன், அள் and து, thus:

அவன், *he,* or *that man.* அவள், *she,* or *that woman.* அது, *it,* or *that thing.*	The remote demonstrative Pronouns, or pointing out the absent person or thing.
இவன், *he,* or *this man.* இவள், *she,* or *this woman.* இது, *it,* or *this thing.*	Demonstrative pronouns pointing out the present person or thing.

2. The masculine and feminine of these pronouns are declined, as மனிதன், thus:

The Singular.

1st, அவன், இவன், *he,* அவள், இவள், *she.*
2d, அவனை, இவனை, *him,* அவளை, இவளை, *her,* &c.

The Plural of both genders is the same, viz.,

1st, அவர், or அவர்கள், *those ;* இவர், or இவர்கள், *these men or women.*
2d, அவரை, or அவர்களை, *those ;* இவரை, or இவர்களை, *these men or women.*

3. அவர்கள், is more commonly used as the plural ; and both அவர் and அவர்கள், are also used by inferiors as honorifics, when speaking of superiors, or by any person when speaking of another respectfully.

4. The Neuter Pronoun is thus declined :

Singular.

1st,	அது,	*that,*	இது	*this.*
2d,	அதை, or அதனை,	*that,*	இதை, or இதனை,	*this.*
3d,	அதினால், or அதனால்,	*by that,*	இதினால், or இதனால்,	*by this.*
	அதினோடு or அதனோடு,	*with that,*	இதினோடு, or இதனோடு,	*with this.*
4th,	அதுக்கு, or அதிற்கு, or அதற்கு	*to that,*	இதுக்கு, or இதிற்கு, or இதற்கு	*to this.*
5th,	அதில், or அதினில், or அதனில் or அதனிலிருந்து, &c.	*from that,*	இதில், இதினில், இதனில், or இதிலிருந்து, &c.	*from this.*
6th,	அதினுடைய or அதனுடைய or அதின் or அதினது.	*of that,*	இதினுடைய or இதனுடைய or இதின் or இதினது.	*of this.*
7th,	அதினிடத்தில் அதில்.	*in, or at that.*	இதினிடத்தில், இதில்.	*in, or at this.*

Plural.

Case	Tamil	English	Tamil	English
1st,	அவை, or அவைகள்,	*those,*	இவை, or இவைகள்.	*these.*
2d,	அவற்றை, or அவைகளை,	*those,*	இவற்றை, or இவைகளை.	*these.*
3d,	அவற்றால், or அவைகளால், அவற்றினால், or அவைகளினால்,	*by those,*	இவற்றால், இவைகளால், இவற்றினால், or இவைகளினால்.	*by these.*
	அவற்றோடு, அவைகளோடு, அவற்றினோடு, or அவைகளினோடு,	*with those,*	இவற்றோடு, இவைகளோடு, or இவற்றினோடு.	*with these.*
4th,	அவற்றுக்கு, அவைகளுக்கு, or அவற்றிற்கு,	*to those,*	இவற்றுக்கு, இவைகளுக்கு, or or இவற்றிற்கு.	*to these.*
5th,	அவற்றில், or அவைகளில், அவற்றிலிருந்து, அவைகளிலிருந்து, or அவற்றினில்,	*from those,*	இவற்றில், or இவைகளில், இவற்றிலிருந்து, இவைகளிலிருந்து, or இவற்றினில்	*from these.*
6th,	அவற்றினுடைய, அவைகளுடைய, அவற்றினது, or அவைகளினது,	*of those,*	இவற்றினுடைய, இவைகளுடைய, இவற்றினது, or இவைகளினது.	*of these.*
7th,	அவற்றினிடத்தில், அவைகளினிடத்தில், அவற்றில், அவைகளில், அவற்றின்கண், or அவைகளின்கண்,	*in, or, at those*	இவற்றினிடத்தில், or இவைகளிடத்தில், இவற்றில், இவைகளில், இவற்றின்கண், or இவைகளின்கண்.	*in, or at these.*

Note 1st.—அவற்றை and இவற்றை, &c., are formed of the demonstrative letters அ and இ, of அற்று, one of the சாரியை, and of the termination.

Note 2d.—The plural of அது and இது has by some been stated to be அதுகள் and இதுகள்; but the native Grammars do not authorize it.

5. The demonstrative letters அ and இ, are also prefixed to any noun, of whatever number, gender, or case. If the noun begins with a consonant, this is doubled after அ and இ; but if it begins with a vowel, those letters are united to it by the letter வ doubled, as:

அம்மனிதன், *that man*, இம்மனிதன், *this man.*
அக்காலம், *that time*, இக்காலம், *this time.*
அவ்வூர், *that village*, இவ்வூர், *this village.*
அவ்வாலயம், *that temple*, இவ்வாலயம், *this temple.*
அவ்விலைகள், *those leaves*, இவ்விலைகள், *these leaves.*

6. அந்த and இந்த are also demonstrative pronouns, and are prefixed as adjectives to any noun, when the usual rules of the increase of letters must be observed.—They are called in Tamil சுட்டுப்பெயரெச்சம்; *i. e., defective demonstrative nouns,* because they do not in themselves point out any particular person, number, gender, or case, and cannot therefore be used by themselves, as:

அந்தச்சேலை, *that cloth*, இந்தத்தானியம், *this grain.*
அந்தவொளி, *that light*, இந்தவிடம், *this place.*
அந்தமலை, *that mountain*, இந்தப்பக்கம், *this side.*
அந்தவழிகள், *those ways*, இந்தக்கத்திகள், *these knives.*

7. A third form of indefinite demonstrative pronouns is அன்ன and இன்ன, which mean *such*, or

such like, when the usual personal terminations are affixed. They also form nouns, and are then regularly declined, as:

அன்னான், *such a man*, இன்னான், *such a man*.
அன்னாள், *such a woman*, இன்னாள், *such a woman*.
அன்னது, *such a thing*, இன்னது, *such a thing*.

The word, இன்ன, is also used adjectively, and thus prefixed to any noun, as:

இன்னமனிதன், *such a man*.
இன்னபெண், *such a woman*.

It is then commonly doubled, as:

இன்னவின்னமனிதன், *such and such a man*.
இன்னவின்னபொருள், *such and such a thing*.
இன்னவின்னவார்த்தைகள், *such and such words*.

8. The Tamulians have also a reciprocal pronoun referring to the படர்க்கைப்பேர், or third person, viz., தான், *himself* and *herself*; and தாங்கள் and தாம், *themselves*. They are thus declined:

	Singular.		Plural. masc. and fem.	masc. fem. and neut.	
1st,	தான்,	*himself, herself and itself.*	தாங்கள்,	தாம்	*themselves.*
2d,	தன்னை,	*himself*, &c.	தங்களை,	தம்மை,	*themselves.*
3d,	தன்னால்,	*by* ———	தங்களால்,	தம்மால்	*by* ———
	தன்னோடு,	*with* ———	தங்களோடு,	தம்மோடு	*with* ———
4th,	தனக்கு,	*to* ———	தங்களுக்கு,	தமக்கு	*to* ———
5th,	தன்னில் தன்னிலிருந்து,	*from* ———	தங்களில், தங்களிலிருந்து,	தம்மில், தம்மிலிருந்து,	*from* ———
6th,	தன், தன்னுடைய, தனது,	*of* ———	தங்கள், தங்களுடைய,	தமது, தம்முடைய,	*of* ———
7th,	தன்னிடத்தில், தன்னில்,	*in*, or *at* ———	தங்களிடத்தில், தங்களில்,	தம்மிடத்தில், தம்மில்,	*in* ro *at* ———

Observe that the plural தாங்கள், is used as an honorific, when an inferior speaks to a superior, as: தாங்கள்சொன்னீர்கள் ; *i. e., you said.*

தாம், is used also as an honorific among equals, or when a superior wishes to honour an inferior, as: தாம்இப்படிச்செய்யவேணடும், *you must do so.*

§ XXI.

1. The வினுப்பேர்ச்சொல், *i. e., interrogative pronoun,* is formed by the letters, எ and யா with the usual personal terminations, as:

எவன்	or யாவன்,	*who?*	*what man?*
எவள்	or யாவள்,	*who?*	*what woman?*
எது	or யாது,	*which?*	*what thing?*

The Plural is:

எவர்கள்	or யாவர்,	*who?*	*what men* or *women?*
எவை	or யாவை,	*which?*	*what things?*

The declension is like அவன், அவள், அது, அவர்கள் and அவை, see § XX.

Note 1.—யாவர், is frequently contracted into யார், which, common use again has changed into ஆர், see § IX. 6, i.

Note 2.—For எவர்கள், also எவர் is used of a single person as an honorific ; like அவர், *which,* see § XX.

2. The interrogative letter எ, is like the demonstative letters அ and இ, prefixed to any nouns and means what? as:

எம்மனிதன்,	*what man?*
எம்மனிதர்கள்,	*what men?*
எப்பட்டினம்,	*what city?*
எவ்வூர்,	*what village?*
எவ்வகைகள்,	*what kinds?*

3. Instead of the simple letter எ the adjective form எந்த is also used in interrogatively, and prefixed to nouns like அந்த and இந்த, (see § XX. 6.) as:

எந்தமனிதன், *what man?*
எந்தப்பிள்ளை, *what child?*
எந்தநெல்லு, *what rice* or *paddy?*
எந்தக்கோவில், *what temple?*
எந்தஊர், *what village?*

4. Of the interrogative letter எ are also formed the common interrogative pronouns என், என்ன, and என்னே, meaning *what?* and again of என்ன, is formed என்னவாய், *how?* used adverbially; likewise, with the சாரியை, (அத்து.)

என்னத்தை *what?* என்னத்திலுலே, *by what?* என்னத்துக்கு, *to what?* or, *for what?*

Note—ஏன் and யேன், have been used for என்; and என்னமாய், for என்னவாய்; but which is incorrect.

5. When the particle உம், is added to any interrogative noun, it changes the interrogative into an affirmative, with a sense of completion.

எவனும்–யாவனும், *every man.*
எவளும்–யாவளும், *every woman.*
எதுவும்–யாவும், *every thing.*
எவர்களும்–யாவரும், *all men* or *women; whosoever.*
எவையும்–யாவையும், *all things whatsoever.*

The singular of this form however, is not much in use. When they are declined, the உம் is always put after the case, as: எவர்களையும், யாவனையும், யாவற்றையும், &c.

6. The addition of ஆகிலும், or ஆனாலும், to either singular or plural, gives to these pronouns an indefinite or exceptive sense thus:

எவனாகிலும், *any one man*
எவளாகிலும், *any one woman* } *of many.*
எதாகிலும், *any one thing*

Thus, also, எப்பட்டினமும், *every city.*

எப்பட்டினங்களும், *all cities whatsoever.*
எவ்வகையும், *every,* or *whatever kind.*
எவ்வகைகளும், *all kinds whatsoever.*
எந்தமனிதனாகிலும், *any man (of many.)*
எந்தமிருகமானாலும், *any beast (of many.)*
எந்தப்பறவைகளானாலும், *any birds (of many.)*

In declining such nouns, the characteristic of the case is put between the noun and உம் or ஆகிலும், as:

எவர்களையும்–எவர்களாலும்–எவர்களோடும், &c.
யாவற்றையும்–யாவற்றினாலும்–யாவற்றிற்கும், &c.
எப்பட்டினத்தையாகிலும்–எப்பட்டினத்தினாலாகிலும், &c.
எந்தமிருகங்களையானாலும், &c.

§ XXII.

1. The எண்ணின்பேர், *i. e., nouns of numbers,* with their appropriate characters, or signs are these:

ஒன்று	௧	1
இரண்டு	௨	2
மூன்று	௩	3
நாலு or நான்கு	௪	4
ஐந்து, vulgarly அஞ்சு	௫	5
ஆறு	௬	6

ஏழு	௭	7
எட்டு	௮	8
ஒன்பது	௯	9
பத்து	௰	10
பதினொன்று	௰௧	11
பன்னிரண்டு	௰௨	12
பதின்மூன்று	௰௩	13
பதினான்கு	௰௪	14
&c. &c.		
பத்தொன்பது	௰௯	19
இருபது	௨௰	20
இருபத்தொன்று	௨௧	21
&c. &c.		
முப்பது	௩௰	30
முப்பத்தொன்று	௩௧	31
&c. &c.		
நாற்பது	௪௰	40
ஐம்பது	௫௰	50
அறுபது	௬௰	60
எழுபது	௭௰	70
எண்பது	௮௰	80
தொண்ணூறு	௯௰	90
தொண்ணூற்றொன்று	௯௧	91
&c. &c		
நூறு	௱	100
நூற்றொன்று	௱௧	101
நூற்றிரண்டு	௱௨	102
நூற்றுமூன்று	௱௩	103
&c. &c.		
நூற்றுப்பத்து	௱௰	110
நூற்றிருபது	௱௨௰	120
நூற்றுமுப்பது	௱௩௰	130
&c. &c.		
இருநூறு	௨௱	200
முந்நூறு	௩௱	300
நானூறு	௪௱	400
ஐந்நூறு	௫௱	500
அறுநூறு	௬௱	600
எழுநூறு	௭௱	700
எண்ணூறு	௮௱	800
தொள்ளாயிரம்	௯௱	900
தொள்ளாயிரத்தொன்று	௯௱௧	901
தொள்ளாயிரத்திரண்டு	௯௱௨	902
&c. &c.		
ஆயிரம்	௲	1000
ஆயரத்தொன்று	௲௧	1001
&c &c.		

ஆயிரத்துப்பத்து	௲௰	1010
ஆயிரத்திருபது	௲௨௰	1020
&c. &c.		
ஆயிரத்தொருநூறு	௲௱	1100
ஆயிரத்திருநூறு	௲௨௱	1200
&c. &c.		
இரண்டாயிரம் or ஈராயிரம்	௨௲	2000
மூவாயிரம்	௩௲	3000
நாலாயிரம்	௪௲	4000
ஐயாயிரம்	௫௲	5000
ஆறாயிரம்	௬௲	6000
ஏழாயிரம்	௭௲	7000
எண்ணாயிரம்	௮௲	8000
ஒன்பதினாயிரம்	௯௲	9000
பதினாயிரம்	௰௲	10,000
இருபதினாயிரம்	௨௰௲	20,000
முப்பதினாயிரம்	௩௰௲	30,000
&c. &c.		
தொண்ணூறாயிரம்	௯௰௲	90,000
நூறாயிரம் or இலச்சம்	௱௲	100,000
இருநூறாயிரம் or இரண்டிலச்சம்	௨௱௲	200,000
&c. &c.		
நூறிலச்சம் or கோடி	——	10,000,000

2. The fractions are thus expressed:

முந்திரி	𑿀	$\frac{1}{320}$	$\frac{1}{320}$
அரைக்காணி	𑿁	$\frac{1}{160}$	$\frac{2}{320}$
காணி	𑿂	$\frac{1}{80}$	$\frac{4}{320}$
அரைமா	𑿄	$\frac{1}{40}$	$\frac{8}{320}$
முக்காணி	𑿆	$\frac{3}{80}$	$\frac{12}{320}$
மா	𑿈	$\frac{1}{20}$	$\frac{16}{320}$
மாகாணி or வீசம்	𑿉	$\frac{1}{16}$	$\frac{20}{320}$
இரண்டுமா or இருமா	𑿋	$\frac{1}{10}$	$\frac{32}{320}$
அரைக்கால்	𑿌	$\frac{1}{8}$	$\frac{40}{320}$
மூன்றுமா	𑿍	$\frac{3}{20}$	$\frac{48}{320}$
மூன்றுமாகாணி	𑿎	$\frac{3}{16}$	$\frac{60}{320}$
நாலுமா	𑿏	$\frac{1}{5}$	$\frac{64}{320}$
கால்	𑿐	$\frac{1}{4}$	$\frac{80}{320}$
அரை	𑿑	$\frac{1}{2}$	$\frac{100}{320}$
முக்கால்	𑿓	$\frac{3}{4}$	$\frac{240}{320}$

3. The cardinal numbers may be considered either as nouns or as adjectives.

i. When they are used as nouns, they are placed after the noun, and regularly declined, as:

கல்லொன்று, *one stone.*
கல்லிரண்டு, *two stones.*
கல்லிரண்டை or கல்லிரண்டினை.
கல்லிரண்டால் or கல்லிரண்டினால், &c.
மரம்மூன்று, *three trees.*
மரம்மூன்றை or மூன்றினை, &c.

ii. They are used as adjectives before neuter nouns, and are then of course not declined, as:

இரண்டுபேர், *two names* or *persons.**
மூன்றுகல், *three stones.*
நூறுதுண்டு, *hundred pieces,* &c.

Observe, that ஒன்று is then changed into ஒரு, as:

ஒருமனிதன், *one man.*
ஒருவீடு, *one house.*

And again ஒரு, is often changed into ஓர், as:

ஓரடையாளம், *one sign.*
ஓராள், *one person.*
ஓர்மனிதன், *one man.*
பதினோர்குதிரை, *eleven horses.*

4. When united with nouns, some of them undergo a change, thus; they either lose a syllable, or shorten or lengthen the vowel, as:

of இரண்டு 2 is made	இரு, as	இருதலை,	*two heads.*
		இருபது,	*twenty.*
மூன்று 3 ———	மூ or மு	மூவாயிரம்,	*three thousand.*
		மூவரசர்,	*three kings.*
		மும்மூர்த்தி,	*the three gods.*
		முக்காலம்,	*the three tenses.*
		முப்பது,	*thirty.*

* When masculine or feminine nouns are added, then the position is thus: மனிதர் இரண்டுபேர், *two men,* புருடர் பத்துபேர், *ten men,* இஸ்திரிகள மூன்றுபேர், *three women,* கூலியாட்கள் ஒன்பதுபேர், *nine labourers, &c.*

of நாலு	4	is made	நால்,	as	நாற்பது,	*forty.*
ஐந்து	5	———	ஐம்	—	ஐங்கலம்,	*five kalams.*
					ஐம்பது,	*fifty.*
ஆறு	6	———	அறு	—	அறுகலம்,	*six kalams.*
					அறுபது,	*sixty.*
ஏழு	7	———	எழு	—	எழுகலம்,	*seven kalams.*
					எழுபது,	*seventy.*
எட்டு	8	———	எண்	—	எண்கலம்,	*eight kalams.*
					எண்பது,	*eighty.*

5. Appellative nouns are formed of the cardinal number, thus :

of ஒரு 1 is made ஒருவன் (vulgarly ஒருத்தன்), one, *a person, a certain man.*

ஒருத்தி, *a female, a certain woman.*

இரு	2	———	இருவர், *two persons.*	whether male or female.
மூ	3	———	மூவர், *three persons.*	
நால்	4	———	நால்வர், *four persons.*	
ஐ	5	———	ஐவர், *five persons.*	

These nouns cannot therefore be placed before other nouns, as adjectives, but must be used either simply as they are, or put after the nouns, as :

அவர்களிருவர், *they both,*
மனிதர்மூவர், *three men,* &c.

6. To express "*one by one, two and two,* &c." they repeat the first syllable of the numbers until ten, with the exception of ஒன்பது, 9, as :

ஒவ்வொன்று, *one by one.*
இவ்விரண்டு, *two and two.*
மும்மூன்று, *three and three.*
நந்நாலு, *four and four.*
ஐவைந்து, *five and five.*
அவ்வாறு, *six and six.*
எவ்வேழு, *seven and seven.*
எவ்வெட்டு, *by eights.*
பப்பத்து, *by tens.*

Of the first four of these, also appellative nouns are formed, thus:

ஒவ்வொருவர், *one after another* or *one by one.*

இவ்விருவர்,
மும்மூவர்
நந்நால்வர், } These however are not much in use; instead of them they say, இருவரிருவராக, மூவர்மூவராக, நால்வர்நால்வராக, &c.

7. Ordinal numbers are formed by adding the future participle ஆம், to the cardinal; excepting ஒன்று; for which முதல், *the beginning* is used, as:

முதலாம், *the first.*
இரண்டாம், *the second.*
மூன்றாம், *the third.*
நான்காம், vulgarly நாலாம், *the fourth.*
ஐந்தாம், vulgarly அஞ்சாம், *the fifth*, &c.
பதினோராம், *the eleventh.*
இருபத்தோராம், *the twenty first.*
முப்பத்தோராம், *the thirty first*, &c.

They are thus used as adjectives, as:

முதலாம்அதிகாரம், *the first chapter*, &c.

To form adverbs of them ஆவது, *a verbal noun*, is added to the cardinal number, as:

முதலாவது, *first.*
இரண்டாவது, *secondly.*
மூன்றாவது, *thirdly.*

§ XXIII.

1. Some indefinite pronouns are ranked among the participles, and called பேரெச்சம், that is, a

word wanting a noun to complete the idea; such are:

சில, *some.*
பல, *many, several, various.*

Others are called வினையெச்சம், *i. e., wanting a verb;* such are:

எல்லாம்,
சகலமும்,
அனைத்தும், } *all.*
முழுவதும்,
முழுமையும்,

2. The former, viz., சில and பல, are used without any change as adjectives to any noun of whatever gender or number, as:

சிலமனிதர், *some men,* சிலகற்கள், *some stones.*
பலபேர்கள், *various persons,* பலமரங்கள், *various trees.*

When used as nouns, the usual personal and neuter terminations of the plural are affixed to them. They are then declined as usual, as:

1st, சிலர், *some persons,* சிலவை, *some things;* பலர், *various persons,* பலவை, *various things.*
2d, சிலரை, *some persons,* சிலவற்றை, *some things;* பலரை, *various persons,* பலவற்றை, *various things.*
3d, சிலரால், *by some persons,* சிலவற்றால், *by some things;* பலரால், *by various persons,* பலவற்றால், *by various things.*
சிலரோடு, *with some persons,* சிலவற்றோடு, *with some things;* பலரோடு *with various persons,* பலவற்றோடு, *with various things.*
4th, சிலருக்கு, *to some persons,* சிலவற்றிற்கு, *to some things;* பலருக்கு, *to various persons,* பலவற்றிற்கு, *to various things,* &c.

Note.—Such is expressed by அப்படிப்பட்ட, and இப்படிப்பட்ட, words composed of அப்படி and இப்படி, *so,* and பட்ட, the participle of படுகிறது, *to be;* அப்படிப்பட்ட, therefore means, *which is (or are) so, i. e., such.* They are prefixed to nouns like சில and பல; thus, அப்படிப்பட்டமனிதன், *such a man;* அப்படிப்பட்டகுருவி, *such a bird.*

The terminations of the pronouns also are affixed to them, and then declined as usual, as:

அப்படிப்பட்டவன், *such a man.*
அப்படிப்பட்டவள், *such a women.*
அப்படிப்பட்டது, *such a thing.*
அப்படிப்பட்டவர்கள், *such persons.*
அப்படிப்பட்டவைகள், *such things.*

The difference between அப்படி and இப்படி, is the same as mentioned, § XX.

3. The words எல்லாம், சகலமும், அனைத்தும், முழுமையும், and முழுவதும், are nouns used, as will be stated in the Syntax, see § CXII.

In the declension of எல்லாம், the ம் is dropt, and the usual termination of the plural substituted, with the particle உம், as:

1st, எல்லாம், *all things.*
2d, எல்லாவற்றையும், *all things.*
3d, எல்லாவற்றாலும், *by all things.*
4th, எல்லாவற்றிற்கும், *to all things.* &c.

The other words are declined in the same way; the உம் is put after the case, thus:

1st, சகலமும், அனைத்தும், முழுமையும், முழுவதும், *all things.*
2d, சகலத்தையும், அனைத்தையும், முழுமையையும், முழுவதையும், *all things.*
3d, சகலத்தாலும், அனைத்தாலும், முழுமையாலும், முழுவதாலும், *by all things*, &c.

Of எல்லாம், சகலமும், அனைத்தும், personal nouns also are formed by rejecting the neuter termination, and adding ரும் the personal termination of the plural; the declension is then as before, thus:

1st, எல்லாரும், சகலரும், அனைவரும், *all persons.*
2d, எல்லாரையும், சகலரையும், அனைவரையும், *all persons.*
3d, எல்லாராலும், சகலராலும், அனைவராலும், *by all persons.*

Note 1.—எல்லாம், has by some been declined as nouns ending in ம், thus: எல்லாத்தையும், எல்லாத்துக்கும், &c., but this is irregular.

Note 2.—When எல்லாம் and சகலம், are used adjectively, they drop the ம, and are then prefixed to the noun, which receives உம் at the end, as: எல்லாமனிதர்களும், *all men*; சகலமரங்களும், *all trees*.

§ XXIV.

It remains to offer a few hints with respect to the formation of nouns. There are various kinds of nouns, as:

1. Primitive nouns; such as மரம், *a tree*, மகன், *a son*, தாய், *mother*, தகப்பன், *father*, &c.

2. Nouns formed from the oblique case and the terminations ஆன், ஆள், as: from

மதம், *a convent*, மதத்தான், *a man of the convent*, மதத்தாள், *a woman of the convent*.
கோத்திரம், *a tribe*, கோத்திரத்தான், *a man of the tribe*, கோத்திரத்தாள், *a woman of the tribe*.
தருமம், *charity*, தருமவான், *a charitable man*.
புண்ணியம், *virtue*, புண்ணியவான், *a virtuous man*.
பட்டினம், *a city*, பட்டினத்தான், *a citizen*, *(masc.)* பட்டினத்தாள், *a citizen*, *(fem.)*
சந்ததி, *offspring*, சந்ததியான், *a male offspring*, சந்ததியாள், *a female offspring*.
ஊர், *a village*, ஊரான், *a villager*, *(masc.)* ஊராள். *a villager*, *(fem.)*

Observe a few nouns insert ம; as நீதி, *righteousness*, நீதிமான், *a righteous man*, with the plural நீதிமான்கள், without changing the ன் into ர், as other nouns do.—The feminine is நீதியுள்ளவள். Thus also,

புத்திமான், *an intelligent man*.
பூமான், *one ruling the earth, a king*.
கோமான், *one ruling the earth, a king*.

3. Personal nouns formed from other nouns by dropping the last syllable, and adding அன் for the masculine and இ for the feminine, as from

அகங்காரம், *anger*, அகங்காரன், *an angry man*, அகங்காரி, *an angry woman.*

உதாரம், *liberality*, உதாரன், *a liberal man*, உதாரி, *a liberal woman.*

கழுத்து, *the neck*, கழுத்தன், *a man with a neck*, கழுத்தி, *a woman with a neck.*

அழகு, *beauty*, அழகன், *a beautiful man*, அழகி, *a beautiful woman.*

உலோபம், *avariciousness*, உலோபன், *an avaricious man*, உலோபி, *an avaricious woman.*

In some words of this class derived from the Samscrit, the termination இ, serves both for the masculine and the feminine, as from

பாவம், *sin*, பாவி, *a sinner.*

கோபம், *anger*, கோபி, *an angry person.*

உலோபம், *avarice*, உலோபி, *an avaricious person*, whether male or female, though, as above mentioned, it has also உலோபன்.

சுத்தம் or பரிசுத்தம், *purity, holiness*, only the masculine பரிசுத்தன், *a holy man*, is formed ; it has also பரிசுத்தவான், and the plural பரிசுத்தவான்கள், without changing the ன், into ர். The feminine is, பரிசுத்தமுள்ளவள்.

4. Personal nouns are formed also by inserting the சாரியை (இன்) between the noun and the termination அன், as:

from வில், *a bow*, வில்லின்ன், *a bow-man.*

பல், *a tooth*, பல்லின்ன், *a man with teeth.*

காது, *an ear*, காதின்ன், *a man with ears.*

from நடை, *a step, walk,* நடையினன், *a man who makes steps,* i. e., *who walks.*

சொல், *a word,* சொல்லினன், *a man who speaks,* i. e., *a speaker.*

5. Some personal nouns are formed by adding to the oblique case the termination காரன், (a Samscrit word, signifying *an agent*) for the masculine, and காரி for the feminine, as :

தோட்டம், *a garden,* தோட்டக்காரன், *a gardener,* mas ; தோட்டக்காரி, *a gardener,* feminine.

வேலை, *a work,* வேலைக்காரன், *a labourer,* masculine ; வேலைக்காரி, *a labourer,* feminine.

ஊழியம், *a service,* ஊழியக்காரன், *a servant,* mas ; ஊழியக்காரி, *a servant,* feminine.

ஆடு, *a sheep,* ஆட்டுக்காரன், *a man who keeps sheep.* ஆட்டுக்காரி, *a woman who keeps sheep.*

கெட்டி, *cleverness,* கெட்டிக்காரன், *a clever man* ; கெட்டிக்காரி, *a clever woman.*

கடன், *debt,* கடன்காரன், *a man who makes debt, whether by borrowing* or *lending* ; கடன்காரி. *a woman who makes debt,* &c.

6. Others are formed by adding ஆளி, to the noun, as :

கடன், *debt,* கடனாளி, *a debtor,* whether male or female.

முதல், *the first,* முதலாளி, *the chief,* masculine and feminine.

கீர்த்தி, *fame,* கீர்த்தியாளி, *a famous man* or *woman.*

வில், *a bow,* வில்லாளி, *a man* or *woman, using the bow, an archer.*

7. Others are formed by adding சாலி, both for the masculine and feminine, as:

> மோட்சம், *heaven*, மோட்சசாலி, *one who enjoys heavenly bliss.*
> யோக்கியம், *cleverness*, யோக்கியசாலி, *a clever, respectable, decent person.*
> புத்தி, *understanding*, புத்திசாலி, *a person of understanding.*

8. Others are formed from numbers, see § XXII. 5.

9. Various nouns are formed from verbs, see § XXXII.

10. Abstract nouns are formed from some obsolete roots, by adding மை to them, as:

from சிறு,	*small,*	சிறுமை,	*smallness,*
அரு,	*difficult, rare,*	அருமை,	*difficulty, rarity.*
கொடு,	*cruel,*	கொடுமை,	*cruelty.*
புது,	*new,*	புதுமை,	*newness, novelty.*
பெரு,	*great,*	பெருமை,	*greatness.*
அடி,	*low,*	அடிமை,	*lowliness.*

From these, appellatives are formed by dropping மை, and adding அன், அவன், ஆன், or ஒன் for the masculine singular; அள், ஆள், or அவள், for the feminine singular; and அர், ஆர், or அவர், for both genders in the plural; அது, or து for the neuter singular; and அவை, or அன, or அ, for the neuter plural; the preceding உ, is then changed into இ, thus:

from சிறுமை—சிறியன், சிறியவன், சிறியான், or சிறியோன், *a small man,*
சிறியள், சிறியவள், or சிறியாள், *a small woman,*
சிறியது, சிறிது, *a small thing,*
சிறியவை, சிறியன, or சிறிய, *small things.*

from கொடுமை—கொடியன், *a cruel man*, &c.
பெருமை—பெரியன், *a great man*, &c.
அடிமை—அடியன் அடியான், *a humble man*, &c.

They are formed also into declinable nouns, called வினைக்குறிப்புப்பேர், by adding the verbal terminations, thus:

from சிறுமை—சிறியேன், *I who am small;* plural: சிறியேம், சிறியோம், or சிறியேங்கள், &c. *we who are small.*
— அடிமை—அடியேன், *I who am a slave;* plural: அடியேம், அடியோம, or அடியேங்கள், &c. *we who are slaves;*
— தாழ்மை—தாழ்மையேன், *I who am a humble person*, plural: தாழ்மையேம், தாழ்மையோம், or தாழ்மையேங்கள், &c. *we who are humble persons.* see § XXXVII.

11. Some nouns of quality are formed by adding தனம் to the simple root; தனம் is contracted from தன்மை, i. e., *nature, character*, &c., thus:

from திருட்டு, *thieving*, திருட்டுத்தனம், *thievishness; a thievish character.*
துஷ்டம், *evil*, துஷ்டத்தனம், *wickedness.*
விளையாட்டு, *playing*, விளையாட்டுத்தனம், *playfulness*, &c.

12. Another termination, derived from the Samscrit, is துவம், which is equivalent to தனம். It is added to words of Samscrit origin, by which they become nouns of condition or quality, as:

from யோக்கியம், யோக்கியத்துவம், *intelligency.*
சீலம், *cold*, சீலத்துவம், *coolness; a meek, quiet disposition.*

from திரி, *three*—திரியத்துவம், when ய is inserted, *a being of three substances.*

VERBS.

§ XXV.

To Tamil verbs belong,

மூவிடம், *i. e., the three persons.*
ஐம்பால், *i. e., the five smaller divisions, implying gender and number.*

பகுதி, *i. e., the root.*
விகுதி, *i. e., terminating particles.*
முக்காலம், *i. e., the three tenses.*
ஏவல், *i. e., the imperative mode.*
வியங்கோள், *i. e., the optative mode.*
எச்சம், *i. e., the indefinite mode.*
தொழிற்பேர், *i. e., the verbal nouns, and*
எதிர்மறை, *i. e., the negative form of the verb.*

The two first of these, viz., மூவிடம், and ஐம்பால் have been already explained, see § XV. XVII. XVIII. XIX. and XX.

§ XXVI.

The பகுதி of a verb is its root, from which all the other modifications proceed, and which as such has no specific meaning, but indicates only the general idea of the verb apart from mode, tense, and person; for example, நட, *walk,* படி, *learn,* விடு, *leave,* போ, *go,* வை, *put,* உண், *eat,* கேள், *hear,* &c.

§ XXVII.

The விகுதி is the affix by which the gender, number, and person of the verb is distinguished.

They are, with certain alterations the terminations of the pronouns, as:

Singular, com.	என், ஏன், அன் or அனென்,			*I.*
do.	ஆய், —	ஐ, or இ, —		*thou.*
masc.	ஆன், —	அனன்,	—	*he.*
fem.	ஆள், —	அனள்,	—	*she.*
neut.	அது, —		—	*it.*
Plural, com.	ஓம், —	அனம், எம், அம் or ஆம்,		*we*
do.	ஈர், —	ஈர்கள் or இர்,	—	*you.*
masc. & fem.	ஆர் —	ஆர்கள், or அனர்,	—	*they.*
neut.	அ or அன,	—	—	*they.*

These affixes are joined to the root after the letters characteristic of the tenses which will be stated in the next Section. Here I shall only observe, that the verbs with these affixes is called முற்றுவினை, *i. e., complete verb;* because it conveys a complete sense, and finishes a sentence.

§ XXVIII.

1. The முக்காலம், or the three tenses, are:
நிகழ்காலம், *i. e., the present tense.*
இறந்தகாலம் or போனகாலம், *i. e., the past tense.*
எதிர்காலம் or வருங்காலம், *i. e., the future tense.*

These tenses are formed by the aid of certain particles, called இடைநிலைச்சொல், *i. e., words standing in the middle,* which are inserted between the root and pronominal affixes, subject to the various changes required by the rules stated in § VI. VII. and VIII. As the pronominal affixes are the same in all tenses, these middle words become the characteristics by which each tense is distinguished. They are these:

2. Of the present tense,

கிறு, கின்று, or ஆநின்று, of which the two former are most commonly used, thus:

Sing.	நடக்கிறேன்	நடக்கின்றேன் or நடவாநின்றேன்,	*I walk.*
	நடக்கிறாய்	நடக்கின்றாய் or நடவாநின்றாய்,	*thou walkest.*
	நடக்கிறான்	நடக்கின்றான் or நடவாநின்றான், நடக்கின்றனன் or நடவாநின்றனன்,	*he walks.*
	நடக்கிறாள்	நடக்கின்றாள் or நடவாநின்றாள், நடக்கின்றனள் or நடவாநின்றனள்,	*she walks.*
	நடக்கிறது	நடக்கின்றது or நடவாநின்றது,	*it walks.*
Plur.	நடக்கிறோம்	நடக்கின்றோம் or நடவாநின்றோம், நடக்கின்றனம் or நடவாநின்றனம்,	*we walk.*
	நடக்கிறீர்கள்	நடக்கின்றீர்கள் or நடவாநின்றீர்கள்,	*you walk.*
	நடக்கிறார்கள்	நடக்கின்றார்கள் or நடவாநின்றார்கள், நடக்கின்றனர் or நடவாநின்றனர்,	*they walk m. & f.*
	நடக்கின்றன or நடவாநின்றன, *they walk, neut.*		

Note. i. The third person plural neut., is always formed with கின்று; between which and the affix அ, ன is inserted. Some use the third person neut., singular also for the plural; likewise நடக்குது for both; but without authority from native Grammarians.

Note. ii. There is no certain rule for inserting the middle particle கிறு, with or without the double க்; in some therefore it is கிறு, in others க்கிறு; but it may be in general assumed that கிறு denotes the intransitive or neuter form; and க்கிறு the transitive or active form, thus:

அழிகிறது, *means to be spoiled, to spoil, to grow corrupt;* but அழிக்கிறது, *to spoil, to destroy.*

அவிகிறது, *to go out, to be extinguished;* but அவிக்கிறது, *to extinguish.*

மேய்கிறது, *to feed, to eat,* as cattle do; but மேய்க்கிறது, *to feed, to make eat,* as the shepherd does.

வளருகிறது, *to grow;* but வளர்க்கிறது, *to make grow, to educate, to rear.*

But there are many exceptions, thus:

அறிகிறது, means	*to know,*	*(a thing).*
சொல்லுகிறது	*to say,*	*(any thing.)*
பேசுகிறது,	*to speak,*	———
எழுதுகிறது,	*to write,*	———
காப்பாற்றுகிறது,	*to protect.*	———

And on the contrary,

நடக்கிறது means	*to walk.*
இருக்கிறது, ——	*to be,* &c.

The transitive or intransitive sense of a verb must therefore be known by use.

Note. iii. The roots வா *come,* and தா *give, become* வருகிறது and தருகிறது.

Note. iv. Roots ending in a consonant conform to the rules by which letters are changed ; as of

எல் is formed எற்கிறது, *to be fit.*
கேள் ——— கேட்கிறது, *to hear.*

3. The past tense is characterized by the middle particles த், ட், ற், and இன்.

The native Grammarians do not point out which roots require the one or the other of these middle particles ; I shall therefore deviate from their course, and rather follow Beschius in describing the formation of this tense ; the only one that has any difficulty.

i. Roots which end with the mute consonants ய் or ர், or with the vowel இ, உ, ஐ, ஊ, or ஆ ; and which form the present tense by க்கிற, always have த்த in the past, as :

மெய்க்கிறேன்,	*I feed,*	மெய்த்தேன்,	*I fed.*
வளர்க்கிறேன்,	*I train up,*	வளர்த்தேன்,	*I trained up.*
தீர்க்கிறேன்,	*I finish,*	தீர்த்தேன்,	*I finished.*
பார்க்கிறேன்,	*I see,*	பார்த்தேன்,	*I saw.*
விரிக்கிறேன்,	*I extend,*	விரித்தேன்,	*I extended.*
படிக்கிறேன்,	*I learn,*	படித்தேன்.	*I learned.*
படுக்கிறேன்,	*I lie down,*	படுத்தேன்,	*I lay down.*
உடுக்கிறேன்,	*I put clothes on,*	உடுத்தேன்,	*I put clothes on.*
படைக்கிறேன்,	*I create,*	படைத்தேன்,	*I created.*
உதைக்கிறேன்,	*I kick,*	உதைத்தேன்,	*I kicked.*
பூக்கிறேன்,	*I flourish,*	பூத்தேன்,	*I flourished*
காக்கிறேன்,	*I preserve,*	காத்தேன்,	*I preserved.*
&c.			

The only exception is இருக்கிறேன், *I am,* which has இருந்தேன், *I was ;* and from எல், *agree,* is formed, எற்கிறேன், *I agree,* and எற்றேன், *I agreed* (for எல்த்தேன்.)

ii. Roots ending in அ and forming the present tense, with க்கிற, receive ந்த் in the past, thus :

மறக்கிறேன், *I forget,* மறந்தேன், *I forgot.*
பறக்கிறேன், *I fly,* பறந்தேன், *I flew.*
பிறக்கிறேன், *I am born,* பிறந்தேன், *I was born.*
மணக்கிறேன், *I join,* மணந்தேன், *I joined, &c.*

iii. Roots ending in க்கு-ங்கு-கு-சு-து-பு-ணு-னு-வு-ழு-டு-று or ளு; and forming the present tense with கிற, receive இன் before the termination, as·

ஆக்குகிறேன், *I make,* ஆக்கினேன், *I made.*
நீக்குகிறேன, *I take away,* நீக்கினேன், *I took away.*
நீங்குகிறேன், *I go away,* நீங்கினேன், *I went away.*
தூங்குகிறேன், *I sleep,* தூங்கினேன், *I slept.*
ஆகுகிறேன், *I become,* ஆகினேன், or ஆயினேன், *I became.*
முடுகுகிறேன், *I hasten,* முடுகினேன், *I hastened.*
பேசுகிறேன், *I speak,* பேசினேன், *I spoke.*
பாய்ச்சுகிறேன், *I water,* பாய்ச்சினேன், *I watered.*
எழுதுகிறேன், *I write,* எழுதினேன், *I wrote.*
திருத்துகிறேன், *I correct,* திருத்தினேன், *I corrected.*
நம்புகிறேன், *I trust,* நம்பினேன், *I trusted.*
நிரப்புகிறேன், *I fill,* நிரப்பினேன், *I filled.*
பண்ணுகிறேன், *I do or make,* பண்ணினேன், *I did, or made.*
பின்னுகிறேன், *I plait,* பின்னினேன், *I plaited.*
உலாவுகிறேன், *I take a walk,* உலாவினேன், *I took a walk.*
பொருவுகிறேன், *I am like,* பொருவினேன், *I was like.*
தும்முகிறேன், *I sneeze,* தும்மினேன். *I sneezed.*
திருடுகிறேன், *I steal,* திருடினேன், *I stole.*
தவறுகிறேன், *I stumble,* தவறினேன், *I stumbled.*
தேடுகிறேன், *I seek* தேடினேன், *I sought.*
கட்டுகிறேன், *I tie,* கட்டினேன், *I tied.*
அண்டுகிறேன், *I approach,* அண்டினேன், *I approched.*
தேற்றுகிறேன், *I comfort,* தேற்றினேன், *I comforted.*
சுற்றுகிறேன், *I surround,* சுற்றினேன், *I surrounded.*
தள்ளுகிறேன், *I push,* தள்ளினேன், *I pushed*
துள்ளுகிறேன், *I leap,* துள்ளினேன், *I leaped.*

Exceptions are:

விள்ளுகிறேன், *I open,* விண்டேன், *I opened.*
ஈனுகிறேன், *I bring forth,* ஈன்றேன், *I brought forth.*
போடுகிறேன், *I put,* போட்டேன், *I put.*
கொள்ளுகிறேன், *I take or get,* கொண்டேன், *I took or got.*

and all words ending in கு, டு, and று, preceded by one short syllable; these double the last consonant, and then receive the terminatins, as:

தகுகிறேன்,	*I am fit,*	தக்கேன்,	*I was fit.*
நகுகிறேன்,	*I laugh,*	நக்கேன்,	*I laughed.*
படுகிறேன்,	*I suffer,*	பட்டேன்,	*I suffered.*
விடுகிறேன்,	*I leave,*	விட்டேன்,	*I left.*
இடுகிறேன்,	*I give,*	இட்டேன்	*I gave.*
பெறுகிறேன்	*I receive,*	பெற்றேன்,	*I received.*
இறுகிறேன்,	*I perish,*	இற்றேன்,	*I perished.*
அறுகிறேன்,	*I go off,*	அற்றேன்,	*I went off.*
But மிகுகிறேன்,	*I increase, has*	மிக்கேன், and மிகுந்தேன்,	} *I increased.*
புகுகிறேன்,	*I enter,*	புக்கேன், and புகுந்தேன்,	} *I entered.*

iv. Roots ending in ண் and ளு, and forming the present tense with கிறு, receive the middle particle ட்; and ளு is changed into ண், as:

உண்கிறேன்,	*I eat,*	உண்டேன்,	*I eat.*
ஆளுகிறேன்,	*I rule,*	ஆண்டேன்,	*I ruled.*
மாளுகிறேன்,	*I perish,*	மாண்டேன்,	*I perished.*
உருளுகிறேன்,	*I roll,*	உருண்டேன்,	*I rolled.*

Except அருளுகிறேன், *I grant,* which has, அருளினேன், *I granted.*
கேட்கிறேன், *I hear* (from the root கேள்) has கேட்டேன், *I heard.*
காண்கிறேன், *I see,* contracts the long vowel & has கண்டேன் *I saw.*

v. Roots ending in ன், லு, ல்லு, and forming the present tense with கிறு, receive the middle particle ற்; when லு and ல்லு are changed into ன், as:

தின்கிறேன்,	*I eat,*	தின்றேன்,	*I eat.*
என்கிறேன்,	*I say,*	என்றேன்,	*I said.*
சுழலுகிறேன்,	*I whirl about,*	சுழன்றேன்,	*I whirled about.*
செல்லுகிறேன்,	*I go on,*	சென்றேன்,	*I went on.*
வெல்லுகிறேன்,	*I overcome,*	வென்றேன்,	*I overcame,*
கொல்லுகிறேன்,	*I kill,*	கொன்றேன்,	*I killed.*
நிற்கிறேன் from நில்லுகிறேன்,	} *I stand,*	நின்றேன்,	*I stood.*

Except சொல்லுகிறேன், *I say,* which has சொன்னேன் and சொல்லினேன், *I said.*

vi. Roots ending in ய், இ, ஐ, கு, and ழு, forming

the present tense, with கிறு, receive the middle particle ந்த்; and ரு and ழு drop the உ, as:

மேய்கிறேன்,	*I feed,*	மேய்ந்தேன்,	*I fed.*
ஈகிறேன்,	*I give,*	ஈந்தேன்,	*I gave.*
அழிகிறேன்,	*I perish,*	அழிந்தேன்,	*I perished.*
அறிகிறேன்,	*I know,*	அறிந்தேன்,	*I knew.*
அடைகிறேன்,	*I get,*	அடைந்தேன்,	*I got.*
கடைகிறேன்,	*I churn,*	கடைந்தேன்,	*I churned.*
வளருகிறேன்,	*I grow,*	வளர்ந்தேன்,	*I grew.*
தீருகிறேன்,	*I finish,*	தீர்ந்தேன்,	*I finished.*
தவிருகிறேன்,	*I remove,*	தவிர்ந்தேன்,	*I removed.*
வாழுகிறேன்,	*I prosper,*	வாழ்ந்தேன்,	*I prospered.*
தாழுகிறேன்,	*I am humble,*	தாழ்ந்தேன்	*I was humble.*
தவழுகிறேன்,	*I creep,*	தவழ்ந்தேன்,	*I crept.*

But there are many exceptions, as:

பெய்கிறேன்,	*I rain,*	பெய்தேன்,	*I rained.*
செய்கிறேன்,	*I do,*	செய்தேன்,	*I did.*
நெய்கிறேன்,	*I weave,*	நெய்தேன்,	*I wove.*
வைகிறேன்,	*I abuse,*	வைதேன்,	*I abused.*
வாருகிறேன்,	*I gather together,*	வாரினேன்,	*I gathered together.*
தருகிறேன்,	*I give,*	தந்தேன்,	*I gave.*
பொருகிறேன்,	*I fight,*	பொருதேன்,	*I fought.*
அழுகிறேன்,	*I weep,*	அழுதேன்,	*I wept.*
உழுகிறேன்,	*I plough,*	உழுதேன்,	*I ploughed.*
தொழுகிறேன்,	*I worship,*	தொழுதேன்,	*I worshiped.*
விழுகிறேன்,	*I fall,*	விழுந்தேன் and வீழ்ந்தேன்,	*I fell.*

vii. A few roots of only one syllable, and forming the present tense with கிறு, have different forms of the past tense, as:

ஆகிறேன்,	*I become,* has	ஆயினேன்,	and ஆனேன், *I became.*
போகிறேன்,	*I go,*	போயினேன்,	and போனேன், *I went.*
சாகிறேன்,	*I die,*	செத்தேன்,	*I died.*
வேகிறேன்,	*I burn,*	வெந்தேன்,	*I burnt.*
நோகிறேன்	*I am in pain,*	நொந்தேன்,	*I was in pain.*

The characteristic middle particle of the past tense being known, the conjugation goes on as in the present tense, thus:

Singular,	நடநதேன் நடநதன்,	*I walked.*
	நடநதாய்,	*thou walkedst.*
	நடநதான் நடநதனன்,	*he walked.*
	நடநதாள், நடநதனள்,	*she walked.*
	நடநதது,	*it walked.*
Plural,	நடநதோம், நடநதனம்,	*we walked.*
	நடநதீர்கள்,	*you walked.*
	நடநதார், நடநதார்கள், நடநதனர்,	*they walked,* (mas. and fem.)
	நடநதன,	*they walked,* (neut.)

Note. 1.—Observe that the 3d person singular neuter of Verbs which have the characteristic இன், should be இனது; but this is changed into இற்று, according to the rules of the changes of letters, thus:

அடங்கினது,	becomes,	அடங்கிற்று,	*it contained.*
சொல்லினது,	———	சொல்லிற்று,	*it said.*
பண்ணினது,	———	பண்ணிற்று,	*it made.*
போயினது,	———	போயிற்று,	*it went.*
ஆயினது,	———	ஆயிற்று,	*it became.*

Note. 2.—The vulgar frequently change ந்த் into ஞ்ச, and த்த into ச்ச, as:

instead of	நடநதேன்,	they say,	நடஞ்சேன்,	*I walked.*
	செய்தேன்,	———	செய்ஞ்சேன்,	*I did.*
	படித்தேன்,	———	படிச்சேன்,	*I learned.*

Thus they say also,

for போயிற்று,	போச்சு,	or	போச்சுது,	*it went.*
— ஆயிற்று,	ஆச்சு,	or	ஆச்சுது,	*it was.*
— சொல்லிற்று,	சொல்லிச்சு	or	சொல்லிச்சுது,	*it said.*

But these forms are incorrect.

4. The *future tense* has only two forms. The characteristic middle-particle of the *first* is ப்ப, which is inserted between the root and the ter-

minations, in verbs, which form the present tense with க்கிற, as:

நடக்கிறேன்,	*I walk,*	நடப்பேன்,	*I shall walk.*
கொடுக்கிறேன்,	*I give,*	கொடுப்பேன்,	*I shall give.*
பொறுக்கிறேன்,	*I forbear,*	பொறுப்பேன்,	*I shall forbear.*
&c. &c.			

The *second* characteristic is வ், which is inserted in verbs forming their present tense with கிற, as:

செய்கிறேன்,	*I do,*	செய்வேன்,	*I shall do.*
பெறுகிறேன்,	*I receive,*	பெறுவேன்,	*I shall receive.*
எழுதுகிறேன்,	*I write,*	எழுதுவேன்,	*I shall write.*
ஆக்குகிறேன்,	*I make,*	ஆக்குவேன்,	*I shall make.*
அறிகிறேன்,	*I know,*	அறிவேன்,	*I shall know.*
தோன்றுகிறேன்,	*I appear,*	தோன்றுவேன்,	*I shall appear.*
அடைகிறேன்,	*I get,*	அடைவேன்,	*I shall get.*
&c. &c.			

Observe the following differences;

i. Roots ending in ண், ன், or ள், or ட், receive a single ப், instead of வ்; because more easily pronounced, as:

உண்கிறேன்,	*I eat,*	உண்பேன்,	*I shall eat.*
காண்கிறேன்,	*I see,*	காண்பேன்,	*I shall see.*
தின்கிறேன்,	*I eat,*	தின்பேன்,	*I shall eat.*
என்கிறேன்,	*I say,*	என்பேன்,	*I shall say,*
கேட்கிறேன்,	*I hear,*	கேட்பேன்,	*I shall hear.*
&c. &c.			

ii. Roots which end in லு, ல்லு, ளு, ள்ளு, or ழு, form the future either regularly, or drop the உ and one of the double consonant, as:

சொல்லுகிறேன்,	*I speak,*	சொல்லுவேன் or சொல்வேன்	*I shall speak.*
கொள்ளுகிறேன்,	*I take,*	கொள்ளுவேன், or கொள்வேன்,	*I shall take.*
ஆளுகிறேன்,	*I reign,*	ஆளுவேன், or ஆள்வேன்,	*I shall reign.*
வாழுகிறேன்,	*I live,*	வாழுவேன், or வாழ்வேன்,	*I shall live.*

iii. The roots ஆ, போ, சா, வே, and நோ, form the future tense regularly; or with the insertion of கு, one of the சாரியை; though the latter is less used, as:

ஆகிறேன்,	*I become,*	ஆவேன்,	and ஆகுவேன்,	*I shall become.*
போகிறேன்,	*I go,*	போவேன்,	— போகுவேன்,	*I shall go.*
சாகிறேன்,	*I die,*	சாவேன்,	— *I shall die.*	
வேகிறேன்,	*I burn,*	வேவேன்,	— வேகுவேன்,	*I shall burn.*
நோகிறேன்,	*I have pain,*	நோவேன்,	— நோகுவேன்,	*I shall have pain.*

In Poetry this கு is inserted also in other verbs, as:

செயகுவேன், *I shall do.* அணிகுவேன், *I shall adorn,* &c.

The conjugation of the future is the same as that of the other tenses, excepting the third person neuter, which has the following variations:

1. Roots, which form the present tense with க்கி று, form the third person neuter, by adding க்கும் to the root. This termination serves for both numbers, thus:

நடக்கும்,	*it or they will walk.*
சேவிக்கும்,	*it or they will serve.*
காண்பிக்கும்,	*it or they will show,* &c. &c.

2. Roots, which form the present tense in கிறு receive உம், in the third person neuter for both numbers; subject to the rules for combining letters, thus:

அடக்கும்,	*it or they will*	*inclose.*
அடங்கும்,	———	*submit.*
வரும்,	———	*come.*
சொல்லும்,	———	*say.*
கொள்ளும்,	———	*take.*
அறியும்,	———	*know,*
மேயும்,	———	*feed,*
காணும்,	———	*see.*
செய்யும்,	———	*do.*

தின்னும்,		*it or they will eat.*	
என்னும்,		———	*say.*
ஆகும்,	or contracted	ஆம்,	—— *become.*
நோகும்,	or	நோம்,	—— *be painful.*
போகும்,	or	போம்,	—— *go.*
சாகும்,	or	சாம்,	—— *die, &c. &c.*

The conjugation of the future tense will then be thus:

Singular,	நடப்பேன், நடப்பன், * நடப்பென்,	*I shall walk,*	பண்ணுவேன், பண்ணுவன்,	*I shall make.*
	நடப்பாய்,	*thou wilt walk,*	பண்ணுவாய்,	*thou wilt make.*
	நடப்பான், * நடப்பன்	*he will walk,*	பண்ணுவான்,	*he will make.*
	நடப்பாள், * நடப்பள்,	*she will walk,*	பண்ணுவாள்,	*she will make.*
	நடக்கும்,	*it will walk,*	பண்ணும்,	*it will make.*
Plural,	நடப்போம், * நடப்பேம், * நடப்பம்,	*we shall walk,*	பண்ணுவோம்,	*we shall make.*
m. & f.	நடப்பீர்கள்,	*you will walk,*	பண்ணுவீர்கள்,	*you will make.*
m. & f.	நடப்பார், — நடப்பார்கள், * நடப்பர் — * நடப்பார,	*they will walk,*	பண்ணுவார்கள்,	*they will make.*
neut.	நடக்கும்,	*they will walk,*	பண்ணும்,	*they will make.*

Note.—The Tamil has no particular forms to express our Perfect and Pluperfect and second Future Tenses, except by the aid of the verb இருக்கிறது. See § LVI. 7, i.

§ XXIX.

The ஏவல், *i. e., the imperative mode,* has two forms; both referring only to the 2d person.

1. The first and most common is, the simple root, for the singular; to this உம is affixed, which is an honorific; and to this the plural termination கள் is added to form the plural. The pronoun is usually prefixed. Thus:

* These forms are used only in Poetry.

நட,	*walking* ——	Sing.	நீ நட,	*walk thou.*
			நீர் நடவும்,	*walk you or thou.*
		Plur.	நீங்கள் நடவுங்கள்,	*walk ye.*
செய்,	*doing* ——	Sing.	நீ செய்,	*do thou.*
			நீர் செய்யும்.	*do you or thou.*
		Plur.	நீங்கள் செய்யுங்கள்,	*do ye.*
படி,	*learning* ——	Sing.	நீ படி,	*learn thou.*
			நீர் படியும்,	*learn thou or you.*
		Plur.	நீங்கள் படியுங்கள்,	*learn ye.*
பேசு,	*speaking* ——	Sing.	நீ பேசு,	*speak thou,*
			நீர் பேசும்,	*speak thou or you.*
		Plur.	நீங்கள் பேசுங்கள்,	*speak ye.*
நில்,	*standing* ——	Sing.	நீ நில்லு,	*stand thou.*
			நீர் நில்லும்,	*stand thou or you.*
		Plur.	நீங்கள் நில்லுங்கள்,	*stand ye.*
வா,	*coming* ——	Sing.	நீ வா,	*come thou.*
			நீர் வாரும்,	*come thou or you.*
		Plur.	நீங்கள் வாருங்கள்.	*come ye.*
தா,	*giving* ——	Sing.	நீ தா	*give thou.*
			நீர் தாரும்,	*give thou or you.*
		Plur.	நீங்கள் தாருங்கள்,	*give ye.*

Note.—The insertion of ர் in the two last instances forms an exception, and is taken from the present tense. See § XXVIII.

2. The other form is made by affixing to the root, the usual terminations of the 2d person, as:

Sing. நீ நடவாய், *walk thou,* படியாய், *learn thou,* வாராய், *come thou.*
நீர் நடவீர், *walk thou,* படியீர், *learn thou,* வாரீர், *come thou.*
Plur. நீங்கள் நடவீர்கள், *walk ye,* படியீர்கள், *learn ye,* வாரீர்கள், *come ye.*

But this form may be easily mistaken for the negative verb, and is therefore not much used.*

§ XXX.

The வியங்கோள், or *optative mode* is used in all persons, and has various forms.

1. The first is க added to the root.—If the root ends in க, that addition is not required. The one

---

* In Poetry the following forms are used:

Sing. போ, or போதி, } *go thou!* Plur. { போமின், போதிர், } *go ye!*

termination serves for all genders, numbers, and persons, thus:

நான், நாம், நீ-நீர்-நீங்கள், அவன், அவள், } அவர்கள்,	கேட்க, *may I you, &c. hear,*	சொல்க, *may I, &c. speak,*	வாழ்க. *may I, &c. prosper.*

Note.—Some have used the Infinitive mode, with the addition of உம், to express the Optative, as: நீர்செய்யவும், நீர்விசாரிக்கவும், &c. &c. but there is no authority for this.

2. Another form is the future tense with ஆக, the infinitive of ஆகிறது, affixed to it, as:

Sing.	நான்நடப்பேனாக,	*may I walk,*	வாழ்வேனாக,	*may I prosper.*
	நீநடப்பாயாக,	*mayst thou walk,*	வாழ்வாயாக,	*mayst thou prosper.*
	அவன்நடப்பானாக,	*may he walk,*	வாழ்வானாக,	*may he prosper.*
hon.	அவர்நடப்பாராக,	*may he walk,*	வழ்வாராக,	*may he prosper.*
	அவள்நடப்பாளாக,	*may she walk,*	வாழ்வாளாக,	*may she prosper.*
	அதுநடப்பதாக,	*may it walk,*	வாழ்வதாக,	*may it prosper.*
Plur.	நாம்நடப்போமாக,	*may we walk,*	வாழ்வோமாக,	*may we prosper.*
hon.	நீர்நடப்பீராக,	*may you walk,*	வாழ்வீராக,	*may you prosper.*
	நீங்கள்நடப்பீர்களாக,	*may you walk,*	வாழ்வீர்களாக,	*may you prosper.*
m. & f.	அவர்கள்நடப்பார்களாக,	*may they walk,*	வாழ்வார்களாக,	*may they prosper.*
neut.	அவைநடப்பனவாக,	*may they walk,*	வாழ்வனவாக,	*may they prosper.*

3. A third form is the infinitive mode, with the defective verb கடவேன், as:

Sing.	நான்நடக்கக்கடவேன்,	*may I walk.*
	நீ —— க்கடவாய்,	*mayst thou walk.*
	நீர் —— க்கடவீர்,	*mayst thou walk* (honor.)
	அவன் —— க்கடவான், or கடவன்,	*may he walk.*
	அவர் —— க்கடவார், or கடவர்,	*may he walk* (honor.)
	அவள் —— க்கடவாள், or கடவள்,	*may she walk.*
	அது —— க்கடவது,	*may it walk.*
Plur.	நாம் —— க்கடவோம்,	*may we walk.*
	நீங்கள் —— க்கடவீர்கள்,	*may you walk.*
m. & f.	அவர்கள் —— கடவார்கள், or கடவர்கள்,	*may they walk.*
neut.	அவை, —— க்கடவன,	*may they walk.*

Note.—There is another optative form common among the people, viz., by adding the word ஒட்டுகிறது, to the infinitive of a verb, thus: அவன் வரவொட்டும், *let him come,* அவன்இருக்கவொட்டும், *let him be,*—which they further contract by rejecting the ஒ, thus: அவன்வரட்டும், அவன்இருக்கட்டும், அவன்போகட்டும்.

§ XXXI.

The எச்சம், *i. e., defect,* comprehends all the indefinite modes of the verb, called in our languages participles, gerunds, infinitives, subjunctives, &c. These defective or indefinite modes are divided into two classes.

1. The *first* is called பெயரெச்சம், *i. e.,* indefinite mode, used with nouns only. They are our participles, with this difference, that they comprehend also the relative pronoun; I shall therefore call them, *relative participles.* They are three in number, corresponding with the three tenses. They are formed by dropping the personal termination of each tense, excepting the future, of which the third person neuter is also the participle future, as:

Pres. நடக்கிறேன், *I walk,* நடக்கிற, *walking,* or *who* or *which walks.*
Past. நடந்தேன், *I walked,* நடந்த, *walked,* or *who* or *which walked.*
Fut. நடக்கும், *it will walk,* நடக்கும், *walking* or *who* or *which will walk.*

Thus also:

Pres.	அடக்குகிறேன்,	*I inclose,*	அடக்குகிற,	*inclosing,* or *who* or *which incloses.*
Past.	அடக்கினேன்,	*I inclosed,*	அடக்கின,	*inclosed,* or *who* or *which inclosed.*
Fut.	அடக்கும்,	*It will inclose,*	அடக்கும்,	*inclosing,* or *who* or *which will inclose.*
Pres.	வளருகிறேன்,	*I grow,*	வளருகிற,	*growing,* or *who* or *which grows.*
Past.	வளர்ந்தேன்,	*I grew,*	வளர்ந்த,	*grown,* or *who* or *which grew.*
Fut.	வளரும்,	*It will grow,*	வளரும்,	*growing,* or *who* or *which will grow.*
Pres.	படிக்கிறேன்,	*I learn,*	படிக்கிற,	*learning,* or *who* or *which learns.*
Past.	படித்தேன்,	*I learned,*	படித்த,	*learned* or *who* or *which learned.*
Fut.	படிக்கும்,	*It will learn,*	படிக்கும்,	*learning* or *who* or *which will learn.*

I add a few other instances of verbs that have some variations, as:

Pres.	சொல்லுகிறேன்,	*I say,*	சொல்லுகிற,	*saying.*
Past.	சொல்லினேன்,	*I said,*	சொல்லிய,	*said.*
or	சொன்னேன்,	*I said,*	சொன்ன,	*said.*
Fut.	சொல்லும்,	*It will say,*	சொல்லும்,	*saying.*
Pres.	போகிறேன்,	*I go.*	போகிற, vulgarly போற,	*going.*
Past.	போயினேன்,	*I went,*	போயின்,	*gone.*
or	போனேன்,	*I went,*	போன்,	*went.*
Fut.	போகும் or போம்,	*It will go,*	போகும் or போம்,	*going.*
Pres.	ஆகிறேன்,	*I become,*	ஆகிற,	*becoming.*
Past.	ஆயினேன் or ஆனேன்,	*I became,*	ஆயின் or ஆன்,	*having become.*
Fut.	ஆகும் or ஆம்,	*It will become,*	ஆகும் or ஆம்,	*becoming.*

The relative participles are prefixed to the noun, as:

நடக்கிறகாரியம்,	*an affair which is going on.*
நடந்தகாரியங்கள்,	*affairs which were transacted.*
நடக்குங்காரியம்,	*the affair which will be transacted.*

2. The *second* class of indefinite modes is called வினையெச்சம், *i. e.*, such as refer to verbs only, which I shall call *verbal participles*. There are five of them.

i. *The first indefinite mode,* (called by Beschius, Gerund,) is formed from the past tense, and ends either in இ, or உ, viz.

Verbs which have இனேன், in the past tense, drop னேன், as:

	அடக்கினேன்,	அடக்கி,	*inclosing* or *having inclosed.*
	பொருந்தினேன்,	பொருந்தி,	*agreeing* or *having agreed.*
	சொல்லினேன்,	சொல்லி,	*saying* or *having said.*
	விரும்பினேன்,	விரும்பி,	*desiring* or *having desired.*
But	போயினேன், has only,	போய்,	*going,* or *having gone.*
	ஆயினேன், ———	ஆய்,	*becoming* or *having become.*

All other verbs drop the personal termination of the past tense; and add உ, as:

படித்தேன்,	படித்து,	*learning* or *having learned.*
அறிந்தேன்,	அறிந்து,	*knowing* or *having known.*
நடந்தேன்,	நடந்து,	*walking* or *having walked.*
விட்டேன்,	விட்டு,	*leaving* or *having left.*
அற்றேன்,	அற்று,	*ceasing* or *having ceased.*

In poetry there are also these forms; செய்பு, செய்யா, செய்யூ, செய்தென, all which are the same as செய்து.

There is no mode in English exactly corresponding to this first indefinite mode in Tamil; it is a kind of verbal participle, used with any gender, number and tense, see § LVI.

ii. The *second indefinite mode*, ends in ஆல் or இல், and answers to our subjunctive mode with *if*.— The *first* form is made from the past tense, by dropping the personal termination, and adding ஆல், as:

நடந்தேன்,	நடந்தால்,	*if I walk, walked,* or *shall walk.*
படித்தேன்,	படித்தால்,	*if I learn,* &c.
அடக்கினேன்,	அடக்கினால்,	*if I suppress,* &c.
விட்டேன்,	விட்டால்,	*if I leave,* &c.
போனேன்,	போனால்,	*if I go.* &c.
ஆனேன்,	ஆனால்,	*if I become,* &c.

The *second* form is made by adding இல், or இன், to the root of verbs, which form the present tense with கிறு; but those which form it with க்கிறு, insert also க்கு, as:

சொல்லு,	சொல்லில்,	or சொல்லின்,	*if I say.*
அடக்கு,	அடக்கில்,	or அடக்கின்.	*if I suppress.*
போடு,	போடில்,		*if I put.*
வேண்டு,	வேண்டில்,		*if I desire.*
ஆகு,	ஆகில்,		*if I become.*
நட,	நடக்கில்,		*if I go.*
படி,	படிக்கில்,		*if I learn.*
அழி,	அழிக்கில்,		*if I destroy,* &c.

But வா has வரின், or வரில், *if I come.*
தா — தரின், or தரில், *if I give.*
போ — போகில் *if I go.*

Note.—In poetry there is another form of this subjunctive, by adding ஆல் or ஏல் to any person of any tense of the verb, or to verbals in து; thus:

செய்கின்றேனால், or செய்கின்றேனேல், செய்தனையேல், &c.
செய்கின்றதேல், செய்ததேல், &c.

iii. The *third indefinite mode*, is formed from the first by adding the particle உம் to it; in which form it corresponds with our subjunctive, with *although*, referring to the *past* time, as:

அடக்கி,	அடக்கியும்,	*although*	*I suppressed.*
சொல்லி,	சொல்லியும்,	———	*I said.*
படித்து,	படித்தும்,	———	*I learned.*
நடந்து,	நடந்தும்,	———	*I walked.*
&c. &c.			

iv. The *fourth indefinite mode*, is formed from the second by adding the particle உம் to it; when it corresponds to the subjunctive mode with *although*, referring to the *future* time, as:

நடந்தால்,	நடந்தாலும்,	*although*	*I should walk.*
படித்தால்,	படித்தாலும்,	———	*I should learn.*
அடக்கினால்,	அடக்கினாலும்,	———	*I should suppress.*
போனால்,	போனாலும்,	———	*I should go.*
ஆனால்,	ஆனாலும்,	———	*I should become.*
சொன்னால்,	சொன்னாலும்,	———	*I should say.*
சொல்லின்,	சொல்லினும்,	———	*I should say.*
ஆகில்,	ஆகிலும்,	———	*I should be,* or *become.*
வரின்,	வரினும்,	———	*I should come.*

v. The *fifth indefinite mode*, ends in அ, and corresponds to our infinitive mode.—அ is added to the root, according to the rules of augmentation of letters, as:

பெறு,	பெற,	*to receive* or *get.*
அழு,	அழ,	*to weep.*
அடங்கு,	அடங்க,	*to be contained.*
அடக்கு,	அடக்க,	*to contain.*
நடத்து,	நடத்த,	*to guide.*
விடு,	விட,	*to leave.*
கொள்ளு,	கொள்ள,	*to take.*
ஆகு,	ஆக,	*to become.*
போகு,	போக,	*to go.*
அறி,	அறிய,	*to know.*
அழி,	அழிய,	*to be destroyed.*
அடை,	அடைய,	*to receive.*
மறை,	மறைய,	*to be hid.*
உண்,	உண்ண,	*to eat.*
என்,	என்ன,	*to say.*
செய்,	செய்ய,	*to do.*
காண்,	காண,	*to see.*
மேய்,	மேய,	*to feed.*
வேய்,	வேய,	*to put on as a crown,* or *flower.*
வே,	வேவ,	*to burn. Here* வ *is inserted for* ய; *an irregularity adopted in a few instances.*
நோ,	நோவ,	*to be in pain.*
சா,	சாவ,	*to die.*

But verbs which form the present tense, with க்கிறு, add க்க to the root, as:

நட,	நடக்க,	*to walk.*
படி,	படிக்க,	*to learn.*
இரு,	இருக்க,	*to be.*
கொடு,	கொடுக்க,	*to give.*
&c.	&c.	

Note.—All the indefinite modes of the second class are used with any person, gender, number and tense, with the exceptions mentioned before. See their use in Syntax. § LVI. LVII. LVIII.

§ XXXII.

The *தொழிற்பெயர், i. e., verbal noun,* is formed from the roots and the participles.

1. Neuter verbal nouns, are formed from the root by adding to it, அல், தல், or கை, in verbs which form the present tense with கிறு, as:

From	அடங்கு,	அடங்கல்,	அடங்குதல்,	அடங்குகை,	*a submitting.*
	அடக்கு,	அடக்கல்,	அடக்குதல்,	அடக்குகை,	*a suppressing.*
	காப்பாற்று,	காப்பாற்றல்,	காப்பாற்றுதல்,	காப்பாற்றுகை,	*a protecting.*
	சொல்லு,	சொல்லல்,	சொல்லுதல்,	சொல்லுகை,	*a saying.*
	விடு,	விடல்,	விடுதல்,	விடுகை,	*a leaving.*
	ஆ or ஆகு,	———	ஆதல் and ஆகுதல்,	ஆகை,	*a becoming.*
	ஆக்கு,	ஆக்கல்,	ஆக்குதல்,	ஆக்குகை,	*a making.*
	படி,	———	படிதல் and படியுதல்,	படிகை,	*a sinking.*
	அடை,	———	அடைதல் and அடையுதல்,	அடைகை,	*a getting.*
	அறி,	———	அறிதல் and அறியுதல்,	அறிகை,	*a knowing.*
	செய்,	செய்யல்,	செய்தல்,	செய்கை,	*a doing.*
	போ or போகு,	———	போதல் and போகுதல்,	போகை,	*a going.*
	தின்,	தின்னல்,	தின்னுதல்,	தின்கை,	*a eating.*
	கேள்,	———	கேட்டல் and கேட்குதல்,	கேட்கை,	*a hearing.*
	தாழ்,	———	தாழ்தல் and தாழுதல்,	தாழ்கை,	*a lowering.*
	&c. &c.				

But if the root forms the present tense with க்கிறு, then த்தல் or க்குதல் or க்கை, is added to the root, as:

From	படி,	படித்தல்,	படிக்குதல்,	படிக்கை	*a learning.*
	படிப்பி,	படிப்பித்தல்,	படிப்பிக்குதல்,	படிப்பிக்கை,	*a teaching.*
	கொடு,	கொடுத்தல்,	கொடுக்குதல்,	கொடுக்கை,	*a giving.*
	பொறு,	பொறுத்தல்,	பொறுக்குதல்,	பொறுக்கை,	*a forbearing.*
	நட,	நடத்தல்,	நடக்குதல்,	நடக்கை,	*a walking.*
	இரு,	இருத்தல்,	இருக்குதல்,	இருக்கை,	*a being.*
	&c. &c.				

2. Some roots of the latter class are formed into verbal nouns by adding ப்பு; others by மை, others by வு, or வி, thus:

From	படி,	படிப்பு,	*a learning.*
	நட,	நடப்பு,	*a walking.*
	இரு,	இருப்பு,	*a being.*
	பொறு,	பொறுமை,	*a being patient, patience.*

From தாழ்,	தாழ்மை,	*a being low, humility.*
அழி,	அழிவு,	*a destroying, destruction.*
அறி,	அறிவு,	*a knowing, knowledge.*
மற,	மறவி,	*a forgetting, forgetfulness.*
பிற,	பிறவி,	*a being born, birth.*
கேள்,	கேள்வி,	*a hearing.*

Note.—In some instances the roots themselves also are used as nouns, as: அடி, மிதி, அறை, குட்டு, சா, &c.

3. From the participles, personal and neuter nouns are formed, by adding the terminations, அன், அள், and அது, in the singular, and அர், and அவை, in the plural to each participle; except the future, as:

From *the Part: present:* நடக்கிற,	Sing.	நடக்கிறவன்,	*he who walks.*
		நடக்கிறவள்,	*she who walks.*
		நடக்கிறது,	*it which walks.*
	Plur.	நடக்கிறவர் or வர்கள்,	*they who walk.*
		நடக்கிறவை,	*they which walk.*
—— *Part: past:* நடந்த,	Sing.	நடந்தவன்,	*he who walked.*
		நடந்தவள்,	*she who walked.*
		நடந்தது,	*it which walked.*
	Plur.	நடந்தவர் or வர்கள்,	*they who walked.*
		நடந்தவை, நடந்தன,	*they which walked.*

As for the future, verbs which have ப்ப or ப as the characteristic of that tense, join the same personal terminations to it, as:

	Sing.	நடப்பவன்,	*he who will walk.*
		நடப்பவள்,	*she who will walk.*
		நடப்பது,	*that which will walk.*
	Plur.	நடப்பவர், or வர்கள்,	*they who will walk.*
		நடப்பவை, நடப்பன,	*they which will walk.*
So also	Sing.	கொடுப்பவன்,	*he who will give.*
		கொடுப்பவள்,	*she who will give.*
		கொடுப்பது,	*it which will give.*
	Plur.	கொடுப்பவர் or வர்கள்,	*they who will give.*
		கொடுப்பவை, கொடுப்பன,	*they which will give.*

So also Sing. கேட்பவன், கேட்பவள், கேட்பது, &c.
காண்பவன், காண்பவள், காண்பது, &c.

But verbs, the characteristic letter of which is வ, receive ப், between it and the root, and then the personal terminations; except the neuter, which omits the ப், probably for the sake of euphony, as:

			Plur.		
Sing.	செய்பவன்,	*he who will do,*		செய்பவர் or செயபவர்கள்,	*they who.* &c.
	செய்பவள்,	*she who will do,*			
	செயவது,	*it which will do,*		செய்வன, செய்பவை,	*they which* &c.
Also	சொல்லுபவன்,	*he who will speak,*	Plur.	சொல்பவர் or சொல்பவர்கள்,	*they who* &c.
	சொல்லுபவள்,	*she who will speak,*			
	சொல்லுவது, or சொல்வது,	*it which will speak,*		சொல்பவை, சொல்வன,	*they which* &c.
and	போபவன்,	*he who will go,*		போபவர் or போபவர்கள்,	*they who.* &c.
	போபவள்,	*she who will go,*			
	போவது,	*it which will go,*		போவன,	*they which,* &c.

Observe, that the 3d person, masculine and feminine, of all the tenses, is also occasionally used as a verbal noun, so that

நடக்கின்றான்,	is the same with,	நடக்கிறவன்.
நடக்கின்றாள்,	———	நடக்கிறவள்.
நடந்தான்,	———	நடந்தவன்.
நடந்தாள்,	———	நடந்தவள்.
நடப்பான்,	———	நடப்பவன்.
நடப்பாள்,	———	நடப்பவள்.
நடப்பார்,	———	நடப்பவர்.
நடபபார்கள்.	———	நடப்பவர்கள்.

4. Sometimes also we meet with the termination ஒன், instead of அன், particularly in the past tense, as:

நடந்தோன்,	for	நடந்தவன்,
செய்தோன்,	—	செய்தவன்,
மீட்டோன்,	—	மீட்டவன், &c.

5. Verbal nouns are also formed by adding மை to the participles of the present and past tenses, as:

நடக்கின்றமை,	*a walking.*
நடந்தமை,	*a having walked.*
சொல்லுகின்றமை,	*a saying.*
சொன்னமை,	*a having said.*
போகின்றமை,	*a going.*
போனமை,	*a having gone,* &c. &c.

All the verbal nouns are regularly declined. The forms நடந்தன, நடப்பன, செய்வன, &c., receive the சாரியை-அற்று, thus: நடந்தனவற்றை, நடந்தனவற்றால், நடந்தனவற்றிற்கு, &c.

§ XXXIII.

1. The எதிர்மறைமொழி, or *negative* of a verb, is made by adding the regular terminations of the three tenses; viz., என், ஆய், &c., to the root, without any middle particle; excepting the 3d, person neuter of the singular which ends in ஆது, and the 3d person neuter of the plural, which ends in ஆ.

2. This form has but one tense, which indeed refers chiefly to future time, but includes also the present and past; and is therefore called முக்காலம், *i. e.*, of three tenses. The conjugation is thus:

Sing.	நான்நடவேன்,	*I shall not*, or *I use not to walk.*
	நீநடவாய்,	*thou wilt not*, or *thou usest not to walk.*
	அவன்நடவான்,	*he will not*, or *he uses not to walk.*
	அவள்நடவாள்,	*she will not*, or *she uses not to walk.*
	அதுநடவாது,	*it will not*, or *it uses not to walk.*
Plur.	நாம்நடவோம்,	*we shall not*, or *we use not to walk.*
	நீங்கள்நடவீர்கள்,	*ye will not*, or *ye use not to walk.*
	அவர்கள்நடவார்கள்,	*they will not*, or *they use not to walk.*
	அவைநடவா, (neut.)	*they will not*, or *they use not to walk.*

Thus also:

நான்படியேன்,	*I shall not* or *I use not to learn*, &c.
நான்செய்யேன்,	*I shall not* or *I use not to do*, &c.
நான்அடங்கேன்,	*I shall not* or *I use not to submit*, &c.
நான்பெறேன்,	*I shall not* or *I use not to receive*, &c.
நான்ஆகேன்,	*I shall not* or *I use not to become*, &c.
நான்வாரேன்,	*I shall not* or *I use not to come*, &c.
நான்தாரேன்,	*I shall not* or *I use not to give*, &c.
நான்காணேன்,	*I shall not* or *I use not to see*, &c.
நான்இரேன்,	*I shall not* or *I use not to be*, &c.

Note. In Poetry the formation of the negative is made by affixing the appellatives இல்லன், or அல்லன், either to the imperative of the positive, or to the past relative participle, and conjugating it throughout all the persons. An ல், is often omitted. Thus: நான்பேசிலேன், *I shall not speak;* நீபேசிலை; அவன்பேசிலன், அவள்பேசிலள், நாம்பேசிலேம், or பேசிலம்; நீர்பேசிலீர், அவர்பேசிலர், அவைபேசில.

i. Besides the above form for all the three tenses, a negative verb may be formed for each tense, by joining the verb இருக்கிறேன், &c., to the negative indefinite mode (the gerund) of any verb, as:

Present.	நான் நடவாதிருக்கிறேன் or நடவாமலிருக்கிறேன்,	*I do not walk.*
	நீ நடவாதிருக்கிறாய் or நடவாமலிருக்கிறாய்,	*thou dost not walk,* &c.
Past.	நான் நடவாதிருந்தேன் or நடவாமலிருந்தேன்,	*I did not walk.*
	நீ நடவாதிருந்தாய் or நடவாமலிருந்தாய்,	*thou didst not walk,* &c.
Future.	நான் நடவாதிருப்பேன், or நடவாமலிருப்பேன்,	*I shall not walk.*
	நீ நடவாதிருப்பாய், or நடவாமலிருப்பாய்,	*thou wilt not walk,* &c.

ii. A negative verb may also be formed by adding the negative இல்லை, to the fifth indefinite mode (Infinitive,) which then refers principally to the past time, thus:

நான், நீ, அவன், &c., &c., நடக்கவில்லை, *I thou,* &c., *did not walk.*
—— —— ———— படியவில்லை, ———— *did not sink.*

iii. இல்லை, is added also to the verbal noun of the present tense, and then negatives the action itself without reference to time, and stands therefore for all the three tenses, as:

அவன்செய்கிறதில்லை, literally, *his doing is not;* meaning, *he does not do, he did not do, he will not do.*
அவள்படிக்கிறதில்லை, *she does not, did not, will not learn.*
நான்செலுத்துகிறதில்லை, *I do not, did not, shall not pay.*
&c.

Note. Some add the same also to the verbal nouns of the past and future tenses, for all persons; thus:

நான்நடந்ததில்லை, *I did not walk.*
நீநடந்ததில்லை, *thou didst not walk.*
அவன்நடந்ததில்லை, *he did not walk,* &c.
நான்நடப்பதில்லை, *I shall not walk.*
நீநடப்பதில்லை, *thou wilt not walk,* &c.

Likewise to any person of any tense, as:

நான்நடக்கிறேனில்லை, *I do not walk.*
—— நடந்தேனில்லை, *I did not walk.*
—— நடப்பேனில்லை, *I shall not walk.*
நீ நடக்கிறாயில்லை, *thou dost not walk.*
—— நடந்தாயில்லை, *thou didst not walk.*
—— நடப்பாயில்லை, *thou wilt not walk,* &c.

But there is no authority for these forms.

3. The Imperative (ஏவல்) of the negative verb is made by adding ஏல் or அல் to the root of any verb, for the 2d person singular, and அன்மின், for the 2d person plural, as:

நீநடவேல், or நடவல், *do thou not walk.*
நீங்கள்நடவன்மின், *do ye not walk.*

But this form is only used in the poetical Tamil. The common form is, to add the imperative of இருக்கிறது, to be, to the negative verbal participle of any verb, as:

நீநடவாதிரு, *do thou not walk.*
நீங்களநடவாதிருங்கள், *do ye not walk.*

Still more common it is to say,

நீநடவாதே, *do thou not walk.*
நீர்நடவாதேயும், *do you not walk,* (honor.)
நீங்களநடவாதேயுங்கள், *do you not walk.*

But this is not elegant.

4. The optative form (வியங்கோள்) of the negative verb is likewise made by adding the optative of இருக்கிறது, to the negative verbal participle, as:

நான்,	விழாதிருப்பேனாக,	*may I not fall.*
நீ,	விழாதிருப்பாயாக,	*mayst thou not fall.*
நீர்,	விழாதிருப்பீராக,	*mayst thou not fall* (honorific.)
அவன்,	விழாதிருப்பானாக,	*may he not fall.*
அவர்,	விழாதிருப்பாராக,	*may he not fall* (honorific.)
அவள்,	விழாதிருப்பாளாக,	*may she not fall.*
அது,	விழாதிருப்பதாக,	*may it not fall.*
நாம்,	விழாதிருப்போமாக,	*may we not fall.*
நீங்கள்,	விழாதிருப்பீர்களாக,	*may you not fall.*
அவர்கள்,	விழாதிருப்பார்களாக,	*may they not fall* (m. and f.)
அவை,	விழாதிருப்பனவாக,	*may they not fall* (n.)

5. The indefinite modes of the negative verb are formed thus:

i. The negative பெயரெச்சம், *i. e.*, relative participle, is formed by adding ஆத or ஆ to the root, as:

நடவாத,	or நடவா,	*not walking,*	for any tense.
செய்யாத,	or செய்யா,	*not doing.*	
பேசாத,	or பேசா,	*not speaking,*	

A negative relative participle for each tense may be formed by adding the relative participles of இருக்கிறது, to the negative verbal participle, as:

நடவாதிருக்கிற,	*not walking,*
நடவாதிருந்த,	*not having walked.*
நடவாதிருக்கும்,	*not be walking.*

ii. Of the வினையெச்சம், *i. e.*, the verbal participles, the *first* is formed by adding ஆது, or ஆமல், to the root, as:

நடவாது, நடவாமல்,	*not walking.*
பேசாது, பேசாமல்,	*not speaking.*
ஆகாது, ஆகாமல்,	*not becoming.*
போகாது, போகாமல்,	*not going.*
சாவாது, சாவாமல்,	*not dying.*

PARADIGM I.

Of a verb forming the present tense with கிற.

	Present.		Past.		Future.	
Sing.	நான் படிக்கிறேன்,	I learn,	படித்தேன்,	I learned.	படிப்பேன்,	I shall learn,
	நீ படிக்கிறாய்,	thou learnest.	படித்தாய்,	thou learnedest.	படிப்பாய்,	thou wilt learn.
	நீர் படிக்கிறீர்,	thou learnest (hon.)	படித்தீர்,	thou learnedest (hon)	படிப்பீர்,	thou wilt learn, (hon.)
	அவன் படிக்கிறான்,	he learns,	படித்தான்,	he learned.	படிப்பான்,	he will learn.
	அவர் படிக்கிறார்,	he learns, (hon.)	படித்தார்,	he learned (hon.)	படிப்பார்,	he will learn, (hon.)
	அவள் படிக்கிறாள்,	she learns.	படித்தாள்,	she learned.	படிப்பாள்,	she will learn.
	அது படிக்கின்றது, or படிக்கிறது,	it learns.	படித்தது,	it learned.	படிக்கும்,	it will learn.
Plur.	நாங்கள் படிக்கிறோம்,	we learn.	படித்தோம்,	we learned.	படிப்போம்,	we shall learn.
	நீங்கள் படிக்கிறீர்கள்,	you learn.	படித்தீர்கள்,	you learned.	படிப்பீர்கள்,	you will learn.
	அவர்கள் படிக்கிறார்கள்,	they learn, m. & f.	படித்தார்கள்,	they learned.	படிப்பார்கள்,	they will learn.
	அவைகள் படிக்கின்றன,	they learn, (neut.)	படித்தன,	they learned.	படிக்கும்,	they will learn.
Rel. Participles,	படிக்கிற,	learning.	படித்த,	learned.	படிக்கும்,	learning.

Verbal Participles.
- 2d. Part. படிக்கில், If I, thou, &c., learn.
- 5th. or Infin. படிக்க, to learn.
- 1st. Part. படித்து, learning.
- 3d. —— படித்தும், although having learned.
- 2d. —— படித்தால், if I, thou &c., learn.
- 4th. —— படித்தாலும், although I, thou, &c., should learn.

Verbal nouns.

	Present.		Past.		Future.	
Abstract.	படித்தல்,	a learning.	படித்தமை,	a having learned.	படிப்பவன்,	a man who will learn.
	படிக்குதல்,	a learning.	படித்தவன்,	a man that has learned.	படிப்பவள்,	a woman who will learn.
	படிக்கை,	a learning.	படித்தவள்,	a woman that has learned.	படிப்பது,	the (bird) which will learn.
Personal.	படிப்பு,	a learning.	படித்தது,	which has learned.	படிப்பவர்,	men or women that will learn.
	படிக்கிறவன்,	a man learning.	படித்தவர்,	men or women that have learned.		
	படிக்கிறவள்,	a woman learning.				
	படிக்கிறது,	the (bird) which learns.	படித்தவை,	things that have learned.	படிப்பவை,	things which will learn.
	படிக்கின்றமை,	the learning.	படித்தன,		படிப்பன,	

Imperative.
- நீ படி, learn thou!
- நீர் படியும், learn thou, (hon.)
- நீங்கள் படியுங்கள், learn you!

Optative.
- நான் படிப்பேனாக, or படிக்கக்கடவேன், may I learn.
- நீ படிப்பாயாக, or படிக்கக்கடவாய், mayst thou learn.
- நீர் படிப்பீராக, or படிக்கக்கடவீர், mayst thou learn &c. &c. &c.

Of a verb forming the present tense with கு.

	Present.		Past.		Future.	
Sing.	பண்ணுகிறேன்,	I make.	பண்ணினேன்,	I made.	பண்ணுவேன்,	I shall make.
	பண்ணுகிறாய்,	thou makest.	பண்ணினாய்,	thou madest.	பண்ணுவாய்,	thou wilt make.
	பண்ணுகிறீர்,	thou makest (hon.)	பண்ணினீர்,	thou madest (hon.)	பண்ணுவீர்,	thou wilt make (hon.)
	பண்ணுகிறான்,	he makes.	பண்ணினான்,	he made.	பண்ணுவான்,	he will make.
	பண்ணுகிறார்,	he makes (hon.)	பண்ணினார்,	he made (hon.)	பண்ணுவார்,	he will make (hon.)
	பண்ணுகிறாள்,	she makes.	பண்ணினாள்,	she made.	பண்ணுவாள்,	she will make.
	பண்ணுகின்றது, or பண்ணுகிறது,	it makes.	பண்ணிற்று,	it made.	பண்ணும்,	it will make.
Plur.	பண்ணுகிறோம்,	we make.	பண்ணினோம்,	we made.	பண்ணுவோம்,	we shall make.
	பண்ணுகிறீர்கள்,	you make.	பண்ணினீர்கள்,	you made.	பண்ணுவீர்கள்,	you will make.
	பண்ணுகிறார்கள்,	they make.	பண்ணினார்கள்,	they made.	பண்ணுவார்கள்,	they will make.
	பண்ணுகின்றன,	they make.	பண்ணின,	they made.	பண்ணும்,	they will make.
Rel. Participles,	பண்ணுகிற,	making.	பண்ணின,	made.	பண்ணும்,	making.

Verbal Participles.
- 2d. Part. பண்ணுகில், If I, thou, &c. make.
- 5th. பண்ண, to make.
- 1st. Part. பண்ணி, making.
- 3d. —— பண்ணியும், although having made.
- 2d. —— பண்ணினால், If I, thou, &c., make.
- 4th. —— பண்ணினாலும், although I thou &c., should make.

Verbal nouns.

Present.		Past.		Future.	
பண்ணல்,	a making.	பண்ணினமை,	a having made.	பண்ணுவான்,	a man who will make.
பண்ணுதல்,	a making.	பண்ணினவன்,	a man who made.	பண்ணுவாள்,	a woman who will make.
பண்ணுகை,	a making.	பண்ணினவள்,	a woman who made.	பண்ணுவது,	a thing which will make.
பண்ணுகிறவன்,	a man making.	பண்ணினது,	the thing which made.	பண்ணுவார்,	men who will make.
பண்ணுகிறவள்,	a woman making.	பண்ணினவர்,	men or women who made.	பண்ணுவன,	things which, &c.
பண்ணுகிறது,	the thing making.	பண்ணினவை,	things which, &c.	பண்ணுவவை,	
பண்ணுகின்றமை,	a making.				

Imperative.
- நீ பண்ணு, make thou!
- நீர் பண்ணும், make thou (hon.)
- நீங்கள் பண்ணுங்கள், make you.

Optative.
- நான் பண்ணுவேனாக, or பண்ணக்கடவேன், may I make.
- நீ பண்ணுவாயாக, or பண்ணக்கடவாய், mayst thou make.
- நீர் பண்ணுவீராக, or பண்ணக்கடவீர், mayst thou, &c., (hon.)

PARADIGM II.

OF THE NEGATIVE FORMS OF THE TWO PRECEDING VERBS.

Common tense for all times.

Sing.	நான் படியேன்,	I shall not learn.
	நீ படியாய்,	thou wilt not learn.
	நீர் படியீர், (hon.)	thou wilt not learn.
	அவன் படியான்,	he will not learn.
	அவர் படியார், (hon.)	he will not learn.
	அவள் படியாள்,	she will not learn.
	அது படியாது,	it will not learn.
Plural	நாங்கள் படியோம்,	we shall not learn.
	நீங்கள் படியீர்கள்,	you will not learn.
	அவர்கள் படியார்கள்,	they will not learn.
	அவைகள் படியா,	they will not learn.

Rel: Participles. படியாத, படியா, } not learning.

Verbal Participles. படியாது, படியாமல், } not learning.

Verbal nouns.
- படியாமை, a not learning.
- படியாதவன், a man who does not learn.
- படியாதவள், a woman who does not learn.
- படியாதது, that which does not learn.
- படியாதவர், men who do not learn.
- படியாதவை, things which do not learn.

Imperative.
- நீ படியாதிரு, or படியாதே, } do thou not learn.
- நீர் படியாதிரும், or படியாதேயும், } do thou not learn. (hon.)
- நீங்கள் படியாதிருங்கள், or படியாதேயுங்கள், } do you not learn.

Optative.
- நான் படியாதிருப்பேனாக, may I not learn.
- நீ படியாதிருப்பாயாக, mayst thou not learn.
- நீர் படியாதிருப்பீராக, mayst thou not learn (hon.)
- அவன் படியாதிருப்பானாக, may he not learn.
- அவர் படியாதிருப்பாராக, may he not learn (hon.)
- அது படியாதிருப்பதாக, may it not learn.
- நாம் படியாதிருப்போமாக, may we not learn.
- நீங்கள் படியாதிருப்பீர்களாக, may you not learn.
- அவர்கள் படியாதிருப்பார்களாக, may they not learn. (m. & fem.)
- அவைகள் படியாதிருப்பனவாக, may they not learn (neut.)

Common tense for all times.

Sing.	நான் பண்ணேன்,	I shall not make.
	நீ பண்ணாய்,	thou wilt not make.
	நீர் பண்ணீர், (hon.)	thou wilt not make.
	அவன் பண்ணான்,	he will not make.
	அவர் பண்ணார், (hon.)	he will not make.
	அவள் பண்ணாள்,	she will not make.
	அது பண்ணாது,	it will not make.
Plural.	நாங்கள் பண்ணோம்,	we shall not make.
	நீங்கள் பண்ணீர்கள்,	you will not make.
	அவர்கள் பண்ணார்கள்,	they will not make.
	அவைகள் பண்ணா,	they will not make.

Relative Participles. பண்ணாத, பண்ணா, } not making.

Verbal Participles. பண்ணாது, பண்ணாமல், } not making.

Verbal nouns.
- பண்ணாமை, a not making.
- பண்ணாதவன், a man who does not make.
- பண்ணாதவள், a woman who does not make.
- பண்ணாதது, that which does not make.
- பண்ணாதவர், men who do not make.
- பண்ணாதவை, things which do not make.

Imperative.
- நீ பண்ணாதிரு, or பண்ணாதே, } do thou not make.
- நீர் பண்ணாதிரும், or பண்ணாதேயும், } do thou not make (hon.)
- நீங்கள் பண்ணாதிருங்கள், or பண்ணாதேயுங்கள், } do you not make.

Optative.
- நான் பண்ணாதிருப்பேனாக, may I not make.
- நீ பண்ணாதிருப்பாயாக, mayst thou not make.
- நீர் பண்ணாதிருப்பீராக, mayst thou not make (hon.)
- அவன் பண்ணாதிருப்பானாக, may he not make, &c.

The *second* and *remaining* verbal participles are formed by adding the verbal participles of the verb இருக்கிறது, to the first negative verbal participle of any verb, as:

the 2d.	நான், நீ, &c.	நடவாதிருந்தால்,	*if I, thou, &c., do not walk.*
—— 3d.	————	நடவாதிருந்தும்,	*although I, &c., do or did not walk.*
—— 4th.	————	நடவாதிருந்தாலும்,	*although I, &c., should not walk.*
—— 5th.	————	நடவாதிருக்க,	*not to walk.*

6. Negative verbal nouns (தொழிற்பெயர்,) are formed,

i. By adding ஆமை, to the root, as:

நடவாமை, *a not walking.*
செய்யாமை, *a not doing.*
பொறாமை, *a not containing, envy.*
வேண்டாமை, *a not desiring, &c., &c.*

ii. By adding the personal terminations to the negative participle, as:

நடவாதவன், *a man who does not walk.*
நடவாதவள், *a woman who does not walk.*
நடவாதது, *a thing which does not walk.*

Having stated the particulars of a verb, I add two Paradigms, to show them to the student in one view; only those terminations are put down, which are most in common use.

§ XXXIV.

The Tamulians form also *causal* verbs,

1. From simple verbs, which have க்கிறு, in the present tense, by substituting ப்பிக்கிறது, for the middle particle, as:

அடி அடிக்கிறேன், *I beat*, அடிப்பிக்கிறேன், *I cause to beat.*
படி படிக்கிறேன், *I learn*, படிப்பிக்கிறேன், *I cause to learn, i. e., I teach.*
நட நடக்கிறேன், *I walk*, நடப்பிக்கிறேன், *I cause to walk, i. e,. I transact.*
போதி போதிக்கிறேன், *I teach*, போதிப்பிக்கிறேன், *I cause to teach.*
&c. &c.

2. From simple verbs which have கிறு, in the present tense, by substituting விக்கிறு as the middle particle, thus:

செய் செய்கிறேன், *I do*, செய்விக்கிறேன், *I cause to do.*
சொல்லு சொல்லுகிறேன், *I say*, சொல்லுவிக்கிறேன், *I cause to say.*
பண்ணு பண்ணுகிறேன், *I make*, பண்ணுவிக்கிறேன், *I cause to make.*
விடு விடுகிறேன், *I leave*, விடுவிக்கிறேன், *I cause to leave, i. e., I deliver.*
வா வருகிறேன், *I come*, வருவிக்கிறேன், *I cause to come.*
அறி அறிகிறேன், *I know*, அறிவிக்கிறேன், *I cause to know. I make known.*

&c. &c.

An exception is காண்கிறேன், I see, which has காண்பிக்கிறேன், *I cause to see, I show.*

These causal verbs are regularly conjugated like படிக்கிறேன், as:

நான் படிப்பிக்கிறேன், *I teach*, &c.
—— படிப்பித்தேன், *I taught*, &c.
—— படிப்பிப்பேன், *I shall teach*, &c.
&c. &c.

§ XXXV.

There are several *defective* verbs, that is, verbs of which some parts only are in use. They are these:

1. Of the root ஒ, *equal* or *agreeing*.

the 3d person neut. fut.	ஒக்கும்,	*it agrees, it is equal.*
the 1st indefinite mood,	ஒத்து,	*agreeing, being equal.*
the 5th indefinite mood,	ஒவ்வ ஒப்ப,	*to agree.*
the perf. participle,	ஒத்த,	*agreed equal.*
the fut. participle,	ஒக்கும்,	*which will* or *which does agree.*
the verbal nouns,	ஒத்தது,	*it which agrees.*
and	ஒப்பு,	*agreement, equality.*

In the negative form, the 3d person neut.	ஒவ்வாது,	*it does not agree.*
the relative participle,	ஒவ்வாத,	*not agreeing.*
verbal participle,	ஒவ்வாது ஒவ்வாமல்,	*in not agreeing.*

Occasionally, however, we meet also with the three tenses, as:

ஒவ்வாநின்றேன்,	*I agree,* &c.
ஒத்தேன்,	*I agreed.*
ஒப்பேன்,	*I shall agree.*

2. Of the root வேண்டு, *necessity,*

the 3d person neut. fut.	வேண்டும்,	*it is necessary, it must.*
the participle of the past tense,	வேண்டிய,	*being necessary.*
the verbal nouns,	வேண்டியது,	*it must,* with respect to the past.
	வேண்டுவது,	*it must,* with respect to the future.
In the negative form,	வேண்டாம்,	*it must not.*

Note 1.—For வேண்டும், the vulgar use வேணும், and for வேண்டாம், வாண்டாம், or வாணும்.

Note 2.—This defective verb must not be confounded with வேண்டு, *desiring*, which is regularly conjugated throughout all the modes and tenses.

3. Of the root மாட்டு, *possibility, ability,* used only in

The negative form,	மாட்டேன்,	*I can, or will not.*
	மாட்டாய்,	*thou canst or wilt not.*
	மாட்டீர்,	*thou canst or wilt not.* (hon.)
	மாட்டான்,	*he can or will not.*
	மாட்டார்,	*he can or will not.* (hon.)
	மாட்டாள்,	*she can or will not.*
	மாட்டாது,	*it can or will not.*
	மாட்டோம்,	*we can or will not.*
	மாட்டீர்கள்,	*you can or will not.*
	மாட்டார்கள்,	*they can or will not.*
The Relative Participle,	மாட்டாத,	*which is not able.*
The Verbal Participle,	{ மாட்டாது மாட்டாமல், }	*not being able.*

Some use this verb also in the affimative form, as மாட்டுவேன், *I can*, மாட்டுவாய், *thou canst*, &c., but there is no authority for it.

4. Of the negative verbal roots இல் and அல், signifying, *not*.

Sing.	இல்லேன்,	அல்லேன்,	*I am not.*
	இல்லாய்,	அல்லாய்,	*thou art not.*
	இல்லான்,	அல்லான்,	*he is not.*
	இல்லாள்,	அல்லாள்,	*she is not.*
	இல்லது, *	அல்லது, *	*it is not.*
Plur.	இல்லோம்,	அல்லோம்,	*we are not.*
	இல்லீர்கள்,	அல்லீர்கள்,	*you are not.*
	இல்லார்கள்,	அல்லார்கள்,	*they are not.*
	இல்லன,	அல்லன,	*they are not.*
Rel. Part.	இல்லாத, *	அல்லாத, *	} *not being.*
	இல்லா, *	அல்லா, *	
Verb Part.	இல்லாது, *	அல்லாது, *	} *not being.*
	இல்லா, *	அல்லா, *	
	இல்லாமல், *	அல்லாமல், *	
	இன்று, *	அன்று or அன்றி *	
Verbal Nouns,	இல்லை, *	அல்ல, *	} *a not being.*
	இல்லாமை, *	அல்லாமை, *	
	இன்மை, *	அன்மை, *	
	இல்லாதவன், *	அல்லாதவன், *	*a man who is not.*
	இல்லாதவள், *	அல்லாதவள், *	*a woman who is not.*
	இல்லாதது, *	அல்லாதது, *	} *a thing which is not.*
	இல்லது, *	அல்லது,	

Note 1.—Only those marked thus * are in common use.

Note 2.—The difference between இல் and அல் is, that இல் denies the existence of a thing; but அல் its quality. See § LXIX.

5. Of உள் denoting *within*.

Rel. Participle,	உள்ள,	*having or containing.*
Verbal Nouns,	உள்ளமை or உண்மை,	*the condition of having.*
	உள்ளவன்,	*a man who has.*
	உள்ளவள்,	*a woman who has.*
	உள்ளது,	*a thing which has.*

3d person for all genders, உண்டு, there is from உள்து.

One of the ள is also omitted; thus அவன் உளன், *he is;* அவர் உளர், *they are,* அது உளது *it is;* அவை யுள, *they are.* But these forms are used more frequently in poetry.

6. Of போது, denoting *sufficiency*,

3d Pers. neut.	போதும்,	*it is enough, sufficient.*
In the Neg. form,	போதாது,	*it is not enough.*
The verb Participle,	போதாத,	*not being enough.*
Verbal noun,	போதாமை,	*the not being enough.*

7. Of the root கட, denoting *necessity, duty,* the whole of the the future tense, thus:

Sing.	கடவேன்,	*I must,* or *may.*
	கடவாய்,	*thou must* or *mayst.*
	கடவீர், (hon.)	*you must* or *may.*
	கடவான் or கடவன்,	*he must* or *may.*
	கடவார் or கடவர், (hon.)	*he must* or *may.*
	கடவாள் or கடவள்,	*she must* or *may.*
	கடவது,	*it must* or *may.*
Plur.	கடவோம்,	*we must* or *may.*
	கடவீர்கள்,	*you must or may.*
	கடவார்கள் or கடவர்கள்	*they must* or *may,* masc. and fem.
	கடவன,	*they must* or *may,* neuter.

In the 3d person neut. plur. the singular, கடவது, is also in use.

Hence also the verbal noun, கடமை, *duty.*

8. Of the root தகு, denoting *fitness, propriety,* the whole future tense, as:

	தகுவேன்,	*I ought, I am fit.*
	தகுவாய்,	*thou ought.*
	தகுவான்,	*he ought.*
	தகுவாள்,	*she ought.*
	தகும்,	*it ought.*
	&c. &c.	
The Infinitive,	தக,	*to be fit.*
Rel. Participle,	தக்க,	*fit,* (past.)
	தகும்,	*fit,* (fut.)
Verbal Nouns,	தகுதி,	} *fitness, propriety.*
	தகைமை,	
	for தகுமை,	
	தககமை,	
	தக்கவன்,	*a man that is fit.*
	தக்கவள்,	*a woman that is fit.*
	தக்கது,	*a thing that is fit.*

The negative form;

The whole tense,	தகேன்,	*I am not fit.*
	தகாய்,	*thou art not fit.*
	&c. &c.	
The Verbal Participles,	தகாது,	*not being fit.*
	தகாமல்,	*not being fit.*
Rel. Paticiple,	தகா	} *not being fit.*
	தகாத,	
Verbal Nouns,	தகாமை,	*the not being fit, unfitness.*
	தகாதவன,	*an unfit man.*
	தகாதவள்,	*an unfit woman.*
	தகாதது,	*an unfit thing.*

§ XXXVI.

The Tamil verbs have two Voices only; viz. தன்வினை, or இயல்புவினை, *i. e.*, verbs, the action of which remains with ourselves, intransitive verbs; and பிறவினை, *i. e.*, verbs, the action of which passes over to another, transitive or active verbs. The passive voice is formed in several ways.

1. By adding படுகிறேன், *I suffer*, in all its modifications, to the infinitive mode of any active verb, as:

அடிக்கப்படுகிறேன், *I am beaten, I suffer beating, &c.*
அடிக்கப்பட்டேன், *I was beaten, &c.*
அடிக்கப்படுவேன், *I shall be beaten, &c.*
&c. &c.

2. By adding பெறுகிறேன், in all its tenses, to the infinitive, as.

அடிக்கபெறுகிறேன், *I get beating*, i. e., *I am beaten.*
அடிக்கப்பெற்றேன், *I got beating*, i. e., *I was beaten.*
அடிக்கப்பெறுவேன், *I shall get beating*, i. e., *I shall be beaten.*
&c. &c.

3. By adding, in some instances, the verb உண்கிறேன், *I eat*, figuratively, to primitive verbal nouns, as:

அறையுண்கிறேன், *lit: I receive stripes;* i. e., *I am beaten.*
அறையுண்டேன், *lit: I received stripes;* i. e., *I have been beaten.*
&c. &c.
குட்டுண்கிறேன், *I am buffetted.*
குட்டுண்டேன், *I was buffetted.*
&c. &c.
அறுப்புண்கிறேன், *I am cut off.*
அறுப்புண்டேன், *I was cut off.*
&c. &c.

The first of these is the most common form, but it does not exactly answer our passive form, because in certain connexions intransitive verbs also may be thus united with படுகிறது, as:

இருக்கப்பட்டேன், *lit: I suffered being*, i. e., *I was.*
நடக்கப்படுவேன், *lit: I shall suffer going*, i. e., *I shall go.*

And again, though the active form be made thus passive, the active verb still retains, in certain cases, its active power; particularly in the participles: *e. g.*,

அவர்கள அதைவைக்கப்பட்டஇடம், *the place in which they put it.* or *the place in which it was put.*

§ XXXVII.

This seems the proper place to state a peculiar kind of appellative nouns, called வினைக்குறிப்புமுற்று, mentioned § XXIV. 10.

They are formed from certain obsolete roots that are still used as adjectives, such as:

> அரு, *hard, difficult,* சிறு, *small,* அடி, *low.*
> கொடு, *cruel,* பெரு, *great,* புது, *new,* உள், *being,* &c. &c.

The final உ, is changed into இ, and the following terminations affixed,

For the 1st person Sing.	ஏன்,	as,	அரியேன்,	*I a hard man.*
2d person,	ஐ,	as,	அரியை,	*thou a hard man.*
3d person, mas.	அன்,	as,	அரியன்,	*he a hard man.*
——— fem.	அள்,	as,	அரியள்,	*she a hard woman.*
——— neut.	து,	as,	அரிது,	*it a hard thing.*
For the 1st person. Plur.	ஏம்,	as,	அரியேம்,	*we hard men.*
or	அம்,	as,	அரியம்,	*we hard men.*
2d person,	ஈர்,	as,	அரியீர்,	*you hard men.*
3d person, mas. fem.	அர்,	as,	அரியர்,	*they hard people.*
neut.	அ	or	அரிய,	*they hard things.*
	அன,	or	அரியன,	*they hard things.*

Thus also,

கொடியேன்,	*I a cruel man,*	சிறியேன்,	*I a little man.*
கொடியை,	*thou cruel man,*	சிறியை,	*thou a little man.*
கொடியன்,	*he a cruel man,*	சிறியன்,	*he a little man.*
கொடியள்,	*she a cruel woman,*	சிறியள்,	*she a little woman.*
கொடிது,	*it a cruel thing,*	சிறிது,	*it a little thing.*
	&c. &c.		

At the same time that these appellatives have the form and regimen of verbs, they have also the form and regimen of nouns; and are then called வினைக்குறிப்புப்பேர். Thus any of the persons may be regularly declined, as:

1st case, கொடியேன், *I who am a cruel man*, அடியேன், *I who am a low man*, i. e., *a humble servant.*
2d case, கொடியேனை, *me who am a cruel man*, அடியேனை, *me who am a low man*, i. e., *a humble servant.*
3d case, கொடியேனால், *by me who am a cruel man*, அடியேனால், *by me who am a low man*, i. e., *a humble servant.*
4th case, கொடியேனுக்கு, *to me who am a cruel man*, அடியேனுக்கு, *to me who am a low man*, i. e., *a humble servant.*
&c. &c.

Thus also the second person.

Ist case, கொடியை, *thou who art a hard person.*
2d case, கொடியையை, *thee who art a hard person.*
3d case, கொடியையால், *by thee who art a hard person.*
4th case, கொடியைக்கு, *to thee who art a hard person.*
&c. &c.

Accordingly we find the following expressions.

கொடியைசிறியேனையடித்தாய், i. e., in plain language.
கொடுமையுள்ளவனாகிய நீ சிறுமையுள்ளவனாகிய என்னையடித்தாய், *thou a cruel man hast beaten me a small man.*
அரியவெளியவாக்குவேன், i. e., in plain language.
அரிமையான்வைகளை எளிமையாககுவேன், *I shall make easy the things that are difficult.*

The use of these concise forms is however nearly confined to poetry. Only some of the forms are in common use, as:

அரிது, *it is difficult.*
சிறிது, and சிறியது, *it is small.*
சிறியன், *he is a small man.*
கொடிது, *it is cruel.*
கொடியான், *he is a hard man.*
அடியான் or அடியேன், } *I your humble servant.*
உளது or உள்ளது, *it is.*
பெரிது, *it is great.*
பெரியன், *he is a great man.*
&c. &c.

§ XXXVIII.

It remains to mention some further particulars respecting the derivation or formation of verbs.

1. From intransitive verbs, formed from the roots as before stated, transitive or active verbs are again made by inserting த்து, before கிற, as:

நடக்கிறது, *to walk,* நடத்துகிறது, *to make walk, to direct.*
இருக்கிறது, *to be,* இருத்துகிறது, *to make to be, to put.*
கிடக்கிறது, *to lie down,* கிடத்துகிறது, *to make to lie down, to lay down.*
படுகிறது, *to suffer,* படுத்துகிறது, *to make to suffer,* i. e., *to affect.*
&c. &c.

In the same way are formed also some verbs from those which are already active, and then the newly formed verb becomes doubly active, or causal, as:

சுமக்கிறது, *to carry, bear a burden,* சுமத்துகிறது, *to make one carry a burden, to put upon.*

If the root end in று or டு, active or causal verbs are formed by doubling the ற் and ட், as:

ஆறுகிறது, *to be composed, comforted,* ஆற்றுகிறது, *to comfort.*
தேறுகிறது, *to be comfortable,* தேற்றுகிறது, *to make comfortable.*
ஏறுகிறது, *to ascend,* ஏற்றுகிறது, *to make to ascend, to lift up.*
ஆடுகிறது, *to play,* ஆட்டுகிறது, *to make one play.*
ஓடுகிறது, *to run,* ஓட்டுகிறது. *to drive.*
வாடுகிறது, *to dry up,* வாட்டுகிறது, *to make dry.*

Roots which end in ங்கு, ம்பு, are formed into active or causal verbs, by changing the ங் and ம் into க் and ப், respectively, as:

அடங்குகிறது, *to be contained,* அடக்குகிறது, *to make to be contained, to retain.*
கலங்குகிறது, *to be troubled,* கலக்குகிறது, *to trouble, to mix.*
முழங்குகிறது, *to sound,* முழக்குகிறது, *to cause to sound.*
திரும்புகிறது, *to return,* திருப்புகிறது, *to turn, to make go back.*
எழும்புகிறது, *to rise,* எழுப்புகிறது, *to make to rise, to raise.*

Lastly, some intransitive verbs, ending in ட், form active verbs by inserting ச்சு, as:

பாய்கிறது,	*to run,*	பாய்ச்சுகிறது,	*to make run, as the water.*
காய்கிறது,	*to become dry,*	காய்ச்சுகிறது,	*to make dry.*
&c. &c.			

2. Verbs are formed from nouns by adding to them படுகிறது, for the intransitive, and படுத்துகிறது, for the transitive; if the noun end in ம், it is dropt. Thus:

குணப்படுகிறது,	*to become healed,*	குணப்படுத்துகிறது,	*to heal.*
சந்தோஷப்படுகிறது,	*to be glad,*	சந்தோஷப்படுத்துகிறது,	*to make glad.*
மகிமைப்படுகிறது,	*to become glorious,*	மகிமைப்படுத்துகிறது,	*tomake glorious.*
&c. &c.			

In a few instances the active form, படுத்துகிறது, is added to the infinitive, and makes the verb active or causal, as:

From தெரிகிறது,	*to know,*	தெரியப்படுத்துகிறது,	*to make known, to acquaint.*
—— அறிகிறது,	*to know,*	அறியப்படுத்துகிறது,	*to make known, to acquaint.*

3. Intransitive verbs are formed from nouns of quality, by adding, ஆகிறது, or ஆயிருக்கிறது, as:

குணமாகிறது,	*to become healed.*
குணமாயிருக்கிறது,	*to be healed.*
நீளமாகிறது,	*to become long.*
நீளமாயிருக்கிறது.	*to be long.*
வெண்மையாகிறது,	*to become white.*
வெண்மையாயிருக்கிறது,	*to be white.*
&c. &c.	

4. Active verbs are formed by joining the verbs ஆக்குகிறது, பண்ணுகிறது or செய்கிறது, to the noun, as:

குணமாக்குகிறது,	*to heal.*
நீளமாக்குகிறது,	*to make long, to lengthen.*
சுத்தஞ்செய்கிறது சுத்தம்பண்ணுகிறது,	} *to make clean, to cleanse.*

தோத்திரஞ்செய்கிறது ——— ம்பண்ணுகிறது,	*to praise.*
நடனம்பண்ணுகிறது.	*to dance.*
பிரசங்கம்பண்ணுகிறது,	*to preach.*
&c. &c.	

5. Active verbs are formed of Samscrit nouns ending in அம், by dropping this syllable, and adding இக்கிறது, &c. as:

From தியானம்,	*meditation,*	தியானிக்கிறது, *to meditate a thing,* தியானிப்பிக்கிறது, *to make another meditate a thing.*
——— தோத்திரம்,	*praise,*	தோத்திரிக்கிறது, *to praise one,* தோத்திரிப்பிக்கிறது, *to make one praise another.*
——— அனுக்கிரகம்,	*favour,*	அனுக்கிரகிக்கிறது, *to favour.*
——— வசனம்,	*word,*	வசனிக்கிறது, *to speak a thing,* வசனிப்பிக்கிறது, *to make another speak a thing.*
——— சுதந்தரம்,	*inheritance,*	சுதந்தரிக்கிறது, *to inherit.*
——— பிரசங்கம்,	*harangue,*	பிரசங்கிக்கிறது, *to preach.*
——— பிரகாசம்,	*light,*	{ பிரகாசிக்கிறது, *to shine.* { பிரகாசிப்பிக்கிறது, *to enlighten.*
——— சந்தோஷம்,	*joy,*	{ சந்தோஷிக்கிறது, *to be glad.* { சந்தோஷிப்பிக்கிறது, *to make glad.*

If the noun end in இ, only க்கிறு is added, as: துதி, *praise* துதிக்கிறது, *to praise.*

The word சுத்தி, *cleanness,* however, receives the addition of கரிக்கிறது, as: சுத்திகரிக்கிறது, from the Samscrit.

ADJECTIVES AND ADVERBS.

§ XXXIX.

The fourth and last part of speech in Tamil, is called உரிச்சொல், *i. e., qualifying* or *descriptive word,* referring either to nouns or to verbs; in the former case, we call them adjectives, and in the latter, adverbs.

§ XL.

Adjectives are variously formed from nouns denoting quality;

1. By adding the relative participles ஆன or உள்ள, to them, as:

நீளம்.	*length,*	நீளமான,	நீளமுள்ள,	*long.*
கோணல்,	*crookedness,*	கோணலான,	கோணலுள்ள,	*crooked.*
செம்மை,	*straitness,*	செம்மையான,	செம்மையுள்ள,	*strait.*
கைப்பு,	*bitterness,*	கைப்பான,	கைப்புள்ள,	*bitter.*
சந்தோஷம்,	*joy.*	சந்தோஷமான,	சந்தோஷமுள்ள,	*joyful.*
கொடுமை,	*cruelty,*	கொடுமையான,	கொடுமையுள்ள,	*cruel.*
இரக்கம்,	*mercy,*	இரக்கமான,	இரக்கமுள்ள,	*merciful.*
&c. &c.				

They always precede the nouns which they qualify, without any further change, as:

நீளமானகோல்,	*a long stick.*
இரக்கமுள்ளமனிதன்,	*a merciful man.*
&c. &c.	

2. If the nouns denoting quality end in ம், this letter is often dropped, and the remainder of the word used adjectively, as:

From சுத்தம்,	*purity,*	சுத்தஇருதயம்,	*a clean heart.*
—— ஞானம்,	*spirituality,*	ஞானபோசனம்,	*spiritual food.*
—— புறம்,	*the outside,*	புறபொருள்,	*an external thing.*
&c. &c.			

3. Nouns ending in a vowel, are often used as adjectives, without the addition or rejection of any letter, as:

மழைகாலம்,	*the rainy season.*
குளிர்காற்று,	*a cold wind.*
பாறைநிலம்,	*a stony ground.*
&c.	

4. Some nouns ending in ம்பு, and ந்து, change the ம and ந respectively into ப and த, and become thus adjectives, as:

From இரும்பு, *iron,* இருப்புக்கோல், *an iron rod.*
—— மருந்து, *medicine,* மருத்துப்பை, *a medicine bag.*

5. Some nouns ending in உமை or இமை, change these syllables into இய, and become adjectives, as:

From கொடுமை, *cruelty,* கொடியமனசு, *a cruel mind.*
—— அருமை, *difficulty,* அரியகற்பனை, *a difficult command.*
—— பெருமை, *greatness,* பெரியமலை, *a large mountain.*
—— புதுமை, *newness,* புதியபொருள், *a new thing.*
—— இனிமை, *sweetness,* இனியபதார்த்தம், *a sweet thing.*
—— உரிமை, *fitness,* உரியகுணம், *a fit disposition.*

In some instances only ஐ is rejected, as:

கொடுந்தமிழ், *difficult Tamil.*
பெருங்கோபம், *great anger,* &c.

Of பெருமை, the last syllable மை, is in certain connexions, rejected and the first vowel lengthened, as: பேராசை, *great desire, insatiableness.*

6. A few words are naturally adjectives, as:

பல, *various,* பலசொற்கள், *various words.*
சில, *some,* சிலகனிகள், *some fruits.*
மற்று, *other,* மற்றொன்று, *another thing.*
மற்ற, *other,* மற்றமனிதர்கள், *other men.*
நல } *good,* { நற்குணம், *good disposition.*
நல்ல, } { நல்லமனசு, *a good mind.*
பொது, *common,* பொதுப்பேர், *a common word.*
புது, *new,* புதுச்சுவாமி, *a new god.*

7. Sometimes the participles of the past tense are used adjectively, thus:

கெட்டமரம், *a corrupt tree.*
செத்தமிருகம், *a dead beast.*
தோன்றியசூரியன், *the risen sun.*
மிகுந்ததிரவியம், *much money.*

§ XLI.

Adverbs are,

1. naturally such, as:

சால,	*much,*	சாலப்பேசினான்,	*he spoke much.*
மற்று,	*otherwise,*	மற்றறிவோம்,	*we shall know otherwise.*
நவ,	*much,*	நவ்வுரைத்தான்,	*he explained much.*

2. Formed from nouns of quality by affixing ஆய் or ஆக, of the verbs ஆகிறது, as:

From கோபம், *anger,* கோபமாய்வந்தான், *he came angrily.*
—— நன்று, *a good thing,* நன்றாய்ச்சொன்னான், *he spoke well.*
—— பக்கம், *the side,* பக்கமாய்ப்போனான், *he went aside.*
—— இறுமாப்பு, *haughtiness,* இறுமாப்பாய்நடந்தாள், *she walked haughtily.*
—— கிருபை, *grace,* கிருபையாயிரங்குகிறார், *he graciously pities.*
&c. &c.

3. Some infinitives are used adverbially, as:

கூட,	*together,*	அவர்கள்கூடவந்தார்கள்,	*they came together.*
ஒருமிக்க, ஒருப்பட,	*together,*	ஒருமிக்கப்போனார்கள்,	*they went together.*
கடுக,	*to be swift,*	கடுகவோடினான்,	*he ran swiftly.*
முடுக,	*to be swift,*	முடுகப்பேசினான்,	*he spoke quickly.*
மெல்ல,	*to be soft,*	மெல்லநடந்தான்,	*he walked softly* or *slowly.*
மிக,	*to be much,*	மிகக்கொடுத்தான்,	*he gave much* or *liberally.*
வலிய,	*to be free,*	வலியக்கொடுத்தான்,	*he gave freely, spontaneously.*

The participle உம், is added to some of the above mentioned words, as:

மிகவுங்கோபித்தான்,	*he was very angry.*
சாலவும்பேசினான்,	*he spoke much.*
மற்றுஞ்சொன்னான்,	*he said otherwise.*

Note.—The Tamil Grammarians divide all the qualities or attributes into 4 classes;

1. The qualities of spirit in connection with bodies are 32; viz. அறிவு, *knowledge*, or perception of any kind; அருள், *kindness*; ஆசை, *desire, love*; அச்சம், *fear*; மானம், *nakedness*; நிறை, *duration*; பொறை, *patience*; ஓர்ப்பு, *desire*; கடைப்பிடி, *retention*; மையல், *confusion*; நினைவு, *thinking*; வெறுப்பு, *aversion*; உவப்பு, *lust*; இரக்கம், *mercy*; நாணம், *shame*; வெகுளி, *anger*; துணிவு, *boldness*; அழுக்காறு, *envy*; அன்பு, *affection, love*; எளிமை, *want*; எய்த்தல், *weariness*; துன்பம், *affliction*; இன்பம், *pleasure*; இளமை, *youth*; மூப்பு, *old age*; இகல், *hatred*; வென்றி, *superiority, victory*; பொச்சாப்பு, *guilt, failing*; ஊக்கம், *courage*; மதம், *haughtiness, pride*; மறம், *unmercifulness, cruelty*; and மறவி, *forgetfulness*.

2. The qualifications of soul and body together are 5; viz., துய்த்தல், *eating*; துஞ்சல், *sleeping*; தொழுதல், *adoring*; அணிதல், *putting on*; and உய்த்தல், *walking*.

3. The qualities common to all bodies are 6; viz.

i. வடிவு, *shape, as*: சதுரம், *a square*; நீளம், *length*; வட்டம், *a circle*; கோணம், *an angle*, &c.

ii. அளவு, *measure*, such as, one, two, three, &c.

iii. வண்ணம், *colour*, such as: வெண்மை, *whiteness*, செம்மை, *redness*, பொன்மை, *gold colour*, கருமை, *black*, பசுமை, *green*, &c. &c.

iv. மணம், *smell*, e. g., நற்கந்தம், *good scent*, துற்கந்தம், *bad smell*.

v. சுவை, *taste*, e. g., கைப்பு, *bitter*, புளிப்பு, *sour*, துவர்ப்பு, *astringency*, உவர்ப்பு, *saltness*, தித்திப்பு, *sweetness*, உறைப்பு, *acrid heat*.

vi. ஊறு, *sensation*, e. g., வெம்மை, *heat*, தண்மை, *cold*, மென்மை, *softness*, வன்மை *hardness*, திண்மை, *weight*, நொய்மை, *lightness*, சீர்மை, *smoothness*, and சருச்சரை, *roughness*.

4. Qualities which spirits have with or without bodies, are 9; viz.

தோன்றல், *visibility*; மறைதல், *concealment*; வளர்தல், *increase*; சுருங்கல், *decrease*; நீங்கல், *motion*; அடைதல், *reception*; நடுங்கல், *trembling*; இசைத்தல், *connexion*; and ஈதல், *giving*.

Adjectives and adverbs may be formed of all these terms, by adding ஆன or உள்ள, ஆய or ஆக.

5. The mode of expressing the comparative and superlative degrees of adjectives and adverbs, will be stated in the Syntax. See § XLVI. 8; § XLVII. 2.

CHAPTER III.

SYNTAX.

§ XLII.

1. Tamil Grammarians do not treat of Syntax specially, but connect it at once with Etymology, calling that chapter, சொல்லதிகாரம், *i. e., the chapter respecting words.*

They make but two principal parts of a sentence, viz., எழுவாய் or கருத்தா, which means *beginning, head,* and expresses what we call *the nominative;* and பயன், which means *end, conclusion,* and expresses the finite verb.

The words which depend upon, or refer to either of these, are called அடைமொழிகள்.

2. As to the position of the parts of a sentence, the subject, or எழுவாய், always precedes the finite verb or பயன், and the latter always concludes the sentence, *e. g.*, கொற்றனவந்தான், *Kotten came,* மரம் வளர்ந்தது, *the tree grew,* &c.

All other words which depend upon these principal parts precede them respectively; so that the most important of the dependent words is placed nearest to its principal, and the least important farthest from it.

It is evident that to this general rule, examples cannot be given in this early part of the Syntax: it will be exemplified throughout; and I mention it in this place to be kept in remembrance during the study of the following rules.

3. Again,

The Adjective always precedes the substantive: as, தயையுள்ளசுவாமி, *gracious God*, &c.

The Noun precedes its governing participle or preposition: as, வீட்டின்மேல், *upon the house.*

The Adverb precedes the verb: as, நன்றாய்ப்பாடினான், *he sang well.*

The Infinitive precedes the governing verb: as, இருக்கச்சொன்னார், *he told to sit down* or *to wait.*

The Negative branch of a sentence precedes the Affirmative: as, வழுவாமற்பத்திரமாய்நட, *walk firmly without slipping.*

மனிதனையல்லப் பராபரனைத் தூஷணிக்கிறான், *he blasphemeth God, and not man.*

The Comparative precedes that which is compared: as, இவனிலும் அவன்நல்லவன், *that man is better than this man.*

The similitude precedes that which is similar: as, சூரியனைப்போல அவன்பிரகாசிக்கிறான், *he shines like the sun.*

The Number precedes that which is numbered: as, பன்னிரண்டுமரங்கள், *twelve trees.*

The Genitive precedes the governing noun: as, மனிதருடையகுணம், *the disposition of men.*

The cause precedes the effect: as, மழையிலேபயிராகும், *seed grows by the rain.*

The reason precedes the inference: as, பராபரன்நல்லவரானபடியினாலே அவர்பாவமுண்டாக்கவில்லை, *God is good; therefore he has not made sin.*

The purpose precedes the determination: as, ஜீவனைக்காக்கும்படிக்குச் சோறுசாப்பிடவேண்டும், *we must eat rice in order to preserve life.*

The condition or supposition precedes the consequence: as, சாப்பிட்டாற்சாவாய், *thou shalt die, if thou eat.*

From these general remarks, it is evident that the order of the parts of speech in Tamil is, on the whole, and in many parts, opposite to that in English; so that the European student has to effect an entire change in the arrangement of his ideas. But let none be discouraged; even a short but diligent application will overcome all the difficulties. I descend now to particulars.

§ XLIII.

1. The nominative and its verb always agree in gender, number and person, as:

நான்சொல்லுகிறேன்,	*I say.*
நாம்போவோம்,	*we shall go.*
நீதூங்காதிரு,	*do not sleep!*
நீர்பேசினீர்,	*you spoke.*
நீங்கள்பயப்படுகிறீர்கள்,	*you fear.*
அவர்சொன்னார்,	*he told.*
தச்சன்வந்தான்,	*the carpenter came.*
பெண்பாடுகிறாள்,	*the maid sings.*
போர்ச்சேவகர்சண்டைபண்ணினார்கள்,	*the troops fought.*
மலையுயரமாயிருக்கின்றது,	*the mountain is high.*
மரங்கள்வளருகின்றன	*the trees grow.*

2. The pronouns are often omitted, as the verb itself sufficiently points out the person; when this is not the case, then the pronoun must be put: as, நீபோகவேண்டும், *thou must go*, &c.

3. The names of superiors, when used by inferiors form an exception to this rule: as, பராபரன், *God*, தேவன், *God*, தகப்பன், *father*, &c. which, because of the respect due to them, may have the verb in the honorific form, though the nouns have the common termination, as:

பராபரன்திருவுளம்பற்றினார்,	*God spake.*
தேவன்எண்ணினார்,	*God thought.*
தகப்பன்வருவார்,	*the father will come.*

It is however more correct to say, தேவர், தகப்பனார்.

4. Though some nouns, masculine and feminine, have the neuter termination, yet their verbs must have the masculine and feminine gender, as:

குருசொல்லுகிறார்,	*the teacher saith.*
கடவுள்அனுக்கிரகித்தார்,	*God has granted.*
ஸ்திரிவருவாள்,	*the woman will come.*
சனங்கள்கூப்பிடுகிறார்கள்,	*the people call.*

However, they may also be construed with the neuter of the future of the verb; though rarely: as,

குருச்சொல்லும், *the teacher will say.*
கடவுள்தயவுசெய்யும், *God will be gracious.*

Note.—The neuter person singular of the present and past tenses, is, in common talk, frequently used with a noun in the plural number: as, காரியங்கள்நடந்தது, (*vulgarly* நடந்துது,) *things happened;* but it is incorrect; because the termination து is evidently singular, neither do the Native Grammarians authorize such a use of it; it must therefore be காரியங்கள்நடந்தன, *things happened,* நாய்கள் குரைக்கின்றன, *dog bark;* Not, குரைக்குது or குரைக்கிறது.

5. The nominative is often used instead of the accusative case. See § XLIV. 2, 3.

6. It is used likewise for the genitive or 6th case in personal nouns, as:

மனிதர்குணம்பொல்லாதது, *the nature of man is bad.*
அவன்வீடுஇடிந்தது, *his house has fallen down.*

7. Two or more nominatives in one sentence must be connected by the conjunction உம், added to every one of them, as:

மனிதருஞ்சுரர்களும்பாடினார்கள், *men and heavenly beings sung.*
புருடர்களும்ஸ்திரிகளும்பிள்ளைகளும்வணங்கினார்கள், *men, women and children, worshipped.*

But such nominatives must be of the same gender; otherwise the sentence must be divided into as many simple sentences as there are nominatives of different genders, or the whole sentence must receive a new form. Thus we cannot say, மனிதருங்குதிரைகளும் அழிந்தார்கள் or அழிந்தன, *men and horses perished; but,* மனிதர் அழிந்தார்கள்குதிரைகளும் அழிந்தன, *men perished; also the horses perished,* or மனிதர்கள்குதிரைகளோடே அழிந்தார்கள், *the men perished with the horses.*

8. In a series of nouns of the same class or species, in whatever case, the connective particle உம்,

may be omitted, and the nouns put in the nominative case, with என்பவர்கள், if they are masculine and feminine; and with என்பவைகள், if they are neuter. These verbal nouns, thus added must be put in the case required, as :

> சாத்தன்கொற்றனென்பவர்கள்புறப்பட்டார்கள், *Satten and Kotten went forth.*
>
> பொன், வெள்ளி, ஈயம், இரும்பென்பவைகள்மிகவும்பிரயோசனமானவைகளாயிருக்கின்றன, *gold, silver, lead and iron, are very useful:*
>
> Instead of சாத்தனுங்கொற்றனும், &c. பொன்னும், வெள்ளியும், ஈயமும். &c.
>
> For என்பவர்கள் and என்பவைகள், the conjunction என்று, with the demonstrative pronouns இவர்கள் and இவைகள், may also be used' as:
>
> சாத்தன்கொற்றனென்றிவர்கள, &c.
>
> பொன், வெள்ளி, ஈயம், இரும்பென்றிவைகள், &c.

See § LXIV. 4.

9. Instead of expressing all the parts of the whole class or kind with உம் or என்பவைகள், &c., only one or two of them may be put in the nominative case, and முதலானவைகள் or முதலியவைகள் added, if they are of the neuter gender ; or முதலானவர்கள், if they are of the masculine and feminine, as :

> பொன்முதலானவைகளுண்டு, *there is gold and such other things*, or *the rest.*
>
> சாத்தன்முதலானவர்கள்வந்தார்கள், *Satten and the rest came.*

As முதல் means first, or the beginning, the meaning is, that class of things, of which gold is the first ; that number of men, of whom Satten is the first, so that the words answer to our etc., etc.,

Instead of the pronominal terminations வைகள் and வர்கள், the noun which is common to the whole class or kind, may be added to முதலான or முதலிய, thus:

முத்துசாமிமுதலியபேர்கள் பிறந்தார்கள், *Moottoosawmy and the rest were born.*
அன்புமுதலானநற்குணங்கள் பாவிகளுக்கில்லை, *love and the other good dispositions are not with sinners.*
தேவேந்திரன்முதலானதேவர்கள் எழும்பினார்கள், *Devendiren and the rest of the Gods rose up.*

Again, when the nouns are neuter, இவை may be prefixed to முதலான, as:

பொன்வெள்ளியிவைமுதலானவைகள், *gold, silver, and the rest.*

10. If the nominatives of the three persons are in one sentence together, the first has the preference ; if only the second and third persons, the second has the preference ; the verb must then be put in the plural of that person.

நானும், நீரும், இவனும், போவோம்வாருங்கள், *I, you, and he, let us go!*
நீயும், அவனும், போங்கள், *go you and he!*

§ XLIV.

1. The second, or accusative case, is required, by all active verbs of whatever kind, as:

சூரியன்இருளைநீக்குகின்றது, *the sun dispels the darkness.*
பராபரன்துன்மார்க்கரைத்தண்டிக்கிறார், *God punisheth the wicked.*
எளியவர்களைத்துன்பப்படுத்தாதிருப்பாயாக, *do not thou afflict the poor!*

Hence also such verbal participles, as are used like our prepositions, (see § XII. 7. b.) and are derived from active verbs, require the accusative case, thus:

தருமகாரியத்தைக்குறித்துப்பேசினார்கள், *they spoke concerning the charity business.*
சன்மார்க்கத்தைவிட்டுவிலகினான், *he forsook the path of virtue,* lit: *he left it and went away.*
பட்டினத்தைச்சுற்றிமதிலிருக்கின்றது, *there is a wall round the city.*

From the same reason also the comparing particle, போல, *as*, must have the accusative, thus:

அதைப்போலஇதுவுங்கெட்டது, *this also is spoiled like that.*

2. Of nouns neuter, when the indefinite article would be used in English, the nominative is often put for the accusative, as:

புத்தகங்கொடுத்தான், *he gave a book.*

If you say, புத்தகத்தைக்கொடுத்தான், it means, *he gave the book.*

This distinction however is not always observed.

3. When the nominative which stands sometimes for the 6th or genitive case, (see the preceding paragraph, Sect. 6,) is liable to be mistaken for the latter, the accusative case must be placed before the nominative case, as:

வீட்டையவன்கட்டினான் or வீட்டைக்கட்டினான், *he built the house.*

If you say அவன்வீட்டைக்கட்டினான், it may be understood the same with அவனுடையவீட்டைக்கட்டினான், *he* (a person) *built* his (another person's) *house.*

4. The accusative case must be placed also before the nominative, when it has many appendages which would remove the nominative too far from its verb. If the nominative however has also many appendages, such place must be given it, as will make the sense least ambiguous.

5. The intransitive verb, சேருகிறது, *to approach*, has sometimes the accusative case, sometimes the 7th case, as:

அவளைச்சேர்ந்தான், *he approached her.*
ஊரிற்சேர்ந்தோம், *we arrived at the village.*

§ XLV.

1. The third case denotes the instrument, or cause, or formation, as:

கண்ணாற்கண்டான், *he saw with the eye.*
ஆயுதத்தால்வெட்டினான், *he smote with a weapon.*
நாழியால் அளந்தான், *he measured with a nárli.*
குயவனாற்குடமுண்டாக்கப்பட்டது, *the water pot was made by the potter.*
அரசனேவினாலேயிதுநடந்தது, *this happened by order of the king.*
சொரூபங்கல்லாற்செய்யப்பட்டது, *the image was made of stone.*
மண்ணாலானகுடம், *a pot made of earth.*
திரிகையாலானகுடம, *a pot made by means of a wheel.*
இந்தவேலையென்னாற்கூடாது, *this business will* (or *can*) *not be* (*done*) *by me*, or *I cannot do this business.*

2. This case when formed with ஒடு, signifies union, harmony, as:

உலகத்தோடேஒப்புரவாகஒழுகுவோம், *we shall be in harmony with the world.*
உங்களோடேயிருப்பேன், *I shall be with you.*

When it means *together with* the word கூட, is often added, as:

தவத்தோடே (கூட) ஸ்நானம்பண்ணுகிறார்கள், *they make ablution with meditation.*
தீயோடு (கூட) ப்புகையிருக்கும், *with fire will be smoke.*
குடையோடே(கூட)நிழலிருக்கும், *with the umbrella will be shadow.*

Of course all verbs denoting union require this case, as:

உன்னோடேகூடினோம், *we joined you.*
மரத்தோடேமரத்தைச்சேர்த்தார்கள், *they joined one piece of wood to another.*
இதினோடே அதுபொருந்தாது, *that does not agree with this.*
பதத்தோடேபதம்புணரும், *one word unites with another.*
மனிதரைப்பராபரனோடேயொப்புரவாக்கினார், *he reconciled men with god.*

§ XLVI.

The fourth, or dative case, is required,

1. By verbs signifying to give, in any wise, thus:

இரப்பார்க்குப்பிச்சைகொடுத்தான், *he gave alms to beggars.*
அஞ்ஞானிகளுக்குஞானத்தைப்போதித்தான், *he taught the ignorant wisdom.*
பிராமணர்சனங்களுக்குப்பொய்களைச்சொல்லுகிறார்கள், *the bramins tell the people lies.*
தேவகட்டளையையுங்களுக்குஅறிவிப்பேன், *I shall make known to you the divine command.*
நீயிதற்குச்சம்மதித்தாய், *thou hast consented to this.*
எங்களுக்குநியாயங்களைச்சொல்லு, *tell us reasons!*

2. By the intransitive verbs போகிறது, *to go*, கிடைக்கிறது, *to happen*, சம்பவிக்கிறது, *to happen*, இரங்குகிறது, *to be merciful*, பயப்படுகிறது, *to fear*, as:

சென்னபட்டினத்திற்குப்போனோம், *we went to Madras.*
கிருபையெனக்குக்கிடைத்தது, *I have found grace;* lit: *grace has happened to me.*
அவனுக்குத்துன்பஞ்சம்பவித்தது, *he has been afflicted;* lit: *affliction has happened to him.*
எனக்கிரங்கும், *have mercy upon me! be merciful to me!*
சனங்கள்மறவருக்குப்பயப்படுகிறார்கள், *the people fear the Maravers.*

3. By the defective verbs, உண்டு, *there is;* வேண்டும், *it is necessary*, தகும், *it is fit*, and their negative forms, இல்லை, வேண்டுவதில்லை, தகாது, as:

எனக்குத்துக்கமுண்டு, *I have sorrow;* i. e., *to me is sorrow.*
உங்களுக்குப்பணமில்லை, *you have no money;* i. e., *to you is no money.*
கூலிக்காரனுக்குப்பத்துப்பணம்வேண்டும், *the cooly wants ten fanams;* i. e., *ten fanams are necessary to the cooly.*
இந்தஅலுவலுக்குஇவ்வளவுபேர்வேண்டுவதில்லை, *so many persons are not necessary for this business.*
இது உனக்குத்தகும், *this suits thee.*
நிந்தைமனிதருக்குத்தகாது, *calumnies are not becoming to men.*

This construction is common in Latin.

4. By all adverbs and adjectives signifying opposition, motion, union, distance, nearness, similarity, suitableness, profitableness, assistance, flattery, pleasure, love, hatred, mercy and the other passions; likewise the feelings of the bodily senses, as, hearing, taste, &c., thus :

இராசாவுக்குவிரோதமாய்ப்பேசுகிறார்கள், *they speak opposed to the king.*
மலைக்குநேராய்ப்போவோம், *we shall go towards the mountain.*
அநீதிக்குநீதியிசைவாயிராது, *righteousness has no connexion with unrighteousness.*
அதுகாஞ்சிபுரத்திற்குத்தூரமாயிருக்கிறது, *that is far from Canjepooram.*
கருத்தாவுக்குச்சமீபமாயிருக்கவிரும்புவாயாக, *desire to be near the Lord!*
இந்தப்புட்பத்திற்குநிகரில்லை, *there is no flower, like this,* i. e., *it is incomparable.*
அவருடையதிருச்சித்தத்திற்குத்தகுதியாய்ச்செய், *do agreeably to his will!*
ஒருவருக்கொருவர்துணையாயிருங்கள், *assist one another ;* or *be assistants one to another.*
அநேகர்பெரியோர்களுக்குஇனிமையாய்ப்பேசுகிறார்கள், *many flatter the great.*
புறங்கூறுகிறவன்எனக்குப்பிரியனல்ல, *the back biter is not pleasant to me, or my friend.*
நமக்குப் பகையாயிருக்கிறவர்களைச் சிநேகிப்போமாக, *let us be friendly to those who hate us.*
பாவிகளுக்குக்கிருபையாயிருப்பார், *he will be gracious to sinners.*
இந்தச்சங்கதியெனக்குக்கேள்வியாயிற்று, *I have heard of this affair.*
இந்தப்பதார்த்தம்நாவுக்குருசியாயிருக்கிறது, *this dish* (or thing) *is tasteful to the tongue.*

5. By the particles கீழ், *under*, மேல், *over*, and பின், *behind*, and by the verbs composed of them, as:

அதைப்பலகைக்குக்கீழேபோடு, *throw it under the board.*
சலம்மலைக்குமேலிருந்தது, *the water was above the mountain.*
அக்காலத்திற்குப்பின (பின்பு,) *after that time.*
சுவாமிக்குக்கீழ்ப்பணியவேண்டும், *we must obey God.*
ஆர்அவர்களுக்குமேற்படுவார்கள், *who will be above them?*
நல்லவர்களுக்குப்பினசெல்லுங்கள், *follow after good people!*

If these verbs be active, they require of course both the accusative and dative cases, as:

நம்முடையவிருப்பங்களைநம்முடையபுத்திக்குக்கீழ்ப்படுத்தவேண்டும் we must subject our desires to our reason.
நீயுன்னையொருவருக்கும்மேற்படுத்தக்கூடாது, thou must not exalt thyself above any body !

The simple particles are often used also with the oblique case. See § LXXXIX.

6. By substantives denoting limit, region, rank, or relation, as:

சமுத்திரம்இந்துதேசத்திற்குஎல்லையாயிருக்கிறது, the sea is the boundary of India.
சென்னபட்டினத்திற்குத்தெற்கேதரங்கம்பாடியுண்டு, south of Madras is Tranquebar.
அவர்எனக்குமுதலாளியாயிருக்கிறார், he is my superior.
நீங்கள்எங்களுக்குச்சிநேகிதர்களாயிருப்பீர்களாக, be ye friends to us!
இவள்எனக்குத்தாய், she is mother to me, i. e., *my mother.*
அவன்அவளுக்குப்பிள்ளையாயிருக்கிறான், he is her child.

7. By verbs which require purpose or design, as:

கூலிக்குவேலைசெய்தான், he laboured for hire.
இதற்குவந்தான், he came for this purpose.

In this sense the infinitive ஆக, is frequently added, as:

கூலிக்காக, இதற்காக, &c.

8. The dative is used in comparisons, where we use the comparative degree, as:

இதற்கு அதுபெரிது, that is greater than this.
மந்திரிக்குஇராசாநல்லவன், the king is a better man than (his) minister.

9. Two dative cases express the particle *between*, as:

தண்ணீருக்குந்திராட்சஇரசத்துக்கும்மிகுந்தவித்தியாசமுண்டு, there is great difference between water and wine.
உனக்குமெனக்குமென்ன? what is there between thee and me? i. e., *what have I to do with thee?* expressing contempt, or hatred.
திரிசிராப்பள்ளிக்கும் பாளையங்கோட்டைக்கும் பத்தொன்பதுகாதம், the distance from Trichinopoly to Palamcottah is 19 *kadams* i. e., 190 miles.

§ XLVII.

The fifth case or ablative of separation and motion is required,

1. By intransitive verbs signifying *removing*, as:

> *ஊரினீங்கினான் or ஊரினின்றுநீங்கினான் or ஊரிலிருந்துநீங்கினான், he removed from the village.*
> *தலையில் (or தலையினின்று) மயிர் தாழ்ந்தது, the hair hang down from the head.*
> *இந்தச்சத்திரத்திலிருந்துபோனான், he went away from this choultry.*
> *பொல்லாதவைகள் இருதயத்திலிருந்துபுறப்படுகின்றன, evil things proceed from the heart.*
> *பட்டினத்திலிருந்துவந்தான், he came from the city.*

2. It is used, like the dative, for the comparative degree, with உம் affixed to it, because it implies that one thing is separated from another, as:

இந்தமலையிலும்அந்தமலைபெரிது,	*that mountain is greater than this.*
அதிலும் இதுமெல்லிது,	*this is finer than that.*

Also without the உம், as: *கொள்ளலினீதலினிது, giving is sweeter than receiving, கொள்ளலில்ஈதல்இனிது.*

3. It denotes in some cases, *possession*, as:

அவன் அறிவிற்பெரியன்,	*he is great in knowledge.*
விசுவாசத்திற்பெலவீனமுள்ளவன்,	*one that is weak in faith.*
பொருளில்எளியன்,	*one poor in goods.*

4. It denotes, though rarely, *similarity, likeness*, as;

பாலின்வெளிதுகொக்கு,	*the stork is as white as milk.*
காக்கையிற்கரிதுகளாம்பழம்,	*the kalām fruit is as black as a crow.*
மின்னினிலையிலையாக்கை,	*the body is as unstable as lightening.*
மின்னினொழியும் இன்பம்,	*pleasure vanishes like lightening.*

5. It expresses *limit*, (எல்லை), as:

திருக்கோவலூரின்றெற்குக்காவிரியாறு, *the river Caviri (is) south of Tirukāveloor.*

Note.—The oblique case having (the சாரியை) இன், must not be confounded with this fifth case. See § XVI. 13, nor with the seventh case. See § XLIX.

§ XLVIII.

The sixth, or genitive case, is required,

1. by nouns, which are the property of another, either as an inherent quality, or as obtained elsewhere; the former is called தற்கிழமை; and the latter பிறிதின்கிழமை, thus:

மாணிக்கவாசகருடையகுணம்,	*the disposition* or *nature of Manikavasager.*
அவருடையஆடை,	*his robe.*
தமது இருதயம்,	*our heart.*
நம்முடையபணம்,	*our money.*
மனிதரதுஇயல்பு,	*the nature of men.*
அரசனுடையஆழி,	*the ring of the king.*

2. It is used also with nouns, of which it expresses the constituent parts, as:

நெல்லதுகுப்பை,	*a heap of paddy.*
மாந்தருடையதொகுதி,	*the total number of men.*
படையதுதொகை,	*the whole number of fighting troops.*
எள்ளதுகூட்டம்,	*a heap of elloo* or *rape seed.*
கிறிஸ்தவர்களுடையசபை,	*the congregation of christians.*

3. This case is also occasionally used when one thing has arisen from another; though the substance remains the same, as:

நெல்லதுசோறு, *the rice of nelloo;* i. e., *boiled rice, which has been prepared of nelloo,* i. e., *rice yet in the husks.*

4. When two or more genitives belong to a noun, they cannot be united by the copulative conjunction as in English.—We cannot say, for instance,

அகத்தியனுடையவும்பிருகுவினுடையவும்மொழிகள், *the sayings of Agattier and of Bhriggoo.*

But the noun to which they belong must be repeated as many times as there are genitives, or the sentence must receive another form.—We must therefore say:

அகத்தியனுடைய மொழிகளும் பிருகுவினுடைய மொழிகளும், *the words of Agattier and the words of Bhriggoo;*—or
அகத்தியனும்பிருகுவுஞ்சொன்னமொழிகள், *the words which Agattier and Bhriggoo spake.*

Or the genitive cases may all be changed into the nominative, and என்பவைகள் or என்பவர்கள் or என்றிவைகள் or என்றிவர்கள், added to the last of them in the genitive case. See § XLIII. 7. 8. as:

சிவப்பு, பச்சை, நீலமென்பவைகளுடையதன்மை, or
சிவப்பு, பச்சை, நீலமென்றிவைகளுடையதன்மை, or
சிவப்பு, பச்சை, நீலமென்றிந்தநிறங்களினுடையதன்மை, *the nature of the red, green,* and *blue colours.*
பிரமா, விட்டுணு, உருத்திரனென்பவர்களுடையநடக்கைகள், *the proceedings of Brooma, Vishtnoo and Ruttiren.*

If the rest be only in general referred to, then முதலானவைகள், முதலானவர்கள், must be used, as:

சிவப்புமுதலானநிறங்களுடையதன்மை, *the nature of the red colour and of the rest.*

5. The nominative case is often used for the genitive, when no ambiguity arises from it, as:

அவன்வீட்டுக்குப்போனேன், *I went to his house,* for அவனுடைய வீட்டுக்கு.
தகப்பன்சொற்படிசெய், *do according to the command of your father.*

But compare § XLIV. 3.

6. The oblique case is frequently used for the genitive case; for instances, see § XVI. 13, and § LI.

Note.—As the genitive case is used in no other instances but those mentioned in this paragraph, it is evident that it does not always correspond with the possessive case in English; and that therefore great discrimination must be used in rendering the latter in Tamil. See the particle *of*, in the Appendix.

§ XLIX.

The seventh case, or ablative of place, is required,

1. by nouns which express things existing in, at, or with others, as:

மணியினிடத்திலொளி (or மணியிலொளி or மணியினொளி or மணியின் கண்ணொளி,) முக்கியமாயிருக்கின்றது, *the splendour of the jewel is beautiful.*

பயிரினிடத்திற்கிள்ளை (or பயிரிற்கிள்ளை or பயிரின்கிள்ளை or பயிரின் கண்கிள்ளை) பயிரைத்தின்கிறது, *the parrot of the cultivated field eats the grain.*

கடலினிடத்திற்றிரை or (கடலிற்றிரை or கடலின்றிரை or கடலின் கட்டிரை) மிகுந்தமணலுள்ளது, *the sea shore is full of sand;* or *very sandy.*

ஆகாயத்தினிடத்திற்பறவை (or ஆகாயத்திற்பறவை, &c.) அநேக விதமாயிருக்கின்றது, *the fouls of the air are very various.*

நாளினிடத்தில்நாழிகை (or நாளின்நாழிகை, &c.) சீக்கிரமாய்ப்போயிற்று, *the hour of the day has quickly passed.*

காரின்கண்முல்லை (or காரின்முல்லை) கண்ணுக்கழகாயிருக்கின்றது, *the vegetation of the rainy season is pleasant to the eye.*

கையினிடத்தில்விரல் (or கையின்விரல், &c.) உபகாரமாயிருக்கிறது, *the finger of the hands is useful.*

நிறத்தின்கண்அழகு (or நிறத்தின்அழகு, &c.) பெரிதல்ல, *the beauty of the colour is not great.*

இளமையின்கண்செல்வம் (or இளமையின்செல்வம், &c.) மூப்பைக் காக்கும், *prosperity in youth will support old age.*

ஆடலின்கண்அழகு (or ஆடலின்அழகு, &c.) மிகவுந்தோன்றவில்லை, *the beauty of the dancing did not much appear.*

2. by verbs signifying to be, to put, to come, to ask, inquire, &c., as:

அவரிடத்தில்மிகுந்தபணமுண்டு, *there is much money with him;* i. e., *he has much money.*

அவன் தன்வஸ்திரங்களை மரத்தினிடத்தில் வைத்தான், *he put his clothes near the tree.*

என்னிடத்தில்வந்தான், *he came to me.*

நாங்கள்துரையினிடத்தில்விசாரிப்போம், *we shall inquire of the gentleman.*

எசமானிடத்திற்கேட்டார்கள், *they asked the master.*
பட்டினத்திற்சேர்ந்தோம், *we arrived at the city.*

§ L.

The eighth, or vocative case, with or without the interjection, ஆ or ஓ, always commences the sentence, as:

ஆ, பராபரனே! எங்களுக்கிரக்கமாயிரும், *Oh God, have mercy upon us!*
ஓ, இராசாவே! நீர்கேட்க, *Oh king, may you hear!*
மிகுந்த கனம்பொருந்தியதுரையே! என் விண்ணப்பத்திற்குச்செவி கொடுப்பீராக, *right honourable gentleman, please to hear my petition!*

§ LI.

The oblique case of nouns is, in the common dialect, used chiefly as already mentioned § XVI. 13. I add a few more instances showing the peculiar use of this case, especially in the poetical dialect, as:

பூணின்மார்பன் or பூண்மார்பன், *a man having an ornament on his breast.*
பெரும்பொருளிற்சாத்தன் or பெரும்பொருட்சாத்தன், *Sattan who possesses great riches.*
பெருந்தயையிற்சாத்தன், *Sattan who has much kindness.*
அஞ்சாமனத்துச்சாத்தன், *Sattan who has a fearless mind.*
அகன்றமார்பிறசாத்தன், *Sattan who has a broad chest;*
கொடுமுகத்துச்சாத்தன், *the savage faced Sattan.*
முற்காலத்துச்செய்தி, *the occurrences of former time.*
இந்நாட்பயிர் or இந்நாளிற்பயிர், *the corn of this time.*

In the same dialect, the oblique form in அத்து is used also for the oblative in இல், as:

அந்தரத்துவாழ்கின்றோம், *we live in the world.*
அறிவாரில்லைநிலத்து, *there are no men in the earth able to know,* (for நிலத்தில்.)

§ LII.

The present tense is used,

1. when the present time is to be expressed, as:

இப்பொழுதுகலக்கமாயிருக்கிறேன், *I am now troubled.*

2. when we wish to express a state or action which is doing at all times; or, which is always the nature of a thing or person, as:

பராபரனிருக்கிறார், *God exists*, i. e., *at all times.*
அரசன் அவனியைத்தாங்குகிறான், *the king sustains the earth.*
மனிதர்பாவஞ்செய்கிறார்கள், *men sin;* viz. *at all times.*

3. It is used also for the future, by reason of விரைவு, *i. e.*, quickness, haste; for instance, if a person is waiting for me, and asks whether I do not yet come, I answer him:

நான்வருகிறேன், *I come,*

although my coming is still future, and I should say:

நான்சீக்கிரமாய்வருவேன், *I shall come presently.*

Thus also:

இப்பொழுதுஇரண்டாம்ஒலையைவாசிக்கிறேன், *I shall now read the second Olei leaf;* lit: *I now read,* &c.

§ LIII.

The past tense is used,

1. when the past time is to be expressed, as:

பூர்வீகத்திலேசலப்பிரளயமுண்டாயிற்று, *formerly there was a deluge.*
சனங்களுக்குநியாயத்தீர்ப்புக்கொடுத்தார், *he gave judgment to the people*, i. e., *he judged the people.*
சுரம்நேற்றுஎன்னைவிட்டுப்போயிற்று, *yesterday the fever left me.*
காலையிலேநான்ஊருக்குப்போனேன், *this morning I went to the town.*

2. On certain occasions it is used for the future, for the same reason as the present tense, viz., to express விரைவு, haste, quickness.—Thus I may say:

> நான்சாப்பிட்டாயிற்று, i. e., *I have done eating;* or
> நான்சமைத்தாயிற்று, i. e., *I have done cooking.*

whilst I am still eating or cooking, but am hastening to finish it; and when I should properly say: "I shall soon have done."

3. Sometimes it is used for the future also to express மிகுதி, *i. e.*, greatness, frequency; viz: when a certain event, usually occurring, does not take place in a particular instance; for example, one avoiding a certain road, on which passengers usually lose their lives by robbers, escapes with his life, I may address him thus:

> இராத்திரியிலேஅங்கேபோனாயானாற்செத்தாய் for சாவாய், *hadst thou travelled there by night, thou wouldst have died.*

Thus also:

> நீகளவுசெய்தாயானாற்கையறுக்கப்பட்டாய், i. e., கையறுக்கப்படுவாய், *hadst thou stolen, thy hand would have been cut off.*

4. Again it is, though rarely, used for the future to express தெளிவு, *i. e.*, clearness, certainty; namely, when the speaker alludes to a future transaction, the event of which is rendered certain by universal experience, *e. g.*,

> எறும்புமுட்டைகொண்டுதிட்டையேறினால்மழைபெய்தது for பெய்யும், *if the ant mount up a heap with an egg, it will certainly rain;* lit: *it has rained.*

Note.—The Perfect and Pluperfect tenses are formed by the help of the verb இருக்கிறது, See LVI. 7. i.

§ LIV.

The future tense is used,

1. to express the future time, as :

நாளைக்குப்புறப்படுவோம், *to-morrow we shall set out.*

2. to express the present time, in cases of இயல்பு, *i. e.*, nature, habit or custom, without any particular cause. Thus, whilst I am going to the Fort, a person asks me :

கோட்டைக்குப்போவீரோ, *will* (or do) *you go to the Fort!* to this I may answer, போவேன், *I shall go;* for போகிறேன், *I go.*

Thus also :

நாங்கள்விளையாடுவதிலேயிவன்வரலாமா, *does this fellow dare to come whilst we are at play?* for விளையாடுகிறகாலத்திலே.
அவனையறிவாயா, *doest thou know him?*
தச்சுவேலைசெய்வேன், *I do Carpenter's business.*

3. For the same reason it expresses also the past time, as :

முன்னோர்கள்பலவிதமானகாரியங்களைச்சொல்லுவார்கள் for சொன்னார்கள், *(our) ancestors said various things (*or *used to say.)*

4. The future tense implies also doubt, uncertainty, as :

சனங்கள் அப்படிச்சொல்லுவார்கள், *the people say so; meaning, that it is not certain what they say.*
இந்தத்துண்டுச்சேலைபத்துமுழமாயிருக்கும், *there will be*, i. e., *there may be about* 10 *cubits in this piece of cloth.*

Note.—The second future tense in English is expressed in Tamil by the help of the verb இருக்கிறது. See LVI. 7. i.

§ LV.

1. The relative participles partake of the nature of adjectives; they retain, however, the same power as the verbs, from which they are derived; and have this peculiarity, that they contain the relative

pronoun, for which the Tamil language has no separate word. That relative pronoun always refers to the noun with which the participle is immediately connected, and must be understood in such a case as the connexion may require.

2. In relative participles of intransitive verbs, or verbs in the passive form, the relative pronoun is always in the nominative case, in whatever case its antecedent may stand, as:

தோன்றியசூரியனைக்குறித்தார், *he described the risen Sun,* i. e., *the Sun which had risen.*
அங்கேநிற்கிறமனிதர்களுக்குவழியைக்காட்டு, *show the way to the men who stand there!*
வருங்கோபாக்கினைக்குத்தப்பிப்போவாயாக, *mayst thou flee from the wrath (which is) to come!*

Qualifying expressions, if necessary, precede these participles, thus:

இத்தனை பிரகாசமாய்த் தோன்றியசூரியன் பராபரனுடையமகிமை யையறிவிக்கிறான், *the Sun, which appears so splendidly, declares the glory of God.*
கோபமாயும் அகந்தையாயும்நடக்கிறமனிதர்களுக்கு விலகு, *avoid men, who walk angrily and proudly!*

3. In relative participles of transitive or active verbs, the relative pronoun may be in any case:

i. When it is in the nominative case, the participle must have another noun in the accusative or any other case preceding it, as:

உலகத்தைப்படைத்தபராபரன் எல்லாரிலும்உயர்ந்திருக்கிறார், *God who created the world (*or *God, the creator of the world) is high above all;* i. e. *is the most high.*
நன்மைசெய்கிறமனிதர்களைக்கடவுள் ஆசீர்வதிக்கிறார், *God blesseth the men who do good.*
பட்டினத்திலே கலகத்தைச்செய்தபேர்களுக்குத் தண்டிப்புவந்தது, *the men, who raised the tumult in the city, have been punished.*

ii. When it is in the accusative case, the participle must have a separate nominative or any other case and circumstance expressed, as:

> நீசெய்தகோணஞ்சரியல்ல, *the angle which thou hast made is not right.*
>
> பூர்வீகத்திலே வேதவியாசர் உண்டுபண்ணின நான்குவேதங்களையும் பிராமணர்ஓதுகிறார்கள், *the Bramins read (sing) the four Vedams, which Vedaviyaser made in ancient times.*

iii. When it is neither in the nominative nor in the accusative, the participle must have these cases expressed separately, and the relative pronoun must be understood with such a case as the connexion requires, as:

> பராபரன்உலகத்தைப்படைத்தவிதம் ஆச்சரியமாயிருக்கின்றது, *the manner in which God created the world is wonderful.*
>
> காவற்காரர் அவ்விரண்டுகள்ளரையுங்கொண்டுபோய் வைத்தவீடெனக்குத்தெரியாது, *I do not know the house, to which the watchmen have brought those thieves.*

4. Every noun or pronoun in a sentence may have relative participles, thus:

> மிகுந்த அன்புள்ளவராகிய கருத்தாவினாலேமகிமையாய்ப்படைக்கப்பட்டமனிதர்யாவரும் அவரைமறக்கிறார்கள், *men, who have all been gloriously created by the Lord, who is full of love, forget him.*
>
> காஞ்சிபுரத்திலிருக்கிற பெரியபெருமாள்கோவிலிலேஊழியஞ்செய்கிற தாசிகள்பொன்னாற்செய்யப்பட்டசுவாமிக்குமுன்பாக நடனம்பண்ணுகிறார்கள், *the female devotees, who serve in the large Peroomal temple, which is in Canjepooram, dance before the Swami, which is made of gold.*

5. More than one relative participle may belong to one noun, in which case all the participles but the last, are put in the form of the first verbal participle, see next §; and then construed in the same manner as the last relative participle, as:

> எண்ணிறந்தநட்சத்திரங்களையுண்டாக்கி, அவைகளைமிகவும்ஒழுங்காய் வைத்தபராபரன்தோத்திரிக்கப்பட்டவர், *God, who has made the innumerable stars, and who has fixed them in the greatest order, is to be praised!*

இவ்வுலகத்திலே தோன்றி, மெய்ஞ்ஞானத்தைப்போதித்து, பலவித தருமங்களைச்செய்துவந்தகருத்தர் எல்லாராலும்விரும்பப்படத்தக்கவர், *The Lord, who appeared in this world, who taught true wisdom, and did various charitable actions, ought to be desired (loved) by all.*

However, if by various intervening clauses the sense should be obscured, it is better to turn such relative participles in to verbal nouns, add to each உம், with ஆய், and add any suitable relative participle of இருக்கிறது, to the last, with which the noun unites, thus:

இவ்வுலகத்திலே மனிதஅவதாரம்பண்ணினவருமாய் மனிதர்யாவருஞ்செய்தபாவங்களை நிவிர்த்தியாக்கும்படிக்குத் தமதுசீவனைவிட்டவருமாய்த் தம்மை விசுவாசிக்கிறவர்களுக்காகப்பரமகதியைச்சம்பாதித்தவருமாயிருக்கிற இரட்சகனை யெல்லாருந்தோத்திரஞ்செய்வார்களாக, *may all men praise the Saviour, who became man in this world, who gave his life to atone for the sins which all men had committed, and who has obtained heavenly bliss for all that believe (in) him!*

The same method ought to be observed when all the principal relative participles have not the same tense, as:

ஆதியிலேமகாதேவனாலுண்டாக்கப்பட்டவைகளுமாய்எப்பொழுதும் பூலோகத்தாருக்கு மிகுந்த பிரயோசனங்களைக்கொடுக்கிறவைகளுமாயிருக்கிற நட்சத்திரங்கள் எண்ணிறந்தசேனையாயிருக்கின்றன, *the stars, which were made at the beginning by the great God, and which are always exceedingly useful to the inhabitants of the world, are an innumerable host.*

Note.—When the sense is not, ஆயிருக்கிறது, *to be; but,* ஆகிறது, *to become*, then the verbal noun does not receive ஆய், *but merely*, உம், and the last of them receives the relative participle ஆன or ஆகிய; f. i. நீதிமான்களாக்கப்பட்டவர்களும் மோட்சத்திற்குத் தகுதியுள்ளவர்களுமானமனிதர்பாக்கியவான்கள், *those men are happy, who have been justified, and become fit for the kingdom of heaven.*

§ LVI.

1. The *first indefinite mode* or *verbal participle* is used for the finite verb of any tense, and is of singular use to render the latter conspicuous. When

a nominative or subject has more than one finite verb, the last only receives the personal termination, all the preceding verbs are changed into this verbal participle. Their tense, number and person must be determined by the last finite verb, thus:

> நான்போய் அப்படிச்சொல்லுவேன், *I shall go and tell so;* i. e., போவேன, &c.
>
> சேவகர்வந்து குற்றவாளிகளைப்பிடித்துக்காவற்கூடத்துக்குக்கொண்டு போனார்கள், *the peons came, took hold of the criminals, and led them to the gaol,* i. e., வந்தார்கள், பிடித்தார்கள், &c.
>
> ஒருசூத்திரனும இரண்டுஸ்திரிகளும் பிரயாணப்பட்டுச்சத்திரத்திலே சேர்ந்து யூராத்திரிதஙகினார்கள், *a Sudra and two women journeyed, came to a choultry, and tarried (there) the night.*
>
> பயிர்விளைந்து அறுப்புக்குப்பருவமாயிற்று, *the fields have grown and become ripe for harvest.*
>
> நானும் நீயும் அவனும் நாளைக்குப்போய்ப், பயிரையறுத்து, க்களத்துக்குக்கொண்டுவந்து, போர்வேய்ந்து, தெளித்து, நெல்லைவிற்று, வரிப்பணத்தைச்செலுத்தக்கடவோம், *I, thou, and he, let us go to-morrow, reap the Paddy, bring it to the floor, make a heap of it, thrash it, sell the grain, and pay the taxes* (or *let you,* and *he,* and *I go,* &c.,)

Occasionally the preceding verbal participle may refer to an action done, whilst the finite verb is in the present or future tense, thus:

> நான் இதைச்செய்துமுடித்துப்போகிறேன் or நான் இதைச்செய்து முடித்துப்பினபுபோவேன் or நான் இதைச்செய்து முடித்தபினபு போவேன, *I shall finish this and then go;* or *when* (or *after) I shall have finished this, I shall go.*

2. When it is desirable to give a peculiar emphasis to the several verbs of a sentence, or to show that the transactions were done at one and the same time, the participle உம், may be added to each verbal participle, and the whole concluded with the finite verb of இருக்கிறது, as:

> சத்துருக்கள் கோட்டையைக்கடடிக்கொண்டும்மிருந்தகூக்குரலிட்டுமிருந்தார்கள், *the enemy besieged the fort, and (at the same time) made a hideous noise.*
>
> அவனையடித்தும்நிந்தித்தும் அவர்மேல்த்துப்பியும்வந்தார்கள், *they (at the same time) beat him, reviled him, and spit upon him.*

Negative verbal participles, when there are more than one, usually receive the உம், as:

> இவ்வூரார்வேலைசெய்யாமலுந் தங்கள்சரீரங்களைச்சுத்தம்பண்ணாமலு மிருக்கிறார்கள், *these villagers neither work, nor clean their bodies.*

Observe that the உம், with affirmative verbs as in the first case, signify *both, also;* and with negative verbs, as in the latter case, *neither, nor.*

3. To avoid ambiguity, affirmative and negative verbal participles should not be intermixed, *e. g.*,

> அவர்கள் பராபரனிடத்தில் அன்புகூர்ந்து அவருக்கூழியஞ்செய்து சன்மார்க்கத்தில்நடவாமற்பொல்லாதவர்களாயிருந்தார்கள்.

It should be:

> அன்புகூராமலும், ஊழியஞ்செய்யாமலும், நடவாமலும், பொல்லாதவர்களாயிருந்தார்கள், *they did not love God, nor serve him, nor walk in the path of virtue, but were wicked.*

In the former, the verbal participles கூர்ந்து, and செய்து, might be understood to be in the negative because of the following, நடவாமல்; but it might also be understood otherwise; which mistake is more likely to occur, when the sense is less apparent from the connexion.

4. Tamulians, in relating successive events, always observe the order in which those events naturally occur; wherefore we cannot say:

> நான்கூலிக்காரனையனுப்பி இந்தவாழைப்பழங்களையுமக்குக்கொடுக்கச் சொன்னேன், i. e., *I sent the cooly and told him to give you the Plantains;*

because the sending him away was after the command, we must say:

> இந்சவாழைப்பழங்களையுமக்குக்கொடுக்கும்படிக்குக் கூலிக்காரனிடத்திற்கொடுத்துஅனுப்பினேன், *I gave the plantains to the cooly, telling* (him) *to give them to you, and sent him away.*

5. After a verbal participle, no new or separate subject can with propriety be introduced in the

same sentence; but there ought to be as many sentences as there are new subjects, either by making the verbal participles finite or by adding participles of time or place, as the sense may admit. Wherefore we cannot say:

அவர்வந்துகாரியம்நடந்தது, *He came and the business went on;* but: அவர்வந்தபொழுது, (or உடனே, or பின்பு,) காரியம்நடந்தது, *when* (or, *as soon as*, or *after*,) *he came, the business went on.*

Thus it is also wrong to say: இராசாபட்டினத்திற்பிரவேசித்துச்சேனைகள்பட்டினத்தைக்கொள்ளையிட்டார்கள். It should be, பிரவேசித்தவுடனே (or பொழுது) *as soon as* (or *when*) *the king entered the city, the troops plundered it.*

சமுத்திரம் ஆரவாரம்பண்ணிப்பூமியதிர்ந்து சனங்கள்பயந்தார்கள், must be, சமுத்திரம்ஆரவாரம்பண்ணிற்று. பூமியதிர்ந்தது. சனங்கள்பயந்தார்கள், *the sea roared, the earth shook, and the people were afraid.*

Only when the new nominative denotes a part of the first nominative, the above irregularity may be admitted, as:

பரதேசிகள்பாதாளத்திற்குப்போகிறமார்க்கத்திற்பிரவேசித்து,அங்கே சிலர் மிகவுந்துன்பப்பட்டார்கள் சிலர் கெட்டுப்போனார்கள், *the pilgrims entered the road leading to the infernal regions; when some suffered severely there; others perished.*

பட்டினத்திற்சனங்கள்பிரிந்து, சிலர்யூதரையுஞ் சிலர்அப்போஸ்தலரையுஞ்சேர்ந்தார்கள், *the people of the city were divided; some held it with the Jews; some with the Apostles.*

Note.—When certain actions are not to be performed immediately one after another, but separately at any time; then the verbal participle cannot be used, but each verb must receive the finite termination. Thus: எப்பொழுதுஞ் சந்தோஷப்பட்டு, இடைவிடாமற்செபம்பண்ணி,எல்லாவற்றிற்காகவுந்தோத்திரஞ்செய்யுங்கள், means *that you shall first rejoice, then pray, and lastly give thanks.*—But if this is not the meaning, then the actions must be separately expressed, as: எப்பொழுதுஞ்சந்தோஷப்படுங்கள். இடைவிடாமற்செபம்பண்ணுங்கள். எல்லாவற்றிற்காகவுந்தோத்திரஞ்செய்யுங்கள்.

6. As adverbs are formed by the verbal participle ஆய், of ஆகிறது, *to become*, it will be proper here to make a few observations on the subject.

Generally speaking, adverbs immediately precede the word which they qualify, as:

இராவணன்சீக்கிரமாயெழுந்துபோனான், *Ravanen rose up hastily and went away.*

But sometimes they may also be separated as:

துரைகோபமாய்என்விண்ணப்பத்தைத்தள்ளினார், *the gentleman rejected my petition with anger.*

In such cases, however, the adverbs may fairly be construed as verbal participles; as, in the last instance: "the gentleman got angry, and rejected my petition."

Again, when more than one adverb belong to a verb, every one of them must receive the copulative conjunction உம், as:

நட்சத்திரங்கள் பிரகாசமாயும் ஒழுங்காயும்நடக்கின்றன, *the stars proceed* (in their course) *shining and in order.*
வானம்உயரமாயும்பிரயோசனமாயுமிருக்கின்றது, *the heaven is high, glorious, and beneficial.*

The உம் often precedes also the ஆய், as:

வானம்உயரமுமாய்மகிமையுமாய்ப்பிரயோசனமுமாயிருக்கின்றது.

If the adverb has another adverb to increase the force of the meaning, the latter precedes the former, as:

தாய்தன்பிள்ளையைமிகவும்அன்பாய்விசாரிக்கிறாள், *the mother cares very lovingly for her child.*

7. The verbs இருக்கிறது, கொள்ளுகிறது, வருகிறது, போடுகிறது, விடுகிறது, இடுகிறது, ஆகிறது, &c., are often added to the verbal participles of other verbs as auxiliaries, for the following purposes.

i. இருக்கிறது, The present of this verb, added to a verbal participle, embraces both the present and past tenses, that is, something of the present time is pointed out besides the past; corresponding in some cases with our *perfect*, as :

> புத்தகத்தைக்கொண்டுவந்திருக்கிறான், *he has brought the book* i. e., *he brought the book and is there.*
>
> அப்போஸ்தலன்இப்படியெழுதியிருக்கிறான், *the apostle wrote thus :* i. e., *he wrote a certain passage which is now existing.*
>
> அந்தவாக்கியம் பேதுருவினுடைய இரண்டாம் நிருபத்திலே சொல்லியிருக்கின்றது, *that passage is* (said) *in the second Epistle of Peter.*
>
> இராமன்கோட்டைக்குப்போயிருக்கிறான், *Ramen is gone to the fort,* i. e., *Ramen went to, and is now in the fort.*

If the past tense be added, the past time to a past transaction will be expressed, in some cases like our *pluperfect*, as :

> ஊர்திப்பற்றியெரிகிறதற்குமுன்னே அங்கேபோயிருந்தான், *he had gone to the village before it was in flames*, i. e., *he went and was there, before etc.*
>
> யூதாவென்பவன்சேவர்களுக்கு அடையாளமாகச்சிலவார்த்தைகளைச் சொல்லியிருந்தான், *Judas had told some words to the servants as a sign.*
>
> அநேகதிரவியங்களையடைந்திருந்தான். தரித்திரனாய்ச்செத்தான், *he had gotten many riches ; but died poor.*
>
> முன்னேநீர்அப்படிச்சொல்லியிருந்தீரானால்நான்இப்படிச்செய்யமாட்டேன், *had you told me so before, I should not have done this.*

If the future be added, a past transaction in the future with another future will be expressed, somewhat like our *second future* tense, thus :

> அவன் கோட்டைக்குப்போயிருக்கும்பொழுது நான்திருநெல்வேலிக்குப்போவேன், *when he shall have gone to the fort, I shall go to Tinnevelly*, i, e., *when he will go and be in the fort*, etc.,
>
> ஒருமணிநேரத்திலேதான்சாப்பிட்டிருப்பேன், *I shall have dined at 1 o'clock*, i. e., *I shall dine and be, as it were, ready at 1 o'clock.*

This form however in some cases implics also doubt, as:

> அந்தப்புத்தகத்தைக்கண்டிருப்பேன், *I may have seen that book.*

Some parts of this verb are also used without any meaning ; for instance :

> எழுந்திருந்தான், *he rose;* here இருந்து, has no meaning ; the expression is the same as எழுந்தான்.
>
> அவன்படுத்திருந்தான், *he was lying down ;* is the same as படுத்தான்.
>
> போகாதிரு, *do not go !* this phrase does not mean, *do not go and sit down* (or be still) but simply *do not go! like* போகாதே.

Note.—On the Perfect, Pluperfect, and second future tenses see the Appendix,—sect. LXVII.

ii. கொள்ளுகிறது, is added to verbal participles, to denote a continued action of the principal verb, as :

> அவனைக்கொலைசெய்யும்படிக்கு யோசனைபண்ணிக்கொள்ளுகிறார்கள், *they are consulting to kill him.*

To this again the present and past tenses of இருக்கிறது are added, for the same reasons as in the former instances :

> இந்தச்சமாசாரத்தைக்குறித்துத்துரைகள் யோசனைபண்ணிக்கொண்டிருக்கிறார்கள், *the gentlemen have been consulting about this matter.*
>
> அவர்கள் யோசனைபண்ணிக்கொண்டிருந்தார்கள், அப்பொழுதுஅவர்களிற்பத்துபேர்எழுந்துபோனார்கள், *whilst they were consulting, ten of them arose and went away.*

கொள்ளுகிறது, is also added to other verbs, to denote that a person did a thing to or for himself and not for another, as:

> வஸ்திரங்களைத்தரித்துக்கொண்டோம், *we put on the clothes.*
>
> ஆஸ்திகளைச்சுதந்தரித்துக்கொள்வோம், *we shall inherit riches.*

iii. வருகிறது, added to verbal participles, denotes the continuance of the transaction, as :

> அந்தவசனம்இப்பொழுதுநிறைவேறிவருகின்றது, *that word is now fulfilling.*
>
> நாம்அவருடையதயவினாலே ஆதரிக்கப்பட்டுவருகிறோம், *we are* (until this moment) *supported by his kindness.*

The verbal participle, கொண்டு, may be inserted before வருகிறது, as:

கருத்தர்இதைநிறைவேற்றிக்கொண்டுவருகிறார், *the Lord is* (now gradually) *fulfilling it.*
அவர்தம்மையாதரித்துக்கொண்டுவருகிறார், *he is* (until this moment) *supporting us.*
இப்படிப்பட்ட வசனங்களைச் சொல்லிக்கொண்டுவந்தான், *he was speaking such words;* or, *he went on talking*, &c.

iv. போடுகிறது, *to cast, throw,* is added to verbal participles to denote the transferring of the action to another, and not to ones self; it is therefore opposed to கொள்ளுகிறது, as:

நான்கொடுத்தநன்மைகளையவன்தள்ளிப்போட்டான், *he rejected* (or cast away) *the good things I gave him.*
உன்வஸ்திரங்களைக்கழற்றிப்போடு, *put off your clothes!*

v. விடுகிறது, *to leave, forsake,* is added to verbal participles, the sense of which admits the idea of leaving, forsaking; simply to strengthen it: and to express the finishing of it, as:

பின்புநான்அவனையனுப்பிவிட்டேன், *afterwards I sent him away.*

vi. இடுகிறது, *to give,* is added in the same way as an expletive, as:

வந்திட்டுப்போனான், *he came and went away.*
போயிட்டான், *he went.*
உண்டிட்டான், *he eat.*
அவனைக்கண்டிட்டேன், *I saw him.*

Some times it is added also to the root, when it has more the meaning of *giving, granting*, as:

சுவாமிவிளங்கிடும், *O Lord! shine forth,* which is the same with விளங்கும், or விளங்கியிடும், or விளங்கியருளும்.
கருத்தாவே, இரங்கிடும், *have mercy! O Lord!*

Note.—This however, as well as the preceding போடுகிறது, is not absolutely necessary; they may be omitted, as the sense is complete without them, only custom has introduced their use as auxiliaries. They are often mere expletives.

vii. The past tense of ஆகிறது, *to become*, is added to verbal participles to denote the full accomplishment of the action, as:

நான் இதைச்செய்தாயிற்று, *I have finished doing it*, or *it is done.*
நீசமைத்தாயிற்று, *hast thou finished cooking?*

Observe, that the verbal participles செய்து, சமைத்து, in these connexions, stand for the finite verb and ought to be thus:

நான் இதைச்செய்தேன் அது ஆயிற்று, i. e., *it is finished* or *done, what I did* or *was doing.*

viii. As there is some difficulty with respect to the use of the auxiliaries, இருக்கிறது, கொள்ளுகிறது &c., I add the following instances.

அத்திமரங்கள்வளர்ந்தன, *the fig trees grew; simply with respect to the past time.*
மரங்கள்வளர்ந்திருக்கின்றன, *the trees are grown;* that is, *their growing is past; and they now stand grown.*
மரங்கள்வளர்ந்திருந்தன, *the trees had grown;* implying that after that something happened respecting them.
மரங்கள்வளர்ந்துவருகின்றன, *the trees are growing*, i. e., *they have been growing and do still grow.*
மரங்கள்வளர்ந்துகொண்டிருக்கின்றன, *the trees have been and are continually growing.*
மரங்கள்வளர்ந்துகொண்டிருந்தன, *the trees had been growing;* implying that afterwards something happened to them.

8. When the particle உம் is added to a verbal participle, the latter bears a past sense, and the former may be translated by *although;* it forms the *third indefinite mode,* or a subjunctive in the past tense, thus:

வெயில்தோன்றியிருந்தும் அவன்போனான், *he went, although the heat of the sun had already appeared;*

நான் அவரிடத்தில் இரக்கத்தைக்கேட்டும், அவர்இரங்கவில்லை, *Although I pleaded* (or asked) *for mercy from him, yet he had no mercy.*

அவர்நீதியாய்நடந்தும், சனங்கள் அவரை விசுவாசிக்கவில்லை, *although he walked righteously, yet the people believed not in him.*

§ LVII.

1. The *second indefinite mode,* or our proper subjunctive, leaves the action doubtful, and only supposes that it may take place; on which account it must always be followed by the future tense, as:

நீவந்தாற்கொடுப்பேன், *if you come I shall give.*

நாம் அவ்வழியாய்நடந்துபோனால்மோசம்வரும், *if we go on that road, we shall come into distress,* or *evil will befal us.*

ணகரத்தின்கீழ்த்தகரம்வரின்தகரம்டகரமாகும், *if* த *follows after* ண, *then* த *changes into* ட.

2. If the conjunction உம் be added to this mode, it expresses the *fourth indefinite mode,* or a future subjunctive, with *although;* in this case likewise the action is only suppositious, thus:

புலிகிடந்தாலும்போவான், *even if* (or *although*) *a tyger should lie there, he will go.*

கொசுக்கடித்தாலும் அழுவான், *even if* (or *although*) *a musqueto should bite* (*him*) *he will weep.*

மன்னிப்பைக்கொடுக்கவேண்டுமென்று நான் கேட்டாலுங்கொடுக்கமாட்டான், *although I should crave forgiveness, he will not grant it.*

அவர் அற்புதங்களைச்செய்தாலுஞ்சனங்கள்விசுவாசிக்கமாட்டார்கள், *although he should do miracles, the people will not believe.*

This latter subjunctive mode must be carefully distinguished from that mentioned under the preceding page, for should you say:

பராபரன்பரிசுத்தராயிருந்தாலும், it would imply not that God was holy, but only supposed to be so.

ஆமைக்குமயிரிருந்தும், likewise implies that the tortoise really has hair; you must therefore say in this instance: மயிரிருந்தாலும்; and in the former, பரிசுத்தராயிருந்தும்.

3. ஆனால், the subjunctive mode of ஆகிறது, is, in common talk, frequently used as a disjunctive conjunction, signifying *but*. It can however be used only when it answers to, *if it be*, which is its proper meaning. The former use of it is therefore not to be recommended in writing, as it is not sanctioned either by Tamil Grammarians, nor by the practice of any elegant writers.

4. If the past or future time is to be particularly expressed in the subjunctive mode, ஆனால் or ஆகில், may be affixed to any person or number of those tenses, thus:

அவர்கள் தங்கள் கடமைகளைநினைத்தார்களானால் இந்தத்துன்பம்வரமாட்டாது, *had they considered their duties, this affliction would not have happened.*

நாம்நீதிசெய்வோமாகில்சவுக்கியம்வாராமலிருக்குமா, *shall we not be happy, if we do righteousness?*

§ LVIII.

The *fifth indefinite mode, i. e.*, our infinitive mode is used,

1. To denote *purpose, end;* referring to the future time, as:

சொல்லவந்தேன், *I came to inform.*
இருக்கச்சொன்னார், *he told (any one) to sit down,* or *to stay.*

If, however, the infinitive is not immediately followed by the finite verb, it is better to use the future participle with a particle denoting purpose or end, instead of the infinitive, in order to avoid ambiguity, as:

நான்மோட்சத்தையடைந்துகொள்ளும்படிக்குத்திரவியங்கள்யாவையுங்குப்பையைப்போலவெண்ணுகிறேன், *I count all riches as dung, that I may obtain heavenly bliss.*

2. To denote *time, state,* or *condition,* with respect to the past time, when it may be rendered by *since, as, when, whilst,* thus:

> இப்படியிருக்க, நாம் அவரோடே சம்பந்தம்பண்ணக்கூடாது, *as it is so, we cannot form any connexion with him.*
>
> அவன் அவர்களைத்தன் னுடனேகூட இழுத்துக்கொள்ள, or இழுக்க அவர்கள்மூவருங்கீழேவிழுந்துநொறுங்கிப்போனார்கள், *as he was pulling them along with him, all the three persons fell down and were dashed to pieces.*
>
> சனங்கள்கரையோரத்திலேநிற்க, குருவானவர் போதித்தார், *whilst the people were standing on the shore, the teacher instructed them.*
>
> குருவானவர்சொல்ல, சீஷர்கள்கேட்டார்கள், *whilst the teacher spoke, the disciples heard.*
>
> புலவர்போற்ற, முதிர்ந்தவயதும்மிகுந்த அறிவுமுடையவேதாந்தப் பிராமணர் மங்கலமானசொற்களினாலே ஆசீர்வாதங்களை முறைமையாய்ச்சொல்லிக்கொண்டிருக்க, ஸ்திரிசனங்கள்இரண்டுபாரிசமுங்கவரிவீச, மற்றஸ்திரிசனங்கள் கீதவாக்கியங்களைப்பாடிநிற்க, பாண்டிய இராசன் சிம்மாசனத்தின்மேலிருந்தான், *whilst the Poets praised, the aged and very learned Bramins around by turns pronounced blessings, some females fanned on both sides, and others stood and sang songs, Pandia Rajah sat on his throne.*

Note.—1. As this use of the infinitive mood, is rather ambiguous, it will often be better to use the proper participle with a particle of time or the ablative of the verbal noun, as:

> அவர்கள்நிற்கையில், or நிற்கிறபொழுது, சொன்னபொழுது or சொன்னபின்பு, &c.

Note.—2. The infinitive கொள்ள, has sometimes been added to the principal infinitive to denote the above meaning *(e. g.,* இப்படியிருக்கக்கொள்ள, *since it is so;)* but it is ungrammatical.

3. The infinitive is an elegant form of the imperative or rather optative mode, chiefly used among respectable people, as:

நீர்சொல்ல,	*may you speak!* or *please to speak!*
நீங்கள்கேட்க,	*may you hear?* or *please to hear!*

§ LIX.

1. The *verbal nouns* cannot be united to a genitive case or a relative participle; because though used as nouns, they retain the power of verbs, thus:

என்னைச்சொஸ்தமாக்குதற்கு உம்மாலே யாகும், *my getting well depends upon you.*
நீதியைச்செய்கிறது நன்றாயிருக்கின்றது, *doing righteousness is good.*
அவன் இவனையடித்தது நல்லதல்ல, *his beating him is not good.*
அங்கேவருகிறவர்கள்சூத்திரர், *they are Soodras, that come there.*
பிராமணர் வேதத்தையோதுகிறவர்கள், *the Bramins (are) the learners of the Vedam.*
நன்றாய்ப்படித்தவன்கனம் அடைவான், *a good scholar will receive honour;*—lit: *he that has learned well, &c.*
அவர் இப்படிச்சொல்லுகையில் ஒருசத்தமுண்டாயிற்று, *when he spake thus, a voice came forth.*
ஞாயிற்றுக்கிழமையிலே நாம்கோவிலுக்குப்போய், ப்பராபரனை நினைத்துச்செபம்பண்ணித்தோத்திரஞ்செய்வது நமக்குப்பிரயோசனமாயிருக்கும், *It will be profitable to us to go on Sundays to church, remember God, pray (to him) and praise (him.)*
நான் ஊருக்குப்போகிறதுநிச்சயமில்லை, *my going to the village is not certain.*

Exceptions are verbal nouns ending in ப்பு, வு, க்கை, and மை. These, when added to the root, do not retain the verbal power; you must therefore say:

என்னுடையபடிப்பு, *my learning.*
நல்லபடிப்பு, *good learning.*
அவனுடையபொறுமை, *his envy.*
மிகுந்த அறிவு, *much knowledge.*
இவர்களுடைய நடக்கை நல்லதல்ல, *the conduct of these men is not good.*

2. The verbal noun in அல் with ஆம் the neuter of the future tense of ஆகிறது, is frequently used as our *may* in asking or giving permission, as:

நீபோகலாம், *thou mayst go.*
நான்போகலாமா, *may I go?*
நீங்கள்அப்படிச்சொல்லலாம, *you may say so.*
சனங்கள்உள்ளேவரலாம, *the people may come in.*

It sometimes expresses *resistance, contempt;* particularly in the form of a question, as:

இவர்கள்நமக்குப்போதிக்கலாமா, *shall these (fellows) teach us?*

3. The verbal and appellative nouns may be also declined, thus:

நீர் இவனைத்தண்டிக்கிறதற்குநிமித்தமில்லையே, *there is no cause for your punishing him.*

ஆறு தன்எல்லையைக்கடந்ததினாலேகுடிகளுக்குமிகுந்த உபத்திரவமுண்டாயிற்று, *the people had much to suffer from the overflowing of the river.*

அவர்கள்பொய்யாய்ச்சொன்னவைகளைநாம்மறக்கக்கடவோம், *let us forget the things which they have falsely spoken.*

§ LX.

The *imperative mode,* is used with or without the pronoun, and mostly also without the interjection ஓய், as:

நீயிங்கேவா,	*come (thou) hither!*
அங்கேபோங்கள்,	*go (ye) thither.*
செம்மையாய்நடவுங்கள்,	*walk (ye) uprightly!*
நீர்கூடவாரும்,	*pray come along!*
ஓய், போசராசனேகேளாய்,	*O hear thou king Bojah!*

§ LXI.

The *optative,* or *polite imperative mode,* is used thus:

நான்தப்பிதத்துக்குட்படாதிருப்பேனாக, *may I not commit a fault!*

அவர் என் விண்ணப்பத்துக்குச்செவிகொடுப்பாராக, *may he listen to my request!*

நீங்கள்வாழ்வீர்களாக, *may you prosper!*

மனைவிதன் நாயகனுக்குக்கீழ்ப்படிவாளாக, *let the wife obey her husband!*

நாம் சமாதானத்தைப் பிரியமாயிருப்போமாக, *may we (or let us) love peace!*

நாம்குடிகளானபடியால் அதிகாரிகளைக்கனஞ்செய்யக்கடவோம், *as we are subjects let us honour those in power.*

ஐசுவரியவான்கள் தருமங்களைச்செய்யக்கடவர்கள், *let the rich do charities!*

நீர்பொறுமையாய்க்கேட்க, *may you hear with patience!*

When we call upon others to join us in doing a thing, the simple imperative may be joined to the optative form in கடவோம், or even to the simple future tense, as:

> நாம் அந்த எளியசனங்களுக்கு உதவிசெய்யக்கடவோம் வாருங்கள், *come, let us help those poor people;* or செய்வோம்வாருங்கள்.

§ LXII.

The *negative* form of verbs for all the tenses is used;

1. In general, for any time; showing the nature or habit, as:

> இவன்திருடான், *this man does not steal;* i. e., *he has not stolen formerly, nor does he steal now, nor will he steal hereafter.*
> விக்கிரகத்துக்குக்கண்ணிருந்துந்தெரியாது, *the idol has eyes, but does not see.*
> துன்மார்க்கர் மோட்சத்துக்குப்போகார்கள், *the wicked do not go to heaven.*

2. In particular, for the future, as:

> அவன்பண்டிகைக்குவாரான், *he will not come to the feast.*
> துன்மார்க்கன்நரகத்தினின்றுநீங்கிஇரட்சிக்கப்படான், *the wicked will not be saved from hell.*

In the foregoing instances the nominatives இவன், கண் &c., are to be construed with the negative verb; but when the present verbal noun is used with இல்லை, that verbal noun is the subject to இல்லை whilst it has its separate nominative &c., of any gender, number, and person, thus:

> இராசேந்திரன்கோபங்கொள்ளுகிறதில்லை, *Rasendiren does not get angry.*
> அநேகமனிதர்கள் ஒருவருக்கொருவர் கீழ் அடங்குகிறதில்லை, *many men do not submit one to another.*

The negative of the past tense is best expressed by இல்லை, with the infinitive mode, as:

அவன்தாழ்மையாய்ப்பேசவில்லை, *he did not speak humbly.*
தச்சன் மாறுத்தரமாக ஒருவார்த்தையுஞ்சொல்லவில்லை, *the carpenter did not say a word in return.*

§ LXIII.

1. The *passive* form of active verbs with படுகிறது, usually requires the instrumental ablative, as:

நாம் தீமையினாலேசெயிக்கப்படக்கூடாது தீமையைநன்மையினாலே செயிக்கவேண்டும், *we must not be overcome by evil, but overcome evil by good!*

இந்தக்காகிதம்என்னாலேயெழுதப்பட்டிருக்கின்றது, *this letter has been written by me.*

அந்தக்குளம்முத்தையனாலேவெட்டப்பட்டது, *that tank was digged by Mootteiyen.*

2. But in the participle form, the infinitive of the active verb still governs the accusative case; and the participle is thus dependent upon the following noun, as:

அவருடையசரீரத்தைவைக்கப்பட்ட இடம், *the place in which his body was laid.*

If it be said, அவருடைய சரீரம்வைக்கப்பட்டவிடம், it will mean, that the body itself placed something and that the place was passive.

இதுபுகையிலைவிற்கப்பட்டகடை, *this (is) the shop in which tobacco* (lit: *smoke-leaf*) *was sold.*

3. Sometimes படுகிறது is used also with the infinitive of intransitive verbs, but as in the above instance only in the relative participle form; and then it implies all times except the future; and must be regarded as an adjective, as:

நான் இருக்கப்பட்டவூர், *the village in which I dwell.*
நீ தூங்கப்பட்ட அறை, *the room in which thou sleepest.*
அவன் நடக்கப்பட்டபாதை, *the road which he went.*

In all which places the literal meaning is, the village which suffered that I dwelled, the room which suffered that I slept, &c.

4. In a similar case the 3d person neuter of the negative form, viz. படாது, is sometimes used for all persons, and means as much as தகாது, கூடாது, as:

நீயிப்படிச்செய்யப்படாது, *thou must not do so.*

§ LXIV.

Some parts of the verb என்கிறது, *to say*, are used in a peculiar sense.

1. The verbal participle என்று, is used as an indicative conjunction, or a particle of quotation, like the Greek ὅτι, or like the mark (" ") in English, when the words of another are to be quoted in his own language. If there be more quotations than one, they all are closed with என்று, and the copulative conjunction உம், after which the narration proceeds, thus :

கருத்தர்நீதியுள்ளவரென்றுவேதஞ்சொல்லுகின்றது, *the Bible saith, God is righteous*, i. e., *that God is righteous.*

விபசாரம் பண்ணுதிருப்பாயாகவென்றும், பொய்சொல்லா திருப்பாயாகவென்றும் உன்சத்துருக்களிடத்தில் அன்புகூர்வாயாகவென்றுங் கருத்தர்கொடுத்த கட்டளைகளை நாம் கைக்கொள்ளவேண்டும், *we must keep the commandments of God*, viz., "*Thou shalt not commit adultery; thou shalt not lie; thou shalt love thine enemies.*"

Observe that in such quotations the Tamulians do not change the person's words as we do in English; for instance, we may say, either *he has commanded that we shall not lie*, or *God's command is: thou shall not lie;* but they can only use the latter mode. பொய்சொல்லாதிருப்பாயாகவென்று அவர்கட்டளையிட்டார் should you say : நாம்பொய்சொல்லாதிருப்போமாகவென்றுபராபரன்கட்டளையிட்டார் it will mean, *that God himself is among those who shall not speak lies.*—If the words of his command are stated indirectly, then நாம் may be used, but என்று must be omitted, and படிக்கு, substituted, as : நாம், பொய்சொல்லாதபடிக்குப் பராபரன் கட்டளையிட்டார் ; thus also :

> நீங்கள் பணத்தைவீணாய்ச்செலவழிக்கக்கூடாதென்று தகப்பன்சொன்னான், *the father said that we should not vainly spend (our) money*, or, *the father said. "Do not spend your money vainly."*
> அவர்கள் கடன்வாங்காமலிருப்பார்களாகவென்றுங் கடன்வாங்கினபின்பு அதைத்தீர்ப்பார்களாகவென்றும் ஞானிகள்உரைத்தார்கள், *wise men have said : "let them not incur debts," and "after they have incurred debts, let them pay them,"* i. e., *wise men have said, that they should not incur debts,* &c.

For the further use of என்று and என, see § LXXXVII.

2. The future relative participle என்னும், is used to identify persons or things ; and is affixed to their names, as :

சிவனென்னுந்தேவன்,	*the God Siven.*
இயோவானென்னுமப்போஸ்தலன்,	*the Apostle John.*
திருச்சபையென்னுஞ்சொல்,	*the word "Church."*
சந்தோஷமென்னுமெண்ணெய்,	*the oil of gladness.*
நீதியென்னும்வஸ்திரம்,	*the garment of righteousness.*
இரட்சண்ணியமென்னுஞ்சால்வை,	*the robe of salvation.*

In all which cases, என்னும் may be rendered by "called." The God called Siven ;—The oil called gladness, &c.,

The relative participles of the other tenses, என்கிற and என்ற, cannot properly be used in the same way, and are interpreted by their proper meaning, thus :

சிவனென்கிறதேவன், means, "*the God who saith Siven.*"
இயோவானென்றஅப்போஸ்தலன், *the Apostle who said,* "*John.*"

But the relative participles of the passive form may be used like என்னும், thus:

சிவனென்னப்பட்டதேவன், *the God who was called Siven.*

3. The subjunctive என்றால் or எனில், *if thou say*, or *ask*, is frequently added to the interrogating adverbs and pronouns, as, என்னத்தினாலென்றால், ஆரென்றால், எப்படியென்றால், என்னவென்றால், &c., the literal meaning of which is, *if you ask, why? from what cause? who? how?* or *what?* They are used either at the beginning of sentences, or they are affixed to verbal nouns at the end of a sentence, in which latter case they mean as much as *thus, as follows*," &c., என்னத்திற்கென்றால், என்னத்தினாலென்றால், may often be rendered "*for, because*," as:

அவன்காவலில்வைக்கப்பட்டான், என்னத்தினாலென்றால், அவன் ஒரு பிள்ளையினிடத்தில் நகைகளைக்கண்டு, அவைகளைப்பறித்துக்கொள்ளும்படியாக அதைக்கொலைசெய்தான், *this man has been put in prison, because, observing jewels upon a child, he killed it in order to rob them.*

With the verbal noun it will be thus:

அவன் காவலில்வைக்கப்பட்டதென்னத்தினாலென்றால், &c. lit: *his being put in prison was because*, &c. or, *if you ask, why he was put in prison? the cause is*, &c.

நீசொல்லவேண்டுவதென்னவென்றால், i. e., *if thou askest what thou shalt say?* or *thou shalt say thus.*

அவனால் அனுப்பப்பட்டவர்களாரெனில், *if thou askest who they are that have been sent by him?* or *those who have been sent by him are these*, &c.

இது நடந்ததெப்படியென்றால், *it happened thus*, or *in this manner.*

The interrogation may also be separated from என்றால், thus:

அது எப்படிநடந்ததென்றால்,
ஆர் அவனால் அனுப்பப்பட்டார்களென்றால்,
நீயெப்படிச்சொல்லவேண்டுமென்றால்,

But as this mode of speaking requires a repetition of the first clause at the end of the answer, viz. அது இப்படிநடந்தது, இவர்களே அனுப்பப்பட்டார்கள், இப்படியே சொல்லவேண்டும், அதினாலே அவன் காவலில்வைக்கப்பட்டான், it is not elegant to use this form when the answer is but short, and without much argument. It would be almost ridiculous to say: இவன்காவலில்வைக்கப்பட்டான், என்னத்தினாலென்றால் ஒருபிள்ளையைக்கொலைசெய்தான். In such cases it is both more clear and elegant to put the causal particle படியினாலே before, thus: இவன் ஒரு பிள்ளையைக்கொலைசெய்தபடியினாலே காவலில் வைக்கப்பட்டான். On this subject, see § CXV.

4. The verbal and appellative nouns என்பது, என்பவன், are used in the same way as என்னும்; but with this difference, that as they are nouns, the whole sentence introduced by them, becomes the subject to the following clause; thus:

மனிதரெல்லாரும் பாவிகளென்பது மெய்தான், *it is certainly true, that all men are sinners.*

அறஞ்செய்யவிரும்பு என்பது நல்லவாக்கியந்தான், *it is certainly a good sentence, " love to do charity."*

சிவனென்பவன் தமிழருக்கு ஒருதேவன், *Siven* (is) *a God among* or *to the Tamulians.*

They may also be declined, as:

அறமென்பதற்குத் தருமமென்று அருத்தமாம், *the meaning of* அறம் *is* தருமம்.

பிரமாவென்பவனுடைய தலைகளிலொன்றைச்சிவன்கிள்ளினான், *Siven pinched off one of the heads of Bramha.*

Note.—In all these instances என்பது and என்பவன், stand for என்று சொல்லப்பட்டது, என்றுசொல்லப்பட்டவன், and, on the contrary, for என்றுசொல்லுகிறான் or சொன்னான், &c. may simply be said என்கிறான் என்றான், &c., in which case the verb both quotes and concludes the sentence, as:

சீக்கிரமாய்வருவேனென்கிறான், *he saith " I shall come quickly," or that he will quickly come.*

§ LXV.

துன்மார்க்கர்கெட்டுப்போவார்களென்றான், *he said, "the wicked shall perish,* or *that the wicked,* &c.

Active verbs formed by the combination of a Samscrit noun with a verb denoting doing, (see § XXXVIII. 5,) must generally be construed as if that noun were the accusative case, which in fact it is; wherefore, though in English they may often be rendered by single active verbs, yet, in Tamil, when other nouns are affected by them, these nouns must be put in such other cases, or receive such additions, as the sense requires, thus:

செபம்பண்ணக்கடவோம், means, "*let us perform the mantram!*" or *say prayers (inwardly)*, but, "*let us pray to God,*" cannot be rendered by, பராபரனைச்செபம்பண்ணக்கடவோம். but by, பராபரனைநோக்கி (or நினைத்து) செபம்பண்ணக்கடவோம், *let us behold,* or *look upon God,* or *think of God, and say prayers.*

அவர்கள்கோபங்கொண்டார்கள், means "*they got angry,*" but, "*they got angry with us,*" must be rendered: அவர்கள் எங்கள் மேற்கோபங்கொண்டார்கள்.

பிரசங்கம்பண்ணினார், *he preached,* lit: *he made a Sermon.*

But, "*he preached Christ,*" கிறிஸ்துவைக்குறித்துப்பிரசங்கம்பண்ணினார்.

"*He preached the resurrection of the dead,*" மரித்தோரெழுப்பப்படுவார்களென்றுபிரசங்கம்பண்ணினார்.

போதகம்பண்ணினார், *he taught;* but "*he taught many people,*" அநேகசனங்களுக்குப்போதகம்பண்ணினார்.

If the noun however be neuter, such verbs may govern it in the accusative, as:

பலபதார்த்தங்களைப்போசனம்பண்ணிறோம், *we eat various things.*
அந்தச்சங்கதியைப்பிரசங்கம்பண்ணினார், *he preached (on) that subject.*

There are a few exceptions, *e. g.*, தோத்திரஞ் செய்கிறது, தியானம்பண்ணுகிறது, and all nouns combined with ஆக்குகிறது, these govern any noun in the accusative case, as:

பராபரனைத்தோத்திரஞ்செய்யக்கடவோம், *let us thank God!*
அவரைத்தியானம்பண்ணுவோம், *we shall meditate (on) him.*
அவர்களைக்குணமாக்கினார், *he healed them.*
மனதைத்தெளிவாக்குவாராக, *may he enlighten the mind!*

Note.—Verbs which are formed of Samscrit nouns, by changing their last syllable, such as தோத்திரிக்கிறது, செபிக்கிறது, தியானிக்கிறது, நிர்மாணிக்கிறது, &c. &c. of course do always require the accusative.

§ LXVI.

1. *Neuter* or *intransitive verbs*, formed with ஆயிருக்கிறது, must be carefully distinguished from those formed with ஆகிறது, and படுகிறது, the word ஆயிருக்கிறது, means *to be*, and gives an adverbial sense to the noun prefixed: but the two latter words mean *to become, to get*, as:

சவுக்கியமாயிருக்கிறேன், *I am well.*
சவுக்கியமாகிறேன் } *I become well; I am getting well.*
சவுக்கியப்படுகிறேன், }

When ஆயிருக்கிறது, relates to more than one noun, the verbal participle ஆய் is separated from இருக்கிறது, and added to every noun with the conjunction உம், either before or after it, as:

கடவுள்நீதியுமாய் இரக்கமுமாயிருக்கிறார், *God is righteous and merciful*, or நீதியாயும் இரக்கமாயுமிருக்கிறார்.

With ஆகிறது, only உம் is added to each noun, as:

அஞ்ஞானிகள் ஞானிகளும் நீதிமான்களுமானார்கள், *the unwise became wise and righteous.*

2. ஆம், the 3d person neuter of the future is occasionally united to any finite verb to denote uncertainty, as:

> அவர்கள் அப்படிச்சொன்னார்களாம், *it seems they said so*, or "*it is said that they said so.*"
>
> அவள்தன்நாயகனைவிட்டுப்போனாளாம், *they say that she left her husband.*

Again ஆம், is sometimes used as an affirming particle *yes*, in answer to a question. But it is not frequent. The usual way of affirmation is, repeating the verb of the question, thus:

> To அப்படிச்செய்தாயா, *hast thou done so?*
> The answer is: செய்தேன், *I have done.*

Some have used ஆம் also as the particle *yea*, or *what is more;* but that is not elegant.

Moreover ஆம் is used in Poetry as a particle without any meaning, merely to fill up the metre, as: பணியுமாமென்றும் பெருமை சிறுமை அணியுமாந்தன்னைவியந்து.

In plain Tamil: பெருமையானது எப்பொழுதும்பணியும். சிறுமையானதுதன்னைவியந்துஅணியும், i. e., *greatness behaves always respectfully; meanness (always) praises and ornaments itself.*

For another use of ஆம், see § LIX. 2.

3. ஆகாது, the 3d person neuter of the negative form, is often added to verbal nouns denoting *it ought not, must not*, as:

> நீ வம்பான வார்த்தைகளைப்பேசலாகாது, *thou must not talk bad words; it is not becoming thee to talk, &c.*
>
> அவர்கள் இரண்டுவிதமாய்நடக்கலாகாது, *they ought not to walk two ways.*

4. ஆவது, the verbal noun of the future tense and its plural ஆவன், are frequently used as par-

ticles of introduction, like the English "*thus, viz. as,*" and is then added to nouns, as:

> அவன்சொன்னதாவது, *he said thus:* or *that which he said,* &c.
> அவர்செய்த அற்புதங்களாவன, *the miracles which he did are these.*
> அவன்கொண்டுவந்தபதார்த்தங்களாவன, *he has brought the following articles.*

Observe, that in this way the sentence must conclude with எ or இவைகளே, thus:

> அவன்கொண்டுவந்தபதார்த்தங்களாவன இரும்பு, செம்பு, மரம், கல், இவைகளே, *the things he brought were iron, brass, wood and stone.*

Thus also: *பொய்யாவதுசத்தியமின்மை, a lie (is) an untruth.*

ஆவது, is also used as the disjunctive particles, *either, or,* and then it is added to two or more nouns which are thus distinguished, as:

> பனைமரமாவதுதென்னைமரமாவதுஅகப்படவேண்டும், *we must get either a palmira or a cocoanut tree.*
>
> வெள்ளியையாவதுபொன்னையாவதுகொண்டுவரவேண்டும், *you must bring either silver* or *gold.*
>
> நீ கல்வியைப்படித்தாவது மற்றொருதொழிலைச்செய்தாவது பிழை, *live either (by) learning seiences,* or *(by) doing any other business.*

5. ஆனவன், ஆனது and ஆவது are used *like* என்பவன் and என்பது (§ LXIV. 4,) as determinating particles, yet retaining the power of nouns *e. g.*

> கொற்றனானவன்நல்லமனிதனல்ல, *Kotten is not a good man.*
>
> மாமரமானதுசுவையுள்ளபழங்களைக்கொடுக்கின்றது, *the mango tree yields delicious fruit.*
>
> பேர்ச்சொல்லாவதுஒருபதார்த்தத்தினுடையபேரைக்குறிக்கின்றது, *the term பேர்ச்சொல், (*or *noun,) denotes the name of any thing.*

Note.—About ஆனாலும் ஆகிலும், &c. see § CIII. and about ஆகையால், ஆதலால், and ஆனபடியினாலே, see § CIX.

§ LXVII.

The verbs ஈதல், தருதல், கொடுத்தல், and இடுதல், mean "*to give;*" but with this difference, ஈதல், is the giving of a superior, தருதல், of an equal, and கொடுத்தல் of an inferior, *e. g.*,

கருத்தாவே, தேவரீர் எனக்கு அருளை ஈயவேண்டும், *O Lord! give me grace!*

கருத்தர் எனக்கு அருளை ஈந்தார், *the Lord has given grace to me.*

நான் உனக்கு அருளை ஈகிறேன், *I give thee grace.*

சிநேகிதரே அந்தப்பசுவை யெனக்குத்தாரும், *O friend, give me that cow!*

நான்பசுவையுனக்குத்தருகிறேன், *I give thee the cow.*

என் மகனே நீ உன்னிருதயத்தைஎனக்குக்கொடு, *my son! give me thine heart.*

நான் என்னிருதயத்தை உமக்குக்கொடுக்கிறேன், *I give my heart to thee.*

But this distinction is often neglected.

இடுதல் is chiefly used in the 3d person, and that only in certain connexions, as, கட்டளையிட்டான், *He gave a commund*, சோறிட்டான், *he gave rice*, பிச்சையிட்டான், *he gave alms*, &c. Its first verbal participle is also added to other such participles, without any meaning, as, வந்திட்டுப்போனான், which is the same as வந்துபோனான், *he came and went.* It is also added to some roots, chiefly to form an imperative, as; இரங்கிடும், *have mercy!* பேசிடும், *speak!* see § LVI. 7. vi.

§ LXVIII.

The verbs வாங்கல், கொள்ளல், ஏற்றல், அடைதல், பெறுதல், mean *to receive, to get, to take*, but with this difference, that the three former require the local ablative, and the two latter the causal ablative, *e. g.*,

எசமானிடத்தில் ஒருபுத்தகத்தைவாங்கினேன், or கொண்டேன் or ஏற்றுக்கொண்டேன், *I received a book from (my) master.*

எசமானால் ஒருபுத்தகத்தையடைந்தேன் or பெற்றேன், *I received a book from my master*, or *through his instrumentality.*

The reason seems to be that வாங்கல், கொள்ளல், and ஏற்றல், mean *to receive*, simply with reference to the person or place from which it is given; but அடைதல் and பெறுதல் mean *to receive*, with reference to the receiver himself, as an addition to what he already has. Hence அடைதல் and பெறுதல், are as much as சேர்த்தல், கூட்டல், which require the causal ablative.

§ LXIX.

சொல்லல்; பேசல், சாற்றுதல், கூறுதல், விளம்புதல், உரைத்தல், அருளிச்செய்தல், திருவுளம்பற்றுதல், என்னல், இசைத்தல், கிளத்தல், கரைதல், நொடித்தல், நவிலுதல், மொழிதல், செப்புதல், நுவலுதல், அறைதல், பாடல், இயம்புதல், பகருதல், all these mean "*to speak*," but are used differently.

All the verbs from இசைத்தல் to the end are used in poetry only; the rest are also in common life.

சொல்லுதல் is used when the meaning is the same as அறிவித்தல், *to inform, to make known, to tell*, thus: அவனோடேசொன்னேன், *I told him;* வாவென்றுசொன்னான், *he said, "come."*

பேசல் is used when it means as much as சம்பாஷணைபண்ணுதல், *to converse, to speak with*, as: நாம் பேசிக்கொண்டோம், *we spoke together;* நான் அவனோடேபேசிக்கொள்வேன், *I shall speak with him.*—நான் எசமானோடேபேசிக்கொண்டு சொல்லு

கிறேன், *I shall converse (*or *speak) with my master, and then tell* or *inform (thee).* This instance shows exactly the difference between the two words.

சாற்றல் is used chiefly in connexion with guilt, as much as "*accuse.*" Thus அவன்மேற்குற்றஞ்சாற்றினான், *he accused him,* lit: *he said a crime against him.*

கூறுதல் is much the same as சொல்லல், thus: அப்படியேயிருக்குமென்றுகூறினான், *he told that it will be so.* Some have used this word for "*to proclaim.*"

விளம்பல் is the same with சொல்லல், and கூறுதல், except that it means also "*to proclaim,*" and hence has come விளம்பரம்பண்ணுகிறது, *to make public.*

உரைத்தல் is the same with சொல்லல், but not so much in use. Its root உரை means also "*explanation.*"

அருளிச்செய்தல் is the same as சொல்லல் with the idea of giving; it literally means "*to do a favour, to be favourable, to be gracious.*" It is hence used with the sense of "*speaking*" of superiors only, particularly of God, thus: நான் உன்னைக்காப்பாற்றுகிறேனென்று அருளிச்செய்தார், *he* (viz. *God) said,* "*I will protect thee.*" It means then also "*to grant,*" as: அவர்நீடியஆயுளை யெனக்கு அருளிச்செய்தார், *he has granted me long life.*

திருவுளம்பற்றல், is composed of திரு, *sacred;* உளம் *the mind,* which stands here for உளத்தில்; and பற்றுதல், which means "*to desire, to will,*" and therefore திருவுளம்பற்றினார் means literally திருவுளத்திலே ஆசைகொண்டார், *he desired* or *willed in (his) sacred mind;* plainly "*he spoke* or *said,*" it is used only of God, or of Kings and other very great men.

என்னல் does not mean simply "*to say,*" but is used in the joint sense of the particle என or என்று and சொல்லுகிறது. Hence என்றான், *he said,* is simply a contraction of என்றுசொன்னான்.

§ LXX.

The defective verb ஒக்கும், &c., is mostly used with the accusative or 2d case, as:

இந்தமலை அந்தமலையை ஒக்கும், *this mountain is equal to that.*

இந்தச்சேலை அந்தச்சேலையை ஒவ்வாது, *this cloth is not equal to that.*

இவன் அவனை ஒத்திருக்கிறான், *this man is equal to that.*

இந்தமரங்களை ஒன்றுக்கொன்று ஒவ்வப்பண்ணு, *make these trees to be equal one with another.*

But the participles ஒத்த and the verbal ஒப்பாய், and sometimes also the negative form, require the dative case, as:

அவருடையமகிமைக்கொத்தமகிமையில்லை, *there is no glory like his.*
பராபரனுக்கொப்பில்லை, *none is equal to God.*

இந்தக்கல் அந்தக்கற்களுக்கொவ்வாமல் வேறுயிருக்கின்றது, *this stone does not agree with those stones, it is different;* or கற்களை யொவ்வாமல், &c.

Note 1.—Sometimes it is used without any case, as:

திணையென்றுஞ்சாதியென்றுவும் ஒக்கும், *it is the same whether you say* திணை or சாதி, i. e., திணை and சாதி *mean the same thing;* thus also:

இதுவும் அதுவும் ஒக்கும், *this and that agree.*

Note 2.—When கொள்ளுதல் is added to the verbal participle ஒத்து, it requires the accusative case, as:

நீயதை ஒத்துக்கொள்ளவேண்டும், *thou must allow, (confess, acknowledge,) that.*

§ LXXI.

The defective verb வேண்டும், &c., is usually construed with the infinitive of another verb, and implies *necessity*, as:

பிள்ளைகள்நன்றாய்ப்படிக்கவேண்டும், *children must learn well.*
நீங்கள்புறங்கூறவேண்டாம், *you must not backbite.*

நான்செய்யவேண்டியதைச்செய்வேன், *I shall do what is my duty to do.*

எனக்குவரவேண்டியபணம்முப்பதுவராகன், *the amount of the money (or the money) which I ought to get,* lit: *which must come to me, is 30 Pagodas.*

அவன் எனக்குத்தீமைசெய்யவேண்டுவதென்ன, *why should he do me evil? what need has he to do, &c.*

Note 1.—The negative வேண்டாம், is used only with the 2d person imperatively, as in the above instance; with the 3d person, கூடாது must be used; see § LXXVIII.

Note 2.—When வேண்டும், &c., is used with the dative case, it is not this defective, but the regular verb வேண்டுகிறது *to desire, to be desirable, to think, a thing necessary,* as:

உம்முடையகிருபையெனக்குவேண்டும், *I desire your favour ;* lit : *your favour is needful to me.*

அவனுடையவீடு எனக்குவேண்டுவதில்லை, *his house is not necessary for me ; I do not want his house.*

In the same sense it is used also with the infinitive, as :

சவுக்கியமாயிருக்கவேண்டுபவர்கள் பராபரனுக்குக்கீழ்ப்படியவேண்டும், *those who desire to be happy , must obey God.*

With கொள்ளுகிறது, it requires the accusative, as :

உம்மைவேண்டிக்கொள்ளுகிறேன், *I beseech you.*

Note 3.—வேண்டியது and வேண்டுவது do not imply that the transaction is already finished, but only that it was, or is necessary, to be done. Hence it is not sufficient to translate, for instance, " *I was obliged to turn him back,*" by நான் அவனைத்திருப்பிக்கொள்ளவேண்டியதாயிருந்தது ; because this does not imply that he actually turned him back ; but only that it was necessary ; hence the additional idea must be expressed, thus : நான் அவனைத்திருப்பிக்கொள்ளவேண்டியதால், அவனைத்திருப்பினேன்.

Note 4.—வேண்டும் being the future tense, implies in certain phrases also *doubt ;* like the English " must," thus :

தோட்டத்திலேயவர் சகலவிருட்சங்களையும்வைத்திருக்கிறபடியினாலே முந்திரிகைச்செடியுமிருக்கவேண்டும், " *as he has planted all kinds of trees in his garden, the vine also must be there,*" though it is still doubtful whether it is actually there or not.

இந்தமண்ணுக்குள்ளே பொன் இருக்கவேண்டும், *there must be gold among this earth ;* implying that naturally it ought to be ; but leaving it doubtful whether it is actually there or not.

§ LXXII.

The defective verb மாட்டேன், &c., denoting *incapability* or *inability,* not so much from want of power, as of will, or suitableness, is used with the infinitive of another verb. Thus to the question :

பராபரன்துன்மார்க்கருக்குப்பரமகதியைக்கொடுப்பாரா, *will God give heavenly bliss to the wicked?* the answer is : கொடுக்கமாட்டார், *he will not give ; he cannot give ;* not because he has no power, but because he will not, and because it would be unsuitable to his nature.

நான்ஊருக்குப்போகமாட்டேன், *I will not go to the village.*
நீநடக்கமாட்டாய், *thou canst not walk; thou art not able, &c.*
மழைபெய்யமாட்டாது, *it will not rain.*

Note.—The affirmative mode மாட்டுவேன், மாட்டுவாய், &c., is used by some, as:

நான் அப்படிச்செய்யமாட்டுவேன், *I may* or *can do so;* but it is not classical. The simple future better expresses the meaning, as: நான் அப்படிச்செய்வேன்.

§ LXXIII.

1. The defective negative verbs இல்லை, &c., and அல்ல, &c., differ from each other, in that இல்லை denies the existence, and அல்ல the quality of a thing.

Thus to the question: அங்கேமாம்பழமுண்டா, *are mangoes there?* The negative answer is, இல்லை, *no, there are no mangoes.* But the question: இது மாம்பழமா? *Is this a mangoe?* the negative answer must be: இதுமாம்பழமல்ல, இதுவாழைப்பழம், *no, it is not a mangoe, but a plantain.* இல்லை always concludes a sentence, and is added to the nominative case; but அல்ல may be added to any case, and always requires a clause to the contrary either expressed or understood, which is done in English by the disjunctive *but;* thus:

சந்தோஷத்தையல்லத்துக்கத்தையுண்டாக்கினான், *he made (or caused) not joy, but sorrow.*

துன்மார்க்கத்தினாலேயல்லச்சன்மார்க்கத்தினாலே பாக்கியங்கிடைக்கும், *happiness arises not from vice, but from virtue.*

2. The relative participles of both require the nominative, as:

அவ்விடத்திலேகுளமில்லாததினால் நாங்கள் அப்புறம்போனோம், *as there was no tank in that place, we went further.*

இவன் நல்லவனல்லாதபடியினாலே இவனுடையசொல்லை நம்பக்கூடாது, *as this man is not a good man, none must believe his word.*

3. The verbal participles இல்லாமல் and இன்றி are frequently used as propositions, meaning *without*, as:

அவனுடைய அநுக்கிரகமில்லாமற் கெட்டுப்போனோம், *(being) without his favour, we perished.*

கோபமின்றி நமக்குப்புத்திசொன்னார், *he admonished us without anger.*

In the first instance it means அநுக்கிரகமில்லாதபடியால். If the sense is future, it must be thus, அநுக்கிரகமில்லாவிட்டாற்கெட்டுப்போவோம்.

4. The verbal participles அல்லாமல் and அன்றி, are likewise used as exceptive particles, meaning, *besides, except, but,* and may be affixed to any case, tense, and person, which receive the expletive particle ஏ ; they are then naturally followed by a negative verb; and that word, which is excepted, receives the negative, as:

துன்பஞ் சம்பவிக்குமேயல்லாமல் இன்பஞ் சம்பவிக்கமாட்டாது, *only affliction will be the consequence, not pleasure,* lit: *except that affliction will be, happiness will not be.*

அவருடைய கிருபையினாலேயல்லாமல் மற்றொன்றினாலும் நாம் பாக்கியசாலிகளாகமாட்டோம், *we shall become happy by nothing, except by his grace.*

நம்மைக்கனஞ்செய்வாரேயன்றி அசட்டைபண்ணமாட்டார், *he will never despise, but honour us.*

நன்மையையேயன்றித்தீமையை விரும்பமாட்டார், *he does not desire evil, but good.*

அவரேயன்றி மற்றொருவரும்நல்லவரல்ல, *none is good, but he.*

Again, அல்லாமல் and அன்றி are also conjunctive; in which case the conjunctive particle உம், and not the exceptive particle ஏ, is inserted after the second noun ; and also after the first, if it be a verbal noun, and then the following verb, may either be in the affirmative or negative form, as:

அவள் பட்சமாய்ப்பேசினதுமல்லாமற் பிச்சைகளையுங்கொடுத்தாள், *besides that she spake kindly, she gave also alms*, or *she not only spoke kindly, but gave*, &c.

பழங்களையல்லாமற்கீரைகளையுஞ்சாப்பிட்டான், *he eat both fruits and greens.*

அன்பினாலன்றி மனத்தாழ்மையினாலும் நற்குணத்தைக்காண்பிக்க வேண்டும், *we must show (our) good disposition not only by love, but also by humility.*

Again, with the addition of உம், they are used as conjunctions in the beginning of a sentence, or added to அது, இது, &c., with உம், as:

அல்லாமலும் (or அன்றியும்) அவர்திருவுளம்பற்றினதாவது, *moreover he spake thus:*

அதுவுமல்லாமல் (or அதுவுமன்றி) அவர்கள்துக்கத்துக்குப்போய் மிகவும்புலம்பினார்கள், *besides, they went to the funeral, and made great lamentation.*

It is evident that great care must be taken not to confound this exceptive particle with இல்லாமல் or தவிர, for which, see § XCV.

5. The verbal noun, அல்லது is sometimes used like அல்லாமல் or அன்றி, but most frequently it is used as the disjunctive or exceptive particle *or* like ஆவது, (§ LXVI. 4,) and may be inserted between any parts of speech, except the verbal participles, the infinitive and subjunctive modes, as:

நாம் அல்லது அவர்கள் அந்தத்துஷ்டரைச்செயித்தால்மிகுந்தநன்மைகிடைக்கும், *much good will follow, if we* or *they overcome those wicked people.*

ஈருள்ளியை அல்லது வெள்ளுள்ளியைஅல்லதுவள்ளிக்கிழங்கை அல்லது முள்ளங்கியைவாங்கவேண்டும், *you must buy onions*, or *garlick*, or *sweet potatoes*, or *radishes.*

நீகல்வியைப்படி அல்லது மற்றொருதொழிலைச்செய், *either learn science*, or *do any other business.*

சன்மார்க்கராகியகல்விமான்களுடனே அல்லது நல்லொழுக்கமுள்ளவர்களுடனேகலந்திருப்பாயாக, *have fellowship with learned men that are virtuous,* or *with (other) men that are good.*

When the sense is not exceptive, it is better to use உம், as:

நீயிப்படிப்பட்டபொல்லாங்குகளைச்சொல்லவும்நினைக்கவுங்கூடாது, *thou must not speak, nor even think such evil things.*

6. The verbal noun இன்மை or இல்லாமை is often used to form negative nouns, as:

இரக்கமின்மை,	*unmercifulness, mercilessness.*
சாக்கிரதையில்லாமை,	*laziness.*
ஊக்கமில்லாமை,	*cowardice,* &c.

§ LXXIV.

The *defective verb* உள்ள, உண்டு, &c. denotes existence; of them

1. உள் or உள்ளே is usually added to the dative case, as a particle denoting *within, into,* as:

வீட்டுக்குள்ளேபோனோம், *we went into the house.*
மனிதரிருதயத்துக்குள்ளே பொல்லாத இச்சைகள்தோன்றும், *evil desires arise within the heart of men.*

Often also the oblique case is used, as:

வீட்டினுள் அடங்கியபொருள்கள், *the things that are in the house.*

In some connexions, it means *of, from, among,* as:

அவற்றினுள் இதுபிரதானமானது, *of them this is the chief.*

With the verb படுகிறது, it means *to submit,* and with படுத்துகிறது, *to subdue;* in both cases requiring the dative case, as:

இராட்சதர்கள் இராவணனுக்குட்பட்டார்கள், *the giants submited to Ravanen.*
அவன் அவர்களைத்தனக்குட்படுத்தினான், *he subdued them under him.*

2. உள்ள, is used like a relative participle, and is added to the fourth or seventh case, when it means *which is* or *was*, as:

வீட்டிலுள்ள யாவுங்கெட்டுப்போயின, *all that was in the house perished.*

பட்டினத்திலுள்ள சனங்கள்கலங்கினார்கள், *the people in the city were troubled.*

Occasionally it stands absolute, without any case, as:

விட்டுணுவானவன் ஐசுவரியத்திலேயாவது வடிவிலேயாவது பின்னு முள்ள மாட்சிமைகளிலாவது எனக்குநிகரானவனோ, *is Vishnoo equal to me in riches, in form, or in any other existing excellencies?*

When it is added to the nominative case it makes of the noun an adjective, and qualifies the other noun with which it is connected, as;

கிருபையுள்ளபராபரன், *the gracious God*, i. e., *God who has grace.*
கோபமுள்ளஇராவணன், *the angry Ravanen.*
அவன் நற்குணமுள்ளவன், *he is a good man.*
அவருடைய இருதயம் தயையுள்ளது, *his heart is kind.*

The word உள்ளது is also used absolute, meaning *it is so, it is truly so*, as:

அவன் அப்படிச்சொன்னது உள்ளதுதான், *it is indeed true that he said so.*

3. உண்டு, means *there is, there was*, as:

அயோத்தியாபட்டினமுண்டு, *there is (or was) the city Ayodian (Oude.)*
என்னிடத்திற்பத்துப்பணமுண்டு, *I have ten fanams.*
பட்டினத்திலே நூறுபேருண்டு, *there are* 100 *persons in the city.*

As a particle of existence it is frequently united with the verbs ஆகிறது, ஆயிருக்கிறது, ஆக்குகிறது and

பண்ணுகிறது; the two latter are used either with the nominative or the accusative case, as:

கலகமுண்டாயிற்று,	*a tumult arose*
கலகமுண்டாயிருந்தது,	*there was a tumult.*
துன்மார்க்கத்தையுண்டுபண்ணினன்,	*he formed a wicked religion.*
கருத்தர்பறவைகளையுமுண்டாக்கினார்,	*God created also the fowls.*

§ LXXV.

The defective verb போதும், &c., requires the dative case, either expressed or understood, as:

அன்னவஸ்திரமெனக்குப்போதும், *food and raiment are sufficient for me.*

இருபதுவராகன்போதாது, *twenty pagodas are not sufficient.*

பன்னீராயிரம்பேருள்ள சேனை யுத்தம்பண்ணுதற்குப்போதாதபடியினாலே சேனையை அதிகமாக்கவேண்டும், *as a corps of 12,000 men is not sufficient for the war, (you) must increase it.*

என்னுடையபெலன் இதற்குப்போதாமையால் நீயெனக்கு உதவி செய்யவேண்டும், *you must assist me, as my strength is not sufficient for this.*

§ LXXVI.

The defective verb கடவேன், &c., always requires the infinitive of another verb, and thus forms the optative mode, implying also necessity, as:

நான் என்னுடையதுற்குணத்தைச்செயிக்கக்கடவேன், *may I overcome my evil nature!*

நீ நன்றாய்ப்பணிவிடைசெய்யக்கடவாய், *mayst thou well perform (thy) service!*

ஒளியுண்டாகக்கடவது, *let there be light!*

Sometimes ஆக is added to it, without altering the sense, as:

நீங்கள்சமாதானமாயிருக்கக்கடவீர்களாக, *may you be peaceful!*

§ LXXVII.

The defective verb தகும் &c., is used,

1. with the dative case, as:

இரங்குகிறது உங்களுக்குத்தகும் or *தகுதியாயிருக்கும், it behoves you to be merciful.*

புறங்கூறுதல்நமக்குத்தகாது, it does not behove us to backbite.

செங்கோலைச்செலுத்துகிறது இராசனுக்குத்தக்கது, it becomes a king to rule righteously; or *to sway a righteous sceptre.*

2. With the Infinitive mode, as:

நீகற்றோரிடத்திலிருக்கத்தகும், it is fit that thou stayest with the learned.

புருடன் தன்மனைவியையடிக்கத்தகாது, a man ought not to beat his wife.

நீசெய்யத்தகாதவைகளைச்செய்தாய், thou hast done things which thou oughtest not to do.

அவர்கள்பேசத்தக்கவைகளைப்பேசவேண்டும், they must speak the things which they ought to speak.

3. Without the dative case or infinitive mode, as:

இவன்தகாதவன், he is an unfit person.
நீ தகாதவிதமாய்ப்பேசக்கூடாது, thou must not speak unbecomingly.

§ LXXVIII.

Of the verb கூடுகிறது, *to join, to agree,* the 3d person neuter of the future tense, both affirmative and negative, viz., கூடும் and கூடாது, with the relative participle of the past tense, கூடிய, or கூடின, are peculiarly used,

1. with the 3d case, or instrumental ablative, when it means *able, fit, possible,* as:

இது என்னாற் கூடும். *I am able to do this*, lit: *this will be (done) by me.*

இந்தச்சுமையைக்கொண்டுபோகிறதற்கு உன்னாற்கூடாது, *thou art not able to carry this burden.*

என்னாற் கூடியமட்டுஞ்செய்வேன், *I shall do as much as I can*, lit: *I shall do so far as it can by me.*

2. With the infinitive mode of other verbs; when the 3d person neuter கூடாது means *must not*, *ought not*, *can not*, implying both impropriety and command, as:

அவர்கள் துரையினுடையசன்னிதானத்திலே பிரவேசிக்கக்கூடாது, *they must not enter into the presence of the gentleman.*
நீ உன் சாதியைக்கெடுத்துப்போடக்கூடாது, *thou must not spoil thy caste.*
நாம் அவர்களைத்துன்பப்படுத்தக்கூடாது, *we must not afflict them.*
நீங்கள்பாவஞ்செய்யக்கூடாதுஆகையாற்பாவத்திற்கேதுவானதற்கு விலகுவீர்களாக, *because you must not commit sin, keep far from every occasion to sin.*

As this verb does not imply ability from strength or power, it cannot be used where that is to be expressed; such words as திராணி, வல்லமை, &c., must be employed, *e. g.*,

I can do that, is not well rendered by நான் அதைச்செய்யக்கூடும், but by நான் அதைச்செய்வேன்,

I cannot (am not able, am too week) to do that, not நான் அதைச்செய்யக்கூடாது, because that implies impropriety or command, but எனக்கு அதைச்செய்யத்திராணியில்லை or அதைச்செய்யஎனக்குத்திராணியில்லை.

You cannot walk so far, உமக்கு அவ்வளவுதூரம் நடக்கத்திராணியில்லை.

3. The difference between கூடாது and மாட்டாது, will be best perceived by stating the following questions with the answers, as:

To நான்போகலாமா, *May I go?* The affirmative answer is: போகலாம், *you may go;* or போ, *go.* The negative answer is, நீபோகக்கூடாது, *thou must not go!*

நாம் திருடலாமா, *may we steal?* நாம் திருடக்கூடாது, *we must not (cannot) steal.*

But to நீ நடப்பாயா, *will you walk* (which implies: *will you be able to walk?)* the affirmative answer is, நான் நடப்பேன, *I shall walk;* the negative answer, is, நடக்கமாட்டேன், *I shall not (be able to) walk,* or *I will not walk.*

நீங்கள் இன்னுந்திருடுவீர்களா, *will you steal again?* திருடமாட்டோம், *we will not steal.*

4. I add a list of the various forms of question and answer in which these defective verbs are used; and from which the correct use of them may be more easily learnt.

To நான் இப்படிச்செய்யலாமா, *may,* or *shall,* or *must I do so?* The affirmative answer, is: செய்யலாம், *you may do so;* negative answer, செய்யக்கூடாது, *you must not (cannot) do so.*

செய்யாமலிருக்கலாமா, *can I be without doing (so)?* affirmative answer, செய்யாமலிருக்கலாம், *you may.*

Negat.—— { செய்யவேணடும், / செய்யாமலிருக்கக்கூடாது, } *you must do,* or *you cannot be without doing (so.)*

	நீ செய்வாயா,	*will you do (so)?*
affirm. ans.	செய்வேன்,	*I will do.*
negat. ans.	செய்யமாட்டேன்.	*I will not do.*

	நான்செய்யவேண்டுமா,	*must I do?*
affirm. ans.	நீ செய்யவேண்டும்,	*you must do.*
negat. ans.	நீசெய்யவேண்டுவதில்லை or வேண்டாம்,	*you must not (need not) do.*

	நான்செய்யக்கூடாதா,	*cannot I do so? may I not? have I no right to do so?*
affirm. ans.	நீ செய்யலாம்,	*you may do so.*
negat. ans.	நீ செய்யக்கூடாது,	*you must not,* or நீ செய்யப்படாது *you must not,* or நீ செய்யத்தகாது, *you ought not to do so.*

Observe that the simple imperative is required when there is no such previous question, either implied or understood.

Note.—Concerning கூட, see § XCIV.

§ LXXIX.

Of the verb போலுகிறது *to be like* the infinitive போல, and the relative participles of the past and future tenses போன்ற and போலும், are used with the accusative case, or sometimes with the nominative, as:

இவனைப்போலச்செய், *do like him.*
மரம்போல்நின்றான், *he stood like a tree.*
சாத்தானைப்போன்ற இராவணன் செத்தான், *Ravanen who was like Satan is dead.*

புலியைப்போலும் பூனைபுறப்பட்டது, *a cat, like a tiger went forth.*
பூனை புலியைப்போலப்பாய்ந்தது, *the cat rushed forth like a tiger.*

Note.—போல் is sometimes used for போல.

§ LXXX.

The Tamil pronouns are used as in our European languages; though occasionally, when no obscurity arises, they may be omitted, particularly in short sentences, as the finite verb itself sufficiently points out the person, thus:

இப்படிச்சொன்னேன், *I said so.*

The particular uses of each pronoun are these:

1. நாம், *we* is used with reference both to the speaker and the persons who are spoken to, as:

நாம்பாவிகளாயிருக்கிறோம், *we are sinners;* this when spoken, *e. g.*, by a minister to his congregation implies, that both the former and the latter are sinners.

However, great men speak of themselves in this plural number. Thus a master will say to his servant:

நாம் உனக்கு இப்படிச்சொல்லவில்லையா, *did I not say so to thee?*

But நாங்கள், *we*, the other form of the plural of the first person, excludes the person or persons to whom we speak, and is therefore properly opposed to நீங்கள், thus:

> நாங்கள்போவோம் நீங்கள இங்கேயிருப்பீர்களாக, *we shall go; (but) do you stay here.*

This also is used by single persons to distinguish themselves still more than நாம் would do.

2. நீ, *thou*, is always used by superiors to inferiors; and on the contrary நீர் and நீங்கள் are used by inferiors to superiors. Thus even a younger brother will say to the elder, நீர்வாரும். But the elder will address the younger by நீ *thou*, as நீ, வா. Again நீங்கள் is more honourable than நீர், the latter is used by equals. To say நீ to a superior or even to an equal, would be an affront.

3. அவன் and இவன், *he*, are distinguished; the former, by being used of a person distant or absent; and the latter, of a person near or present. The same is to be observed of அது, *that*, and இது, *this*. Also in writing, when two subjects immediately preceding, are referred to, அவன் and அது, refer to the first of them, and இவன் and இது to the second, as:

> சாத்தனுங்கொற்றனும்வந்தார்கள், இவன்துஷ்டன் அவன்நல்லவன், *Sutten and Kotten came;* the latter (was) *a wild man,* (but) *the former a good man.*

> நீங்கள் பத்திலொரு பாகத்தைச்செலுத்தியும், இரக்கத்தைக்காண்பிக்கவில்லை இதை நீங்கள்செய்யவேண்டும் அதையும் விட்டுவிடக்கூடாது, *you do indeed pay tithes, but you show no mercy; this you ought to do, and that you must not leave undone.*

> பொன்னும்வெள்ளியும் உயர்ந்தவிலைபெறறலோகங்கள். அதுமஞ்சள் நிறமுள்ளது இது வெண்மைநிறமுள்ளது, *gold and silver are precious metals;* that *has a yellow*, this *a white colour.*

But this way of speaking is obscure to a Tamulian, and used chiefly in poetry. In common life, it is better to repeat the nouns, particularly when they are remote.

தகப்பனுங்குமாரனும் வீட்டிலேபிரவேசித்தபொழுது, இவன் என்மகனென்றுதகப்பன்சொன்னான், *when father and son entered the house, the father said this is my son.* If you say here அவன், it will mean a person not then present.

சேனைகள் கோட்டையைப்பிடித்து, அதிற்பிரவேசித்தார்கள், *the troops took the fort and entered it.* If you say, இதில், it will mean some thing different from the fort; as if the speaker pointed to a house or some other place before him, into which they entered.

இக்காலத்துமனிதர் அதிகமாய்ப்பொய்பேசுகிறார்கள், *the men of this time* (meaning the present) *are great liars.* If you say அக்காலத்து, it refers to any former time.

It is evident from hence, that these pronouns are always demonstrative, and never merely personal.

Note 1.—Sometimes to affect humility when speaking with others, a person will use the 3d person இவன் of himself, instead of நான், *e. g.*, இவனுக்கென்னதெரியும், *what does this person know? instead of* எனக்கென்னதெரியும், *what do I know?*

Note 2.—அவர், இவர், in high Tamil are used as the plural number; but in common life merely as an honorific of a single person, as: அவர் என்மேல்தயவாயிருந்தார். Again the plural அவர்கள் is used as a still higher honorific, by an inferior to a superior, when it is often added to the noun denoting the rank, as: துரையவர்கள் அப்படிக்கட்டளையிட்டார்கள். If the speaker literally means more than one, துரைமார்கள் should be substituted.

Note 3.—When அவன் or அவர் or அது, is put twice, as: அவனவன் அவரவர், it means *every one, each one*, respectively. The last only is put in the case required, as:

பராபரன் அவனவனுக்குத்தக்கதாகப்பலனை அளிப்பார், *God will recompense so as is due to every one.*

மரங்களுக்கு அதற்கதற்கேற்றவிதமாய்ச்செய்யவேண்டும், *you must treat the trees according to their respective natures.*

4. The reciprocal or reflective pronouns தான், தாங்கள், &c., are used instead of அவன், &c., when the nominative of the sentence and not another noun is to be referred to, thus:

> ஆசாரியன்தன்வஸ்திரத்தையுடுத்திக்கொண்டான், means, *the priest put on his (own) garment;* if you say, அவனுடைய வஸ்திரத்தை, it means, *the garment of another person.*

> ஞானிகள்தங்களைவீணராக்கிக்கொண்டார்கள், *the wise men rendered themselves fools.*

> அவன் தனக்குக்கொடுத்ததடியை முறித்தான், *he broke the stick which (one) had given him.* Here தனக்கு, *to himself.*

> ஜனங்கள் தங்கள்பூரணமனதோடுந்தம்மிடத்தில் அன்புகூரவேண்டுமென்று கருத்தர்கட்டளையிட்டார், *the Lord has commanded that the people shall love him with their whole heart.* Here தம்மிடத்தில், refers to the principal nominative கருத்தர்; and தங்கள் to ஜனங்கள், the nominative of the inserted instance.

Note 1.—Neuter nouns usually do not require the reciprocal pronoun, as:

> மரங்கனிகொடுக்கின்றது, *the tree gives (its) fruit.*

Yet plural neuter nouns, when their respective natures are referred to, receive it; in which case the reciprocal pronoun is doubled, as:

> மரங்கள் தமதுதமதுசாதியின்படி கனிகொடுக்கின்றன, *trees give fruit according to their (own respective* or *several) kind.* Observe that in the high language தமது தமது is contracted into தந்தம்.

Note 2.—When the plural தாம் is used as an honorific to a single person, its preceding noun must be likewise in the honorific form, thus:

> அவர்தம்முடையநீதியைவெளிப்படுத்தினார், *he has made known his (own) righteousness.*

It is also used instead of நீர், by equals: ஐயா தாம் அனுப்பினமனிதன் சுகமாயிருக்கிறான், *Sir, the man whom you sent, is in health.*

Note 3.—The plural தாங்கள் is used as a still greater honorific by an inferior to a superior, instead of நீங்கள், as:

துரையே தாங்கள்கொடுத்த உத்தரவின்படி அடியேனை யிரட்சிக்க வேண்டும், *O! Sir, you must save (your) humble servant according to your word.*

Observe; that when a native uses, வேண்டும் in such a connexion, he does not mean properly *must*, but, *I beseech you, it is desirable.*

Note 4.—தான் also is used sometimes as an honorific, when a superior writing to an inferior, wishes to avoid the blunt address of நீ, *i. e.*, தான் எழுதியனுப்பின காகிதம்வந்துசேர்ந்தது, *the letter which you wrote and sent has arrived;* or simply, *your letter has come to hand.*

Note 5.—The indeclinable particles தான் and தாம், must not be confounded with this pronoun. See § CX.

5. Of the indefinite demonstrative pronouns அன்ன and இன்ன, the former is not in common use. The use of the latter will appear from the following instances:

அந்தமனிதன் இன்னானென்று எனக்குத்தெரியாது, *I do not know who that man is.*

பூர்வீகத்திலே இன்னவின்னவைகள் நடந்தனவென்றுசொல்லு, *say what things happened in ancient times.*

In the same way is used, இப்படிப்பட்ட, as:

கருத்தர் இப்படிப்பட்டபோதகங்களைச்செய்தாரென்று எங்களுக்கு அறிவிக்கவேண்டும், *inform us what instructions the Lord gave.*

From these instances, it will be observed, that it would be wrong to use the interrogative pronouns, as in the English. Some do say, அந்தமனிதன் ஆரென்று எனக்குத்தெரியாது. பூர்வீகத்திலே என்னநடந்ததென்றுசொல்லு. கருத்தர் என்னபோதகங்களைச்செய்தாரென்று அறிவிக்கவேண்டும்; but this is not elegant. The interrogative can however be used, when the closing verb means, *inquire, ask,* &c.; for instance: அந்தமனிதர் ஆரென்றுகேள், *ask who those men are?* பூர்வீகத்திலே என்னநடந்ததென்று விசாரித்துக்கொள்.

Inquire what happened in ancient times, &c., and then the preceding clause suggests the question to be put.

Note.—We meet with அவன்நாயனானான், he is like a dog; but this அன்னான, in not the pronoun, but அன்ன the particle of similarity, and ஆன the personal termination. See § XII. 5, and § XX. 7.

§ LXXXI.

1. The interrogatives, எவன், யாவன், எந்த, எ, &c., are used the same as in our languages, thus:

எவனோடேபேசினாள், *with whom did she speak?*
இவன் எவளுடையநாயகன், *whose husband (is) this man?*
எதற்காகவந்தான், *what did he come for?*
எந்தக்குதிரையின்மேலேறுவீர், *what horse will you mount?*
இன்றைக்கு ஆரிடத்துக்குப்போய்ச்சாப்பிடுவீர், *with whom will you go to-day and dine?*

எவ்விடத்திலிருந்துவருகிறாய், *from what place do you come?*

நீயெப்படிப்பட்டதானியத்தைக்கொடுத்தாய், *what kind of grain did you give?*

2. In point of position, யாவன், எவள், எது &c., in the nominative case only, are often placed at the end of the sentence, in which case the substantive verb *to be* is omitted in Tamil, thus:

அவன் எவன் (or யாவன்,) *who (is) he?*

இந்தப்பணத்தைக்கொண்டுவந்தவனெவன் (or யாவன்,) *who has brought this money?* lit; *who (is) he that brought*, &c.
இதெது, *what (is) this?*

Sometimes however the dative of the neuter interrogative எதற்கு, என்னத்துக்கு is used in the same manner, as:

இதென்னத்துக்கு, *what for (is) this?*
அதெதற்கு, *what for (is) that?*

3. The gender and number must be well observed in every instance; though the common people usually say:

> அவனார், *who (is) that man?*
> அவளார், *who (is) that woman?*

Instead of அவரார், or அவன்யாவன் அவள் எவள், &c., Thus they also say:

> அவனைக்கண்டதார், *who has seen him?*

for அவனைக்கண்டவன்யாவன்; *or* கண்டவர்யார்.

4. The interrogative particle ஓ, connects the interrogative pronoun, எவன், எவள், எது, with a following demonstrative pronoun, and thus forms the compound pronoun *whoever, whatever*, thus:

களவுசெய்கிறவர்கள் எவர்களோ அவர்கள் துன்மார்க்கர், *whoever steal, they (are) wicked people.*

அவனை விசுவாசிக்கிறவனெவனோ அவன் கெட்டுப்போகமாட்டான், *whoever believeth in him, shall not perish.*

நூறு கோட்டைநெல்லுக்கொண்டுவருகிறவர்களெவர்களோ அவர்களுக்கு ஐந்துவராகனை சந்தோஷமாகக்கொடுக்கப்படும், *whoever shall fetch* 100 *kotas of rice, to them will 5 pagodas be given as a present.*

வருத்தப்படுகிறவனெவனோ அவன் என்னை நோக்கிக்கூப்பிடக்கடவன், *whoever is in trouble, let him call upon me.*

நீ அளக்கிற அளவு எதுவோ அதினாலே உனக்கும் அளக்கப்படும், *with the same measure that thou measurest with, it shall be measured unto thee.*

நான்போகிற இடமெங்கேயோ அங்கேநீயும்வரவேண்டும், *wherever I go, there thou must come also.*

Note.—Some separate the ஓ from the interrogative pronoun, thus:

நீ எதினாலேயளக்கிறாயோ அதினாலே உனக்கும் அளக்கப்படும். நான் எங்கேபோகிறேனோ அங்கே நீயும் வரவேண்டும்; but this is not only inelegant, but evidently confusing ideas; because the following demonstrative pronouns do not correspond to the immediately preceding question, இருக்கிறாயோ அதிலே—போகிறேனோ அங்கே, are dissimilar to each other.

5. The particle உம், forms the interrogative pronouns எவன், and யாவன், into distributive pronouns, *every one, all,* as:

> எவனும் வரலாம், *every one may come.*
> யாவருங்கோவிலுக்குப்போகவேண்டும், *every one* (or *all*) *must go to church.*
>
> எளியவர்கள் யாவருக்கும் பிச்சைகொடுக்கலாம், *we may give alms to any poor man.*
>
> நீயெங்குந்திரியலாம், *you may rove about any where,* or *every where.*

6. Thus also the addition of ஆகிலும், or ஆனாலும், changes the interrogative into the indefinite pronouns, *any one, at least one, whoever,* as:

> எவனாகிலும்போகவேண்டும், *one* or *the other must go.*
> யாவரானாலும் மோட்சத்தையடையவேண்டிற் பராபரனையறியவேண்டும், *whoever wishes* (or *if any one wishes*) *to attain heavenly bliss, must know God.*

Note 1.—The difference between உம் and ஆகிலும் is that உம் fixes the meaning on every one and all; whereas ஆகிலும் takes one out of the number. Thus எவனும்போகவேண்டும், means, *all without exception, must go;* but எவனாகிலும்போகவேண்டும், means, *at least one of them must go;* all need not go. It is then equivalent to ஒருவனாகிலும்.

Note 2.—ஆகிலும் or ஆனாலும், in its contracted form of the subjunctive mode, is often detached from the interrogative noun, and postfixed to the verbal participle; the meaning remains the same, as:

> எவன்வந்தாலுஞ்சந்தோஷத்தைப்பெறுவான், *whoever comes shall receive a present.*
>
> எப்போதுகேட்டாலுங்கொடுப்பார், *he gives whenever* (*one*) *asks;* or *whenever he is asked.*

7. The interrogative noun என்ன, *what? why?* may stand either before the finite verb, or after the neuter verbal noun, as:

> அவர் என்னசொன்னார், *what did he say?*
> அவர் சொன்னதென்ன, *what was it that he said?*

When it is declined, it may stand wherever the force of the sense requires it, thus:

என்னத்துக்காக இதைக்கொடுத்தார், *for what purpose (or why) did he give this?*

அவர் என்னத்தினாலேயித்தனைகோபமாயிருந்தார், *on what account was he so angry?*

நீயிப்படிச்செய்ததென்ன, *why hast thou done so?*

8. The interrogative particle ஏன், is not much used in common language; the vulgar have changed it into என், or யேன், and this they use not only like, என்ன, or என்னத்தினாலே, but also as an emphatic particle of entreating, நீசொல்லேன், *pray, say on!* Sometimes they add it also to the future 3d person masculine, as சொல்வானேன்போவானேன், &c.; and thus used with any person, as:

நீயிப்படிச்சொல்வானேன் *why do you say so?*
நாம அப்படிப்போவானேன், *why shall we go that way?*

But this is not classical, and ought not to be imitated. You should say instead, என்னத்தினாலே அப்படிச்சொல்லுகிறாய், or, நீயப்படிச்சொல்லவேண்டுவதென்ன, &c.

§ LXXXII.

1. The particle படி, *as, according to*, is affixed to any relative participle, or to any noun in the general oblique case, in இன், thus:

அவர்கட்டளையிட்டபடிசெய்வேன், *I shall do as he has commanded.*

தேவவசனத்தின்படிநடப்பீர்களாக, *may you walk according to the word of God.*

2. படி, means *manner, measure;* and when used in the oblative case, படியால், or படியினால், becomes the particle, *because, on account of, by reason of, as, since*, and is used only with the present and past relative participles, as:

நீ இப்படிச்செய்தபடியாற் சபிக்கப்பட்டாய், *because thou hast done this, thou hast been cursed.*

அவன் அவலட்சணமானவைகளை நடப்பிக்கிறபடியால், என்முகத்துக்குமுன்பாகவரக்கூடாது, *he must not come into my presence, because he practices indecent things.*

சருவவல்லமையுள்ளவர் நம்முடையபங்கிலிருக்கிறபடியால் நாம் பயப்படவேண்டுவதில்லை, *we need not fear, as the Almighty is with us.*

3. When it is used in the dative case, படிக்கு, or in the adverbial form படியாய், படியாக, it denotes *purpose, end, effect;* and must be rendered by *that, so that, to the end that, in order to.* It is then naturally used with the relative participle of the future tense, as:

தேவர்களைச்செயிக்கும்படிக்கு இராவணன் மிகுந்தசேனையைக்கூட்டிக்கொண்டு புறப்பட்டான், *in order to overcome the gods, Ravanen collected a large host and went forth.*

கங்கையிலே ஸ்நானம்பண்ணும்படியாக அநேகசனங்கள் காசிக்குப்போனார்கள், *many people went to Kási (Benares) to bathe in the Ganges.*

In this sense, படி also is simply used—படிக்கு is, on the other hand, added also like படி, to nouns in the oblique case, meaning the same, as:

அவருடைய வசனத்தின்படிக்கு or
அவருடைய வசனப்படிக்குச்செய்தோம், } *we did according to his word.*

§ LXXXIII.

The particle எ is used in the following instances.

1. To give emphasis to any word, which is called தேற்றம்; *i. e.*, certainty, it means then *certainly, doubtless*, as:

> நற்புலவருக்கேதற்றேபுகழ், *praise is doubtless (indeed) due to good poets.*
>
> நீங்கள் சாவதேயில்லை, *you shall certainly not die.*

2. As a conjunctive conjunction, like உம், when it is added to several nouns in succession, as:

> நிலமே, நீரே, தீயே, வளியே, ஆதியிலுண்டாயின, *earth, water, fire,* and *wind, got into existence at the beginning.*

3. As a disjunctive conjunction, which is called பிரித்தல்; it may then be rendered by, *none other, but, only*, as:

> இராசனே கொடுத்தான், *none other but the king gave.*
>
> இந்தத்துண்டுச்சேலையையேயெடுத்துக்கொள், *take none other, but this piece of cloth.*

4. As an interrogative particle, in which sense it is however not commonly used, as:

> நீயேயிதைத்தந்தாய், *was it you who gave this?*
>
> அறிவேயிப்படிச்செய்கிறது, *is this doing knowledge?* i. e., *did you do this with understanding?*

5. As an euphonic particle, called இசைநிறை, as:

> அம்பு யானையின்மார்பிற்பாய்ந்தொளித்ததே, *the arrow flew and lodged in the Elephant's breast.*

In this way it is commonly added to any words without any particular meaning, as: படியிருலே, படியே &c. It is however better to avoid it.

6. It is the sign of the vocative case, as:

> துரையே! *O gentleman!*
> தகப்பனே! *O father!*

7. It is a particle of exclamation, at the beginning of a sentence, chiefly in poetry, and then it is often doubled, as:

ஏயேயிவளொருத்திபேடி, *Oh! Oh! this woman alone is an idiot.*

§ LXXXIV.

The interrogative particle ஓ, has eight applications, and is annexed to the word to which it refers, viz.

1. It simply interrogates, (வினா), as:

அவனோவல்லவன்,	*is he the strong person?*
அவன் வல்லவனோ,	*is he powerful?*
மதுரைக்குப்போகிறானோ,	*does he go to Madura?*
மதுரைக்கோபோகிறான்,	*does he go to Madura?* meaning, not to another place.

என்னிடத்திலோதயவாயிருப்பான், *will he be kind to me?* or, to another?

If there be a question about several subjects, each of the nouns receives ஓ, and an interrogative pronoun usually follows, as:

கொத்தனோசாத்தனோஎவன்வந்தான், *who came, Kotten, or Saten?*
உன் பாவம்மன்னிக்கப்பட்டதென்றுகட்டளையிடுகிறதோ உன் படுக்கையையெடுத்துக்கொண்டுபோவென்று கட்டளையிடுகிறதோ எது எளிது, *which is easier to say (or command), thy sins are forgiven thee, or take up thy bed and walk?*

புதுச்சேரியையோ வேலூரையோ எந்தக்கோட்டையைப்பிடித்தார்கள், *which fort did they take, Puduchery or Vellore?*

Sometimes the concluding interrogative pronoun is also omitted, as:

அங்கேயிருக்கிறமரங்கள் ஆலமரமோ மாமரமோ, *are those trees Banian or Mangoe trees?*

Note.—Europeans are apt to put the interrogating pronoun in Tamil at the beginning, as in English, e. g. ஆர் அங்கேவருகிறான் சாத்தனோ கொற்றனோ, but this is improper.

2. It negatives (எதிர்மறை), as:

நான்வந்தேனோ, *I did not come*, lit: *did I come?*
புண்ணியஞ்செய்தானோ, *he did not perform acts of charity*, lit: *has he performed acts of charity?*

சத்திரங்களையுங் கோயில்களையுங் குளங்களையுஞ் செய்தோ, மோட்சத்துக்குட்போனான், *he did not go to heaven by constructing choultries, temples and tanks.* செய்தோ is here for செய்ததினாலோ.

3. As an exceptive particle (பிரித்தல்), as:

யானோசொன்னேன், *I did not speak*, viz., I in a company, separating myself from the rest.

This however differs very little form the last mentioned subject, எதிர்மறை.

4. As a particle of doubt (ஐயம்,) when the question is between several subjects. It may then be rendered by *whether, and, or*, as:

அதுஆலமரமோமாமரமோ, *(I don't know) whether it is a Banian* or *a Mangoe tree.*

Observe that this is not a question, as in Sect. 1., though the form is the same. For instance, A asks B, அது ஆலமரமோ மாமரமோ. *Is that a banian or a mangoe tree?* Here it is a proper question. B doubts about it, and says, அது ஆலமரமோ மாமரமோ தெரியாது, *I do not know whether it is a banian or a mangoe tree.* But though the question and answer appear the same on paper, yet there is a wide difference in the manner of speaking them.

5. As an interjection both of wonder and pity, (சிறப்பு,) as:

ஓஓபெரியன், *Oh! Oh! what a great man!*
ஓஓகொடியன், *Oh! Oh! what a cruel man!*

6. It rejects that which is expressed and means another (ஒழியிசை,) as:

வேலைசெய்யவோபோகிறாய், *you do* (not) *go to work* (but to play.)

7. ஓ, is used at the end of a sentence to express regret at something that is gone or lost; hence it is called கழிவு. For instance, suppose a person travels alone, and is killed on the road. A messenger informs me of it, saying, அவன்கள்ளராலே கொலைசெய்யப்பட்டான், *(he has been killed by robbers.)* To this I reply, நாலுபேர்கூடப்போனாலோ, meaning நாலுபேர்கூடப்போனார்களானால்அவன்சாவமாட்டான் or நாலுபேர்கூடபோகாததினாலே செத்தான். ஓ, means here therefore as much as அப்படியாகுமோ? viz., *if four men had gone along with him, would it be so?* or it means அல்லவோபிழைப்பான், *would he not have lived if four men had gone along with him?*

A master gives orders to all his servants to come at an appointed time. One of them does not come, and is fined 3 rupees. This he relates to me the next day, saying, எசமானவர்கள்என்னிடத்தில்மூன்று ரூபாய் அபராதமவாங்கினார்கள். To this I reply, நீநேற்றுவந்தாலோ, meaning நீ நேற்றுவாராததினாலே பணம் போயிற்று, or நீநேற்றுவந்தாயானால், பணம்போகாது.

A person ruins himself by not seeking his real good. Another tells me of it, saying, அவன் உறுதியை யுணராமற்கெட்டான், *he perished, not having known (his) real good.* To this I say, ஓ ஓ தமக்கோருறுதியுணராரோ, meaning தமக்கோருறுதியுணர்ந்தாரானாலஉறுதி கிடைக்குமே உணராததினாலே உறுதிபோயிற்று.

Thus also தைதவின்றிநல்லறஞ்செய்தாலோ, meaning, *if he did virtuous deeds without evil, would he not live?*

8. It is a mere expletive, without any meaning இசைநிறை, as: ஓ ஓ உவமன், *reconciliation.*

Note.—The particle ஓ, has, by several foreign writers, been used to express the English particle *but*. For this, however, I find no authority, nor do the natives so use it, unless ஓ, in any of the preceding instances, may in some way or other be brought to mean *but*. Thus it is said :

> இவர்களெல்லாருந் தருமங்களைச்செய்தார்கள் கொற்றனோ செய்யவில்லை, *all these persons did charity ; but Kotten*, or only *Kotten did not*. Here the English requires *but*, or some such particle ; but because of the repetition of the verb it is not necessary in Tamil. The Tamulian says : இவர்களெல்லாருந் தருமஞ்செய்தார்கள். கொற்றன்செய்யவில்லை, or கொற்றன்மாத்திரஞ் செய்யவில்லை.

Note.—Concerning another peculiar use of ஓ, see § LXXXI. 4.

§ LXXXV.

The particle ஆ, is likewise used as an interrogation and as an interjection ;

1. As an interrogation, it is added like ஓ, to the word, about which the question is made, as :

வந்தாயா,	*hast thou come?*
இப்படியாசெய்தாய்,	*hast thou done so?* (or otherwise.)

Note.—ஆ, is more frequently used as a imple interrogation than ஓ, because it is less ambiguous.

2. As an interjection it stands like ஓ before the vocative case, as : ஆசுவாமீ, *O swamy !*

§ LXXXVI.

The particle உம், has likewise various applications ;

1. It is a proper conjunctive conjunction, like *and*, in which sense every word to be connected, or numbered up, as it were, must receive உம் ; it can therefore never be united to one word only in this sense. With the exception of the genitive and vocative cases, the relative participle and the finite

verb, all other words may be thus connected by உம் ; as has been sufficiently shown in the preceding pages: see § XLIII, 7. 8. § XLVIII. 4.

However, though it is usually necessary and elegant to add this conjunction to all the nouns that are to be connected, it may be omitted in all but the last; and then the preceding nouns must be in the nominative; whatever case the last noun may have, thus:

அடகு புலால் பாகு பாளிதமுமுண்டான், *he eat leaves, meat, milk and sugar.*

வீடு, தோட்டம், குளம், குதிரைகளையும் அழித்தான், *he destroyed the house, garden, tank and horses; instead of,* வீட்டையுந் தோட்டத்தையுங்குளத்தையுங்குதிரைகளையும், &c.

2. It is used singly in the following instances;

i. To point out a negative, called எதிர்மறை, when it means *even*, as:

அவன்வருதலுந்தீது, *even his coming is an evil* implying that his not coming is an evil. See § LVI. 8. and § LVII. 2. about உம் added to the second verbal participle.

ii. To point out something understood, called எச்சம், as:

இராமனும்வந்தான், *Ramen also has come;* implying that others not mentioned, had come before him.

iii. To point out *completion, entireness, fullness,* called முற்றும், as:

தமிழ்நாட்டுமூவேந்தரும்வந்தார்கள், *(all) the three kings of the Tamil country came;* implying that there were no more than three kings.

கண்ணிரண்டுஞ்சிவந்தன, *both eyes were red*, implying that a man has but two eyes.

காலமூன்றுங்கண்டான், *he has seen the three times;* viz., the past, the present, and the future. There are no more times than these three.

If உம் be omitted in these sentences, it will mean that there were more than three kings in existence; that there are more than two eyes, and three times. Thus also, if a person possesses no more than two cows, we must say இரண்டுபசுவையும் or பசு இரண்டையுங்கொண்டுவா, *bring both the cows.* But *if he has more than two,* then we must say, இரண்டுபசுவைக் கொண்டுவா, omitting உம்; which implies that *he has more than two.*

Again:

> என்னங்கைக்குமயிரும்முயற்கோடும் ஆமைமயிரும்முன்புமில்லை இக்கழுதைக்குங்கோடில்லை, *also in former times, hair was not in the hollow of the hand; nor had the hare a proboscis, nor the tortoise hair; also this ass has no proboscis.* Here, if உம be not added to முன்பு, nor to இக்கழுதைக்கு, the meaning will be that though there were no such things in existence formerly, yet they are now; though this ass has no proboscis, yet others have.

Under this head may be noticed all interrogative words which by the addition of உம், cease to be interrogatives and become as it were complete, or entire in sense, as:

எவன்,	*who?*	எவனும்,	*every one, all.*
யாவர்,	*who?*	யாவரும்,	*all, without exception.*
எப்படி,	*how?*	எப்படியும்,	*howsoever.*
எவ்வளவு,	*how much?*	எவ்வளவும்,	*how much, or how little soever.*
எப்பொழுது,	*when?*	எப்பொழுதும்,	*always.*
எங்கு or எங்கே,	*where?*	எங்கும்,	*every where.*
எக்காலம்,	*what time?*	எக்காலமும்,	*at all times, &c.*

iv. To point out an extraordinary circumstance called சிறப்பு, as:

> இதுகுறவரும்மருளுங்குன்றம், *this is a mountain of which even its own inhabitants are afraid;* implying that it must therefore be a very bad place to reside in.

v. To make the comparative degree by being

added to the 5th case, in this sense it is called ஆக்-கம், and must be rendered by *than, more than*, as:

புலியினுங்கொடியன், *(he is) more cruel than a tiger.*
கடலினும்பெரிது, *(this is) greater than the sea.*

vi. To point out assurance, certainty, as:

இதுநன்றுமல்ல, *this is certainly not a good thing.*
இதுதீதுமல்ல, *this is certainly not a bad thing.*

Observe, that if these two sentences be united thus:

இதுநன்றுமல்லத்தீதுமல்ல, the meaning is, *this is neither good nor bad.*

§ LXXXVII.

The particles என்று and என are used,

1. As indicative conjunctions; like *that*, as:

அவன் நிலைநிற்பானென்றுகாண்பி, *show that he will stand firm.*

For further particulars, see § LXIV. 1.

2. As particles of similarity, when they may be rendered by *as, like*, thus:

இவன் அவனைத்தகப்பனென்றுகனம்பண்ணினான், *he honored him as his father.*

மையெனத்திரியேல், *do not rove about like a sheep.*

3. As numbering conjunctions like *and*, as:

கல்லென்று முள்ளென்று செடியென்றுசொன்னான், *he said, stone, thorn and shrub.*

ஒன்றென இரண்டென மூன்றென எண்ணினான், *he counted one, two and three.*

Note.—உம் may also be added to each.

4. என is used as an infinitive, of the verb என்கிறது, as:

> ஊரெனப்படுவது உறையூர், *Ooreiyoor is that which is called a town;* i. e., *that has every thing belonging to a town, and therefore worthy to be called a town.*

With என்று, the verb சொல்ல, must be added, as: ஊரென்றுசொல்லப்படுவது, &c.

5. As an adverb,

> திடீரென (திடீரென்று) எழுந்தான், i. e., சடுதியாய் எழுந்தான், *he rose on a sudden.*

> எனக்குப்பகீரென்று இருந்தது, } i. e., எனக்குமிகுந்த
> என் வயிற்றிலே பகீரெனவிருந்தது, } நோவாயிருந்தது,
> which may be rendered, *it was tearing my bowels;* or, *my bowels yearned.*

> படபடவென்றுவேலைசெய்; i. e., இடைவிடாமல் or சீக்கிரமாய் வேலைசெய், *do the work without intermission, quickly.*

6. In certain cases it means *calling*, or giving a sound, as:

> கூவென (கூவென்று) ஓடினான், *he ran, calling out koo.*

> வீடு மடமடவென்றுவிழுந்தது, *the house fell with a crackling sound;* i. e., *it fell*, saying as it were, *mada, mada.*

Note.—The native Grammars state 8 modes, by which nouns may follow each other in succession; viz., by putting them without any conjunction at all; and by adding to each noun either உம், ஏ, என்றா, என, என்று, எனா, or ஒடு,—all which mean *and.*

The total number of the nouns, with உம், must be added after the last noun, when they are put together without any conjunction at all, or when ஏ, என்று, or எனா has been added to each, as:

> சாத்தன் கொற்றனிருவரும்வந்தார்கள், *both Sáten* and *Kotten came.*

> சாத்தனேகொற்றனேபிரகாசனேமூவரும்வந்தார்கள், *Sáten, Kotten,* and *Prakasen came.*

> நீயென்று அவனென்று இருவரும் போவீர்கள், *both you* and *he shall go.*

நானென்று நீயென்று அவனென்று மூவரும்வந்தோம், *I, thou*, and *he came.*

Again உம், என்று and என, may be followed by the total number after the last noun, or not, as :

நிலமும் நீரும்நல்ல or நிலமுநீரு மிரண்டும்நல்ல, *earth* and *water are good things.*

சாத்தனென்று கொற்றனென்று சொல்லப்பட்டவர்கள் வரவில்லை, *the persons called Sáten* and *Kotten have not come.*

நிலமென நீரென வேண்டும், *both earth* and *water are necessary.*

Again, என்று, and என may be added only to the last noun, with the addition of the total number, with or without the demonstrative letter இ, or இந்த, as :

வினை, பகை, யென்றிரண்டினுங்கேடில்லை or வினைபகையென்றிவ்விரண்டினுங்கேடில்லை, *there is nothing worse than evil actions* and *hatred.*

The total may also be omitted, and a noun common to all the preceding nouns substituted with the demonstrative pronoun, thus :

வினைபகையென்றிந்தீமைகளினுந்தீமையில்லை, *there is no greater evil than wicked actions* and *hatred.*

சாத்தன் கொற்றனென்றிம்மனிதர்கள் பயிரிட்டார்கள், *Sáten* and *Kotten tilled the ground.*

Again when என்று, is added to every noun உம் may be added to it, as :

கொற்றனெனும் பிராகாசனென்றுஞ்சொல்லப்பட்டவனிருந்தான், *there was a man called Kotten* and *Saten.*

Note.—Observe that only உம், என்று and ஓ are used as conjunctions in common language.

§ LXXXVIII.

இன்னம் and இன்னும், *still, still longer, yet, until now*, are used,

1. With reference to the future time, meaning இன்மேலும், as :

அவன்வரும்படிசொன்னேன் வரவில்லை இன்னம்பார்ப்பேன், *I told him to come ; but he did not come ;—I shall still wait.*

2. With reference to the present time, meaning இதுவரைக்கும், as :

அவன்வரும்படிசொன்னேன் இன்னும்வரவில்லை, *I told him to come ; but he has not yet come.*

Observe that this word cannot, like *yet*, be used with reference to the past time. For instance it would be wrong to say அவன் இன்னம் அடித்தான், *he beat him still* (or yet) more ; here பின்னும் must be used.

§ LXXXIX.

The particles முன், முன்பு, முன்னர், or முன்னம், *before, in the presence of,* பின், பின்பு, பின்னர், *after, behind,* கீழ், *under, below,* and மேல், *above* are used,

1. With the dative case, in regard to place ; when the things spoken of are still at some distance from each other, thus :

நமக்குமுன்பு மலைகள்தோன்றின, *mountains appeared before us ; or, we got mountains in sight*

வீட்டுக்குப்பின்பு இரண்டுதெருக்களுண்டு, *there are two streets behind the house.*

வானத்துக்குக்கீழேபூமியுண்டு, *beneath the sky is the earth.*

நம்முடையதலைகளுக்குமேலே குருவிகள்பறக்கின்றன, *birds fly over our heads.*

In this sense ஆக is often added to them, as :

முன்பாக, பின்னாக, கீழாக, மேலாக.

2. With the oblique case, when the things spoken of are closer to each other, thus:

என்னுடைய வீட்டின்முன் மூன்றுகதவுகளுண்டு, *there are three doors in the front of my house.*

அதின்பின் ஒருகதவுமாத்திரமுண்டு, *behind it there is but one door.*

அவனுடையகாலின்கீழே கொப்புளமுண்டு, *he has blistens under his foot.*

கல்லைத்தலையின்மேல் எறிந்துபோட்டான், *he threw stones upon the head;* if you say, தலைக்குமேலே எறிந்துபோட்டான், *it means over the head.*

Nouns ending in ன், may have these particles annexed in the nominative case, as:

அவன்முன், *before him.*
அவன்பின், *behind him.*
அவன்கீழ், *beneath him, under him.*
அவன்மேல், *upon him.*

Also the before mentioned difference between the use of the two cases with these particles is not always strictly observed.

3. முன் and பின் are used also with respect to time, mostly with the dative case, as:

அதற்குமுன்னே, *before that, previous to that.*
அந்தக்காலத்திற்குப்பின்பு, *after that time.*
எனக்குமுன்னமேயிருந்தான், *he was before me.*
உனக்குப்பின்பிறந்தேன், *I was born after you.*

Note 1.—முன் may be added to the verbal noun of any tense in the dative case, as;

நான்பேசுகிறதற்குமுன்னே, *before I speak.*
நான்பேசினதற்குமுன்னே, *before I spoke.*
நான்பேசுவதற்குமுன்னே, *before I shall speak.*

However the present verbal noun, or the common verbal noun is used for any time, as:

நான்பேசுகிறதற்கு } முன்னேவந்தான்,
—— பேசுதற்கு —} *he came before I spake.*

But பின் naturally requires always the verbal noun of the past tense, as:

நான்போனதற்குப்பின்பு, *after I had gone.*

Again முன் may be added to the relative participle of the future tense, and பின் to that of the past tense, as:

நான் சொல்லும்முன்னேபோனான், *he went before I spake.*
நான் போனபின்புகூக்குரலிட்டான், *he made a noise after I had gone.*

Note 2.—முன்னே has also been used with the verbal noun of the negative verb, as: நான் சொல்லாததற்குமுன்னே, *before I spake;* but it is not elegant.

Note 3.—For பின், the common people use also பிறகு, பிற்பாடு; which is likewise not classical.

4. முன்னே, முன்பு, and பின்பு, are also used adverbially at the beginning of a sentence, meaning *formerly*, and *afterwards*, as:

முன்னேயவன்நல்லவனாயிருந்தான் பின்புகெட்டவனானான், *formerly (or at first) he was a good man; but afterwards he became bad.*

5. முன், பின், கீழ் and மேல் are used also adjectively, as:

முற்பக்கம், *the front*, or *the four part.*
பிற்பக்கம், *the hinder part.*
கீழ்ப்பக்கம், *the lower part.*
மேற்பக்கம், *the upper part.*

6. பின்னும், மேலும் are used as conjunctions, meaning *moreover*, *again*, *besides*, as:

பின்னும் (or மேலும்,) அவன் சொன்னதாவது, *again, (moreover) he said thus.*

7. முன் and பின் are also used substantively, when they are declined, as:

முன்னேப்போலப்பேசினுன், *he spoke as before, in former time.*
முன்ஞலேபோனுன், *he went before.*
பின்ஞலேபோ, *go behind!*

Note.—When கீழ் and மேல் are used as substantives, மை is affixed to them; as கீழ்மை lowliness, subjection; மேன்மை, excellence.

8. மேல் is used also as a particle meaning *upon, concerning*, with the oblique case, as:

கடலின்மேல்நடந்தார், *he walked on the sea.*
கருத்தர்மேலேபாடினுன், *he sang concerning the Lord*, (or கருத்தரைப்பாடினுன்,)

Concerning கீழ் and மேல், see § XLVI. 5.

9. மேல் is often used twice with உம், as மேன்மேலும், which means, *more and more, increasingly*, as:

மேன்மேலும் ஏறினுர்கள், *they ascended more and more*, or *higher and higher*

§ XC.

The particles மட்டும், வரையில், வரைக்கும், பரியந்தம் and அளவும், all meaning *until, as, far as*, are used with the nominative case:

1. மட்டும் or மட்டுக்கும், refers principally to place only, as:

அவ்வூர்மட்டும்போவோம், *we shall go as far as that village.*

2. வரையில், வரையிலும் or வரைக்கும் and பரியந்தம் refer both to time and place, as:

நாங்கள் சென்னேபட்டினம்வரையிற்சென்றபொழுது, *when we had come as far as Madras.*

என்னுடையபன்னிரண்டாம்வயசுவரைக்கும் அடிக்கடிசுரங்கொண்டிருந்தேன், *I was frequently sick of fever until my twelfth year of age.*

எதுவரைக்கும் என்னைவருத்தப்படுத்துவீர்கள், *how long will you trouble me?*

மரணபரியந்தம் உண்மையாயிருந்தான், *he was faithful until death.*

3. They are used also with the relative participles, but most frequently with that of the future tense, as:

நீ அவ்வூருக்குவருமட்டுஞ்சாமான்களைவிட்டுப்போகாதிருப்பாயாக, *do thou not leave the baggage until thou comest to that village.*

மனிதர்கள்மனந்திரும்புமளவும் பரமசதியில்லாமலிருப்பார்கள், *men will be without heavenly bliss until they repent.*

மகா இராசாமரணம் அடையும்பரியந்தந்தருமஞ்செய்துகொண்டு வந்தார் *the king performed charity until his death.*

நான் திரும்பிவருகிறவரைக்கும் என்வீட்டுக்காரியங்களை விசாரித்துக்கொள், *take care of my household affairs until I return.*

§ XCI.

The particle மற்று, *otherwise,* with or without உம் is used adverbially, thus:

மற்றநேககாரியங்களைப்பேசினர், *the spake besides many things.*
மற்றுந்தூஷணமானவார்த்தைகளை யெழுதியிருக்கிறன், *he has likewise written other blasphemous words.*

மற்ற, is used adjectively like *other*, as:

மீன்களையுங் கீரைகளையும் மற்றப்பதார்த்தங்களையுங் கொடுத்தார்கள், *they gave fish, greens, and other things.*

Observe, that மற்ற must be used when the preceding nouns are put in the required case with உம், as in the above instance, but when they are stated in the nominative case without உம், then முதலானவைகள் must follow, as:

மீன் கீரைமுதலானபதார்த்தங்களைக்கொடுத்தார்கள், *they gave fish, greens, and other such things.*

Observe farther the difference between மற்ற and வேறு; the latter means *other*, with respect to kind or distributively, but மற்ற, with respect to the whole number; wherefore if of ten persons, two go to the east, but all the rest go southward, you must use மற்ற to signify the rest; but if two of them go to the east, some others to the south, and again some others to the west, வேறு or சிலர் must be used.

§ XCII.

The particle இனி or இனிமேல் *hereafter, henceforth*, refers always to the future time; and must therefore have the verb always in the future tense, as:

இனிநான் இப்படிப்பேசமாட்டேன், *I shall not hereafter speak thus.*

இனிமேல் அதிகதண்டனைவரும், *In future you will get greater punishment*, lit: *more punishment will come.*

§ XCIII.

The commiserating particle ஐயோ is used as, *oh! alas!* thus:

ஐயோ எத்தனை அநியாயம், *alas! how much injustice!*

ஐயோசகலத்தையும் இழந்துபோனான், *alas! he has lost every thing.*

ஐயோ has been used to express also the English *woe!* and then affixed to the dative case, as உனக்கு ஐயோ, *woe be to thee!* But this is incorrect. It can never be used as a noun; in this sense வேதனை, தண்டனை, or any other such word, must be added, as:

ஐயோ உனக்குவேதனைவரும், *woe be to thee*, lit: *alas! there will come distress to thee!* or *alas! thou shalt be unhappy* or *miserable.*

§ XCIV.

கூட *together*, is frequently added to the social ablative, either in ஒடு or உடனே, as:

> அவனோடேகூடப்போனேன், *I went along with him.*
>
> என்னுடனேகூடப்பத்துப்பேரிருக்கிறார்கள், *there are ten persons with me;* i. e., *united with me.*

§ XCV.

தவிர and ஒழிய, *except*, are used either with the nominative or accusative, as:

> இவ்விரண்டுசேலைகளைத்தவிர மற்றயாவையுமெடுத்துக்கொண்டுபோ, *take all the cloths, except* (or *but*) *these two.*
>
> சாத்தன் கொற்றனென்பவர்களொழிய, மற்றயாவருங்கீழ்ப்பட்டிருக்கிறார்கள், *all have submitted except Satten and Kotten.*

Note.—The word ஒழிய has also been used for *unless*, and thus added to the subjunctive mood, as: நீங்கள் மறுபடியும் பிறந்தாலொழிய, *unless you be born again;* but it is not classical, and the negative verb, with விட்டால், ought to be substituted, as: நீங்கள்மறுபடியும்பிறவாவிட்டால்.

§ XCVI.

ஏறக்குறைய, *about, more or less,* is placed before the number to which it refers, as:

> ஏறக்குறைய ஏழுவருஷத்துக்குப்பின்பு, *after about seven years.*
>
> ஏறக்குறைய நாலாயிரம்வருஷத்திலே கிறிஸ்துப்பிறந்தார், *Christ was born in about the 4000th year.*
>
> கிறிஸ்துப்பிறந்து ஏறக்குறைய முந்நூறுவருஷத்துக்குப்பின்பு கொனிஸதந்தின இருந்தான, *Constantine lived about 300 years after Christ.*
>
> கிறிஸ்துப்பிறந்ததற்குஏறக்குறைய எழுநூறுவருஷங்களுக்குமுன்னே ஏசாயாத்தீர்க்கதரிசியிருந்தார், *the prophet Isaiah lived about 700 years before Christ.*

§ XCVII.

அற *off, from, without*, is used with the nominative case, as:

அவனைக்காதறவெட்டினான், *he cut off his ear*, lit: *he cut him so that the ear fell off.*

என்னுடையசந்தேகமறப்பேசினார், *he spoke so as to remove my doubt.*

In common life the ignorant use அற also in this way,

என்ன அறப்படித்தவனாகப்பேசுகிறாய், *what do you talk as one that has learnt much?*

அய்யா அறக்கொடுமைசெய்தான், *Sir, he has done much cruelty.*
In which examples, அற means மிகுதியாய்.

§ XCVIII.

சூழ, சூழ்ந்து, or சூழ்ந்துகொண்டு, and சுற்றி, *round about, surrounding*, require the accusative case, as:

என்னைச்சூழவாருங்கள்
என்னைச்சூழ்ந்துவாருங்கள்
என்னைச்சுற்றிவாருங்கள், } *come around me!*

Note.—Sometimes சுற்றிலும் (the ablative with உம் of சுற்று) has been used for சுற்றி, without necessity, and without authority, சுற்றிலும் means *also around;* for instance, கோட்டையின்சுற்றிலும்போங்கள், *go also around the fort*, (not only within). In this case சுற்று is a noun.

§ XCIX.

கடுக, and முடுக, *quickly, hastily*, and மெல்ல, *slowly*, are used adverbially, thus:

கடுகவந்தான், *he came hastily!*
முடுகப்போனான், *he went quickly.*
மெல்லநடந்தான், *he walked slowly.*
மெல்லச்செய்பவன்நன்றாய்ச்செய்வான், *he who works (or does a thing) gently, will do it well.*

§ C.

வலிய *spontaneously, freely*, precedes a verb, as:

வலியத்தந்தான், *he gave of his own accord, spontaneously.*
வலியப்போனான், *he went of himself.*

This must not be confounded with வலிய, the adjective meaning *strong*, which is joined to nouns, and does not require the following க, ச, த, or ப to be doubled, as:

வலியசருப்பம், *the strong serpent.*

§ CI.

குறித்து, *concerning, about, with respect to,* requires the accusative, as:

இந்தச்சங்கதியைக்குறித்து நான் என்னசொல்லலாம், *what shall I say concerning this affair?*
உன்னைக் குறித்துயோசனைபண்ணுவேன், *I shall consider about you.*
நீங்கள் என்னைக்குறித்து அழவேண்டுவதில்லை, *you need not weep about me.*

Note.—பேரிலே has been used instead of குறித்து, which is however not Tamil; it seems to have come from the Teloogoo.

§ CII.

Concerning இல்லாமல், and அல்லாமல், see § LXIX. 3, 4, as for இல்லாவிட்டால், *if not, unless*, it is always added to the nominative, or used absolutely with reference to the preceding verb, as:

பணமில்லாவிட்டால் எப்படிப்பிழைப்போம், *how shall we live unless we have money? or without money?*

நீஇதைச்செய் இல்லாவிட்டால்த்தண்டிக்கப்படுவாய், *do this, or you will be punished.*

§ CIII.

1. The subjunctives ஆனாலும், ஆயினும், ஆகிலும், meaning, *although it be,* are used as disjunctive conjunctions, at the commencement of a sentence, meaning *but, although, yet.* But here the same distinction must be observed which has been pointed out, § LVI. to be between the 2d and 4th subjunctives; for, as ஆனாலும், or ஆகிலும், implies merely supposition, it cannot be used when the thing actually exists, or has been already done; in which case அப்படியிருந்தும், must be used. ஆகிலும் &c. always require the following verb to be in the future tense, with a negative, either expressed or understood, as:

> பாவிகள் நரகத்துக்குப்போவார்கள் ஆகிலும் புத்தியடையமாட்டார்கள், *sinners will go to hell; yet they will not get good sense;* meaning, *although sinners go to hell, they will not improve.* Here போவார்கள் ஆகிலும், *is the same as* போனாலும்.
>
> பாவிகள் மோட்சத்திற்குப்போனாலுந் துற்குணராகவேயிருப்பார்கள், *sinners will remain wicked though they should go to heaven.*

But,

> பாவிகள் நரகத்திற்குப்போவார்களென்றுகருத்தர்சொன்னார் அப்படியிருந்தும், மனிதர்கள்மனந்திரும்பவில்லை, *the Lord has said, that sinners shall go to hell; yet, they do not repent.*

2. Again ஆகிலும், or, ஆனாலும், is affixed to nouns in succession, when it denotes *either, or;* and with a negative verb, *neither, nor;* as:

> இராசாவானாலும் பிச்சைக்காரனானாலும் பராபரனிடத்தில் மனந்திரும்பாவிட்டால் மோட்ச இராச்சியத்திற் பிரவேசியார்கள், *neither the king nor the beggar will enter the heavenly kingdom, unless they turn unto God.*

Note.—In this sense என்கிலும் has been used instead of the last ஆகிலும்; but upon no proper authority.

3. Again ஆகிலும், or ஆனாலும் may be added only to one noun; and then signifies *at least, even;* as:

> அவனையாகிலும்வரச்சொல்லு, *tell him at least to come.*
> ஒருபணத்தையாகிலுங்கொடுக்கக்கூடாதா, *cannot you give even a fanam?*

Concerning its being affixed to words of interrogation, see § LXXXI. 6.

§ CIV.

The particles ஏனும் and ஆனும், signify the same as ஆகிலும், in the following instances.

1. When affixed to a single noun, they mean, *even, at least*, as:

> சற்குணன் எவ்வளவேனும்புத்தியடையமாட்டான், *Sarkunnen will not get sense in the least.* Here எவ்வளவேனும் is the same as எவ்வளவாகிலும்.
> பத்துப்பணமேனுங்கொடு, *give at least ten fanams.*

2. When added to two or more nouns, ஏனும், means *either, or;* and if the following verb be negative, *neither, nor,* as:

> முன்னின்றமெய்யின்மேல் அகரமேனும் இகரமேனும்வரும், i. e., அகரம் or இகரம் (அ or இ) *is put on the preceding consonant.*
> பொன்னேனும் வெள்ளியேனுஞ்செம்பேனுங்கொடு, *give (me) either gold,* or *silver,* or *copper.*
> அரிசியேனும் பருப்பேனுங்கொடாவிட்டால் என்பசிதீராது, *if you give me neither rice, nor pulse, my hunger will not be satisfied* (or *unless you give me either rice or pulse.*)

3. ஏனும், is also added, though rarely, to the finite verb, when it means *although,* as:

> புரையூரார் புத்தியோடே நடந்தார்களேனுந்துன்பம்நீங்காது, *although the people of Pureiyoor should walk wisely, persecution will not cease.*
> சிங்கங்கள்கருச்சித்தனவேனும் நீயங்கேபோகவேண்டும், *you must go thither, although the lions roar.*

Note.—ஆனும், is not much used in common life.

§ CV.

மாத்திரம், அளவு, தனை, and துணை, are words denoting *measure;* and are used with the demonstrative and interrogative pronominal prefixes, as:

அம்மாத்திரம்,	அவ்வளவு,	அத்தனை,	அத்துணை,
இம்மாத்திரம்,	இவ்வளவு,	இத்தனை,	இத்துணை,
எம்மாத்திரம்,	எவ்வளவு,	எத்தனை,	எத்துணை,

They all mean *that quantity, this quantity, what quantity?* or *thus much,* &c. They are used,

1. Substantively, as:

இந்தநெல்லு எம்மாத்திரம், *how much paddy is this?*
இப்பணம் எவ்வளவு, *how much money is this?*
இப்பணம் எத்தனை, *how much money is this?*
பூமியின்சுற்றளவு அம்மாத்திரமே, *thus much is the circumference of the earth.*

வருஷம் எத்தனை, *how many years?*

2. Adjectively, thus:

இவ்வளவுபணத்தை நீசெலவழிக்கலாமா, *ought you to have spent so much money?*
அம்மாத்திரந்தானியத்தைக்கொடுத்தான், *he gave so much grain.*
எத்தனை நாட்பிரயாணம், *how many days journey?*
இந்தக்குழி அம்மாத்திரம் ஆழமாயிருக்கின்றது, *this ditch is so deep.*
அந்தத்துண்டுச்சேலை இவ்வளவுநீளமாயிருக்கின்றது, *that piece of cloth is so long.*

3. Again மாத்திரம், is used as a particle of restriction, meaning *only, but,* and is then affixed to nouns in any case, thus:

நான்மாத்திரம்வந்தேன், *I only have come.*
இதைமாத்திரஞ்சொல்லு, *say this only.*
பராபரனுக்குமாத்திரஞ்சருவவல்லமையுண்டு, *God only has Almighty power.*

4. Again மாத்திரம், in the ablative of location, added to participles, means *as soon as, immediately, at the instant,* thus:

மழைபெய்தமாத்திரத்திலே ஒளித்துக்கொண்டோம், *we hid ourselves as soon as it began to rain.*

மின்னுண்டானமாத்திரத்திலே இடிமுழக்கமுமுண்டாகும், *the thunder follows immediately upon the lightning.*

5. அளவு, and தனை, with the conjunction உம், added to each, are affixed also to the future participle, and mean *until*, *whilst*, as:

நீவருமளவும் இருப்பேன், *I shall wait till you come.*

தேவகிருபை வருந்தனையுஞ்செபிக்கவேண்டும், *we must pray, until we obtain grace.*

§ CVI.

புறம், and பால், which mean *apart*, *the side*, are, with the prefixes of the demonstrative pronominal letters, used as adverbs, viz., அப்பால் and அப்புறம், *further on that side*, இப்பால் and இப்புறம், *hither, on this side*, as:

அப்புறஞ்சொல்லு,	*say on!* or *further.*
இப்புறம்வா,	*come hither!*
அப்பாலேபோ,	*go further!*
இப்பாலேவை,	*put (it) this way*, or *this side.*

When united with nouns of place, they require the dative case, as:

ஆற்றுக்கப்புறம் போனோம் or ஆற்றுக்கப்புறத்திலே போனோம், *we went to the other side the river.*

சென்னைபட்டினத்திற்கிப்பாலே பல்லக்குவந்தது, *the palankeen came on this side Madras.*

Again, in opposition to உள், *within, inside*, புறம் means *without, outside*, and is thus used:

உள்ளும்புறமும், *within and without.*

புறத்திலேயிதைச்சொல்லாதிருப்பாயாக, *do not say this out of doors.*

வீட்டுக்குப்புறத்திலே (or புறத்து) ப்போ, *go out of the house!*

Hence is also the appellative புறத்தியான், *a man who is not of the family but a stranger*, புறத்தியாள், *such a woman* &c.; however these are not classical words.

§ CVII.

பொருட்டு, the contracted form of பொருள்து, is used with the future participle, to express *purpose, design;* and means *that, in order to, for the purpose of.* It can therefore be used only of rational beings, as:

அவர் நமக்குநீதிசெய்யும்பொருட்டு வந்தார், *he came in order to render justice to us.*

For பொருட்டு, also பொருட்டாக is used.

As a noun it is added to the 6th case of the neuter pronouns, as: அதின்பொருட்டு, இதின்பொருட்டு, *for that—this purpose.*

§ CVIII.

நிமித்தம், or நிமித்தமாக, *for the sake of, on account of,* is used with the nominative or general oblique case, as:

அவர்நிமித்தமாகப்பராபரன்அனுக்கிரகஞ்செய்கிறார், *for his sake, God is gracious.*

நீதியினிமித்தந்துன்பப்படுவீர்கள், *you will be persecuted on account of righteousness.*

§ CIX.

ஆகையால், ஆதலால், ஆனபடியினாலே, are words used as causal conjunctions, *wherefore, therefore,* at the beginning of a sentence, as:

கருத்தர்கிருபைசெய்வார் ஆதலாற்சந்தோஷமாயிரு, *the Lord will be gracious; therefore be glad!*

Or they may be regarded as concluding the clause which contains the cause or reason for the admonition, &c., and then they may be rendered by *for, because, since,* as:

மழைபெய்யும் ஆகையாற்பிரயாணமாய்ப்போகக்கூடாது, *we cannot commence our journey, because it will rain, &c.*

§ CX.

The particles தான் and தாம், with or without ஏ, affixed, the former with singular nouns, and the latter with plural nouns, are used emphatically to denote *certainty, reality;* and mean *indeed, very, self.* They may be added to nouns in any case, as:

அவன்தான்வந்தான், *he himself came.*
அந்தப்பையைத்தானேகொண்டுவா, *bring that very bag.*

அவன்அப்படிச்செய்யவேண்டியதுதான், *he ought indeed to have done so.*

கருத்தர்தாமேயுங்களைத்தண்டிப்பார், *the Lord himself will punish you.*

Note.—மெய்தான் or அதுமெய்தான், i. e., *that is true, truly, certainly,* is put in Tamil always at the end of the sentence of which it is an affirmation, and not before or in the middle, as in English. மெய்தான் must follow a verbal noun; but அதுமெய்தான், any finite verb, as:

பாண்டிய இராசாவுக்கு மாணிக்கவாசகர் மந்திரியாயிருந்தது மெய்தான், *it is indeed true that Manikavasagar was minister to Pandiya Rajah.*

சூரியன்பூமியைச்சுற்றியோடுகிறான் அதுமெய்தான், *the sun certainly moves round the earth.*

§ CXI.

தோறும் (or தொறும், as used in poetry), is a particle which means *every one, without exception,* and unites with nouns in the nominative case, and with the relative participle of the future, *e. g.*

நாடோறும் (நாள்தோறும்) வா *come every day*, i. e., *daily.*

நான் வருகிறேனென்று வீடுகள்தோறும் போய்ச்சொல்லு, *go to every house and say that I am coming.*

சொற்றொறும் (or சொற்கள்தோறும்) தேன்பொழிகின்றது, *from every word flows (or drops) honey;* where சொல்த்தொறும் stands for சொற்கள்முழுவதிலுமிருந்து.

அவர்சொல்லுந்தோறும் நீகேட்கவேண்டும், *whenever he speaks, you must hear.*

அவர் புறப்படுந்தோறும்மழைபெய்கின்றது, *whenever he sets out, it rains.*

Note.—In this latter sense some have used பொழுதெல்லாம், thus அவர்சொல்லும்பொழுதெல்லாம், but this is not a proper composition, தோறும் must not be confounded with ஒவ்வொரு, the latter means *one by one, separately of every kind*, e. g.

ஒவ்வொரு புத்தகங்கொடும், *please to give a book of every kind. If we say* புத்தகந்தோறுங்கொடும், it will mean: *give me books of all kinds, or of every sort.*

வேலைக்காரருக்கு ஒவ்வொருபணமாகக்கொடு, *give to every labourer a fanam*, lit: *give fanam by fanam to the labourers.* We cannot say: ஒவ்வொருவேலைக்காரனுக்கு ஒருபணங்கொடு, neither பணந்தோறும்; but we may say, ஒவ்வொரு மனிதனுக்கு ஒவ்வொருபணங்கொடு, *give to every man a fanam*, lit: *give fanam by fanam to man by man.*

§ CXII.

The nouns, எல்லாம், (neut.) எல்லாரும் (m. and f.) முழுவதும், and முழுமையும், (neut.) சகலமும், (neut.) அனைத்தும், (neut.) அனைவரும், (m. and f.) யாவும் (neut.) யாவரும், (m. and f.) mean *all* with respect to number. Of சகலம், the oblique case சகல is like an adjective always prefixed to a noun of any gender, and requires உம், at the end of the noun. முழுவதும், அனைத்தும், அனைவரும், யாவும் and யாவரும், are always affixed to nouns and then put in any case that may be required. எல்லாம், and எல்லாரும், may be either prefixed or affixed; the manner of doing this has been explained § XXIII. *e. g.*

மிருகங்களெல்லாம்,
மிருகங்கள்முழுவதும்,
மிருகங்கள்முழுமையும்,
சகலமிருகங்களும்,
மிருகங்களனைத்தும்,
மிருகங்கள்யாவும், } *all beasts.*

மனிதர்களெல்லாரும்,
சகலமனிதர்களும்,
மனிதர்களனைவரும்,
மனிதர்கள்யாவரும், } *all men.*

Of these words, முழுவதும் and முழுமையும், only can be used to denote *the entireness of a thing*, which thing is then put in the singular number, as:

இருதயம்முழுவதும், *the whole heart.*
வேஷ்டிமுழுவதுங்கிழிந்துபோயிற்று, *the whole cloth is torn.*

கிணற்றுத்தண்ணீர்முழுவதும் இறைத்தாயிற்று, *all the water of the well is already drawn out.* In this instance, தண்ணீரெல்லாம் is also used; probably from the consideration that water consists of many drops.

தோட்டம்முழுவதும் நீர்ப்பாய்ச்சினேன், *I have watered the whole garden;* here also தோட்டமெல்லாம் may be said, meaning தோட்டத்திலுள்ள இடங்களெல்லாம், *all the places of the garden.*

Note 1.—முழுமையும் and முழுவதும், unite only with neuter nouns, and these only when signifying inanimate creatures. We cannot therefore translate *he eat a whole sheep* by ஆடு முழுவதையுஞ்சாப்பிட்டான், but by ஓராட்டிறைச்சிமுழுவதையுஞ்சாப்பிட்டான், i. e., *he eat all the flesh of a sheep,* the former means: *he eat all the sheep (of a flock.)* Thus also *the Lion swallowed a whole cow,* must be rendered by சிங்கம்மாட்டைவிழுங்கிற்று, and not, மாடுமுழுவதையும், which means *all the cows.* So neither can we translate *the whole man is corrupt,* by அம்மனிதன் முழுவதுங்கேடுள்ளவன், but by மனிதனுடைய ஆத்துமா சரீரம்முழுவதுங்கேடுள்ளவைகள், i. e., *the whole body and soul of the man are corrupt,* ஆத்துமாமுழுவதும், *the whole soul,* சரீரம்முழுவதும் *the whole body,* may be said; but முழுவதும் does not agree with மனிதன். Hence it is incorrect to say அந்த மனிதன் முழுவதுங்கெட்டுப்

போறான், though we sometimes hear the common people say so; அவன்கெட்டுப்போறான் is quite enough.

Note 2.—Some have abridged முழுமை and எல்லாம், and put them as adjectives before nouns to express entireness, thus, முழு இருதயமும், எல்லா இருதயமும், *all the heart or the whole heart;* but this is incorrect.

Note 3.—The word சருவமும் all, has sometime since been introduced into the Tamil from the Samscrit. It is used the same as சகலமும், thus சருவவல்லமையுமுடைய கருத்தா, *the Almighty God.*

§ CXIII.

Two negatives destroy each other; wherefore if the clause containing the purpose or design of a subject, be in the negative, the following clause leading to it cannot be in the negative too; but must be in the affirmative form, and *vice versa,* if the latter clause be in the negative, the former must be in the affirmative form, as:

கண்ணுக்குச்சேதம்வாராதபடிக்கு இவ்விடத்திலே நில்லு, *remain in this place lest your eye be injured;* or கண்ணுக்குச்சேதம் வரும்படிக்கு இவ்விடத்தை விட்டுப்போகாதே, *do not leave this place, lest your eye be injured.*

The propriety of this will appear plain, if you separate and invert the clauses, thus:

நீ யிவ்விடத்தை விட்டுப்போகாதிருப்பாயாக. போனால், கண்ணுக்குச்சேதம்வரும், *and the former sentence* இவ்விடத்திலே நில்லு நின்றுற்கண்ணுக்குச்சேதம்வாராது.

Note.—This must not be confounded with such sentences as these: நீ பணம்வாங்காமல்வாராதே, *do not come without bringing the money,* நீ படியாமலிராதே, *do not be without learning.*

§ CXIV.

The clause containing the *resolution, determination, assertion* or *command,* always follows the *purpose, design* or *end* of that resolution, thus:

நீங்கள் பராபரனுடையபிள்ளைகளாயிருக்கும்படிக்கு, உங்கள்பகைஞரிடத்தில் அன்பாயிருப்பீர்களாக, *love your enemies, that you may be the children of God.*

மிகுந்த மோசங்கொடுக்கத்தக்கதாக அந்தப்பாதையிலே அநேக கள்ளரிருக்கிறார்கள், *there are many thieves on that road, so that there is great danger.*

This order can never be deviated from, because a sentence in Tamil never closes without a finite verb, except in cases of ellipsis which will be stated hereafter. Hence if in the course of a narrative, the clause stating the purpose, end or design cannot conveniently precede the other, stating the resolution, &c., the former may succeed the latter, but it must be followed by the repetition of the principal verb of the preceding clause, or a suitable substitute ; thus :

உங்கள்பகைஞரிடத்தில் அன்புகூருவீர்களாக. நீங்கள்பராபரனுடைய பிள்ளைகளாயிருக்கும்படிக்கு அப்படிச்செய்யுங்கள், *love your enemies. (Do so) that you may be the children of God.*

§ CXV.

The clause containing the *effect* or *inference* generally follows that containing the *cause* or *reason*, as :

காற்றுமிகவும் அடித்தபடியினாலே நாம்துரிதமாய் நடக்கவில்லை, *we did not proceed quickly, because the wind blew hard.*

பராபரன் மிகுந்தகிருபையுள்ளவராகையால் அவரிடத்தில்நம்பிக்கையாயிருங்கள், *trust ye in God ; for he is very gracious.*

பரமண்டலத்திலே யுங்களுக்குமிகுந்தபலன் வருவதாற், சந்தோஷமாயிருப்பீர்களாக, *rejoice ; for your reward will be great in heaven.*

Unless the sentence be very long, to invert this order, as in English, and say, நாம் துரிதமாய்நடக்கவில்லை, என்னத்தினாலென்றால் காற்றுமிகவும் அடித்தது, or, பராபரனிடத்தில்நம்பிக்கையாயிருங்கள், என்னத்தினாலென்றால் அவர் மிகுந்த கிருபையாயிருக்கிறார், is awkward and feeble.

§ CXVI.

Respecting *Ellipsis* in Tamil.

1. When the attributive noun signifies the same thing or person as the subject; or when the sentence ends in a pronoun, or interrogative pronoun, the finite verb ஆயிருக்கிறது, is properly omitted, as:

அவன்திருடன்,	*he (is) a thief.*
இதுஞானம்,	*this (is) wisdom.*
நான்பாவி,	*I (am) a sinner.*
நீயே அவன்,	*thou (art) he.*
அவனெவன்,	*who (is) he?*
இது எவ்வளவு,	*how much (is) this?*
எதுபொன்,	*which (is) gold?*

2. But when the attributive noun expresses only a quality or an attribute of the subject, the finite verb must be used, as:

பராபரன்மகிமையாயிருக்கிறார், *God is glorious,* If you say: பராபரன்மகிமை, it means, *that the glory itself is God.*

அவன்திருடனாயிருக்கிறான், *he is a thief,* i. e., *a thief by habit;* thievery is his quality.

பூமியழகாயிருக்கின்றது, *the earth is beautiful;* should you say, பூமியழகு, it would be unintelligible.

அவள்சந்தோஷமாயிருக்கிறாள், *she is joyful;* should you say, அவள்சந்தோஷம்; it will mean, *that she is the person called Sandòsham.*

ஒளிநன்மையாயிருந்தது, *the light was good,* ஒளிநன்மை, means *the light is goodness itself,* but, ஒளி ஒருநன்மை, means *the light is one of the things that are good.*

In some sentences however both forms may be used without difference in the sense, as:

இதுஎவ்வளவு and இதுஎவ்வளவாயிருக்கின்றது, *how much is this?*

It may easily be ascertained whether the verb is required or not, by exchanging the nouns; *i. e.* by putting the first for the second, and the second for the first; if both make sense ஆயிருக்கிறது, may be omitted; if not, it must be added.

3. Excepting this ellipsis of ஆயிருக்கிறது, not so much for brevity's sake, as for expressing a particular sense, no others are used in Tamil; for avoiding the repetition of a word in the same sentence, can hardly be called an ellipsis; because, though the word itself may not be repeated, yet a suitable substitute is usually put, thus:

He is a wise and good man, அவன்ஞானமும்நற்குணமுமுள்ளமனிதன், here மனிதனை is not repeated, but the conjunction உம், with உள்ள, sufficiently supplies its place. அவன் ஞானமுள்ளமனிதனுமாய் நற்குணமுள்ள மனிதனுமாயிருக்கிறான், is also allowable, though not elegant.

Wherever precision and perspicuity are at stake, repetition cannot be avoided in Tamil, as an instance I shall add the passage, Matth. v. 34, 35, which has in the Greek and in the other European languages repeated ellipsis; but which cannot be imitated in Tamil without greatly obscuring the sense. It ought to be rendered, thus:

நீங்கள் எவ்விதத்திலுஞ்சத்தியம் பண்ணக்கூடாது. வானம் தேவஆசனமாயிருக்கிறபடியால் வானத்தின்மேற் சத்தியம்பண்ணலாகாது. பூமி பராபரனுடையபாதப்படியாயிருக்கிறபடியாற்பூமியின்மேற் சத்தியம் பண்ணலாகாது. எருசலேம் பெரியஇராசனுடையபட்டினமானபடியால் எருசலேமின்மேற் சத்தியம்பண்ணலாகாது, &c.

Thus also, உன்னைப்போலப்பிறனிடத்தில் அன்புகூருவாயாக, is not clear; and may even be misunderstood, so as to mean *love thy neighbour, who is like thyself*. It is better therefore to repeat the verb thus: உன்னிடத்தில் அன்புகூருகிறதுபோலப் பிறனிடத்திலும் அன்புகூருவாயாக.

§ CXVII.

When something is said of a subject both negatively and affirmatively; the negative always precedes the affirming clause, by which the use of a disjunctive conjunction becomes unnecessary, thus:

> இந்தப்பையல் சாக்கிரதையாயிராமற் சோம்பலாயிருக்கிறான், *this boy is not diligent, but lazy.*
> சூரியன்பிரகாசங்கொடாமல்மறைந்திருந்தான், *the sun did not shine but was hid.*
> எனக்குப்பின்செல்லுகிறவன் இருளிலேநடவாமல் ஒளியையடைந்திருப்பான், *he that follows me, shall not walk in darkness but will have light.*

In English, the clause may be inverted, thus: *this boy is lazy and not diligent*, &c., but this cannot be done in Tamil; a circumstance which must be attended to. Hence also the fine passage 1 John i. 5.

> *God is light, and in him is no darkness at all*, must be rendered thus: பராபரன் எவ்வளவாகிலும் இருளில்லாமல் ஒளியாயிருக்கிறார்.

In a few cases this order need not be observed, but then the negative must not be the opposite of the affirmative, and the latter must close with an auxiliary verb, thus:

> தயவுள்ளசிருட்டிகரை நீங்கள்விசுவாசித்துக்கொண்டு, அவருடையகற்பனைகளைத்தள்ளாதிருப்பீர்களாக, *believe in your beneficent creator, and do not break his commandments.*

§ CXVIII.

In comparisons the thing compared must follow that with which it is compared, thus:

> அவன்சொன்னதுபோல நீயுஞ்சொல்லு, *say thou, as he said.*
> பள்ளத்திலுள்ளகுளிர்ச்சியிலும் மலைகளிலுள்ள குளிர்ச்சியதிகமாயிருக்கின்றது, *the cold on the mountains is greater than in the valley.*
> என்னிலும் மகனையும் மகளையும் அதிகமாய்ச்சிநேகிக்கிறவன்எனக்குப்பாத்திரனல்ல, *he that loveth son or daughter more than me, is not worthy of me.*

If you put the latter sentence thus: மகனையும் மகளையும் என்னிலும் அதிகமாய்ச்சிநேகிக்கிறவன், &c., it will mean, *he that exceeds me in loving son and daughter*, &c.

உன்மேல்அன்புகூருகிறதுபோலப்பிறனிடத்திலும்அன்பாயிரு, *love (thy) neighbour as thyself, (or as thou lovest thyself.*

உம்முடையதிருவசனம்பொன்னிலும் அதிகவிலையேறப்பெற்றதாயிருக்கின்றது, *thy word is more precious than gold.*

§ CXIX.

As for the proper position of words in a sentence, it may be observed, as a general rule, that the words belonging to the nominative and those belonging to the finite verb must not be mixed together, but kept distinct, and that those words which are the least important must be placed first, and the most important last, that is, nearest to the words to which they refer. A few instances will elucidate this rule.

சென்னைபட்டினத்திலேசங்கரலிங்கமென்பவனிருந்தான், this means: *there was a certain Sankaralingam in Madras;* the most important part of it is "*the person,*" and not the city. But, சங்கரலிங்கமென்பவன் சென்னைபட்டினத்திலேயிருந்தான், means: *Sankeralingam was in Madras;* the principal relation being, not that such a person was, *but that that person was in Madras.*

அவருடைய வாயிலிருந்து கபடமொன்றும் புறப்படவில்லை, *no deceit whatever proceeded out of his mouth.* This sentence would be weakened by placing கபடமொன்றும், before; unless you mean to say, that no deceit proceeded *out of his mouth.*

அதிகதிரவியங்களைத்தேடுகிறவன் தன்குடும்பத்தை வருத்தப்படுத்துகிறான், *he that seeketh great riches troubleth his household.* It would be very obscure to say: தன்குடும்பத்தை அதிகதிரவியங்களைத்தேடுகிறவன்வருத்தப்படுகிறான்.

அந்த விளக்குகள் சுற்றியிருந்தகுடிசைகளிலேமங்குதலான ஒளியைக்கொடுத்தன, *those lamps cast but a faint light upon the surrounding huts.* Here, if you place the மங்குதலான ஒளியை, before சுற்றி, &c., the sentence will not express clearly the author's mind.

ஆண்டவரே இராசரிக்கத்தை நீர் இஸரவேலருக்கு இக்காலத்திலோ திரும்பக்கொடுப்பீரொன்றுகேட்டார்கள், *they asked, Lord, wilt thou at this time restore the kingdom (or government) to Israel?* As the principal part of the question is the time, இக்காலத்திலோ, is properly placed immediately before the finite verb. If இஸரவேலருக்கு, be put in its place, the meaning will be: *wilt thou give it at this time to Israel or some other nation?* and again, if இராசரிக்கத்தை, be put immediately before the verb, it means, *wilt thou give at this time to Israel the kingdom or something else?*

APPENDIX.

As much depends upon a right understanding and use of the prepositions, conjunctions, and other such particles, each of which has in most languages many significations, I shall in this Appendix particularly point out the manner in which the Tamulians express the various meanings of each of the English particles, whereby the student will see much of the Tamil idiom, and the necessity of ascertaining well the meaning of the English particle before he translates it. I shall also at last notice a few other peculiarities of the English language, and show how they must be disposed of in Tamil.

The Particles are arranged alphabetically.

1. *The Articles A and The.*

The Tamil has no Articles.

1. The *indefinite* Article, however, is well expressed by the numeral ஒரு, when the meaning is one among many, or any, thus:

Give (me) a book, ஒருபுத்தகத்தைக்கொடு.
He run off with a piece of cloth, ஒரு துண்டுச்சேலையையெடுத்து ஓடிப்போனான்.
A man brought a fowl, ஒருமனிதன் ஒரு கோழியைக்கொண்டுவந்தான.

When it points out one of a certain class of men, it is better to express it accordingly, thus:

A Poligar revolted, பாளயக்காரரிலொருவன் கலகஞ்செய்தான்.
A Pharisee invited Christ to supper; பரிசேயரிலொருவன் தன்னுடனே சாப்பிடும்படிக்குக்கிறிஸ்துவை வேண்டிக்கொண்டான்.
A fruit seller stands without, பழங்களைவிற்கிறவர்களிலொருவன் (or பழங்கள்விற்கிறமனிதனொருவன) வெளியிலேநிற்கிறன்.

2. The *definite* article may often be expressed by the demonstrative pronouns அந்த and இந்த, as:

Bring (me) the book, அந்தப்புத்தகத்தைக்கொண்டுவா.
The country is not fertile, இந்தத்தேசஞ்செழிப்புள்ளதல்ல.
Thou art the man, நீயேஅந்தமனிதன்.

Personal nouns, and particularly nouns of Office are often pointed out without அந்த or இந்த, by having ஆனவன் affixed, as:

The King has given orders, இராசாவானவர்கட்டளைகளைக்கொடுத்தார் (or *simply* இராசா.)

The Priest came in high style, ஆசாரியனானவன் மிகுந்தகோலத்தோடேவந்தான்.

3. When the noun is qualified, neither ஒரு nor அந்த is required, as:

The man who brought fruits is gone, பழங்களைக்கொண்டுவந்த மனிதன்போய்விட்டான்.

He is an agreeable companion for me, அவன் என் உயிர்ப்பாங்கன் or உயிர்த்தோழன்.

She (is) a good woman, அவள்நல்லபெண்.

He is the best friend I have, எல்லாரிலும் அவன் எனக்குநல்லசிநேகிதனாயிருக்கிறான்.

In some cases however they may be added, thus:

A good man came here (this) morning, நல்லகுணமுள்ள ஒருமனிதன் காலமேயிவ்விடத்துக்குவந்தான்.

He smote the rich King, அவன் ஐசுவரியமுள்ள அந்த இராசாவையடித்தான்.

4. The different virtues, vices, qualities, sciences, arts, metals, &c., require no article; though ஆனது may be affixed to them, as:

Prudence is commendable, விவேகம் (or விவேகமானது) புகழப்படத்தக்கது.

Falsehood is odious, பொய் (or பொய்யானது or பொய்பேசுகிறது) அருவருக்கப்படத்தக்கது.

Anger ought to be avoided, கோபத்திற்கு விலகவேண்டும்.

Astronomy (is) a very useful science; சோதிடசாஸ்திரம்பிரயோசனமானகல்வி.

To proper names என்பவன், *or* ஆனவன், may be affixed, as:

In the opinion of all good men, Alexander was a great robber, அலெசந்தர் (or அலெசந்தரென்பவன்) பெரிய கள்ளனாயிருந்தானென்று நல்லமனிதர்களெல்லாருந்தீர்மானிக்கிறார்கள். If this sentence be translated, thus: நல்ல மனிதரெல்லாருடைய தீர்மானத்தின்படி அவன் பெரியகள்ளனாயிருந்தான், the meaning will be, *that all good men resolved on his being a great robber, and that he was one accordingly.*

2. *About.*

1. When it means *around* is rendered by சுற்றி, the verbal participle of சுற்றுகிறது; *or by* சூழ, the infinitive of சூழுகிறது; both require the accusative case, as:

The people came about me, சனங்கள்என்னைச்சுற்றிவந்தார்கள்.

2. When it means *more or less, nearly,* with respect to number, ஏறக்குறைய, *or* சற்றேறக்குறைய, expresses it. Examples, see § XCVI.

3. When it means, *concerning, with regard to,* &c. குறித்து, is used, as:

Various opinions exist about the author of the book of Job, யோபென்னும் புத்தகத்தை யெழுதினவனைக்குறித்துப்பலபயவிதமாய்ச்சொல்லிக்கொள்ளுகிறார்கள்.

Other examples, see § CI.

4. When it means, *engaged in*, *employed in*, &c., the Tamulian has no particular expression for it, but changes the phrase altogether. Thus:

What is this to you? go about your business! இதிலேயுனக்கென்ன, நீ உன்னுடையவேலைசெய்யப்போ, lit: *what is it to thee from (or by) this go to do thy business!*
I am about my business, என்வேலைசெய்கிறேன்.

3. *Above.*

May frequently be rendered by the comparative or by மேல், some times the phrase must be altogether changed.

1. When it means, *higher in place.*

You are above the door, நீ கதவிலும் உயரமாயிருக்கிறாய்.

2. *More in quantity and number.*

In this piece of cloth there are above twelve yards, இந்தத்துண்டுச்சேலைபன்னிரண்டுமுழத்துக்குமேலேயிருக்கின்றது.

3. *Higher in rank or excellence.*

The king is above the ministers, இராசா மந்திரிகளுக்கு மேலானவர், or மந்திரிகளிலும் இராசா மேன்மையுடையவர்.
Love is above faith, அன்பு விசுவாசத்துக்கு மேலானது.

4. *Unattainable by.*

The Samscrit language is above my reach; சமஸ்கிருதபாஷை படிக்க என்னாற்கூடாது, or சமஸ்கிருதபாஷை எனக்கு எட்டாததாயிருக்கிறது, i. e., *to learn the Samscrit language is too difficult for me.*
It is above my power to give you hundred Pagodas, உமக்கு நூறுவராகன் கொடுக்க என்னாலே கூடாது or உமக்கு நூறுவராகன் கொடுக்க எனக்குத்திராணியில்லை.
This doctrine is above my comprehension, இந்த உபதேசம் என் புத்திக்குமேலானது or எட்டாதது.

5. *Superior to.*

She is above disguise, இவள் வஞ்சனைசெய்யமாட்டாள், i. e., *she cannot disguise* or *deceive* or இவள் வஞ்சனையைக்கடந்தவள், *she has passed deceit.* Observe, that if you here would say lit: இவள் வஞ்சனைக்குமேலானவள், the sense would be, *she is even worse than disguise itself;* i. e., *she is exceedingly hypocritical.*

4. *After.*

Is usually expressed by பின், பின்பு, பின்னாலே, see § LXXXIX. when it means,

1. *Behind*, with regard to place.

He came after me, அவன் எனக்குப்பின்நடந்துவந்தான்.

In this connection, it may be expressed by numerals, as :

First came the king ; after him followed the priest ; after the priest came the servant, முதலாவது இராசாவும் இரண்டாவது குருவும் மூன்றாவது ஊழியக்காரனும் நடந்துவந்தார்கள், or முதலாவது இராசாவும் அவருக்குபின்பு குருவும் அவருக்குப்பின்பு, &c.

2. *According to.*

After this manner, he has acted for four years, இவ்விதமாய் (or இந்தப்பிரகாரமாய்) அவன் நாலுவருஷஞ்செய்துகொண்டு வந்தான்.

3. *In imitation of.*

Believe after Abraham's example, ஆபிரகாம்விசுவாசித்ததுபோல் நீயும் விசுவாசித்துக்கொள்.

5. *Against.*

1. When it refers to hostile opposition, விரோதமாய், with the dative usually expresses it, as :

All are against me, எல்லாரும் எனக்கு விரோதமாயிருக்கிறார்கள்.
He wrote against idolatry, விக்கிரக ஆராதனைக்கு விரோதமாயெழுதினான்.
This is against the laws of the country, இது தேசத்தின்பிரமாணங்களுக்குவிரோதமாயிருக்கின்றது.

2. When it means, *opposite in place*, the words எதிரே, எதிராய், express it, as :

The Ships anchored against the mouth of the river, ஆற்றுமுகத்துவாரத்துக்கெதிராய்க்கப்பல் மனிதர் நங்கூரம்போட்டார்கள், lit : *the sailors cast the anchor opposite to the opening of the river*. The Tamulian would not say merely, *the ship*.

3. When it refers *to the hurt of a person*, the Tamulian expresses it accordingly, as :

This circumstance will be against me ; இந்தக்காரியம் எனக்குச்சேதமுண்டாக்கும் or நஷ்டங்கொடுக்கும்.

4. When it means, *in expectation of*, it must be paraphrased, as :

We are provided against the time of famine, பஞ்சகாலத்திலே நமக்குக்குறைச்சல் வாராதபடிக்கு வேண்டியவைகளிருக்கின்றன, or

பூரணமாயிருக்கிறது, lit: *we have enough (or plenty), so that we shall have no want in time of famine.*

6. *Ah! Alas! Oh!*

These interjections are commonly expressed by ஆ, ஓ, ஐயோ, ஐயையோ. Of them ஆ, signifies joy and admiration; the rest pity and woe, as:

Ah! are you come, ஆ, வந்தீரா.
O virtue! how amiable art thou! ஆ புண்ணியமே! நீ யெத்தனை அன்புகூரப்படத்தக்கது.
Oh! I have alienated my friend, ஐயோ எனசிநேகிதனையெனக்கு அந்நியனாகச்செய்தேன் (or செய்தேனே.)
Alas! I fear for life! ஐயோ எனசீவன்போகுமே, *I fear* cannot well be expressed without making the lamentation to concern his fear and not his life, as: ஐயோ என் சீவன்போகுமென்று பயப்படுகிறேனே.
Oh! what a worthless fellow! ஓ சண்டாளன்.
Ah! woe me! ஐயையோ எனக்குவேதனைவரும்.

7. *Already.*

1. When it means *at this present time,* it is expressed by இப்பொழுது, or simply by the present tense, as:

He is already come, அவன் இப்பொழுது வந்திருக்கிறான், or அவன் வந்திருக்கிறான்.

If it refer to the present time in the past, it cannot be rendered, thus:

He had already commenced speaking, when the soldiers entered the hall; அவன் பேசத்தொடங்கினபொழுது, போர்ச்சேவகர் சாலையிற்பிரவேசித்தார்கள்.

2. When it means *so soon* it is expressed by இத்தனைசீக்கிரமாய், as:

Are you already come? நீர் இத்தனை சீக்கிரமாய்வந்தீரா.

3. When it implies *accomplishment before the present time,* it must be expressed by ஆயிற்று, added to the verbal participle of the verb, as:

I have already told him the affair, நான் அந்தச்சங்கதியையவருக்குச்சொல்லியாயிற்று.
When I came, divine worship was already finished; நான்வந்தபொழுதுதேவாராதனைசெய்தாயிற்று.

4. When it means *before the present,* it must be expressed by இதற்குமுன்னே or முன்னே, as:

The sun must be already risen, சூரியன் இதற்குமுன்னே தோன்றியிருப்பான்.

5. When it means *until now,* இதுவரைக்கும், is required, as:

All the world shall be filled with the knowledge of the Lord. Already many nations have received it, கருத்தாவையறிகிற அறிவு உலகமெங்கும்நிரம்பும். இதுவரைக்கும் அநேகதேசத்தார் அதைப்பெற்றுக்கொண்டிருக்கிறார்கள்.

8. *Also.*

Is expressed by உம் added to any part of the sentence, to which it belongs, excepting the finite verb, which never can receive it, as:

He also gave money to the poor, அவனும் ஏழைகளுக்குப்பிச்சை கொடுத்தான்.
He gave money also to the poor, அவன் ஏழைகளுக்குப்பணத்தையுங் கொடுத்தான்.
He gave money to the poor also, அவன் பணத்தை ஏழைகளுக்குங் கொடுத்தான்.

9. *Although*, see Though.

10. *Among.*

Is usually expressed by the dative with உள்ளே, as:
There are thieves among them, அவர்களுக்குள்ளே திருடரிருக்கிறார்கள்.

When it means *associated with*, the ablative social with கூட, may also be used, as:

The king was amongst them, இராசா அவர்களுடனேகூடவிருந்தார், or (அவர்களுக்குள்ளே,)

11. *As.*

Requires various renderings.

1. When it stands unconnected with any other particle,

i. Meaning *because, since,* படியினாலே or ஆகையால், expresses it, *e.g.*
As this is a case of great moment, we must be circumspect, இந்தக்காரியம் மிகவுங்கனமாயிருக்கிறபடியால் (or இது பெரியகாரியம் ஆகையால்) நாம் சாவதானமாயிருக்கவேண்டும்
As the matter rests upon me, I shall attend to it, அந்தக்காரியத்தை நானே விசாரிக்கவேண்டியபடியால் (or வேண்டுவதால், or அந்தக்காரியம் எனக்கே யொப்புவிக்கப்பட்டிருக்கிறபடியால்) நான் அதை விசாரிப்பேன்.

ii. meaning *like,* போல், ஒப்பாய், must be used, as:
This is as the overthrow of Sodom, இது சோதோமூர்கவிழ்க்கப்பட்டதுபோலிருக்கின்றது.

iii. Meaning *thus, in this manner*, when quotations are made, the Tamulian uses ஆவது, with the singular; ஆவன, with the plural, என்னவென்றால், with any number, &c., as:

He spoke various evil words, as : you are a thief, a robber, and so on, அவன் பற்பலபொல்லாதவசனங்களைப்பேசிக்கொண்டான் என்னவென்றால, நீதிருடன், நீகொள்ளைக்காரன் முதலானவைகளே. But it is often more idiomatic, to invert the order of the clauses, and say thus : நீதிருடன் நீகொள்ளைக்காரன என்றிவை முதலான பற்பல பொல்லாதவசனங்களைச்சொன்னான்.

He told another parable, as : அவர் வேறொரு உவமையைச்சொன்னார், அதாவது.

He told other parables, as : அவர் வேறு உவமைகளைச்சொன்னார், அவையாவன.

iv. When it means, *according to,* படி, must be used, as :

He did as God commanded him, பராபரன் கட்டளையிட்டபடி அவன்செய்தான்.

2. When it stands connected with other particles, *e. g.*

i. With *as,* meaning similarity in quality, போல், படி, or any other suitable word must be used ; thus :

She is as amiable as her sister, இவள் தன் சகோதரியைப்போல் அன்புகூரப்படத்தக்கவள்.

He is as good as his word, அவன் தன் வார்த்தையின்படியே செய்வான், *or* அவனுடைய வார்த்தையைப்போல் அவனுடைய செய்கை.

I am as well as can be expected, நான்கூடியமட்டுஞ் சவுக்கியமா யிருக்கிறேன், or ஒருவாறுசவுக்கியமாயிருக்கிறேன்.

You must give a reason for this as well as far that ; இதற்காகவும் அதற்காகவும் நியாயஞ்சொல்லவேண்டும். But if the sense be, that for the one, the reason has already been given, and that he must likewise give one for the other, it must be expressed, thus : அதைக்குறித்து நீ நியாயஞ்சொன்னதுபோல் இதைக்குறித்தும் நியாயஞ்சொல்லவேண்டும்.

But when it means equality in number, it is expressed thus :

Give him as many hoes as he wants, இவனுக்குவேண்டிய மண்வெட்டிகள் எவ்வளவோ அவ்வளவுகொடு.

ii. With *so* following, as :

As the stars so shall thy seed be, நட்சத்திரங்களெத்தனையோ அத்தனையாய் உன்சந்ததிபெருகும்.

As the sun gives us light by day so does the moon by night, சூரியன் பகலிலே நமக்கு ஒளியைக்கொடுக்கிறதுபோலச்சந்திரன் இராவிலே ஒளியைக்கொடுக்கின்றது.

As the one dieth so dieth the other, எல்லாருஞ் சாகிறார்கள், i. e., *all die,* or சாவாமலிருக்கிறவர்கள் ஒருவருமில்லை.

If you say literally, ஒருவன் மரிக்கிறதுபோல் மற்றவனும் மரிக்கிறான், then the particular kind or manner of death will be pointed out.

iii. With *so* preceding.

I desire to see thy glory, so as I have seen it in thy sanctuary பரிசுத்தஸ்தலத்திலே உம்முடைய மகிமையைக் கண்டதுபோல் இன்னுங்காணவிரும்புகிறேன்.

Pompey was not so great a man as Cæsar, கைசார்போலப்பொம்பேயுபெரியவனல்ல.

My house is not so large as your's, என்னுடைய வீடு உம்முடைய வீட்டைப்போலப்பெரிதல்ல.

iv. With *such* when it is in fact a relative pronoun, the Tamulian uses the verbal noun in this case, or the relative participle with a noun or pronoun, as:

Let such as presume to advise others, look well to their own conduct, மற்றவர்களுக்குப் புத்திச்சொல்லத் துணிகிறவர்கள் தங்கள் சொந்தநடக்கையை நலமாய்நோக்கக்கடவர்கள்.

v. With *for*, or *to*, meaning *with respect to*, it is not expressed, thus:
As for this horse, it was starved to death, இந்தக்குதிரைபட்டினியினாலே செத்துப்போயிற்று.

As for that matter, we must farther consider it, அந்தக்காரியத்தைக்குறித்து நாம் இன்னும் (or அதிகமாய்) யோசனைபண்ணவேண்டும்.

vi. With *though* or *if*.

He acted as though he were his own master, தானேதனக்கு எசமானென்றெண்ணிச்செய்தான் or better தானே எசமானைபோலச்செய்தான்.

We beseech you as though God did beseech you, பராபரன் உங்களை வேண்டிக்கொண்டாற்போல் நாங்கள் உங்களை வேண்டிக்கொள்ளுகிறோம், or *better* பராபரன் உங்களை வேண்டிக்கொண்டால் எப்படியோ அப்படியே நாங்கள் &c.

12. *At.*

Has likewise various significations;

1. When it means *near*, it must be expressed by அருகே, சமீபமாய், &c.

He is at the river, அவன் ஆற்றின் அருகேயிருக்கிறான்.

2. When it means *in a place*, the locative ablative must be used, as:

When we arrived at Madras, we saw the superstition of the natives, நாங்கள் சென்னைபட்டினத்திற்சேர்ந்தபொழுது, சனங்களுடைய அவபத்தியைப்பார்த்தோம்.
He lives at Pondicherry, அவன் புதுச்சேரியிலேவாசமாயிருக்கிறான்.

3. Before a word signifying *time* or *business*, the same ablative is used, as:

He rose at 10 *o'clock,* பத்தாம்மணிநேரத்திலே யெழுந்திருந்தான்

This boy is busy at his task, இந்தப்பையல் தன்வேலையிற் சாக்கிரதையாயிருக்கிருன்.

4. Signifying *the condition of a person* it should be expressed by the adverbial form, as :

Let us be at peace with all men, நாம் எல்லாமனிதரோடுஞ் சமாதானமாயிருக்கக்கடவோம.

5. Signifying *in immediate consequence of* it is expressed variously, thus :

He went to Jaffna at my request, நான் கேட்டபடியினுலே அவன் யாழ்ப்பாணத்திற்குப்போனுன்.
He swooned at the sight of the fire; நெருப்பைக்கண்டமாத்திரத்திலே or கண்டவுடனே or simply கண்டு, சோர்ந்துபோனுன்.
At one blow he cut off his head, ஒரேவெட்டாக அவனுடைய தலையை வெட்டினுன்.
He came at a call, நான் கூப்பிட்டவுடனே அவன் வந்தான்.

6. Signifying *subjection,* as much as *under,* thus :

These things are all at my command, இந்தக்காரியங்கள்யாவும் என் அதிகாரத்துக்குட்பட்டவைகள்.

7. When connected with *all,* it is rendered by எப்படியும், எவ்விதத்திலும், எவ்வளவும், or any such word denoting entireness, as :

At all events I shall come to-morrow, நான் எப்படியும் நாளைக்கு வருவேன் or என்னவிருந்தாலும் நான் நாளைக்குவருவேன்.
He did not do this business at all well, இந்த வேலையையவன் எவ்வளவாகிலும நன்றுய்ச்செய்யவில்லை.
He must not go there at all, அவன் ஒருக்காலும அங்கே போகக்கூடாது or அவன அங்கேபோகவேகூடாது.

Not at all may be rendered also by, பரிச்சேதம் or ஒருவிதத்திலும் or ஏகதேசமாயாகிலும், with a negative verb, as :

He must not marry at all, அவன் பரிச்சேதம் (or ஏகதேசமாயாகிலும்) விவாகம்பண்ணக்கூடாது.

13. *Before.*

Is usually expressed by, முன்னே முன்பு முன்பாக முன்னுலே, when referring to *place,* as :

My house is before that of the Doctor's, என்வீடு வயித்தியருடைய வீட்டுக்குமுன்னே (or முன்னுக) இருக்கின்றது
They are gone to the camp before us, அவர்கள் எங்களுக்கு முன்பாகப்பாளயத்துக்குப்போனுர்கள்.
We halted before the mountain, மலையின் அடியிலே இறங்கினேம்.
Stand before him! அவனுக்கு முன்பாகநில்லு.

When it means *in presence of,* particularly *of God,* or *of great men,* it is better expressed by சன்னிதானத்திலே, as :

Let us go before God with thanksgiving! துதிச்சலோடே பராபரனுடைய சன்னிதானத்திலே செல்வோமாக.

The phrases *before your eyes, before your face, before you, may be literally rendered by*, உங்கள் கண்களுக்குமுன்பாக, உன்முகத்துக்குமுன்பாக, உனக்குமுனபாக; or by நீங்கள்பார்க்கத்தக்கதாக, &c.

The phrase *from before thee*, means from thy sight or from thy face, which must be expressed accordingly, as:

I will drive them out from before thee, அவர்கள் உன்னைவிட்டோடிப்போகும்படி செய்வேன், or அவர்கள் உனக்கு முன்னில்லாதபடிக்கு அவர்களைத்துரத்துவேன்.

ii. When it refers to *time*, முன்னே or முன்னமே is used, as:

I arrived here before you, நான்உமக்குமுன்னே இங்கேசேர்ந்தேன்.
He died before him, இவனுக்குமுன்னமே அவன் இறந்துபோனான்.

iii. When it means *in preference to*, the phrase must be expressed in various ways, as:

Abel was accepted before Cain, காயினையல்ல ஆபேலை அங்கிகரித்தார், i. e., *He accepted, not Cain, but Abel.* If it be literally rendered, காயினுக்குமுன்னே ஆபேலை அங்கிகரித்தார், it means *that Cain also was accepted only later than Abel.*

14. *Behind.*

Like *after* is translated by பின், பின்பு, பின்னாலே. I mention here only such phrases as require a different rendering.

At my leaving England, I left various things behind me; நான் இங்கிலந்தைவிட்டுப்புறப்பட்டபொழுது, பலவகையான பதார்த்தங்களைவிட்டு வந்தேன். If it was from forgetfulness, then it must be thus: பலவகையான பதார்த்தங்களை மறந்து விட்டு வந்தேன், because the former implies design.

He is not behind him in doing good, தருமங்களைச்செய்கிறதில் அவனுக்கு இவன் தாழவில்லை

15. *Beneath* or *Below.*

When it means,

1. *Under, lower in place*, கீழ், expresses it, as:

It stands beneath the table, அது பலகையின்கீழ்நிற்கின்றது.
The earth is beneath the sky, பூமிவானத்திற்குக்கீழிருக்கின்றது.

2. *Under*, as overborne or overwhelmed by some pressure, the phrase must have another form, as:

I sink beneath the oppression of that man, அந்தமனிதன்செய்கிற

துன்பத்தினாலே சோர்ந்துபோகிறேன், or கெட்டுப்போகிறேன், *I faint because of the oppression,* &c., or அந்தமனிதன் செய்கிறதுன்பமாகியசுமைக்குள்ளாயிருக்கிறேன்.

3. *Lower in rank, excellency,* &c., தாழ்கிறது, expresses it, as:

The minister is below the king, மந்திரியானவன் இராசனுக்குத் தாழ்ந்திருக்கிறான்.

4. *Unworthy of, unbecoming,* the phrase must be given accordingly, as:

To slander is beneath the character of a virtuous man, மற்றவர்களை நிந்திக்கிறது நல்லமனிதனுக்கேற்றதல்ல or உரியதல்ல or தகாது or நல்லமனிதனுக்கேலாது.

16. *Besides.*

1. As a preposition, when it means,

i. *Near,* the Tamulian uses, அருகே, கிட்ட, பக்கத்திலே, as

He stood beside me, அவன் என்னருகேநின்றான் or என்பக்கத்திலே நின்றான் or என்மருங்குநின்றான்.

ii. *Over and above,* அல்லாமல், or அன்றி, is used, as:

Besides the congregation there were also two Priests, சபையாரல்லாமல் இரண்டுகுருக்களுமிருந்தார்கள்.

Is there a God beside me? என்னையன்றி வேறுதேவனுண்டா.

2. As an adverb, at the beginning of a sentence, அல்லாமலும், or அன்றியும், expresses it. See § LXXIII.

17. *Between.*

Is usually expressed by putting the two nouns in the Dative case with உம், affixed to each, thus:

What is the distance between Madras and Madura? சென்னைப்பட்டினத்துக்கும் மதுரைக்கும் எவ்வளவுதூரம்.

But observe, that though *between* usually requires two things or persons, the English often expresses only one of them, implying the other; in Tamul this cannot be done, without obscuring or changing the sense; both must be expressed, as:

Between us there is no difference, உனக்கும் எனக்கும் வித்தியாசமில்லை, *between thee and me,* &c., *we may indeed say,* நமக்கு வித்தியாசமில்லை, but that is ambiguous.

18. *Beyond.*

When it means,

1. *On the further side of,* அப்புறம், அப்புறத்திலே, or அப்புறமாய், is proper, as:

We went beyond the town, நாம் ஊருக்கப்புறம்போனோம்.
We halted beyond the river, ஆற்றுக்கப்புறத்தில் தங்கினோம். If the shore be particularly meant, then அக்கரையிலே must be used.

2. *Exceeding, above, surpassing,* the phrase must receive another form, as :

He was afflicted beyond measure, அளவில்லாத உபத்திரவத்தை யடைந்தான்.

Do not act beyond your sphere, உன்னுடைய நிலைமைக்குமேலே நடவாதிருப்பாயாக or உன்னுடைய கடமைக்கு மிஞ்சினதாக ஒன்றுஞ்செய்யாதிரு.

19. *Both.*

Is expressed by affixing, உம், to both nouns, as :
Let them both come, அவனையும் அவளையும்வரச்சொல்லு or இரண்டுபேரையும்வரச்சொல்லு.

He killed both the tyger and the elephant, புலியையும் யானையையுங்கொலைசெய்தான், (or புலியானை இரண்டையும்.)

20. *But.*

When it means,

1. *Except,* the Tamulian uses, தவிர, ஒழிய, or இன்றி, as :

All came but Vedamootoo, வேதமுத்துத்தவிர எல்லாரும் வந்தார்கள்.

He brought every thing but one box ; ஒரு பெட்டி தவிரமற்றப்பண்டங்களெல்லாவற்றையுங்கொண்டுவந்தான்

2. When it means *only, nothing more than,* மாத்திரம் expresses it, as :

He spoke but two sentences, இரண்டு வாக்கியங்களைமாத்திரஞ்சொன்னார்.

Stay but one day, ஒருநாள்மாத்திரம்பொறு, that is, if *stay* mean *be patient,* but if it mean, *to stop, to remain,* பொறுத்திரு or தங்கியிரு, must be said instead of பொறு.

3. When it means *not more than, even,* the Tamulian expresses it by தான், or தானே, or merely by the emphatic ஏ, as :

Your demand is but reasonable, நீ கேட்டுக்கொண்டது நியாயந் தான் or நியாயமே.

It is but what is necessary, இதுவேண்டுவதுதான்.
He came but now, அவன் இப்பொழுதுதான் வந்தான்.

4. When meaning *otherwise than,* the Tamulian uses the emphatic, ஏ, as :

I cannot but cry out, i. e., *I must cry out,* நான்சத்தமிட வேண்டுமே or நான் சத்தமிடாமலிருக்கக்கூடாதே.

5. When it follows a negation, the Tamulian changes it and the negative into the positive form, as :

There is no day but he comes to my house, i. e., *he comes every day to my house*, அவன் நாடோறும் என் வீட்டுக்கு வருகிறான் to say, அவன் என் வீட்டுக்கு வாராத நாளில்லை, would define or determine the time rather than his coming.

There is none but knows it, யாவரும் அதையறிவார்கள் or அதையறியாதவர்கள் ஒருவருமில்லை.

6. When it merely connects two sentences, or simply points out a contrary condition or circumstance, the Tamulian does not particularly express it, as :

I went to see him, but he was not at home, நான் அவனைக்கண்டு பேசப்போனேன் அவன் வீட்டிலேயில்லை.

He is not diligent, but lazy, அவன் சாக்கிரதையாயிராமற் சோம்பலாயிருக்கிறான்.

He told me the affair, but I would not believe it, அவன் இந்தக்காரியத்தையெனக்குச்சொன்னான், நான் அதை நம்பவில்லை

He came not to do evil but to do good, as, அவன் தீமையையல்ல நன்மையைச்செய்ய வந்தான்.

This will not be done by human power, but by the power of God, இது மனிதருடைய வல்லமையினாலேயல்ல, பராபரனுடைய வல்லமையினாலேயாகும், or இது மனிதருடைய வல்லமையினாலே யாகமாட்டாது பராபரனுடையவல்லமையினாலேயாகும் or இது பராபரனுடைய வல்லமையன்றி மனிதருடையவல்லமையினாலே ஆகமாட்டாது.

Note.—It is evident that *but* in such sentences is expressed by the negative. When however *but* heads a new sentence in an argument it is by no means proper to use ஆனால், as is frequently done ; because, ஆனால் being the subjunctive mode of ஆகிறது, means properly *if it be so*; but by ஆனாலும், ஆகிலும் அப்படியிருந்தும், in the application of which the sense must be considered, and the use discriminated according to § CIII. LVI. 8, LVII. 2. 3.

21. *By*.

When it denotes,

1. The *agent* or *cause*, by which any thing is effected or obtained, the instrumental ablative expresses it, as :

This flower was plucked by me, இந்தப்பூ என்னாலே பறிக்கப்பட்டது or இது நான் பறித்த பூ.

The fever came by a cold, குளிர்ச்சியினாலே சுரம் வந்தது.

2. When it means *the instrument*, the same ablative instrumental is used, or கொண்டு, with the accusative case ; or the phrase is turned altogether, as :

The wound was made by a knife, இந்தக்காயங்கத்தியினாலுண்டா யிற்று. Observe, the Tamulian would not say, உண்டாக்கப் பட்டது, because the knife was not the active instrument, which was a person. If the phrase be *he wounded me by (with) a knife,* then he would say thus, அவன் ஒரு கத்தியைக்கொ ண்டு (or எடுத்து) என்னைக்காயப்படுத்தினான்.

3. When it means *the method* in which any progressive action is performed, as:

The business was done by little and little, இந்தக்காரியங்கொஞ்சங் கொஞ்சமாய்ச்செய்யப்பட்டது.

4. When it means *quantity*, the noun must be doubled, as:

I bought these chairs by the dozen, பன்னிரண்டு பன்னிரண்டாக இந்த நாற்காலிகளைவாங்கினேன்.

This house fell by pieces, இந்தவீடுதுண்டுதுண்டாக இடிந்துபோ யிற்று.

5. When it denotes *the object of explanation;* the Tamulian changes the phrase altogether, as:

What do you mean by spirit? ஆவியென்பதற்கு அருத்தமென்ன or ஆவியென்பதென்ன or ஆவியாவதென்ன, should you say ஆவி யைக்கொண்டு நீ நினைக்கிறதென்ன, the meaning will be, *what do you think* by means of (or through the spirit).

6. When denoting *place,* மேல், or some other suitable preposition is required, as:

They fought by sea, சமுத்திரத்தின்மேல் (or சமுத்திரத்திலே) யுத்தம்பண்ணினார்கள்.

7. When denoting *permission,* படி, படியினாலே, or another form is required, as:

You may go by my leave, நான் உத்தரவுகொடுத்தபடி (or கொடு த்தபடியினாலே) நீ போகலாம் or நான் உத்தரவு கொடுத்தேன் நீ போகலாம்.

8. When denoting *the difference* between two things, the Tamulian turns the phrase, as:

Rice is now cheaper than formerly by a fanam a marcal, முன் னிலும் ஒருமரக்கால் அரிசிக்கு ஒரு பணம் நயமாயிருக்கிறது.

9. When denoting *passage,* வழியாய் with the oblique case is required, as:

We came hither by Tranquebar, நாங்கள் தரங்கம்பாடியின் வழி யாய் இவ்விடத்துக்குவந்தோம்.

10. When denoting *near to* அருகே, இடத்தில் or any such word is required, as:

The General stood by the King, சேனாபதி இராசாவருகே (இராசாவினிடத்தில்) நின்றான்.

11. When denoting *the absence of all others,* the Tamulian uses தனியே; or turns the phrase altogether, as:

He came by himself, அவன் தனியேவந்தான்.
They came by themselves, வேறொருவரில்லாமல் வந்தார்கள் or தாங்கள்மாத்திரம் வந்தார்கள்.

12. When denoting *the solemn form of swearing,* it must be expressed in Tamil according to the sense of the connexion, as:

By my life! thou shalt die, நீசாவாயென்று என்சீவன் மேலே யாணையிட்டுச்சொல்லுகிறேன்.

13. When it denotes, *within a short time,* it must be rendered accordingly, as:

He will come by and by, கொஞ்சக்காலத்துக்குள்ளே (or கொஞ்சக்காலத்துக்குப்பின்பு) வருவான்.

Note.—*By the by,* a phrase to call the attention of another, cannot be well expressed in Tamil; perhaps we may say, இன்னம் ஒருபேச்சிருக்கிறது கேள், i. e., *There is still another subject; hear!*

14. When denoting *substitution,* or *by proxy of,* the Tamulian circumscribes it, as:

He appeared by his attorney, அவன் தான்வாராமல்த்தன் காரியக்காரனையனுப்பினான், i. e., *he himself did not come; he sent his attorney.*

22. *Either, or.*

When they mean *both,* it is expressed by adding உம் to both nouns or actions, as:

Averse either to contradict or to blame, எதிர்த்துப்பேசும்படிக்குங் குற்றஞ்சாற்றும்படிக்கும்மனசில்லாமல்.

But when they mean separate things, the Tamulian expresses them by adding ஆவது to both nouns, &c., as:

Either this man or that woman is guilty of the crime, இந்தமனிதனாவது அந்தஸ்திரீயாவது இந்தக்குற்றஞ்செய்திருப்பார்கள்.

But frequently they are expressed by அல்லது or அல்லவென்றால், placed before every clause that is proposed, except the first, thus:

Either stay to see the end of the affair, or *go and be silent about it,* இந்தக்காரியத்தின்முடிவை யறிகிறவரைக்கும் இரு அல்லவென்றால் இதைக்குறித்து ஒன்றும்பேசாமற்போ, lit: *stay! till you see the end of the affair. If not,* (i. e., *if you say, I will not stay,*) *then go,* &c.

Either gold or silver or brass will be found here, இங்கே பொன் அல்லது வெள்ளி அல்லது பித்தளை காணப்படும்.
We must (either) believe or perish, நாம் விசுவாசிக்கவேண்டும். அல்லது கெட்டுப்போகவேண்டும்.

23. *Except.*

When it means *but, exclusively of,* it is expressed as stated § XCV.

When it means *unless* it is expressed by the negative verb with விட்டால், as:

Except a man be born again, he cannot see the kingdom of God, ஒருமனிதன்மறுபடியும்பிறவாவிட்டால் மோட்ச இராச்சியத்தைக்காணமாட்டான்.

24. *For.*

1. The *conjunction,* is expressed by படியினாலே, with a relative participle, or by the causal ablative of the verbal noun, or by ஆகையால், ஆதலால் or ஆனபடியினாலே, added to any sentence which states the cause or reason of some effect or consequence. This sentence usually precedes that containing the effect, &c., as:

I will send an angel before thee; for I will not go up in the midst of thee, for thou art a stiff necked people, நீங்கள் வணங்காதகழுத்துள்ள சனங்களானபடியினாலே நான உங்களுடனேகூடவரமாட்டேன். ஆதலால் ஒருதூதனை யுங்களுக்கு முன்நடக்க அனுப்புவேன. This last ஆதலால் is even not required; and the sentence may be given thus, நான் கூடப்போகாமல், ஒருதூதனை யுங்களுக்குமுன்னடக்க அனுப்புவேன்.

See farther on the subject and other instances § §. LXXXII. CIX. CXV.

When a long argument follows, the effect may be first stated, and the causal sentences introduced by என்னத்தினாலென்றால், or எப்படியென்றால் or என்னத்திற்கெனில், as the sense may require. But even then it is proper at the end of the argument to repeat the effect. See § CXV.

2. The *preposition* is variously rendered,

i. When it means *for the sake of, in advantage of, in order to,* &c., the Dative case with ஆக, or the relative participle with படிக்கு expresses it, as:

Labour not for the meat that perisheth, அழிந்துபோகும் போசனத்துக்காக (or போசனம் அடையும்படிக்கு) ப்பிரயாசப்படாதிருங்கள்.

He wrote for money, பணத்துக்காக எழுதினான்.

ii. When it means *duration,* and is united with words of time, the Tamulian expresses it by the nominative, as:

He has not come for many days, அநேகநாள் அவன்வரவில்லை.

iii. When it means *accommodation, adaptation, belonging to, becoming, capability, in proportion to,* the Dative case expresses it, as:

I am not fit for this work, நான் இந்தவேலைக்குத்தகுதியானவனல்ல.
Commanding is for the king. Obedience for the subjects. கட்டளையிடுதல் இராசாவுக்குங் கீழ்ப்படியுதல் குடிகளுக்கு மேற்றவைகள்.

It is hard for me to learn, படிக்கிறது எனக்கரிதாயிருக்கிறது, or வருத்தமாயிருக்கிறது.

He is tall for his age, இவனுடைய வயசுக்குத்தக்க வளர்த்திக்கு மேலாயிருக்கிறான், or உயர்ந்திருக்கிறான் or இவன் நெட்டையன்.
He is small for his age, இவனுக்கு வயசுக்குத்தக்கவளர்த்தியில்லை, or இவன் குட்டையன்.

iv. When it means *in exchange, instead of,* the dative with either ஆக or பதிலாக is used, as:

I gave him a ground for his house, அவன் வீட்டுக்காக (or வீட்டுக்குப்பதிலாக) ஒருநிலத்தைக்கொடுத்தேன்.

v. When it means *in remedy of, in search of,* or when it stands connected with certain verbs, it must be expressed accordingly, as:

This medicine is for the fever, இந்தமருந்து சுரத்தை நீக்கும் or இது சுரத்துக்குரியமருந்து.

He went for the sheep, அவன்ஆடுகளைத்தேடப்போனான்.
He waited for the Gentleman, துரை வருகிறவரைக்குங்காத்திருந்தான்.

They lay for dead three days, மூன்றுநாள் அவர்கள்செத்தவர்கள் போலக்கிடந்தார்கள்.

He wished for peace, சமாதானத்தைவிரும்பினான்.

25. *From.*

Has also many significations as:

1. Its primary meaning of *away,* denoting privation, separation, transmission, emission, is expressed by the locative ablative with இருந்து, or நின்று, or by the accusative with விட்டு, as:

The land was taken from him, தேசம் அவனிலிருந்து நீக்கப்பட்டது.

My friend departed from me, and united himself to another, என் சிநேகிதன் என்னைவிட்டு, வேறொருவனுடனே இசைந்தான்.
The Governor sent troops from Madras, பெரியதுரை சென்னைபட்டினத்திலிருந்த சேனைகளையனுப்பினார்.

2. When it means *reception* or *attainment,* the ablative இடத்தில் expresses it, as:

I learned this from him (of him,) நான் இதை யவரிடத்திற்கற்றுக்கொண்டேன்.

He got only ten thousand Rupees from me, அவன்பதினாயிரம் ரூபாய்மாத்திரம் என்னிடத்திற்பெற்றுக்கொண்டான்.

3. When it denotes *procession* or *descent*, the instrumental ablative is used, as:

From ignorance of the true God proceeds wickedness, மெய்யான தேவனையறியாமலிருக்கிறதினாலே துன்மார்க்கமுண்டாகும்.

His lavishness proceeds from kindness, தயவினாலே அவர் ஆஸ்திகளைச்செலவழிக்கிறார், lit: *he spends (his) riches from kindness.*

From thee, kings shall proceed, உன்னாலே இராசாக்கள் தோன்றுவார்கள்.

But David descended from Abraham, தாவீது ஆபிரகாமின் சந்ததியிலேபிறந்தான், i. e., *David was born in the posterity of Abraham.*

4. When it means *exemption*, the Tamulian uses இல்லாமல், as:

Christ was free from sin, கிறிஸ்துபாவமில்லாதவராயிருந்தார்.

5. When it implies *succession of time,* முதல் or முதற்கொண்டு, must be used, as:

The gentleman was engaged from morning till night, துரை உதயமுதல் இராத்திரிவரைக்கும் அலுவலாயிருந்தார்.

From the beginning of the world such things have not been heard, உலகமுண்டானது முதற்கொண்டு இப்படிப்பட்ட காரியங்கள் கேள்விப்படவில்லை.

Note.—The phrase *from generation to generation*, is expressed, thus: தலைமுறை தலைமுறையாய்.

6. When it is united with verbs denoting *deliverance*, it is sometimes expressed by the ablative of motion with இருந்து, or நின்று; sometimes by the dative, sometimes the phrase must receive a different form, as:

See that you be saved from your sins, உன்பாவங்களினின்று நீங்கி இரட்சிக்கப்படும்படிக்குப்பார்ப்பாயாக or simply உன் பாவங்களை நீக்கும்படிக்குப்பார்ப்பாயாக.

Christ only can deliver us from hell, நாம் நரகத்திற்குப்போகாதபடிக்குக்கிறிஸ்துமாத்திரம்நம்மை யிரட்சிக்கத்தக்கவர். Observe that you cannot say here, நரகத்தினின்றுநம்மை யிரட்சிக்கும்படிக்கு, &c., because this supposes that we are already in it. This is to be observed also in the following sentence;

Sir, deliver us from prison; if we are already in it, we may say, ஐயா இந்த க்காவற்கூடத்தினின்று எங்களை விடுதலையாக்க வேண்டும். But if we are not yet in, it must be rendered, ஐயா, நாங்கள் காவற்கூடத்துக்குப்போகாதபடிக்கு எங்களைக்காப்பாற்றவேண்டும்.

Deliver us from this dangerous sickness, மோசத்தைக்கொடுக்கும் இந்தவியாதிக்கு எங்களை விலக்கவேண்டும்.

The poor people have been exempted from paying taxes, ஏழைச்சனங்கள் வரிசெலுத்தாதபடிக்கு உத்தரவு பெற்றார்கள், i. e., *the poor people have received permission* (or *order*) *not to pay taxes.*

26. *How.*

1. When the sentence is properly *interrogative*, it is rendered by எப்படி, எவ்வளவு, எத்தனை, எவ்விதமாய், எதினாலே, &c., according to the connexion, as:

How can these things be? இவை யெப்படியாம்.
How large was the sum? எவ்வளவுபணம் இருந்தது.
How did this come to pass? இது எவ்விதமாய் நடந்தது.

2. When it simply denotes *the manner*, the Tamulian omits the interrogation, as:

How a seed grows up into a tree, and how the mind acts upon the body, are mysteries which we cannot explain, விதை மரமாகிற வகையும் மனது சரீரத்தை நடப்பிக்கிறவகையும் நம்மாற்சொல்லக்கூடாத இரகசியங்களாயிருக்கின்றன.

Remember how kind he was to us, அவர் நமக்குத்தயவாயிருந்ததை நினைத்துக்கொள், (or எத்தனை தயவாயிருந்தாரென்று).

3. When it is used in exclamation to denote *greatness* and *wonder*, the interrogative may be used with ஓ, or ஆ, prefixed, as:

How dreadful is this place! ஆ, இந்தத்தலம் எத்தனைபயங்கொடுக்கிறதாயிருக்கின்றது.

How admirably is this done! ஆ, இது எவ்வளவு ஆச்சரியப்படத்தக்கதாய்ச்செய்யப்பட்டது.

O God how excellent is thy name in all the earth! ஆ, பராபரனே உம்முடைய திருநாமம் பூமியெங்கும் எத்தனைமேன்மையாயிருக்கின்றது.

But when the wonder is at any thing which causes regret or sorrow it is better to use, ஐயோ, without the interrogative, thus:

How few can be found whose activity has not been misemployed! ஐயோதங்கள் திராணிகளை வம்பாய்ச்செலுத்தாதபேர்கள் சிலர்மாத்திரங்காணப்படுகிறார்கள். If we say எவ்வளவுபேர், it will be ambiguous, meaning *as well many as few.*

How wretchedly is this man going on! ஐயோ இந்தமனிதன் மிகவுங்கெட்டநடத்தைக்காரனாயிருக்கிறான்.

27. *However.*

1. When it means *in whatsoever manner*, எப்படியும், எப்படியாகிலும், எவ்விதத்திலும், or எவ்விதமாகிலும், expresses it, as:

I must however go thither, எப்படியாகிலும் நான் அங்கே போக வேண்டும்.

2. When it means *at all events, happen what will*, as:

However ill I may be, I shall go to Canjepooram, எனக்கு எவ்வளவு வியாதியிருந்தாலுங்காஞ்சிபுரத்துக்குப்போவேன்.

3. When it means *nevertheless, yet, but*, &c. அப்படியிருந்தும், அப்படியிருந்தாலும், ஆகிலும், ஆனாலும், will express it.

The body was ordered to remain there for many days; in the night, however, it was taken down, சரீரம் அங்கே அநேக நாளிருக்கும்படிகட்டளைபிறந்தது அப்படியிருந்தும், இராத்திரியிலே யது இறக்கப்பட்டது, lit: *order was given that the body should remain there for many days; nevertheless it was taken*, &c. &c.

The intentions of that Gentleman were always good; however he was a man of lavish expence, அந்தத்துரை எப்பொழுதும் நல்ல விருப்பமுள்ளவராயிருந்தும், மிகுந்த பணத்தை வீணாயச்செலவழித்தார்.

28. *If.*

Is expressed by the subjunctive mood of the verb in ஆல், or இல், as:

If he be but discreet, he will succeed, அவன்புத்தியாய் (or விவேகமாய்) நடந்தால் அவனுடையகாரியஞ்சித்திக்கும்.

If she is sincere, I shall be happy, அவள் உண்மையுள்ளவளானால் (or வளாயிருந்தால்) எனக்குச்சந்தோஷமுண்டாயிருக்கும்.

When not *supposition* but *time* is implied, the sense must be given accordingly, as:

If thou be afflicted repine not, உனக்குஉபத்திரவம்வருங்காலத்தில் (or வரும்பொழுது) விசனப்படாதிருப்பாயாக.

When *if* is connected with *not*, it must be rendered by இல்லாவிட்டால் or better by repeating the verb negatively and adding விட்டால், as:

If he come, I will speak with him; if not, I cannot help him, அவன் வந்தால் அவனோடே பேசுவேன், அவன் வாராவிட்டால், நான் அவனுக்கு உதவிசெய்யேன். Here observe that இல்லாவிட்டால் merely, refers to either வந்தால் or பேசுவேன்.

29. *In.*

1. When it denotes *the place or time where and when any thing is present*, the ablative in இல், (6th case,) is used, as:

He is in the house, வீட்டிலேயிருக்கிறான்.
He lives in Madras, அவர் சென்னைபட்டினத்திலே வாசம்பண்ணுகிறார்.

This happened in the same year, இது அந்தவருஷத்திலே நடந்தது.
He is steady in the pursuit of that science; அந்தக்கல்வியை யடைந்துகொள்ளத்தேடுகிறதில் உறுதியாயிருக்கிறான்.

2. When denoting *the state or thing present at any time,* the Tamulian puts the noun which expresses the state or condition, in the form of a verb or adverb, as:

He is in prosperity, அவர் வாழ்ந்திருக்கிறார் or அவர் வாழ்வை யுடையவர் or வாழ்விலிருக்கிறார்.
He went away in anger, அவன் கோபமாய்ப்போனான், or கோபத்தோடே, &c.
I will lie down in peace and dwell in safety, நான் சமாதானத்தோடே படுத்துக்கொண்டு பத்திரமாயிருப்பேன்.
The upright in heart, உண்மையுள்ள இருதயமுடையவர்கள் or கபடமில்லாத இருதயமுள்ளவர்கள்.
He came in haste, அவன் தீவிரமாய்வந்தான்.
It is in his power to do it, அவன் இப்படிச்செய்ய வல்லமையுடையவன் or இது அவனாலே நடக்கும்.
It was useful in promoting domestic concord, சமுசாரத்திற் சமாதான சவுக்கியமுண்டாகிறதற்கு இது பிரயோசனமாயிருந்தது.

3. When connected with *behalf,* meaning *for,* the dative with ஆக, expresses it, as:

He spoke in my behalf, அவர் எனக்காகப்பேசினார்.

4. In several phrases the causal case expresses it, as:

In that he said a new covenant, he abolished the old, புதிதான உடம்படிக்கையென்று அவர்சொன்னதினாலே பழய உடம்படிக்கையை நீக்கினார்.
In as much as all men are sinners, they are all under condemnation, எல்லா மனிதர்களும் பாவிகளாயிருக்கிறதால் அவர்களெல்லாரும் ஆக்கினைக்கேதுவாயிருக்கிறார்கள்.

Into is more particularly expressed by the dative with உள், often also by the ablative: in இல், as:

The Lady returned into the room, அம்மாளவர்கள் அறைக்குள்ளே திரும்பவந்தார்கள்.

In this, as in all other particles, much depends upon the verb with which it stands connected, agreeably to which it must be expressed, thus:

He introduced me to his family, அவர் தம்முடைய மனைவியையும் பிள்ளைகளையும் எனக்குக்காட்டினார், lit: *he showed me his wife and children.*
The fatigue threw me into a fever, இளைப்பு எனக்குச்சுரம்வரும் படிக்கேதுவாயிருந்தது, or இளைப்பு என்னைச்சுரத்துக்குள்ளே தள்ளிற்று.

30. *Lest, or That not.*

Is often expressed by the negative participle with படிக்கு, as:

I hide it, lest it should be lost, இது இழந்துபோகாதபடிக்கு மறைக்கிறேன்.

He gave him medicine, lest he should die, அவன் சாவாதபடிக்கு (or சாவாதிருக்கும்படிக்கு) அவனுக்கு மருந்துகொடுத்தார்.

But when the other part of the sentence also has a negative, this mode will be very ambiguous. The Tamulian makes two sentences of it, and repeats the verb in the subjunctive mode, as:

Ye shall not eat of the fruit, lest ye die, நீங்கள் அந்தக்கனியைச்சாப்பிடக்கூடாது சாப்பிட்டாற்சாவீர்கள், lit: *you shall not eat the fruit; if you eat, you will die.*

Love not sleep, lest thou come to poverty, தூக்கத்தை விரும்பாதிருப்பாயாக விரும்பினால்த்தரித்திரனாவாய்.

Do not go up the mount to fight, lest ye be slain, யுத்தம்பண்ணும்படிக்கு மலையின்மேலேறிப்போகாதிருங்கள், ஏறிப்போனால் அடிக்கப்படுவீர்கள்.

31. *More.*

The particle denoting the comparative degree, answered by *than*, see the article *than*.

32. *Most.*

1. The adjective *most*, when it signifies the *superlative* of some or many, is expressed by எல்லாம், and by எல்லாரும், the noun being then put in the ablative இல், with உம், as:

Leprosy is the most dreadful disease, எல்லாவியாதிகளிலுங்குட்டவியாதியே பொல்லாதது.

Ramasamy is the most obstinate of mankind, எல்லாமனிதர்களிலும் இராமசாமி முருட்டாட்டமுள்ளவனாயிருக்கிறான்.

God is most high, பராபரன் எல்லாரிலும் மேலானவர்.

The ablative of comparison may be followed also by மிகவும், or மிகுந்த, as, in the above instances, மிகவும்பொல்லாதது, மிகுந்தமுருட்டாட்டமுள்ளவன் &c.; but this is not necessary.

2. When it is used as a substantive, அதிகம், அநேகம், or மிகுதி, will answer it, thus:

Most of the churches were pulled down, கோயில்கள்மிகுதியாய் இடிக்கப்பட்டன, or the Tamulian will rather say கோயில்கள் பாதிக்குமேலாக இடிக்கப்பட்டன, i. e., *more than half of the churches.*

Ten fanams is the most I will give, பத்துபணத்துக்கு அதிகமாய்க்கொடுக்கமாட்டேன்.

3. When it is used adverbially with *at*, it must be variously rendered, thus :

His downfal will be protracted a few days at the most, அவன் கெட்டுப்போகிறதற்கு அதிகநாட்செல்லாது.

A hundred rupees at most will suffice for the building, வீடுகட்ட வேண்டுமானால் நூறுரூபாய்க்குமேலே செல்லமாட்டாது, lit: *if you will build the house, it will not cost beyond* 100 *rupees.* Here வேண்டுமானால் is necessary, because of மாட்டாது. But if the phrase were in the affirmative, as: *It will cost* 100 *rupees to build the house*, then the dative will be proper, as: வீடு கட்டுகிறதற்கு நூறுரூபாய்செல்லும்.

33. *Neither, Nor*

Are expressed by உம், affixed to the nouns, with the verb in the negative form, as :

Neither light nor air entered our room, ஒளியுங்காற்றும் எங்கள் அறையில் வரவில்லை.

Ye shall neither eat of it, nor touch it, நீங்கள் அதைப்புசிக்கவுந்தொடவுங்கூடாது.

Neither despise nor oppose what thou doest not understand, உனக்குத்தெரியாததை நீ அசட்டைபண்ணவும்விரோதிக்கவுங்கூடாது.

The dog would neither eat the straw himself, nor suffer the ox to eat it, நாயானது இந்தவைக்கோலைத்தான்தின்னவுமில்லை மாடு தின்னும்படிக்கு இடங்கொடுக்கவுமில்லை.

When the verb is in the future tense ஆகிலும், or ஆனாலும், may be used for உம், as :

Neither good nor evil shall be done to you, நன்மையாகிலுந்தீமையாகிலும் உனக்குச்செய்யப்படாது.

Neither gold nor silver nor estates will make you truly happy, பொன்னாகிலும் வெள்ளியாகிலும் நிலங்களாகிலும் உனக்கு மெய்யான பாக்கியத்தைக்கொடுக்கமாட்டாது.

In this instance உம், or ஆவது, will do as well.

34. *Notwithstanding* or *Nevertheless*

Is generally expressed by the third verbal participle, as :

Notwithstanding all the opposition which exists in Ireland to the cause of Bible education, it is on the increase, தேவவசனத்தின் படிபிள்ளைகளைவளர்க்கிறதற்கு ஐருலந்துதேசத்தில் மிகுந்த விரோதமுண்டாயிருந்தும், தேவவசனத்தின்படியே வளர்க்கிறது மென்மேலும்வழக்கமாகின்றது.

Notwithstanding this, he came, அப்படியிருந்தும் அவன் வந்தான்.

35. *Now*

Is literally expressed by இப்பொழுது, but it cannot be used unless the present time be indeed meant, as:

Now seek to be saved, இப்பொழுது இரட்சிப்பையடையும்படி தேடு.

When, therefore, *now* is used merely as an emphatic or expletive particle, it requires no rendering in Tamil. It may often be regarded as a conjunction, to introduce an explanation of the preceding sentence, and then it may be rendered by a corresponding word in Tamil, இதைக்குறித்து, or such like, as:

This man asserts that Vishtnoo is the true God; now you must understand that, &c., விட்டுணு மெய்யாய்த்தேவனாயிருக்கிறானென்று இவன்சொல்லுகிறான் அதைக்குறித்து நீஙகள் அறியவேண்டியதென்னவென்னில்,

When it is unitedwith *then*, the Tamulian expresses it by அடிக்கடி, as:
Now and then he said, there is a Ghost there, அங்கே ஆவேஷமென்று அவன் அடிக்கடி சொன்னான்.

36. *O! Oh!* See under *Ah!*

37. *Of.*

This preposition also has in English many significations, which must be duly considered and expressed in Tamil accordingly.

1. When it denotes possession, the 6th (or Genitive) case, or the oblique case இன், is used, as:

The justice of God is unimpeachable, பராபரனுடைய நீதி குற்றஞ்சாற்றப்படாததாயிருக்கிறது.
The goodness of God is very great, பராபரனுடையதயவு மிகுதியாயிருக்கின்றது.
Jacob was the son of Isaac, இயாக்கோபு ஈசாக்கின்குமாரன்.

Europeans are apt to use the 6th case in Tamil indiscriminately for the genitive case in English, or Greek; by whieh the language is not a little obscured, and the sense misinterpreted. Here are a few instances.

The righteousness of God: is பராபரனுடைய நீதி, namely, the attribute of God; but in Rom. iii. 21, the same expression must be rendered, பராபரனுக்கேற்றநீதி, or பராபரனுக்குமுன்பாகச்செல்லுகிற நீதி, or பராபரன் உண்டுபண்ணினநீதி, *the righteousness which is accepted of God,* or *which God has made.*
The faith of Jesus Christ is, இயேசுக்கிறிஸ்துவினுடைய விசுவாசம, namely, the faith which Christ himself had; but in Rom. iii. 21, it must be இயேசுக்கிறிஸ்துவைப்பற்றும் விசுவாசம், *the faith which lays hold on Christ.*

The knowledge of God, பராபரனுடைய அறிவு, means, the knowledge which God, himself has; but if the meaning be *our knowledge of God*, it must be, பராபரனையறிகிற அறிவு.

The fear of God, cannot be rendered, பராபரனுடைய பயம், which means, the fear which God himself has; but பராபரனுக்குப்பயப்படுகிறபயம்.

The praise of the Saviour, இரட்சகருடைய துதி, means, the praise which he himself sets forth; but இரட்சகரைத்துதிக்கிற துதி, *the praise which praises him*,

The zeal of God, in Rom. x. 2, is evidently *the zeal for God*, and must therefore he rendered accordingly, பராபரனுக்காக வயிராக்கியம்.

The stone of stumbling, இடறுதற்குத்தக்ககல், not இடறுதலினுடையகல்.

2. When it denotes *from among*, *out of*, the ablative in இல் with சில, or some such word, must be used, as:

You may eat of all the fruits in the garden, தோட்டத்திலுள்ள சகல பழங்களிலுஞ்சில சாப்பிடலாம்.

He is a friend of mine, இவர் என் சிநேகிதர்களிலொருவர்.

At last all the people of the world shall be judged, கடைசியிலே உலகத்திலுள்ளயாவரும் நியாயத்தீர்ப்பையடைவார்கள்.

Take 12 pieces of the 24, அந்த இருபத்திநான்கு துண்டுகளிற் பன்னிரண்டு துண்டுகளையெடுத்துக்கொள்.

3. When it means *concerning*, *relating to*, குறித்து is used, as:

When I told him of the affair, he was amazed, நான் இந்தக்காரியத்தைக்குறித்து அவனுடனேபேசினபொழுது அவன் ஆச்சரியப்பட்டான் or இந்தக்காரியத்தையவனுக்குச்சொன்னபொழுது.

4. When it is the sign of a Genitive, qualifying its governing word, என்னும் must be used, as:

The land of Judea, யூதேயா என்னுந்தேசம், or merely, யூதேயா தேசம்.

He anointed him with the oil of gladness, சந்தோஷமென்னுந் தயிலத்தை அவருக்கு அபிஷேகம்பண்ணினார்.

He has clothed me with the garment of righteousness, நீதியென்னும்வஸ்திரத்தை யெனக்குடுத்தினார்.

5. When it denotes *property* or *condition*, meaning as much as *having*, the Tamulian uses உடைய, உள்ள; and if the meaning be negative, இல்லாத, as:

He is the king of glory, அவரேமகிமையுடைய இராசா, (or மகிமையுள்ள.)

He is a man of fortune; அவன் ஆஸ்திகளையுடையவன்.

He has no coach of his own, சொந்தமானபண்டியவருக்கில்லை.

She is a woman of great abilities, அவள்மிகுந்தபுத்தியையுடையவள்.

6. When it denotes *power* or *choice*, as the cause of a thing, the ablative causal is used, as:

Of ourselves we can do no real good, நம்மாலே மெய்யானநன்மை செய்யத்திராணியில்லை.

7. When it denotes *extraction*, or *belonging to*, and in a few other connexions, it must be given according to the sense in Tamil, thus:

He is of an ancient family, அவன் பூர்வீகமான குடும்பத்திற்பிறந்தவன்.

This is an affair of the cabinet, இது இராசசபைக்கேற்றகாரியம்.
I am of the Tamil nation, நான்தமிழன்.
Of necessity, வேண்டுவதாய், அவசியமாய்.
Of a truth, மெய்யாய், நிச்சயமாய்.
Of late he has not come, போனமாதத்திலே (or போனவாரத்திலே) அவன்வரவில்லை or சிலகாலம் அவன்வரவில்லை.

38. *On*, or *upon*.

1. With regard to place or situation, it must be rendered by மேல, or by the ablative of place, as:

A city set on a hill cannot be hid, மலையின்மேல் (or மலையில்) உண்டாக்கப்பட்ட பட்டினம் மறைவாயிருக்கமாட்டாது.
Bombay stands on a island, பம்பைப்பட்டினம் ஒருதீவிலே இருக்கின்றது.

The guilt be upon your head, இந்தக்குற்றம் உன் தலையின்மேலிருப்பதாக.

2. When it denotes *a particular day*, the same case in இல் must be used, as:

He died on the 12*th of March,* அவன் பங்குனிமாதம் ௰௨ தேதியிலே யிறந்துபோனான்.

3. When it means *in immediate consequence of*, மாத்திரத்திலே or உடனே expresses it, as:

Upon one kind word he was reconciled as: நல்லவார்த்தைகளில் ஒரேவார்த்தையைச்சொன்னமாத்திரத்திலே(or சொன்னவுடனே) அவன்சமாதானப்பட்டான்.

The ablative causal may also be used, particularly when it means simply *in consequence of*, as:

He valued himself much upon his high birth, தான் உயர்குலத்திற் பிறந்ததினாலே (or உயர்குலத்தானானதினாலே) மிகவும் மேன்மை பாராட்டினான்.

4. **When it means** ***relating to, with respect to,*** **குறித்து, must be used, as:**

Locke wrote upon Government, உலொக்கென்பவர் துரைத்தனஞ்செய்கிறதைக்குறித்து எழுதினார்.
I was silent upon questions which I did not understand, எனக்குத்தெரியாதகாரியங்களைக்குறித்து நான்பேசாமலிருந்தேன்.

5. **When it means** ***in consideration of,*** **the Tamulian usses நினைத்து, ப்பார்த்து, கேட்டு, நம்பி, or any other verb suiting the connexion, as:**

He surrendered upon splendid promises, மிகுந்தபிரயோசனமுள்ள வாக்குத்தத்தங்களையவன்கேட்டு ஒப்புக்கொடுத்தான்.
I do it upon your word, நான் உம்முடையவார்த்தையை நம்பிச்செய்கிறேன், or நீர் சொன்னதினாலே செய்கிறேன், or உம்முடைய வார்த்தையின்மேல் இதைச்செய்கிறேன்.

6. **When it denotes** ***by, the means of support,*** **the causal ablative must be used, as:**

He lives solely upon water and rice, சோற்றினாலுந்தண்ணீரினாலும்மாத்திரம் பிழைக்கிறான் or சோறுந்தண்ணீரும்மாத்திரஞ்சாப்பிட்டுப்பிழைக்கிறான்.

7. **In different connexions, it must be differently expressed; a variety of instances is here given, as:**

Upon such terms I also would undertake the business, இப்படியானால், நானும் இந்தவேலையைச்செய்வேன்.
On God's providence our hopes depend, பராபரன் விசாரிப்பாரென்று நாம் நம்பிக்காத்துக்கொண்டிருக்கிறோம், or merely நம்புகிறோம், or பராபரனுடையவிசாரிப்பின்மேலே நம்பிக்கையாயிருக்கிறோம்.
They went on foot, காலால்நடந்துபோனார்கள்.
I came on horseback, குதிரையின்மேலேறிவந்தேன் or குதிரையின்மேல்வந்தேன்.
It happened on a sudden, இதுசடுதியாய்நடந்தது.
He did this on purpose, அவன்மனதறிய இப்படிச்செய்தான்.
Do not go there on pain of death, மரணத்துக்குத்தப்பவேண்டில் அங்கேபோகாதிரு, or நீயங்கேபோகக்கூடாது. போனால்,உனக்கு மரண ஆக்கினைவரும்.
From on high, உயரத்திலிருந்து.
On the contrary, அதற்கெதிராக.
She played on the harp, வீணையைவாசித்தாள்.
On my part, there is no objection, நான் ஒரு விரோதமுஞ்சொல்லமாட்டேன்.
Upon this he said as follows, அதின்பின்பு (or அதைக்கேட்டு) அவன்சொன்னதாவது.

39. *Or.*

For the meaning of this conjunction, when it answers to *either*, see *Either*.

When it stands alone, and denotes opposition, it must be rendered by இல்லாவிட்டால், or அல்லவென்றால், thus:

> *Give me to eat*, or *I die*, எனக்குச்சாப்பாடுதரவேண்டும். இல்லாவிட்டாற்சாவேன்.
> *Repent*, or *you will perish*, மனந்திரும்பு அல்லவென்றாற்கெட்டுப்போவாய்.

When it signifies distribution, ஆவது will express it, which must be added to every word or clause which is distributed, thus:

> *Send (me) gold*, *silver*, *copper* or *lead*, பொன்னையாவது, வெள்ளியையாவது, செம்பையாவது, ஈயத்தையாவது, அனுப்பு.

Or அல்லது may be prefixed to every such word, except the first, thus:

> *Let the carts bring lime* or *sand* or *stones*, பண்டிகள்சுண்ணும்பை அல்லது மணலை அல்லது கற்களைக்கொண்டுவரட்டும்.
> *These subjects are usually taken from the scriptures* or *from the life of some saint*, இப்படிப்பட்ட பொருள்களைத்தேவவசனத்திலிருந்தாவது ஒருமுனியினுடைய நடக்கைப் புத்தகத்திலிருந்தாவது எடுத்துக்கொள்வார்கள். If அல்லது be used, then எடுத்துக்கொள்வார்கள் must be put also after the first இருந்து, thus: தேவவசனத்திலிருந்து எடுத்துக்கொள்வார்கள், அல்லது ஒருமுனியினுடைய, &c. &c.

40. *Otherwise* or *Else*

Is literally expressed by மற்றப்படி, or வேறுபிரகாரமாக, but neither will always suit; the former is the least proper; the latter may be used when *otherwise* stands adverbially, as:

> *If you act otherwise, I shall get angry*, நீ வேறு பிரகாரமாய்ச் செய்தாற்கோபமாயிருப்பேன், (or வேறுவிதமாய்)

But in other cases, the Tamulian repeats the verb of the preceding action, which is affected by *otherwise* or *else*, put in the subjunctive mode, as:

> *Thou desirest not sacrifice, else I would give it*, பலிகளைத்தேவரீர் விரும்பமாட்டீர் விரும்பினாற்செலுத்துவேன்.
> *He did not pay the money; otherwise I should have given him the goods*, பணத்தையவன் செலுத்தவில்லை, ச்செலுத்தினானாற் பண்டங்களையவனுக்குக்கொடுப்பேன்.

41. *Over.*

1. With regard to *place*, is expressed by மேல், as:

He poured water over my head, அவன் என்தலையின்மேற்றண்ணீர் வார்த்தான்.

2. When it denotes *superiority,* மேலாய், or மேன்மையாய், with the dative, expresses it, as:

The king is over his ministers, இராசாத்தன்னுடைய மந்திரிகளுக்கு மேலாயிருக்கிறான்.

3. When it means *through, diffusely,* எங்கும், is used, as:

His fame spread all over the country, அவருடையகீர்த்தி தேசமெங்குஞ்சென்றது or பரவிற்று.

42. *Out.*

1. When it means *outside* adverbially, it is expressed by, வெளியே, புறம்பே, as:

He is out, அவன்வெளியேயிருக்கிறான்.

2. When united with *of,* it must frequently be differently expressed; though வெளியே, &c., may often be used when it is opposed to inside; yet much depends upon the verb with which it stands connected, as:

He is out of the house, அவன்வெளியிலேயிருக்கிறான்.
He went out of the house, அவன் வீட்டைவிட்டுவெளியேபோனான்.
He is out of the camp, அவன்பாளயத்துக்குப்புறம்பேயிருக்கிறான்.
In the morning all the ships were out of sight, காலமே (காலையில்) எல்லாக்கப்பல்களுங்கண்ணுக்கு எட்டாததூரமாய்ப்போயின.
He is out the king's favour, இராசாவினுடையதயவை யிழந்தான்.
He is out of humour, அவன்பிரமைகொண்டிருக்கிறான், or அவன் சஞ்சலமுள்ளவனாயிருக்கிறான்.
He is now out of debt, அவனுக்கிப்பொழுதுகடனில்லை, or அவனுடையகடன் இப்பொழுதுதீர்ந்தது.
I went out of the way, வழியைவிட்டுவிலகினேன்.
He is out of danger, அவனுக்குமோசமில்லை.
The fire is out, நெருப்புஅவிந்துபோயிற்று.
He was distressed out of measure, அவன் அளவில்லாத உபத்திரவப்பட்டான், or if the sense be active, அவன் மிகவும் மிகுதியாய் உபத்திரவப்படுத்தப்பட்டான்.

3. When *out of* means the same as *because of,* the causal ablative is required, as.

I gave him 20 pagodas out of compassion, இரக்கத்தினாலே நான் அவனுக்கு (உ௰) வராகனைக்கொடுத்தேன், or நான் அவனுக்கிரங்கி உ௰ வராகனை, &c.

4. Sometimes it means *from,* when the ablative of place with இருந்து or இருந்த, is required, as:

He plucked the book out of my hands, என்கையிலிருந்த புத்தகத்தைப்பிடுங்கினான்.

He took the things out of the box, பெட்டியிலிருந்து பண்டங்களையெடுத்தான்.

This history is taken out of the Bible, இந்தச்சரித்திரஞ்சத்தியவேதத்திலிருந்தெடுக்கப்பட்டது, or வேதத்திலெடுக்கப்பட்டது.

43. *Perhaps*

May be rendered by ஒருவேளை, but it often happens that it cannot be rendered at all, and the sentence must either receive another form, or when the word means *it may be*, the simple future tense will express it, thus :

Perhaps he will come, ஒருவேளை வருவான்.

It was perhaps negligence which brought him into these embarrassments, அவன இப்படிப்பட்டவருத்தத்தில் அகப்பட்டதற்கு தாமதம் ஏதுவாயிருக்கும்.

The simplest method, perhaps, will be to dismiss him, அவனைத் தள்ளிவிட்டால்நன்மையாயிருக்கும், or நன்மையாயிருக்குமென்று தோன்றுகின்றது.

44. *Rather.*

Cannot be rendered by any particular word in Tamil ; the sense must be determined and accordingly rendered, thus.

It would rather retard than promote instruction, அது அறிவு சீக்கிரமாய் வரும்படிக்கல்லத் தாமதமாய் வரும்படிக்கேதுவாயிருக்கும்.

I had rather you go and ask for the bill, நீபோய்ப்பணப்பத்திரத்தைக்கேட்டுக்கொண்டால் எனக்குச்சந்தோஷமாயிருக்கும்.

Rather than lose my soul, I shall give up sin, என்னாத்துமா நித்தியவாழ்வையிழந்துபோகாதபடிகுப்பாவத்தை விட்டுவிடுவேன்.

This is rather to much rain, இந்தமழைதகுதிக்கதிகமாயிருக்கும்.

45. *Since.*

1. When it means *from* முதல், or முதற்கொண்டு, expresses it, as :

Since times immemorial, men have departed from the way of truth, நமக்குத்தெரியாத பூர்வீககாலம்முதற்கொண்டு மனிதர்கள் சத்தியமார்க்கத்தைவிட்டு விலகியிருக்கிறார்கள்.

2. When adverbially used, meaning *ago, before this,* முதல், with the corresponding particle, வரைக்கும், or பரியந்தம், may be used, or simply the verbal participle, as :

It is now twelve years since the earthquake took place, பூமி யதிர்ந்துண்டானதுமுதல் இதுவரைக்கும் பன்னிரண்டு வருடமாயிற்று, or பூமியதிர்ந்துண்டாகி ப்பன்னிரண்டு வருடமாயிற்று.

3. When it means *because that, whereas, as,* படியினாலே, with a relative participle, or the causal ablative must be used, as :

Since then great circumspection is required, be careful to use it, மிகவுஞ்சாவதானமாயிருக்கவேண்டியபடியால் (or வேண்டுவதால்) நீ சாவதானமாயிரு.

Since ye believe in Christ, do as he has commanded you, நீங்கள் கிறிஸ்துவை விசுவாசிக்கிறபடியால், அவர்கட்டளையிட்டதைச்செய்வீர்களாக.

The expression *ever since* is sufficiently expressed by முதற்கொண்டு, as in the before mentioned instances.

46. *Still.*

When this adverb means *nevertheless, notwithstanding*, the subjunctive mode expresses it, as:

நான் அவனுக்குப்புத்திசொல்லியும், அவன் அப்படிச்செய்தான்.

When it means *in an increasing degree* பின்னும், will express it, as:

He went on still faster, அவன்பின்னும் அதிகவிரைவாய்நடந்தான்.

When it means *in continuance*; பின்னும், will be proper, as:

He still studies the Veda, அவன்பின்னும் வேதத்தைப்படிக்கிறான்.

If இன்னம் be put, the sense will be, *that hitherto he did not get on in learning, and that therefore he still learns.*

When it means *besides,* இன்னம் expresses it, as:

I have still another piece of news இன்னம் ஒருசெய்தியுண்டு.

47. *Than.*

Is expressed in Tamul by the dative, and by the ablative in இல், with உம், without any change in the adjective or adverb, though occasionally அதிக, or அதிகமாய், may be added, as:

This is better than that, இதற்கு அது நல்லது, or நலமாயிருக்கின்றது.

I am greater than he, அவனிலும் நான்பெரியவன்.

This writing is worse than the other, அந்தஎழுத்திலும் இது அவலட்சணமாயிருக்கின்றது;

Observe that these forms imply that both have the same quality, only the one is better or worse; when therefore the sense is that the one, with which another thing is compared, has nothing of the quality at all, or one contrary to it, the comparative form cannot be used in Tamil; one of the qualities must be directly denied, thus:

It is better to say the truth than to lie, பொய்பேசாமற்சத்தியமானதைச்சொல்லுகிறதே நலம். Here if you say பொய் பேசுகிறதிலும், it implies that to a certain degree falsehood also is good.

It becomes us more to love than to hate our neighbour, பிறனைப்பகைக்கிறதல்ல, அவனிடத்தில் அன்புகூருகிறதே நமக்குத்தகுதியாயிருக்கிறது.

It is better to suffer than to do evil, தீமையைச்செய்கிறதல்ல, தீமையைச்சகிக்கிறதேநல்லது.

Note.—Concerning the comparative degree, see § XLVI. 8. and XLVII. 2.

48. *That.*

This conjunction is expressed,

1. When it means *because* or *on account of*, by the dative, with ஆக, or by குறித்து, as:

I am sorry that I cried out, நான்கூக்குரல்பண்ணினதற்காக மனஸ்தாபப்படுகிறேன், or பண்ணினதைக்குறித்து.

2. When it refers to *a consequence*, the clauses must be inverted, and the causal particle used, as.

He was so frightened that he fled, அவன் மிகவும்பயத்தினாலே (or *simply* பயந்து) ஓடிப்போனான்.

3. When it quotes another sentence, என்று and other modifications of என்கிறது are used, or the mere verbal noun in such a case as the following verb may require, as:

Acknowledge that men are sinners, மனிதர்கள் பாவிகளாயிருக்கிறார்களென்பதையொத்துக்கொள்.

Know this day that Jehovah is God, பராபரனே தேவனென்று இந்நாளிலே அறிந்துகொள்.

Remember that thou wast a servant in Egypt, எகிப்துதேசத்திலே நீஅடிமையாயிருந்ததை நினைத்துக்கொள்.

I shall demonstrate that the earth moves round the sun, பூமிசூரியனைச்சுற்றியோடுகிறதென்பதற்கு உதாரணங்களைச்சொல்லுவேன் or என்றுதிருட்டாந்தப்படுத்துவேன்.

4. When it denotes *a final end*, படி, படிக்கு, or படியாய் expresses it, as:

Do thou work, that they may live, அவர்கள் பிழைக்கும்படிக்கு நீ வேலைசெய்.

49. *Then.*

1. When it means simply *at that time*, or *after that*, is expessed by அப்பொழுது, or அக்காலத்திலே, அந்நேரத்திலே, அதற்குப்பின்பு.

2. When it means *that time*, the Tamulian expresses it thus, as:

Till then, let us watch, அக்காலம்வரைக்கும் (or அதுவரைக்கும்) நாம் விழித்திருக்கக்கடவோம்.

3. When it means *if it be so*, it must be expressed accordingly, as:

Then let me go and smite him, அப்படியானால், நான்போய் அவனை யடிக்கும்படிக்கு இடங்கொடு.
What shall I then do? அப்படியானால்நான் என்னசெய்யலாம்.

Note.—When *then* follows after a subjunctive, the former need not be expressed in Tamil, as:

If it be so, then I shall come, அப்படியானால் நான் வருவேன்.
Sometimes it is proper to translate it by, அப்பொழுது.

50. *Thence, Thenceforth.*

These adverbs mean *from that place or time*, or, *for that reason*, and must be expressed accordingly, as:

Thence we departed, அந்த இடத்தைவிட்டுப்புறப்பட்டோம்.
Thenceforth they did not join us any more, அதுமுதல், (or அந்தக்காலம்முதல்) அவர்கள்மறுபடியும் எங்களைச்சேரவில்லை, or எங்களோடேவந்துசேரவில்லை.
Thence it was that I rejected his offer, அதினாலே (or அந்தமுகாந்திரத்தினாலே) நான் அவனுடையசொல்லைத்தள்ளினேன்.

51. *There, thereabout, thereafter, thereas, thereby, therefore, therefrom, therein, thereinto, thereof, thereto, thereupon and therewith.*

1. The adverb *there* is in most acceptations expressed by அங்கே, or அவ்விடத்திலே. When it is used as an exclamation directing something at a distance, it may be expressed by அதோ, as:
There he comes! அதோவருகிறான்.

When it is expletive, it cannot be rendered, thus:
There was a man in Sadras, whose name was Subaroyen, சதுராங்கபட்டினத்திலே ஒருமனிதனிருந்தான் அவனுக்குச்சுப்பராயனென்றுபேர்.

2. *Thereabout.* When it means, *near that place*, is expressed by அவ்விடத்திலே, or அவ்விடத்திற்குச்சமீபமாய். When it means, *nearly*, ஏறக்குறைய must be used. When it means, *concerning that matter*, அதைக்குறித்து will be proper.

3. *Thereafter.* When it means *according to that*, or *accordingly*, அந்தப்படி, expresses it.

4. *Thereat.* When it means *at that place*, அவ்விடத்திலே must be used. But when the meaning is *at that, on that account*, it must be rendered by அதினாலே, அதினிமித்தம்.

5. *Thereby* is well rendered by அதினாலே, அதின்மூலமாய்.

6. *Therefore* (and *wherefore*) are expressed by, ஆகையால், ஆதலால், ஆனபடியால், அதினாலே, ஆனதால், see § CVI.

Besides these, ஆனதுகொண்டு has also been used, but upon no authority.

7. *Therefrom* is expressed by அதிலிருந்து, அதினின்று, or அதுமுதல்.

8. *Therein* and *thereinto* are rendered by அதில், or அதற்குள்ளே:

9. *Thereof*, for instance, *the earth and all the fullness thereof*, பூமியும் அதிலுள்ளயாவும், or, பூமியும் அதில்நிறைந்திருக்கிறயாவும்.

10. *Thereon* is rendered by அதின்மேல்.

11. *Thereto* and *thereunto* are expressed by அதற்கு.

12. *Thereunder*, is rendered by அதின்கீழ்.

13. *Thereupon*, when it means *upon that*, is expressed by அதின்மேல்; when it means *in consequence of that*, அதினாலே expresses it. When it means *immediately*, உடனே must be used.

14. *Therewith*, when it signifies *with that*, அதினோடே expresses it; when it means *immediately* உடனே will be suitable.

15. *Therewithal*, when it means *at the same time*, அக்காலத்திலே expresses it; when it signifies *with that*, அதினோடே must be used.

52. *Though or Although.*

Is expressed both by the verbal participle with உம், and by the subjunctive mood with உம், the difference between them, which ought to be carefully observed, is pointed out in § LVI. and LVII.

He shall live though he die, அவன் மரித்தாலும் பிழைப்பான், which implies that he is not yet dead.

He will not renounce Christ though he should die, அவனுக்குமரணம்வந்தாலும் (or அவன்மரணம் அடைந்தாலும்) கிறிஸ்துவை மறுதலிக்கமாட்டான்.

Although my house is not large, yet I remain in it, என்வீடு சிறிதாயிருந்தும், நான் அதிலேயிருக்கிறேன். Here the smallness of the house is a certainty.

But although the house should not be large enough, I shall take it, அந்த வீடுசிறிதாயிருந்தாலும் நான் அதைவாங்குவேன், where the smallness of the house is still a doubt.

53. *Through.*

1. When it denotes *passage*, வழியாய் expresses it, as:

We passed through Tanjore on our way to Cochin, நாங்கள் தஞ்சாவூர்வழியாய் (தஞ்சாவூரின்வழியாய்) க்கொச்சிக்குப்போனோம்.

Go through the strait gate, நெருக்கமான வாயிலின்வழியாய்ப்போங்கள்.

2. When it means *from end to end*, உருவ, the infinitive of உருவுகி றது, or some other suitable phrase, expresses it, as :

An axis is imagined to pass through the earth, ஓரச்சுப்பூமியை யுருவப்போகின்றதென்று பாவிக்கிறார்கள் or பூமியின்மத்தியிலே போகிறதென்று, &c.
He pierced him through the body, அவனுடைய உடலையுருவக்குத் தினான்.
We went through the town, நாம்பட்டினத்திற்கு ஊடேபோனோம்.

3. When it signifies *by means of*, the causal ablative, or adverbs denoting cause, as மூலமாய், will express it, thus :

It was through indolence that he became so poor, சோம்பலினாலே இவனுக்கு இவ்வளவுதரித்திரமுண்டாயிற்று.
Through this man is forgiveness of sins preached unto you, இவர் மூலமாய்ப்பாவமன்னிப்பு உங்களுக்கு அறிவிக்கப்படுகிறது. Here you cannot say இவராலே, because that would refer to the preaching.
He helped them much that had believed through grace, கிருபையி னாலேவிசுவாசிகளானவர்களுக்கு மிகவும் உதவியாயிருந்தான்.

54. *To.*

i. As an adverb ;

1. When it denotes the infinitive mode, simply pointing out the verb, the fourth indefinite or infinitive mode expresses it, as :

I begin to fear, நான்பயப்படத்தொடங்குகிறேன்.
You ought to go thither, நீயங்கேபோகவேண்டும்.
I love to read, நான்படிக்கவிரும்புகிறேன்.

2. When the infinitive mode in English is the subject of the sentence, the Tamil verbal noun must be used, as :

To relieve the indigent, to comfort the afflicted, to protect the innocent, to reward the deserving, are humane and noble employments, ஏழைகளுக்கு த்தருமஞ்செய்கிறதுந் துக்கப்படு கிறவர்களைத்தேற்றுகிறதுங் குற்றமில்லாதவர்களைக்காப்பாற்றுகிற தும் பாத்திரவான்களுக்குப்பலனைக்கொடுக்கிறதும மனிதருக்கே ற்றபெரியகிரியைகளாயிருக்கின்றன, or தருமஞ்செய்தலுந், தேற்ற லுங், காப்பாற்றலுங், கொடுத்தலும், &c.

3. When it is the object of another verb, the same verbal noun in the accusative case must be used, as :

I hate to steal, திருடுகிறதைப்பகைக்கிறேன்.
Cease to do evil, தீமைசெய்கிறதைவிடுங்கள்.

4. When it denotes *intention* or *purpose,* படிக்கு, with a future participle, must be used, as:

He came to kill me, என்னைக்கொலைசெய்யும்படிக்கு வந்தான்.
as the verb வந்தான் is here alone, the simple infinitive also will do, கொலைசெய்யவந்தான்.

They spoke thus to destroy me, என்னை யழிக்கும்படிக்கு அப்படிப்பேசினார்கள்

Christ came to save sinners, பாவிகளை யிரட்சிக்கும்படிக்குக்கிறிஸ்துவந்தார்.

5. When it simply denotes *tendency,* the verbal noun in the dative case with or without ஏதுவாக expresses it, as:

This will serve ouly to inflame the passions, இது துராசைகளை யெழுப்புகிறதற்குமாத்திரம் ஏதுவாயிருக்கும்.

Why should you blaspheme the name of God to destroy your soul? உன் ஆத்துமாவைக்கெடுக்கிறதற்கேதுவாக நீ பராபரனுடைய திருநாமத்தைத்தூஷணிக்க வேண்டுவதென்ன, or உன்னாத்துமாவைக்கெடுக்கத்தக்கதாக.)

ii. As a Preposition.

1. When it denotes *motion towards a place,* or *opposition to,* the dative is used, as:

I went yesterday to town, நேற்றுநான் ஊருக்குப்போய்வந்தேன்.

Note.—The Tamulian usually adds வந்தேன், *I came,* because the speaker says this after his return from town.

He sent fifty asses to Vannarpettah, அவர் ஐம்பது கழுதைகளை வண்ணார்பேட்டைக்கனுப்பினார்.

Note.—When it is connected with journeying to a place, the Tamulian puts நோக்கி, with the accusative, as:

He travelled to Kasi, (i. e., *Benaris,)* அவன் காசியைநோக்கிப் போனான்.

2. When it denotes *motion towards a person,* the ablative loc: with இடத்தில் (or இடத்திற்கு,) is required, as:

I went to the Gentleman, நான் துரையினிடத்திற் (or இடத்திற்குப்) போனேன்.

Take the money to the Guru, பணத்தைக்குருவினிடத்திற்குக்கொண்டுபோய்க்கொடு.

I have given (to) him the Pooranas, புராணங்களை யவனிடத்திற்கொடுத்தேன், or அவருக்குக்கொடுத்தேன.

3. When it stands in a peculiar connexion, the phrase must be expressed according to the sense, thus:

My friend was true to his trust, என்சிநேகிதன் தனக்கொப்புவிக்கப்பட்டதை யுண்மையாய்க்காத்துக்கொண்டான்.

The king sent him troops to the number of 60,000 men. இராசா அறுபதினாயிரம்போர்ச்சேவகரை அவரிடத்துக்கனுப்பினான்.

55. *Towards.*

1. When it means *in direction to* the Tamulian uses, நோக்கி with the accusative, or நேராய் with the dative, as:

He proceeded towards the south, அவன் தென்றிசையைநோக்கிப் போனான்.

We are journeying towards Madras, நாங்கள் சென்னபட்டினத்தைநோக்கிப்போகிறோம்.

The currents drive towards the sea, நீரோட்டஞ்சமுத்திரத்திற்கு நேராயிருக்கின்றது.

2. When it means *in direction to a person, near to,* சமீபமாய், or அருகே, or the ablative with இடத்தில், is used, as:

The danger now comes towards him, மோசம் இப்பொழுது அவனுக்குச்சமீபமாய்வருகின்றது, or அவனிடத்தில்வருகின்றது, or அவனருகேவருகிறது.

3. When it means *with respect to,* it is expressed by the dative or local ablative, with a suitable verb, thus:

His love towards us was great, அவர் நமக்குக்காண்பித்த அன்பு பெரிதாயிருந்தது, or நம்மிடத்தில்வைத்த அன்பு, or நமதுமேல் வைத்த அன்பு.

This was the first act towards a breach, பிரிவுண்டாகிறதற்கு இது வேமுதற்செய்கையாயிருந்தது.

56. *Under.*

1. When it means *in a state of subjection, inferiority, below in place, opposition,* கீழ், தாழ் or உள் with a suitable verb, must be used, as:

We are all under the king, நாமெல்லாரும் இராசாவுக்குக்கீழ்ப்பட்டவர்கள் or இராசாவுக்குட்பட்டவர்கள்.

The sword was under the cloak, கட்கஞ்சால்வையின் கீழிருந்தது.

A Soodra is under a Bramin, சூத்திரன் பிராமணனுக்குத்தாழ்ந்திருக்கிறான், or கீழிருக்கிறான்.

I am a man under authority, நான் அதிகாரத்திற்குக்கீழ்ப்பட்டவன்.

We are all under sin, நாமெல்லாரும் பாவத்திற்குட்பட்டவர்கள். or நாமெல்லாரும் பாவமுள்ளகுணத்தையுடையவர்கள்.

2. In a variety of phrases, *under* must be rendered according to the sense, as:

The sword was under his cloak, கட்கம் அவனுடையசால்வையில் மறைந்திருந்தது, but if the sense be that the sword lay on a place, and the clock upon it; கீழ, may be used, as under No. 1.

He acted under a misconception of my order, அவன் என்னுடைய கட்டளையின்பொருளையுணராமல் நடத்தினான்.

It was sold under twenty Pagodas, அது இருபது வராகனுக்குள்ளாகவிற்கப்பட்டது, where *under* means *for less than* or *within.*

Nothing under royalty contented him, இராசப்பட்டமன்றி வேறொன்றுக்கும் அவன் சம்மதிக்கவில்லை.

He escaped under the appearance of a messenger, அவன் ஒருதூதனைப்போலவந்துதப்பிப்போனான், or அவன்ஒருதூதன வேஷத்தைத்தரித்துத்தப்பிப்போனான்.

He fainted under his load, தன்மேலிருந்தசுமையினாலே சோர்ந்துபோனான், or if the place merely is to be referred to, அவன்தன்சுமையின்கீழ்ச்சோர்ந்துபோனான்.

I was under great anxiety, நான் மிகுந்த விசாரமுள்ளவனாயிருந்தேன், or நான்மிகுந்தவிசாரத்தை யடைந்துகொண்டிருந்தேன், or விசாரத்துக்குள்ளிருந்தேன்.

He acts under legal restraints, நீதி நியாயங்களினாலே (or இராசாவின்கட்டளையினாலே) கட்டப்பட்டுச்செய்கிறான்.

He sunk under his father's influence, அவன் தன் தகப்பனுடைய செய்கையினாலே அமிழ்ந்துபோனான், or அழிந்துபோனான்

I am under fifteen years of age, என்வயசு பதினைந்துக்குள்ளிருக்கின்றது.

Under your direction I am safe, உம்மாலேநடத்தப்பட்டு நான் பத்திரமாயிருக்கிறேன்.

This took place under Constantine, இதுகொன்ஸ்தன்டீனென்னும் இராயனுடையகாலத்திலே நடந்தது.

It is mentioned under two heads, அது இரண்டு வகுப்புக்களிற்சொல்லியிருக்கின்றது.

I gave it under my hand, நான் என்கையெழுத்துப்போட்டு இதைக்கொடுத்தேன்.

All this was under consideration, இவையெல்லாவற்றையுங்குறித்து யோசனைபண்ணிக்கொண்டிருந்தார்கள்.

Their hopes are in you under God, முதலாவது பராபரனமேலும் இரண்டாவது உம்முடையமேலும் நம்பிக்கையாயிருக்கிறார்கள்; or பராபரனுக்குப்பின்பு உம்முடையமேலே நம்பிக்கையாயிருக்கிறார்கள்.

He was under his uncle's care, அவன் தன் சிறியதகப்பனுடைய விசாரிப்புக்குள்ளிருந்தான்.

57. *Unless.*

Is expressed, like *if not* or *except,* by the negative verb with the subjunctive mode of இருக்கிறது, or விடுகிறது, as:

Unless the Lord had been my support, I should have perished, கருத்தர் என்னை ஆதரித்துக்கொள்ளாதிருந்தாரானால், நான் கெட்டுப்போவேன்.

Do not go thither, unless you wish to expose yourself, நீ யுனக்குத்தீங்கைவருவிக்கவிரும்பாவிட்டால், (or மனதில்லாவிட்டால்,) அங்கே போகாதிருப்பாயாக.

58. *When, Whenever,* &c.

1. The adverb *when*, is expressed by the noun, பொழுது, as a particle of time, added to any relative participle, thus:

When he comes to Madura, அவன் மதுரைக்குவருகிறபொழுது.
When he came to Madura, அவன் மதுரைக்குவந்தபொழுது.
When he will come to Madura, அவன் மதுரைக்குவரும்பொழுது.

When it means *whilst, during,* the verbal noun in the ablative case is also used, as:

When he entered the fort, the troops gave a shout, அவன் கோட்டைக்குட்பிரவேசிக்கையிற் சேனைகள் ஆரவாரம்பண்ணினார்கள், (or பிரவேசிக்கிறபொழுது.)

When it is used *interrogatively,* எப்பொழுது, எந்நேரத்திலே, or எக்காலத்திலே is required, as:

When did he come? எப்பொழுதுவந்தான்.

2. *Whenever* or *whensoever,* meaning *at whatsoever time,* is expressed by தோறும், added to the future verbal participle. See தோறும் § CXI.

But if the meaning is simply *at the time when,* then பொழுது is sufficient, thus:

Whenever men shall begin to despise the Bible, their morals will decrease, மனிதர்கள் வேதத்தை யசட்டைபண்ணத்தொடங்கும் பொழுது அவர்களுடைய நல்லொழுக்கங்கள் குறைந்துபோம, or தொடங்குங்காலத்திலே

59. *Whence, Whensoever.*

1. *Whence,* when it means *from a place,* is expressed by அதிலிருந்து, or அதைவிட்டு, thus:

Whence he proceeded to Calcutta, அதிலிருந்து, (or அதைவிட்டு) கற்கத்தாவுக்குப்போனான்.

When it means *from a person,* the pronoun in the same case must be used, viz., அவனிலிருந்து, அவனைவிட்டு.

When it means *from a cause* or *a source,* அதினாலே, is required, or அந்த ஏதுவினாலே, or அந்தமுகாந்திரத்தினாலே, or இந்தக்காரணத்தினாலே, or any other such word as suits the connexion.

When it is *interrogatively* used, எங்கிருந்து, எங்கேயிருந்து or எவ்விடத்திலிருந்து, is required, as:

Whence do you come? எங்கேயிருந்துவருகிறாய்.

2. *Whencesoever* is variously expressed accordingly to the connexion.

Whencesoever you may have got the squirrel, you must take it back again, நீயிந்த அணிற்பிள்ளையைவாங்கிக்கொண்டுவந்த இடமெதுவோ அதிற்கு அதைத்திரும்பக்கொண்டுபோகவேணடும்.
Whencesoever the people came, we must receive them, அந்தச்சனங்கள் எவ்விடத்திலிருந்து வந்திருந்தாலும் நாம் அவர்களையேற்றுக்கொள்ளவேண்டும்.

60. *Where, whereas, whereabout, wherever, wheresoever, wherefore, whereof, whereupon, and wherewith.*

1. The adverb *where* is expressed,

When it is used *interrogatively*, by எங்கே, as:

Where is the man? அந்தமனிதன் எங்கே.

When it means *at which* or *what place*, or *at the place in which*, it is expressed like the relative pronoun *which* by the participles, as:

The place where the body was laid, தேகத்தை வைக்கப்பட்ட இடம்.

The house where the robbers entered, கள்ளர்பிரவேசித்தவீடு.
The corner where the birds made their nest, குருவிகள் கூடு கெட்டினமூலை.

When it is answered by *there*, எங்கேயோ அங்கே, is required, as:

Where the slain are, there is the eagle, கொலைசெய்யப்பட்டவர்களெங்கேயோ அங்கே கழுகு இருக்கும்.

When it is united with *any*, எங்கேயாகிலும் will be proper, thus:
You may stay any where, நீ யெங்கேயாகிலுமிருக்கலாம்.

2. *Whereas.* When it means *but on the contrary, yet, or but*, the particle அப்படியிருந்தும், must be used, as:

Thou hast done me good; whereas I have done thee evil, நீ யெனக்குநன்மைசெய்தாய், அப்படியிருந்தும் நான் உனக்குத்தீமைசெய்தேன், or நீ யெனக்குநன்மைகளைச்செய்தும், நான், &c. &c., or நீயெனக்குநன்மைசெய்தாய், நான் உனக்கு, &c.

When it means *since, because,* படியினாலே, should be used, as:

Whereas it is commanded that no man shall injure another, we ought carefully to obey the command, ஒருவன் மற்றொருவனுக்குத்தீமையைச்செய்யக்கூடாதென்று கட்டளையிட்டிருக்கிற படியினாலே நாம் அதின்படியே செய்யும்படிக்கு எச்சரிக்கையாயிருக்கவேண்டும்.

3. *Whereabout,* when it is used *interrogatively*, is expressed by எங்கே, thus:

Whereabout did you drop the Rupee, வெள்ளிக்காசை நீ எங்கே இழந்துவிட்டாய்.

When it means *about which, or concerning which, near which place,* it must be expressed by a relative participle, as:

Let no man know any thing of the business, whereabout I send thee, நான் உன்னை யனுப்புகிறகாரியத்தை ஒருவருக்குந்தெரியப் படுத்தாதிருப்பாயாக.

The town whereabout the battle took place, யுத்தம்நடந்தபட்டினம்.

4. *Wherever, and wheresoever,* answered by *there,* will be expressed by தோறும், or எங்கேயோ அங்கே, thus:

Wherever the rain drops, there is a hole made, மழைத்துளிகள் விழுகிற இடங்கள்தோறுங்குழியாகும், or simply, மழைத்துளிகள் விழுகிற இடத்திலேகுழி, &c.

Wheresoever the carcase is, there will the eagles be gathered together, பிணமெங்கேயோ அங்கே கழுகுகள்கூடிவரும்.

Without *there,* எங்கே and the subjunctive with உம் will be proper, thus:

Wherever the thief may be, we must go and find him out, அந்தக் கள்ளன் எங்கேயிருந்தாலும நாம்போய் அவனைக்கண்டுபிடிக்க வேண்டும்.

5. *Wherefore,* see *therefore,* § 51, 6.

6. *Whereof,* meaning *of which,* and } are expressed by the relative
7. *Whereupon,* meaning *upon which,* } participle, as:

The business whereof I told you, நான் உனக்குச்சொன்னகாரியம்.
The text whereupon I enlarged in my last discourse, கடைசியான பிரசங்கத்திலே நான் விவரித்துக்காட்டின வாக்கியம்.

When it commences a sentence, *whereupon* may be rendered by அதின்பின்பு.

8. *Wherewith* or *wherewithal,* meaning *with which,* must be rendered by the relative participle, thus:

The hammer wherewith the smith struck the anvil, கொல்லன் அடை கல்லின்மேல் அடித்தகூடம்.

The sword wherewith he pierced the rogue's body, அவன் அந்தக் கள்ளனுடையதேகத்தை யுருவக்குத்தினகட்கம்.

When it is used *interrogatively,* meaning *with what?* எதினாலே must be used, as:

Wherewith shall I pay the debt? எதினாலே நான் கடனைச்செலுத்துவேன்.

61. *Whether.*

1. When it is answered by *or,* is expressed by a repetition of the subjunctive mood with உம், as:

Whether you come or not, I shall go, நீ வந்தாலும் வாராதிருந்தாலும் நான்போவேன்.

Whether you send the horse back to me or keep it, I shall be glad, குதிரையை நீர் என்னிடத்திற்குத்திரும்ப அனுப்பினாலும்நீர் அதை வைத்துக்கொண்டாலுஞ்சந்தோஷமாயிருப்பேன்.

If in this case, *whether* and *or* refer to nouns, then, ஆனாலும் or ஆகிலும் or ஆவது, must be added to each of them, as:

Whether you or he come I shall be glad; நீயானாலும் அவனானாலும் வந்தாற்சந்தோஷமாயிருப்பேன்.

2. In interrogative sentences, *whether* and *or* are expressed by ஓ added to each part of the sentence, followed by என்று and a pronoun, or without either, thus:

Tell me whether you will come or not? நீ வருவாயோமாட்டாயோ இரண்டிலொன்றைச்சொல்லு, lit: *tell me one of two things, will you come or not.*

I do not know whether this will be good for you or not? இது உனக்குநன்மையாயிருக்குமோ தீமையாயிருக்குமோ அது எனக்குத் தெரியாது.

Note.—In English the negative part of the question is often omitted; but in Tamil it must be expressed, as:

Let me know whether you will purchase the Elephant? யானையை வாங்குவீரா. வாங்கமாட்டீரா. அதையறிவிக்கவேண்டும்.

Whether he be a sinner I know not, அவன்பாவியோ (அல்லவோ) அதையறியமாட்டேன். If you translate it by அவன் பாவியென்பதைநான் அறியேன், the sense is, *that he is a sinner; only you knew it not.*

62. *With.*

1. Denotes primarily *connexion,* in which sense the Tamil ablative social, with or without கூட, corresponds with it, as:

He went with them, அவன் அவர்களுடனேகூடப்போனான், (or அவர்களோடேகூட.)

I have made an agreement with him, நான் அவனோடேஉடம்படிக்கைபண்ணினேன்.

2. If it mean *in the same place,* the ablative of place, இடத்தில், is used, as:

You were with me where it occurred, அதுநடந்தபொழுது நீ யென்னிடத்திலிருந்தாய்.

It is difficult to live with bad men, பொல்லாதவர்களிடத்தில் வாசம்பண்ணுகிறது அரிது.

I shall be with you within an hour's time, ஒருமணிநேரத்துக்குள்ளே உம்மிடத்திற்சேர்வேன்.

3. **When it means *on the side of*, *on the part of*, பங்கிலே or பக்கத்திலே is required, as :**

Fear not! I am with thee, பயப்படாதிரு, நான் உன்பங்கிலிருக்கிறேன் or உனக்குடனேயிருக்கிறேன்.

We have many enemies, but God is with us, அநேக சத்துருக்கள் நமக்குண்டாயிருந்தும் பராபரன் நமது பங்கிலிருக்கிறபடியினாலே பயமில்லை. This last additional clause is implied in the English, though not expressed ; in Tamil we must express it.

4. **When it means *the cause* or *means*, the causal ablative is required, as :**

I am sick with sorrow, சஞ்சலமாகிய வியாதிப்படுகிறேன், i. e., *I have the sickness which is sorrow.*

He won him over with sweet promises, அவன் இன்பமான வாக்குத்தத்தங்களினாலே யவனைச்சம்பாதித்தான், or அவன் அவனுக்கு இன்பமானவசனங்களைச்சொல்லி, யவனைச்சம்பாதித்தான.

He was stricken with a hailstone கன்மழையினாலேயவன் அடிக்கப்பட்டான், or கன்மழைபெய்து அவனையடித்தது.

With God all things are possible, பராபரனாலே யெதுவுமாகும், or எல்லாமாகும்.

63. *Without.*

i. **When it stands *singly as an adverb*, வெளியே, வெளியிலே, or புறம்பே, expresses it, as :**

Without are the unclean, அசுத்தர் புறம்பேயிருக்கிறார்கள்.

ii. **As a preposition,**

1. **When it means *outside, not within,* the same words are used, as :**

Without the city, பட்டினத்துக்குப்புறம்பே, பட்டினத்தின்வெளியே.

2. **When it means *non existence,* இல்லாமல், இல்லை, or இன்றி, is required, as :**

The place shall be without men and without beast, இந்தத்தலம் மனிதரில்லாமலும் மிருகங்களில்லாமலுமிருக்கும்.

They abode without a king, அவர்கள் இராசாவில்லாமலிருந்தார்கள்.

I am without clothes, எனக்குவஸ்திரமில்லை, or நான் வஸ்திரமில்லாமலிருக்கிறேன்.

My mind was many days without peace, என்மனது அநேகநாட் சமாதானமில்லாமலிருந்தது, or அநேகநாள் என்மனதுக்குச்சமாதானமில்லை.

Without doubt, he is afraid to come, அவன் வரப்பயப்படுகிறானென்பதற்குச்சந்தேகமில்லை.

However when the verb is negative, *without* is also expressed in this sense by அன்றி, அல்லாமல், as :

Without me you can do nothing, என்னையன்றி நீங்கள் ஒன்றுஞ்செய்யமாட்டீர்கள்.

64. *Yea.*

When it means *yes, truly,* மெய்யாய், expresses it, as:

Yea, the God of this world has blinded their eyes, மெய்யாய் இவ்வுலகத்தின்தேவன் அவர்களுடைய கண்களைக்குருடாக்கினான்.

When it means *not only so but more than so,* அன்றி, with உம், expresses it:

He brought costly spices, yea, and gold too, விலைபெற்ற சரக்குகளையன்றிப்பொன்னையுங்கொண்டுவந்தான்.

They reviled him, yea, they spit in his face, அவனைநிந்தித்தார்கள், அதனறி அவனுடையமுகத்திலுந்துப்பினார்கள், or அவனைநிந்தித்தும் அவனுடையமுகத்தில்த்துப்பியும்வந்தார்கள்.

Note.—Some have interpreted *yea* like *yes,* by ஆம், but this is incorrect.

65. *Yes and No.*

These particles are most frequently expressed by repeating, in the answer, the word contained in the question either in the affirmative or negative, as may be required, thus:

Is he come? வந்தானா.
Yes, வந்திருக்கிறான்.
No, வரவில்லை.

The words ஆம் and உண்டு, are also used to express *yes,* and அல்ல and இல்லை, *no;* ஆம் and அல்ல, affirm or deny the same quality or quantity of a thing, and உண்டு and இல்லை, affirm or deny the existence of a thing. This distinction must be carefully observed. The following instances will elucidate the subject.

Is this rice? அது அரிசியா.
Yes, அதுதான் or இது அரிசிதான், or (ஆம்.)
No, (*it is wheat*) அல்ல இது கோதும்பை.

Is there rice? அரிசியுண்டா.
Yes, உண்டு.
No, இல்லை.

Is not this what you said? இது நீங்கள்சொன்னதல்லவா.
Yes, it is, ஆம் or இது நாங்கள்சொன்னதுதான்.
No, it is not, இது நாங்கள்சொன்னதல்ல.

Did you not say this? இதை நீங்கள்சொல்லவில்லையா.
Yes, சொன்னோம்.
No, சொல்லவில்லை (or இல்லை.)

Did you not say this? இதையல்லவோ நீங்கள்சொன்னீர்கள்.
Yes, ஆம் or இதைத்தான் (or இதையே) சொன்னோம்.
No, இதையல்ல.

Did you not say this? இதை நீங்களல்லவோசொன்னீர்கள்.
Yes, ஆம் or நாங்களேசொன்னோம்.
No, நாங்களல்ல.

When *yes* is used emphatically, like *yea indeed*, the particle ஏ, is affixed to the word on which the emphasis is to be, thus:

Yes, my friend, the hour of your relief is come, என் சிநேகிதனே, உனக்கு ஆதரவுகொடுக்கிறநேரமேவந்தது.
Yes, you despise the man, நீயந்தமனிதனை யசட்டையே பண்ணுகிறாய்.

66. *Yet.*

1. The conjunction, is rendered in the same way as *neverthless, notwithstanding;* which see.

2. The adverb is variously rendered according to the connexion. When it means *beside, over and above,* இன்னம், will express it, thus:

This furnishes us with yet one more reason, இது இன்னம் ஒருநியாயத்தைநமக்குக்காட்டுகிறது.

When it means *still, without any alteration,* it cannot be separately expressed; the sense is contained in the present tense, as:

While they were yet heathen, அவர்கள் அஞ்ஞானிகளாயிருக்கையில்.

When it means *once more,* இன்னம் expresses it, as:
Yet a moment I will wait for you, உனக்காக இன்னம் ஒரு நிமிஷங் காத்திருப்பேன்.

When it means *at this time,* or *so soon,* with a negative before it, it cannot be expressed but by the present tense, as:

Thales, being asked when a man should marry, said: young men not yet, old men not at all, மனிதர் எப்பொழுது விவாகம்பண்ண வேண்டுமென்று ஒருவன் தாலேசென்பவனிடத்திற்கேட்டபொழுது, வாலிபராயிருக்கையிற் பண்ணத்தகாது விருத்தாப்பியரான பின்பு பரிச்சேதம்பண்ணக்கூடாது. For பரிச்சேதம், we may also say, ஒரு விதத்தினும் or ஏகதேசமாயானும்.

When it means *hitherto,* இதுவரைக்கும் or இன்னம் will express it, as:
The master is not yet come, எசமான் இதுவரைக்கும்வரவில்லை, or இன்னம்வரவில்லை.

When it means *continuance and extension,* it must be expressed according to the nature of the sentence, thus:

The storm grew louder and yet louder, பெருங்காற்று அதிகமதிகமாய் இரைந்தது.

When it means *even, after all,* connected with a negative, it cannot be expressed, but by changing the phrase, thus:

The tiger is not far off, but yet not near, புலிகிடக்கிற இடந்தூரமுமல்லச்சமீபமுமல்ல, lit: *the place where the tiger lies, is neither far nor near.*

It is not difficult to learn the Tamil language, but yet it cannot be called easy, தமிழ்ப்பாஷையைப்படிக்கிறது அரிதல்ல, எளிதென்றுஞ்சொல்லக்கூடாது.

I shall now notice a few other particulars, which may facilitate the translation of our European ideas into Tamil.

67. *Certain Verbs.*

Many of the English prepositions are also used adverbially, and therefore belong to the verb with which they are connected. Verbs so connected have often very different meanings from the simple verb, as, *undertake, understand,* &c. Tamil prepositions are not used in this manner. Prepositions and verbs united together, retain, with very few exceptions, their original meaning, as may be observed from the following specimen.

உட்படுகிறது,	*to get in, to submit.*
மேற்படுகிறது,	*to be over, to excel (intrans.)*
கீழ்ப்படுகிறது,	*to be under, to submit, obey*
புறம்பாகிறது,	*to be out, to be excluded.*
உட்படுத்துகிறது,	*to cause to go under, to subdue.*
மேற்படுத்துகிறது,	*to cause to be over, to exalt.*
கீழ்ப்படுத்துகிறது,	*to cause to be under, to subject.*
புறம்பாக்குகிறது,	*to cause to be out, to exclude.*
உட்கொள்ளுகிறது,	*to take in; to keep.*

The sense of the adverbial prepositions in English ought therefore to be well ascertained, when those verbs are to be rendered in Tamil. Sometimes a simple and sometimes a compound word answers to the English verb and preposition; and consequently will often require a different government from that of the English compound verb, as:

He under-took the business, இத்தக்காரியத்தை யேற்றுக்கொண்டான்.

He sent-for me, என்னையழைப்பித்தான் or என்னை யழைக்கும்படி ஆள் அனுப்பினான்.

He under-valued the piece of ground, அந்த நிலத்தின் விலையைக் குறைத்து மதித்தான்.

He under-stood me; நான்சொன்னது அவனுக்குத்தெரிந்தது.

It was imprinted on wax, அதுமெழுகிலேபதிக்கப்பட்டிருந்தது.

He forbore to upbraid me, அவன் என்னைக்கடிந்துகொள்ளாதபடிக்குப்பொறுத்தான்.

God has forbidden stealing, திருடக்கூடாதென்று பராபரன்கட்டளையிட்டார்.

Throw the parcel by, இந்தக்கட்டைப்பக்கத்திலேவைத்துப்போடு.

Throw the letter out, இந்தக்காயிதத்தை யெடுத்துப்போடு, or தள்ளிப்போடு.

He cast the plate down, பீங்கானைக்கீழேதள்ளினான்.

Be not cast down, விசனப்படாதிரு, or சஞ்சலப்படாதே.

Let us carry-on the business, இந்தத்தொழிலைநாம் செய்யக்கடவோம்.

Let the water in, தண்ணீர் உள்ளேவரப்பண்ணு.

When prepositions coalesce with neuter verbs, the verb usually governs the same case as the preposition, as:

அவருக்குட்பட்டிரு or அவருக்குக்கீழ்ப்பணிந்திரு, *submit to him.*
அவருக்கு மேற்படுவாயாக, *may you exceed him.*
அவருக்குப்பின்செல்லு, *follow him!*

But when the verb is active, both the verb and preposition govern their proper cases, as:

They excluded him from the congregation, அவனைச்சபைக்குப்புறம்பாக்கினார்கள்.

We subdued them, அவர்களை நமக்குக்கீழ்ப்படுத்தினோம்.

They exalted me above others, அவர்கள் என்னை மற்றவர்களுக்கு மேற்படுத்தினார்கள்.

The judge consigned him to punishment, நியாயாதிபதி அவனை ஆக்கினைக்குட்படுத்தினான்.

68. *Parenthesis.*

The *parenthesis,* so frequently used in European languages, cannot be admitted into a Tamil sentence. If parenthetic clauses are to be rendered in Tamil, separate sentences must be made of them, unless they can be otherwise conveniently united with the principal sentence. I shall add a few instances.

Seven or eight (Sozomus makes it ten) months Julian staid at Constantinople, இயூலியானென்னுமிராயன் கொனஸ்தந்தின்புரியிலே ஏழெட்டுமாதமிருந்தான், பத்துமாதமிருந்தானென்று சொசொமுவென்பவன் சொல்லியிருக்கிறான்.

Know then this truth, (enough for man to know,) virtue alone is happiness below, இவ்வுலகத்திலே சன்மார்க்கத்தினாலேமாத்திரம் பாக்கியமுண்டாகுமென்பது மெய்தான், அதையறிந்துகொள். இதுமனிதர் அறிவுக்கு அமைந்தது.

69. *Peculiar expressions.*

In translating from one language into another, it will always be found that there are some peculiar and happy expressions which cannot be rendered exactly. The genius of the Tamil and English languages are so different, that instances of this kind will continually meet and perplex the student. In such cases, it will be proper to weigh the literal meaning of the English word apart from its metaphorical sense; and to consider the precise signification which it bears in the sentence under translation. If this be done, it will be usually found, that there exists some proper Tamil word, which may well supply its place; but if such word be altogether wanting, or if it be antiquated and uncommon, it will be necessary to new-mould the sentence altogether. I subjoin a few instances of such difficulties with their solution, in order to convince the student that the road, though sometimes rough, is not impassable, thus:

Of himself, man is confessedly unequal to his duty, தங்கள் கடமைகளெல்லாவற்றையும் நிறைவேற்றுகிறதற்கு வேண்டியபெலன் மனிதருக்கில்லை, யாவரும் இப்படிச்சொல்லுகிறார்கள், lit: *man is destitute of the strength which is needful to enable him to fulfill his duties, this all admit (or confess.)*

This is a dangerous road, இது மோசங்கொடுக்கிற மார்க்கமாயிருக்கிறது.

This is a very pernicious error, இது மிகுந்த துன்பத்திற்கேதுவானதப்பிதமாயிருக்கின்றது.

It is a frightful place, அதுபயமுண்டாக்குகிற இடம்.

The idea of thankfulness is rendered by தோத்திரம், துதி, which literally means *praise*, thus:

For all blessings be thankful to God, ஆசீர்வாதங்களெல்லாவற்றிற்காகவும் பராபரனைத்தோத்திரஞ்செய்.

Be thankful to men also for their favours, மனிதர்கள்செய்யும் உபகாரங்களுக்காக அவர்களையுந்தோத்திரஞ்செய்.

But when the person himself is addressed, the expression is varied, as:

Sir! I thank you for your great kindness, ஐயா! நீர்பெரியஉபகாரத்தைச்செய்தீரோ நீர் நன்றாயிருப்பீராக, lit: *Sir you have done (me) a great favour, may you be well!*

Note.—That as தோத்திரம், lit: means *praise*, it cannot be used in this place. If it be used உண்டாவதாக, or உண்டாகக்கடவது, must be added, thus: ஐயா! உமக்குத்தோத்திரம் (or புகழ்ச்சி,) உண்டாவதாக.

Observe further, that when I say to a person, நீர் எனக்குப்பெரிய உபகாரத்தைச்செய்தீர், உம்மைப்போல் இரக்கமுள்ளவனொருவனையும் நான்காணவில்லை, this is in fact praising him (தோத்திரம் or புகழ்ச்சி,) when I add: நீர்நன்றாயிருக்கக்கடவீர், உம்முடைய வாழ்நாள் குன்று

திருப்பதாக, or such like, that is வாழ்த்தல் or expressing good wishes towards him. By both expressions I show him my thankfulness. In common life the natives express their thanks by சலாம் ஐயா! which is evidently a foreign word.

It is a curious circumstance that none before Columbus discovered America, கொலும்பெனபவருக்குமுன்னே ஒருவரும் அமெரிக்காக்கண்டத்தைக்காணாதது ஆச்சரியமாயிருக்கின்றது.

It is curiously wrought, இது விசித்திரமாய்ச்செய்யப்பட்டது.

These are curious people, இந்தச்சனங்கள் வேடிக்கைபார்க்கவிரும்புகிறவர்கள்.

He is a curious man, அவன் ஒரு விதமான குணமுள்ளமனிதன்.

The administration of justice in England is good. இங்கிலந்துதேசத்திலே நீதிநன்றாய்ச்செலுத்தப்படுகிறது, or இங்கிலந்துதேசத்திலே துரைகள் நீதியைச்செம்மையாய்ச்செலுத்துகிறார்கள்.

That man's character is not good, அந்த மனிதனுடைய நடக்கை நல்லதல்ல.

Christ Jesus is applied to by his people in the character of an advocate, இயேசுக்கிறிஸ்து தம்முடைய சனங்களுக்குக்காரியக்காராய் அவர்களால் வேண்டிக்கொள்ளப்படுகிறார், or கிறிஸ்துவினுடையசனங்கள் அவரைத்தங்கள் காரியக்காரரென்று அறிந்து அவரை வேண்டிக்கொள்ளுகிறார்கள்.

70. The Tenses.

It is necessary to say a few words more about the tenses. In § LVI. 7, it has been observed that by the help of the verb இருக்கிறது something like the Perfect, pluperfect and the second future tenses, are formed. I now observe further,

1. That the perfect tense in English cannot always be expressed by joining இருக்கிறேன் to a verbal participle, nor is it necessary; the Tamil past tense will often be sufficient. For instance,

I have finished my letter, is well expressed by, நான் காகிதத்தையெழுதிமுடித்தேன். The Tamulian does not say simply காகிதத்தைமுடித்தேன், but inserts எழுதி, *writing*, leaving out என்.

I have seen the person that was recommended to me, நல்லவனென்று அறிவிக்கப்பட்ட மனிதனைக்கண்டேன்.

I have been there this morning and done what was necessary, அங்கேபோய்வேண்டியதைச்செய்தேன்.

He has travelled much this year, இந்த வருஷத்திலே அவன் அநேக இடங்களுக்குப்பிரயாணமாய்ப்போனான்.

2. So also the Pluperfect is often sufficiently expressed by the simple Past, as:

I had finished my letter before he arrived, அவன்வருகிறதற்குமுன்னேகாகிதத்தையெழுதிமுடித்தேன்.

They had not yet gone far, when a tiger sprung forth, அவர்கள் கொஞ்சத்தூரம்போனபின்பு ஒரு புலிபாய்ந்தது.

When he had spoken those words, he lifted up his eyes and said thus, அந்தவார்த்தைகளைச்சொன்னபொழுது அவர் தம்முடைய கண்களையுயர்த்திச்சொன்னதாவது. Here, however, in order to express the finishing of the saying the Tamulian adds முடிக்கிறது to the verbal participle, as, அந்தவார்த்தைகளைச்சொல்லிமுடித்த பொழுது, &c., i. e., *when he had finished saying those words.*

3. The second future tense is frequently well expressed by the simple future; sometimes also by the past, as:

The Parliament will have finished their business, when the King comes to prorogue it, இராசாவானவர் சங்கத்தாரை அனுப்பிவிடும் படிக்குவரும்பொழுது அந்தச்சங்கத்தார் தங்கள் அலுவலை முடித் துவைத்துக்கொண்டிருப்பார்கள். Here வைத்துக்கொண்டு, must be inserted in order to express the finishing of the business, before the King's coming.

When we shall have done all that we were commanded to do, let us say we are unprofitable servants, நமக்குக்கட்டளையிடப்பட் டவைகளெல்லாவற்றையுஞ் செய்தபின்பு நாம் அப்பிரயோசன மான ஊழியக்காரரென்று சொல்லிக்கொள்ளக்கடவோம்.

When you will have done this work, then do that, இந்தவேலையைச் செய்தபின்பு அதைச்செய். Here பின்பு, sufficiently expresses the futurity of the action.

When you will have gone about 4 kadams you will meet with a large stone, நீங்கள் நாலு காததூரம் நடந்தபின்பு ஒரு பெரிய கல்லைக்காண்பீர்கள்.

When you will have become 16 *years of age, then you may think on marrying,* நீ பதினாறு வயதுள்ளவளாயிருக்கும்பொழுது, விவா கத்தைக்குறித்து யோசனைபண்ணலாம் (or உனக்குப்பதினாறுவய து ஆனபொழுது,)

4. When the action is still continuing, the verb should be in the present tense, as:

My brother is writing, என்சகோதரன் எழுதுகிறான்.
She is knitting, அவள் தைக்கிறாள்.

5. In the same case the Imperfect is expressed by the present tense or by adding வருகிறது, to the verbal participle, as:

When my brother was writing, a thunder bolt struck him dead, என் சகோதரன் எழுதுகையில் (or எழுதிவருகையில்) இடி அவ னைக்கொலைசெய்தது.

My sister was playing the piano, when the postman came in, என் சகோதரி இன்னரத்தைவாசித்துவருகையில் (or வாசிக்கையில்) தூதுக்காகிதக்காரன்வந்தான்.

Whilst we were walking, it began to rain, நாங்கள் நடந்துபோ கையில் (or நடந்துவருகையில்) மழைபெய்யத்தொடங்கிற்று

6. The auxiliary *shall be*, added to the present participle, requires the addition of கொண்டிருக்கிறது, in the future to the verbal participle, as :

When you will come to morrow I shall be writing, நீ நாளைக்குவரும்பொழுது நான் எழுதிக்கொண்டிருப்பேன்.
When our friends arrive, we shall be drinking tea, நம்முடைய சிநேகிதர்வந்து சேரும்பொழுது, நாம் தேயிலைத்தண்ணீர்சாப்பிட்டுக்கொண்டிருப்போம.

7. The auxiliary *do, did*, in reply to some one who asserts that we *do not* or *did not* a certain action, is expressed by addinng ஏ to the verbal participle, as :

She doth walk, அவள் நடந்தேவருகிறாள்.
I did eat the rice, நான் சோறுசாப்பிட்டுக்கொண்டேயிருந்தேன்.
We often do go to his house, நாங்கள் அடிக்கடி அவனுடைய வீட்டுக்குப்போயேயிருக்கிறோம.
We did tell her of the danger, அவளுக்கு மோசம்வருமென்று அவளுக்குச்சொல்லியேயிருந்தோம்.
He did speak a lie, அவன் பொய்சொல்லியேயிருந்தான் or அவன் ஒரு பொய்யைச்சொன்னதுண்டு.

71. *The Modes and Participles.*

About the indicative, imperative and infinitive modes, enough has been said in the syntax. But the potential and subjunctive modes and the participles require a little more elucidation.

1. The potential mode in its various forms will be best explained by the following phrases.

It may rain, மழைபெய்யுமே.
He may go or stay, அவன் போகலாம் அல்லது இருக்கலாம்.
I can ride, நான் குதிரையின்மேலேறிப்போவேன் or குதிரையின்மேலேறிப்போக என்னாற்கூடும.
He would walk, அவன் நடக்கமனதாயிருக்கிறான்.
They should learn, அவர்கள் படிக்கவேண்டும, i. e., it is necessary that they learn.
They might have done better, அவர்கள் (இதை) அதிக நன்றாய்ச்செய்யலாமே or செய்வார்களே.
We may always act uprightly, நாம் எப்பொழுதும் உண்மையாய் நடக்கலாமே.
He was generous and would not take revenge, அவன் நல்லவனாகையாற் பழிவாங்கமனதில்லாதிருந்தான்.
We should resist the allurements of vice, துன்மார்க்கத்திற்கு நம்மையிழுக்கிறகாரணங்களோடே எதிர்த்துநிற்கவேண்டும்.
I could formerly indulge myself in things of which I cannot now think but with pain, இப்பொழுது நினைக்குந்தோறும் நோவைக் கொடுக்கிற அநேககாரியங்களை முன்னே சந்தோஷத்தோடே செய்வேன்.

2. On the subjunctive mode, see §§ LVI. and LVII. Here are a few more instances:

I will respect him, though he chide me; அவன் என்னைக்கடிந்துகொண்டாலும் நான் அவனைக்கனஞ்செய்வேன்.

Were he good he would be happy, அவன் நல்லவனாயிருந்தாற் பாக்கியமுள்ளவனாயிருப்பான்.

If he desire it, I will perform the operation, அவன் விரும்பினால், நான் அந்தவேலையைச்செய்வேன்.

If he were present, he was highly culpable, அவன் கூடியிருந்தானானால் அவனுக்கு மிகுந்தகுற்றமுண்டு.

3. The participles are often expressed by the verbal participle, or by the relative participle with a particle, as:

Knowing him to be a mischievous man. I avoided him, அவன் பொல்லாதவனென்று நான் அறிந்து அவனுக்கு விலகினேன், or (அறிந்தபடியினாலே.)

Admired and applauded he became vain, அவன் ஆச்சரியத்தையும் புகழ்ச்சியையும் அடைந்து (or அடைந்ததினாலே) வீணானான்.

Having finished his work, he submitted it for examination, அவன் தன் வேலையைமுடித்தபொழுது (or பின்பு) அதைச்சோதிக்கிறதற்கு ஒப்புக்கொடுத்தான்.

When the participle has a different nominative from that of the sentence, the Tamil relative participle must have, subjoined to it, one or the other of the before mentioned particles, as

The cooly having brought the fire, the cook boiled the rice, கூலிக்காரன் நெருப்பைக்கொண்டுவந்தபின்பு, மடைப்பள்ளிக்காரன் சோறாக்கினான்.

It being still hot, we cannot go up the mountain, வெய்யிலாகையால் (or வெய்யிலானபடியால்) நாம் மலையின்மேலேறக்கூடாது.

The sun having set, we descended from the mountain, சூரியன் அஸ்தமித்தபின்பு நாம் மலையிலிருந்திறங்கினோம்.

The moon rising, we commenced our journey, சந்திரோதயமாகையில் (or சந்திரன் உதயமானபொழுது, or நிலவு தோன்றினபொழுது) நாங்கள் பிரயாணமாய்ப்புறப்பட்டோம்.

The infinitive mode may also be used in these instances, as:

The teacher having delivered various doctrines, the disciples put many questions, குருவானவர்பல உபதேசங்களைச்சொல்லச்சீஷர்கள் அநேகம்வினாவினார்கள்.

When the participles stand as substantives, they must be rendered accordingly, or by a relative participle with a particle, thus:

The generals being attached to the king secured his crown, சேனாதிபதி இராசாவைப்பற்றிக்கொண்டது இராசாவினுடைய முடியைக்காக்கிறதற்கு ஏதுவாயிருந்தது, or பற்றிக்கொண்டதினாலே இராசாவினுடைய கிரீடங்காக்கப்பட்டது.

John's having been writing a long time had wearied him, யோவான்மிகுந்தகாலமிருந்து எழுதினதினாலே ஆயாசமடைந்திருக்கிறான்.

72. *The Personal Pronouns.*

The English *to me*, *my*, is not always required in Tamil, when the other parts of the sentence, naturally imply these pronouns, the Tamulian omits them, as:

Give (me) the book, அந்தப்புத்தகத்தைக்கொடு. Here to add எனக்கு would be stiff. It means none else, if another person is meant, then அவனுக்கு, &c., must be added,

I have finished my letter, நான் காகிதத்தை யெழுதி முடித்தேன். Here என் is not necessary; it is sufficiently implied in நான்.

Thus also the second personal pronoun *thee* in imperative phrases is not necessary in Tamil, as:

Make (thee) an ark, ஒருபேழையைச்செய்வாயாக. Here உனக்கு is unnecessary and stiff; unless *thee* be rendered *for thee* then உனக்காக may be said.

Hew (thee) two tables of stone, இரண்டு கற்பலகைகளைச்செய்.

Go, get (thee) down, நீயிறங்கிப்போ.

Thus also the reciprocal Pronouns *his*, *its*, *it*, are unnecessary, as:

A tree bringeth forth (his) fruit in (his) season, தகுதியானகாலத்திலே விருட்சமானது கனிகளைக்கொடுக்கின்றது, here தன் கனி, தன்காலத்திலே, would not be Tamil.

He broke the stick I gave (him,) நான்கொடுத்த தடியைமுறித்தான். Here தனக்குக்கொடுத்த is unnecessary.

73. *Certain Phrases.*

The dog barks,	நாய் குரைக்கின்றது.
The hog grunts,	காட்டுப்பன்றி உறுமுகின்றது.
The pig squeaks,	பன்றி இரைகின்றது.
The horse neighs,	குதிரை கனைக்கின்றது.
The cock crows,	சேவல் கூவுகின்றது.
The ass brays,	கழுதை கத்துகின்றது or கூப்பிடுகிறது.
The cat purrs,	பூனை உறுமுகின்றது.
The kitten mews,	பூனைக்குட்டி கூப்பிடுகிறது or மியா மியாவென்று கூப்பிடுகிறது.
The bull bellows,	காளை கனைக்கிறது.
The cow lows,	பசு கனைக்கிறது.
The calf bleats,	கன்று கூப்பிடுகிறது.
The sheep bleats,	ஆடு கூப்பிடுகின்றது or கனைக்கிறது.

The lion roars,	சிங்கம் கருச்சிக்கின்றது.
The wolf howls,	கோணாய் ஊளையிடுகின்றது.
The elephant roars,	யானை கருச்சிக்கின்றது.
The tiger growls,	புலி கருச்சிக்கிறது.
The fox barks,	நரி ஊளையிடுகின்றது or கூப்பிடுகிறது.
Mice squeak,	எலிகள் கூப்பிடுகின்றன.
The frog croaks,	தவளை இரைகின்றது or கூப்பிடுகிறது.
The sparrow chirps,	அடைக்கலன்குருவி கூப்பிடுகின்றது.
The swallow twitters,	தகைவில்லான்குருவி கூப்பிடுகின்றது.
The rook caws,	காகங்கத்துகின்றது, கூப்பிடுகிறது.
The pigeon cooes,	புறாக்கூப்பிடுகின்றது.
The turkey gobbles,	வான்கோழி கத்துகின்றது கூப்பிடுகிறது.
The peacock screams,	மயில் கூவுகின்றது.
The beetle (or wasp) hums,	வண்டு இரைகின்றது.
The duck quacks,	தாராக்கூவுகின்றது.
The goose cackles,	வாத்துக்கூவுகின்றது.
Monkies chatter,	குரங்குகள் கூப்பிடுகின்றன.
The owl hoots,	ஆந்தை கூப்பிடுகின்றது.
The screech owl shrieks,	சாகுருவி கூப்பிடுகின்றது.
The snake hisses,	பாம்புஇரைகின்றது.

MISCELLANIA.

74. *The Measures.*

The largest grain-measure is called கலம் or கலன்; and is marked ள.

1. *Kalam is marked,* ௧ள or கள.
2. ——— .... ௨ள.
3. ——— .... ௩ள.
4. ——— .... ௪ள, &c. &c.

A kalam is divided into 12 smaller measures called மரக்கால் or குறுணி, and marked ப;

2.	குறுணி *is called* பதக்கு, *and marked*	ஹு.
3.	.... முக்குறுணி, ...	ங.
4.	.... தூணி, ...	தூ.
5.	.... ஐங்குறுணி, ...	தூப.
6.	.... தூணிப்பதக்கு, ...	தூஹு.
7.	.... எழுகுறுணி, ...	தூங.
8.	.... இருதூணி, ...	௨தூ.
9.	.... இருதூணிக்குறுணி, ...	௨தூப.
10.	.... இருதூணிப்பதக்கு, ...	௨தூஹு.
11.	.... இருதூணிமுக்குறுணி, ...	௨தூங.
12.	.... கலம்	௧ள.

A குறுணி is again divided into 8 parts, called நாழி or படி and marked டெ.

1. நாழி, *is called* ஒருநாழி, *and marked* டெ.
2. ——— .. .. இருநாழி, ... உடெ.
3. ——— .. .. முந்நாழி, ... ௩டெ.
4. ——— .. .. நானாழி, ... ௪டெ.
5. ——— .... ஐந்நாழி, ... ௫டெ.
6. ——— .... அறுநாழி, ... ௬டெ.
7. ——— ...... எழுநாழி, ... ௭டெ.
8. ——— .... குறுணி, ... ப.

A நாழி or படி is divided into 8 smaller parts, one of which is called ஆழாக்கு, marked ஹு.

2. ஆழாக்கு, *is called* உழக்கு, or காற்படி, *marked* ஞ.
3. ——— .. .... உழக்காழாக்கு, ... ஞஹு.
4. ——— ...... உரி or அரைப்படி, ... வீ.
5. ——— .... உரியாழாக்கு, ... வீஹு.
6. ——— ...... மூவுழக்கு or முக்காற்படி, ௩ஞ.
7. ——— ...... மூவுழக்காழாக்கு, ... ௩ஞஹு.
8. ——— ...... நாழி, ... டெ.

A ஆழாக்கு is subdivided into 5 parts called செவிடு (vulg. சுவடு and சோடு,) and marked ஒ.

1. செவிடு, *is called* ஒருச்செவிடு, கஒ.
2. ——— ...... இருச்செவிடு, .. உஒ.
3. ——— ...... முச்செவிடு, .. ௩ஒ.
4. ——— ...... நாற்செவிடு, .. ௪ஒ.
5. ——— ...... ஆழாக்கு, ... ஹு.

Observe that when the term கலம், is united with any of the above subdivisions, the ம் is changed into ன் and ே is added, thus: இருகலனேதூணி முக்கலனேயிருதூணி, &c. &c. In general also கலன is more in use than கலம்.

75. *Days, Months, and Years.*

The day, distinguished from the night, is called பகல், and the night இரா.

A day consisting of 24 hours in called நாள், when considered as a part of the month; but கிழமை, when it is considered as a part of the week; தேய்தி, or தேதி, the day or date of the month, marked உ, it is called திதி, with respect to the age of the moon.—The day is divided into 60 parts, called நாழிகை; (vulg: நாழி, which is equal to our 24 hours; and a நாழிகை is divided into 360 parts called நொடி or நிமிடம். The night, viz., from sun set to sun rise, is divided into 4 parts, called சாமம் or யாமம். Therefore முதலாஞ்சாமம, is from 6 o'clock in the evening till 9 o'clock; இரண்டாஞ்சாமம், from 9 to

12. (Midnight is called நடுச்சாமம்,) மூன்றுஞ்சாமம், is from 12 to 3 o'clock: and நாலாஞ்சாமம், from 3 to 6 o'clock in the morning.

The week is called கிழமை or வாரம். It consists, like ours, of 7 days; which receive their names from the 7 Planets, called கிரகம்; in which the natives include the sun; to which the term கிழமை is added, as:

ஞாயிறு,	*the Sun,*	ஞாயிற்றுக்கிழமை,	*Sunday.*
திங்கள்,	*the Moon,*	திங்கட்கிழமை,	*Monday.*
செவ்வாய்,	*Mars,*	செவ்வாய்க்கிழமை,	*Tuesday.*
புதன்,	*Mercury,*	புதன்கிழமை,	*Wednesday.*
வியாழம்,	*Jupiter,*	வியாழக்கிழமை,	*Thursday.*
வெள்ளி,	*Venus,*	வெள்ளிக்கிழமை,	*Friday.*
சனி,	*Saturn,*	சனிக்கிழமை,	*Saturday.*

The month is called மாதம், or மாசம், and marked ௴. The first month of the year is சித்திரை, corresponding to nearly half of our April and May.

———	வைகாசி,	do.	*May and June.*
———	ஆனி,	do.	*June and July.*
———	ஆடி,	do.	*July and August.*
———	ஆவணி,	do.	*August and September.*
———	புரட்டாசி,	do.	*September and October.*
———	ஐப்பசி (vulg: அற்பசி)	do.	*October and November.*
———	கார்த்திகை,	do.	*November and December.*
———	மார்கழி,	do.	*December and January.*
———	தை,	do.	*January and February.*
———	மாசி,	do.	*February and March.*
———	பங்குனி,	do.	*March and April.*

The year is called வருஷம், or ஆண்டு, and marked ௵ But when the age of a person is meant, வருஷம், is not used, but வயது, or வயசு, or பிராயம்; which literally signifies *age:* For instance, *I am* 10 *years old,* must be rendered by எனக்குப்பத்துவயதாண்டு, not பத்துவருஷம்; but, *I was born* 10 *years ago,* must be expressed by வருஷம், viz., நான் பிறந்துபத்துவருஷமாயிற்று.

The Hindoos have also a kind of cycle, consisting of 60 years, to each of these years, they give a separate name, subjoined is a list of them, with the year according to our reckoning.

1	பிரபவ,	வருஷம்,	1807—8.
2	விபவ,	௵	1808—9.
3	சுக்கில,	,,	1809—10.
4	பிரமோதூத	,,	1810—11.
5	பிரசோற்பத்தி,	,,	1811—12.
6	ஆங்கீரச,	,,	1812—13.
7	ஸ்ரீமுக,	,,	1813—14.

8	பவ,	வருஷம்,	1814—15.
9	யுவ,	ஷ	1815—16.
10	தாது,	,,	1816—17.
11	ஈச்சுர,	,,	1817—18 பவா.
12	வெகுதான்னிய,	,,	1818—19.
13	பிரமாதி,	,,	1819—20 பிர.
14	விக்கிரம,	,,	1820—21.
15	விஷு,	,,	1821—22.
16	சித்திரபானு,	,,	1822—23.
17	சுபானு,	,,	1823—24.
18	தாரண,	,,	1824—25.
19	பார்த்திவ,	,,	1825—26.
20	விய,	,,	1826—27.
21	சருவசித்து,	,,	1827—28.
22	சருவதாரி,	,,	1828—29.
23	விரோதி,	,,	1829—30.
24	விகிருதி,	,,	1830—31.
25	கர,	,,	1831—32.
26	நந்தன,	,,	1832—33.
27	விசய,	,,	1833—34.
28	சய,	,,	1834—35.
29	மன்மத,	,,	1835—36.
30	துன்முகி,	,,	1836—37.
31	ஏவிளம்பி,	,,	1837—38.
32	விளம்பி,	,,	1838—39.
33	விகாரி,	,,	1839—40.
34	சார்வரி,	,,	1840—41.
35	பிலவ,	,,	1841—42.
36	சுபகிருது,	,,	1842—43.
37	சோபகிருது,	,,	1843—44.
38	குரோதி,	,,	1844—45.
39	விசுவாவசு,	,,	1845—46.
40	பராபவ,	,,	1846—47.
41	பிலவங்க,	,,	1847—48.
42	கீலக,	,,	1848—49.
43	சவுமிய,	,,	1849—50.
44	சாதாரண,	,,	1850—51.
45	விரோதிகிருது,	,,	1851—52.
46	பரிதாவி,	,,	1852—53.
47	பிரமாதீச,	,,	1853—54.
48	ஆநந்த,	,,	1854—55.
49	ராட்சத,	,,	1855—56.
50	நள,	,,	1856—57.
51	பிங்கள,	,,	1857—58.
52	காலயுத்தி,	,,	1858—59.
53	சித்தார்த்தி,	,,	1859—60.

54	ரவுத்திரி,	வருஷம்,	1860—61.
55	துன்மதி,	ஷை	1861—62.
56	துந்துமி,	,,	1862—63.
57	ருத்திரோத்காரி,	,,	1863—64.
58	இரத்தாட்சி,	,,	1864—65.
59	குரோதன,	,,	1865—66.
60	அட்சய,	,,	1866—67.

They use these names chiefly in legal transactions; but in family concerns, which are for perpetuity, as well as in the inscriptions of temples, they join to the name of the year, the year of the æra of Sālivāɹana and that of the 4th age. About the Hindoo ages I shall give an account presently.

As for the epoch of Sālivāhana (சாலிவாகனம்,) it is the most memorable among the Hindoos, from which they reckon their years. This epoch dates from the death of Sālivāhana, king of Visnagar, which happened in the 3179th year of the 4th age, and corresponds with the 78th year of the Christian æra, சாலிவாகனம், means the vehicle of the cross, or crossbearer. Who can help thinking that this alludes to our Lord Jesus Christ? Many circumstance coincide to make us believe that the whole account of சாலிவாகனம் is a perversion of the history of Christ. See more on this subject in the Asiatic Researches, vol.

Moreover the Hindoos make the duration of the world to be 4 ages, called யுகம், each of which consists of a large number of years.

The first யுகம், is called கிரேதாயுகம், i. e., the age of innocence; the golden age of the Greeks. It consisted of 1,728,000 years; in it the bull of justice stood on 4 legs. The second யுகம், is called திரேதாயுகம், or the silver age; consisting of 1,296,000 years. It was inferior to the former; and the bull stood on three legs. The third யுகம், is called துவாபரயுகம் or the brazen age; consisting of 864,000 years. It was still worse, and the bull had only two legs. The fourth யுகம், is called கலியுகம், i. e., the age of strife and misery; the iron age; consisting of 432,000 years. This is the age in which we now live; and the bull is left standing on only one leg; which allegory aptly represents the tottering state of virtue, and the prevalence of sin.

In the kanda puranum, we are informed of the manner in which these ages have been calculated. It is thus:

The time that is necessary for the middle finger resting on the thumb, to be taken off quickly, is one instant, equal to the twinkling of an eye; this time is called மாத்திரை or கண்ணிமை.

2.	மாத்திரை,	*make*	1 நிப்புரம்.
10.	நிப்புரம்,		1 கணம்.
12.	கணம்,		1 விநாடி.
60.	விநாடி,		1 நாழிகை.
7.	நாழிகை,		1 சாமம், or *the 8th part of a day.*
8.	சாமம்,		1 நாள், or *day.*
15.	நாள்,		1 பக்கம், or *half a month.*

2.	பக்கம்,	*make*	1 மாதம், or *a month.*
12.	மாதம்,		1 வருஷம், or *a year.*

100 வருஷம் is the common term of the life of man.

These 100 years multiplied by 360 (because each year contains so many days) make 36,000. This number multiplied by 6, on account of the 6 subdivisions, மாத்திரை, க்ஷிப்ரம் &c. makes 216,000 which is the basis of the calculations, respecting the durations of the 4 ages. The calculation then proceeds thus :

216,000 multiplied by 2, in honour of the quality of virtue, and of vice, gives the number of 432,000, which expresses the duration of the கலியுகம், or fourth age in which we now live.

216,000 multiplied by 4 in honour of the 4 vedams makes 864,000, which is the number of years of the த்வாபரயுகம், or third age.

216,000 multiplied by 6 in honour of the six Shastrams, makes 1,296,000, which is the number of the years of the திரேதயுகம், or second age, and lastly,

216,000 multiplied by 8 in honour of the eight points of the compass, produces 1,728,000, being the number of years of the கிரேதயுகம், or first age.

The united years of these 4 ages make the number of 4,320,000 called சதுராயுகம், i. e., the 4 ages of the world.

2000 சதுராயுகம், (i. e. 8,640,000,000,) make 1 day, and 1 night of Brahma, or 24 of his hours ; 60,000, சதுராயுகம், are one of his months; 12 such months, one of his years, and 100 such years are the term of his life.

The duration of the life of Brahma makes only 1 day of Vishtnoo's existence ; 30 of such days form one of his months, and 12 such months, one of his years, after 100 such years, he will die, and then Siven alone will exist.

This calculation is certainly ingenious ; but at once points out what we have to think of the boasted antiquity of the Hindoos. It does not rest on any history whatever, and is a mere invention of the brain.

The Bramins prepare annually an almanac, which is called பஞ்சாங்கம், a sanscrit word, composed of பஞ்ச, i. e., five, and அங்கம், a member : It is so called, because it contains five points of information, viz. 1. It shows the திதி, the day according to the age of the moon ; 2. வாரம், i. e., the day of the week. 3. நட்சத்திரம், i. e., the constellation in which the moon enters every day, 4. யோகம், i. e. the good and bad days ; 5. கரணம், divination, augury.

76. *The Points of the Compass and Signs of the Zodiac.*

A region, or point in the horizon is called திசை or திக்கு. The 4 chief points are:

கிழக்கு or கீழ்திசை or கீழைத்திசை,	*the East.*
மேற்கு or மேற்றிசை or மேலைத்திசை,	*the West.*
தெற்கு or தென்றிசை,	*the South.*
வடக்கு or வடதிசை,	*the North.*

The 4 intervening angles are called மூலை, viz.

தென்கிழக்கு,	*between*	*East and South.*
தென்மேற்கு,		*South and West.*
வடமேற்கு,		*West and North.*
வடகிழக்கு,		*North and East.*

In each of these 8 points, the Hindoos imagine a God to reside, whom they call திக்குப்பாலகர், the keepers or guardians of the points. They are these:

இந்திரன்,	*the chief of the gods, in the East.*
அக்கினி,	*the god of fire, in S. E.*
இயமன்,	*the god of death, in the South.*
நிருதி,	*a king whom they esteem the most potent and liberal, in S. W.*
வருணன்,	*the God of the waters, in the West.*
வாயு,	*the God of the winds, N. W.*
குபேரன்,	*the God of riches, in the North.*
ஈசானன்,	*Siven himself, in N. E.*
ஈசானம்,	*is one of the fire faces of Siven:*

The above terms, are also used as adjectives, thus:

கீழ்தேசம், *the eastern country* or *region.*
கீழ்கடல், *the eastern sea.*
மேல்தேசம் or மேற்றேசம் or மேலைத்தேசம், *the western country.**
மேல்கடல் or மேலைக்கடல், *the western Sea.**
தென்றேசம், *the southern country.*
தென்கடல், *the south sea.*
வடதேசம், *the north country.*
வடகடல், *the north sea.*
கீழ்ப்பக்கம், *the east side.*
மேல்பக்கம் or மேலைப்பக்கம், *west side**
தென்பக்கம் *south side*
வடபக்கம், *north side*

---

* If these words be written மேற்றேசம், it will mean *the upper country*; மேற்கடல் *the upper sea*; மேற்பக்கம் *the upper side.*

The signs of the Zodiac are called இராசி. Their names are these:

மேஷம் or மேடம்,	*Aries,*	*in March.*
ரிஷபம் or இடபம்,	*Taurus,*	*in April.*
மிதுனம்,	*Gemini,*	*in May.*
கற்கடகம்,	*Cancer,*	*in June.*
சிங்கம்,	*Leo,*	*in July.*
கன்னி,	*Virgo,*	*in August.*
துலாம்,	*Libra,*	*in September.*
விருச்சிகம்,	*Scorpio,*	*in October.*
தனுசு,	*Sagittarius,*	*in November.*
மகரம்,	*Capricornus,*	*in December.*
கும்பம்,	*Aquarius,*	*in January.*
மீனம்,	*Pisces,*	*in February.*

77. *Terms of Consanguinity.*

The Tamulian's call their relationship முறை or உறவு; for instance, உங்களுக்குள்ளே முறையென்ன, *of what relation are you (to each other)?* Particulars are these

The father is called, தகப்பன், அப்பன், தந்தை, or பிதா.
The father's brothers, do do.
But *the elder brother of the father,* பெரியப்பன்.
—— *younger* do. சிற்றப்பன்.
The mother, தாய், ஆயி, அம்மாள், ஆய்ச்சி, அம்மை.
The mother's sister, do. do.
But *the mother's elder sister,* பெரியஆயி.
do. *younger,* do. சின்னஆயி.
The grand father, both on the father and mother side, பாட்டன்.
The grand mother, both on the father and mother's side, பாட்டி; பேர்த்தி.
The father's sister
The mother of one's wife or *husband.* } அத்தை.
The brother of the mother, அம்மான், தாய்மாமன்.
Brothers and sisters, கூடப்பிறந்தவர்கள் or சகோதரர்கள்.
The elder brother (of the same father and mother) அண்ணன், தமையன்.
The younger brother of do. தம்பி.
The elder sister of do. அக்காள் or தமக்கை.
The younger sister (of the same father and mother,) தங்கச்சி, or தங்கை.
A man, புருடன், மனிதன், ஆண்சாதி.
A woman, ஸ்திரி, பெண், பெண்சாதி.
The husband, நாயகன், கணவன், மணவாளன், கொழுநன், பருத்தா, or பத்தா, அகம்புடையான், (vulg: ஆம்புடையான்,) &c.
The wife, பெண்டாட்டி, மனைவி, நாயகி, தாரம்.

A brother in law, மைத்துனன், (vulg: மச்சினன், மச்சான்,) it means also a cousin who is the mother's brother's son or the father's sister's son.

A sister in law, மைத்துனி, (vulg: மச்சினி, மச்சினிச்சி,) also the wife's younger sister, or the younger brother's wife; also a cousin who is the mother's brother's daughter, or the father's sister's daughter.

The wife's elder sister, கொழுந்தி.
The husband's brother, கொழுந்தன்.
The husband's sister நாத்தனூர்.
Persons who have married two sisters call each other, சகலன்.
Persons who have married two brothers, are called, ஓப்பிடியார், ஓரகத்திமார்.
Several women, married to one man, call each other, சக்களத்தி;
A father in law, மாமன்,
A mother in law, மாமி.
A son in law, மருமகன்; also the son of a man's sister or of a woman's brother.
A daughter in law, மருமகள், also the daughter of a man's sister, or of a woman's brother.
A grandson, பேரன், பேரப்பிள்ளை.
A granddaughter, பேர்த்தி, also a sister's grand son.
A grandson's son, பூட்டன்.
A grandson's daughter, பூட்டி.

Note.—That the Tamulians often add ஆர், as an honorific to these several terms, as:

தகப்பனார், தாயார், மாமனார், மாமியார், தமையனார், தமக்கையார். &c., மார், or மார்கள், is also added to form the Plural, as: மாமன்மார்கள், பேரனமார்கள், பேர்த்திமார்கள், &c.

78. *On Figures.*

The natives often employ figurative language, especially in poetry; where they sometimes run into extravagance. I shall state a few instances of each particular figure with notes.

1. The figure, called, *metaphor*, (உருவகம்,) *e. g.*,
A good Minister is the pillar of a state நல்லமந்திரியானவன் இராச்சியத்தின் தூண், (or ஸ்தம்பம்.) Were we to say தூணையிருக்கிறான், we make a simile; and lessen the beauty of the sentence.

I will be unto her a wall of fire round about, நான் அவளைச்சுற்றி அக்கினிக்கோட்டையாயிருப்பேன், the finite verb here is necessary on account of அவளைச்சுற்றி. If it be expressed with the dative, it is not necessary, as: நான் அவளுக்கு அக்கினிக்கோட்டை, which does not define any time, but only the bare fact.
Thy word is a lamp to my feet, and a light to my path, lit: உம்முடைய வசனம் என்பாதத்துக்குத்தீவெட்டியுமாய் என்வழிக்குப்

பிரகாசமுமாயிருக்கிறது, this is not good in Tamul. The Tamulian questions the propriety of giving a தீவெட்டி, to the பாதம், *because the foot cannot see*, the தீவெட்டி, *is for the eye*, Besides no lamp is without light; but in this sentence the light is separated from the lamp, and both clauses are united as if the lamp and the light were two different things. It is better therefore to express it thus: உமது திருவசனம் என்பாதவழிக்குப்பிரகாசங்கொடுக்கிறதீவெட்டி, or make two sentences of it thus: நான் செம்மையாய்நடக்கிறதற்கு உமதுவசனம் ஒருதீவெட்டி. என் பாதவழிக்கு அது பிரகாசம்.

There is not a single view of human nature, which is not sufficient to extinguish the seeds of pride, lit: மனிதசுபாவத்தினுடைய நோக்கங்களிலொன்றிலும் அகந்தையினுடைய விதைகளை அவிக்கிறதற்குப்போதாததல்ல; this is unintelligible, the English also is improper, making two inconsistent metaphors meet on one object; for a *view* does not *extinguish;* nor are *seeds* to be *extinguished.* It ought to be: அகந்தையாகிய விதைகளையழிக்கிறதற்கு மனிதசுபாவத்தை யாராய்கிற நோக்கங்களிலொன்றே போதும். The affirmative form போதும், is better here than போதாததல்ல.

The Tamulians have many instances of this figure, thus:

A strong man is called காளை, a bull, as: அதோகாளைவருகிறான் *behold! the bull comes* (meaning the mighty man.) It is an honorable term.

பழியஞ்சான்வாழும் பகடு, i. e., பழிக்கு அஞ்சாதபடிக்கு வாழுகிறபகடு *an ox that lives fearless of sin;* meaning a man that does so.

பான்மொழி, *a word as sweet as milk*, பான் is பால்.

தேன் மொழி, *a word as sweet as honey.*

2. Allegory and simile (called உவமை,) is very common in Tamil. The native books are full of fables, parables, and comparisons. They make animals and inanimate objects, speak and act like men. I shall adduce only a few instances of the simile, as:

The actions of Princes are like those great rivers, the course of which every one beholds, but their springs have been seen by few, lit: இராசாக்களுடைய செய்கைகள் பெரிய ஆறுகளைப்போலிருக்கின்றன. அவைகளின் ஓட்டத்தை யாவரும் பார்க்கிறார்கள். அவைகளின் ஊற்றுச்சிலருக்குமாத்திரந் தோன்றுகின்றது; but it is better to invert the sentence thus: பெரிய ஆறுகளின் ஓட்டத்தை யாவரும்பார்க்கிறார்கள். அவற்றின் ஊற்றுச்சிலருக்குமாத்திரந்தெரியும்: இப்படியே இராசாக்களுடையசெய்கைகளுமிருக்கின்றன.

As the mountains are round about Jerusalem, so the Lord is round about his people, மலைகள் எருசலேமைச்சூழ்ந்திருக்கிறதுபோலப் பராபரன் தம்முடைய சனங்களைச்சூழ்ந்திருக்கிறார்.

As wax would not be adequate to the purpose of signature, if it

M 2

had not the power to retain as well as to receive the impression, the same holds of the soul, with respect to sense and imagination. Sense is its receptive power; imagination its retentive. Had it sense without imagination, it would not be as wax but as water; where though all impressions are instantly made, yet as soon as they are made, they are instantly lost, மெழுகானது முத்திரையைப் பெறுதலன்றி, அதைப்பற்றிக்கொள்ளுந் தன்மையுமுள்ளதாயிராவிட்டால், முத்திரைக்குத் தகுதியாயிருக்கமாட்டாது. அதுபோல ஆத்துமா அறிவும் யோசனையுமுடையதாயிருக்கவேண்டும். அறிவானது ஒன்றைப்பெறுதற்கான கருவி. யோசனையானது அதைப்பற்றிக்கொள்ளுதற்கான கருவி. யோசனையாகிய கருவியின்றி அறிவாகிய கருவி மாத்திரமுடையதானால் ஆத்துமா மெழுகைப்போலல்லச் சலத்தைப்போலிருக்கும். எப்படியெனிற் சலத்திலே எதையாகிலுஞ் சீக்கிரமாய்ப்பதிக்கலாம்: பதித்தவுடனே அதுதோன்றாமற்போம்.

A few instances from the Tamil.

அரிமந்திரம்புகுத்தாலானைமருப்பும்,
பெருகொளியமுத்தும்பெறலாம்,
நரிநுழையில்,
வாலுஞ்சிறியமறியெலும்புங்கத்தவத்தின்
றோலுமல்லால்வேறுண்டோசொல்.

In plain Tamil:

சிங்கத்தினுடைய குகையிற்பிரவேசித்தால் ஆனையின் மருப்பையும் மிகவும் பிரகாசிக்கிற முத்துக்களையும் பெறலாம். நரியினுடைய நுழையிலே சிறியமறியின் வாலும் எலும்புங் கழுதையினுடைய தோலுமேயன்றி வேறுண்டோ சொல்லு, i. e. "*If thou enter the Lion's den, thou wilt obtain ivory and brightly shining pearls; but, in the hole of a fox, tell! whether thou wilt find there any thing else but (ass's) tails, colt's bones, and ass's skin?*" The moral drawn from this is: Associating with the noble and good, thou wilt enrich thy body and mind, but conversation with the mean and wicked yields nothing but trash. அரி, *is Lion;* மந்திரம, *a mansion,* அரி மந்திரம் stands for அரியினுடையமந்திரத்தில் or குகையில்; ஆனைமருப்பு, for ஆனையினுடைய மருப்பு, *the horn of an Elephant,* i. e., ivory; பெருகொளிய, is பெருகு, and ஒளிய; நரிநுழை, is நரியினுடையநுழை, *the hole of a fox.* சிறிய மறி, for மறியினுடைய, *the colt of an ass;* கத்தவம், *an ass;* அல்லால், is for அல்லாமல்.

புலிபசித்தாற் புல்லைத்தின்னுமா, *If the tyger be hungry, will he eat grass?* i. e., will a great man when he is in distress go (for relief) to a mean person?

3. Metonomy, or the cause for the effect, &c. Tamulians use this figure, but not to the extent as in English; for instance they will say:

திருநெல்வேலிமுழுவதும் இங்கேவந்திருக்கிறது, *All Tinnevelly is come together here.*

வானத்துக்கு (or பரமண்டலத்திற்கு) விரோதமாகக்குற்றஞ் செய்தேன், *I have sinned against heaven.*

பானைபொங்கிற்று, *Has the pot boiled?*

இந்தப்பானை எத்தனைபடியரிசிபொங்கும், *how many measures of rice will this pot boil?*

செங்கோலைப்பிடித்தார் *He assumed the sceptre.*

But they could not use the following speeches :

They read Milton, lit : அவர்கள் மில்த்தோனை வாசிக்கிறார்கள், *they will say* மில்த்தோன் செய்யுளைவாசிக்கிறார்கள், the Poetry of Milton.

Grey hairs should be respected, lit : நரைமயிரைக்கனஞ்செய்ய வேண்டும், they say மூத்தோரை or விருத்தாப்பியரைக்கனஞ்செய்யவேண்டும்.

4. Synecdoche, where the whole is put for a part, or a part for the whole. The Tamulians use this figure also, but not in all cases like in English, thus :

A fleet of twenty sail, இருபதுபாயுள்ள கப்பற்கூட்டம்; they say better, இருபதுகப்பலுள்ள கூட்டம்.

How many hands are there? எத்தனைகையுண்டு, they rather say எத்தனைவேலைக்காரருண்டு.

But the following phrases are common.

ஊரிலே எத்தனைதலைக்கட்டு, lit : *how many heads (or pieces of heads) are in the village?* i. e., how many persons are there.

தலை யெண்ணிச்சம்பளத்தைக்கொடு, lit : *count the heads* (i. e. the persons) *and give (them) their wages.*

வெண்டிரைசூழ்ஞாலம், *the earth surrounded by the white wave;* where திரை, *the wave*, is for சமுத்திரம், *the sea*, சூழ is the root for சூழ்ந்த.

வெற்றிலை நட்டான், *he planted the beetle leaf* (instead of the branch.)

அறுபதம்முரலும், *the six feet make a noise*, அறுபதம், i. e. ஆறுபாதம், 6 feet instead, வண்டு, the wasp with 6 feet.

விளக்குமுறிந்தது, *the light burst ;* for விளக்குத்தண்டு, *the candle-stick*.

நெஞ்சுநொந்தது, *the mind pained ; for* மார்பு, *the chest.*

5. Personification or Prosopopocia is frequent. The Tamulian will well understand, for instance, the following.

The ground thirsts for rain, நிலம் மழையின்மேல்த்தாகமாயிருக்கிறது.

The earth smiles with plenty, பூமி சம்பூரணத்தினாலே நகைக்கின்றது, The Tamulian would not say, சம்பூரணத்தோடே.

Ambition is restless, இறுமாப்பு அமைதலில்லாமலிருக்கிறது.

When Israel went out of Egypt, the sea saw it and fled ; Jordan was driven back ; the mountains skipped like rams, and the little hills like lambs. What ailed thee, O thou sea! that thou fleddest? Thou Jordan, that thou wast driven back? ye mountains, that ye skipped like rams, and ye hills like lambs? Tremble, thou earth! at the presence of the Lord, கடலானது இஸ்ரவேலர் எகிப்பத்தை விட்டுப்புறப்படுகிறதைக்கண்டு விலகிப் போயிற்று. யோர்தான்பின் தள்ளப்பட்டது. மலைகள்கிடாய்களைப் போலவுங் குன்றுகள் ஆட்டுக்குட்டிகளைப்போலவுங்குதித்தன. ஓ, கடலே, நீ விலகிப்போகிறதற்கும் ஓ யோர்தானே, நீ பின்னாகத் தள்ளப்படுகிறதற்கும் ஓ, மலைகளே, நீங்கள் கிடாய்களைப்போலவுங் குன்றுகளே நீங்கள் ஆட்டுக்குட்டிகளைப்போலவுங் குதிக்கிறதற்கும உங்களுக்கென்னகேடுவந்தது. ஓ, பூமியே, நீ பராபரனுடைய சன்னிதிக்குமுன்பாக நடுங்கு..

Here are some purely Tamil instances:

பூ நகைக்கிறது, *the flower laughs.*
பள்ளிக்கூடம் முழங்குகிறது, *the school roars,* i. e., the boys in the school, &c.
உம்முடைய மனமேசொல்லும், *thy own mind will tell.*
முல்லைகள் முறுவலித்துக்காட்டின, *the Mullei-shrub laughs and points out* (viz. the coming of rain.)
அரசனாணையெங்குஞ்செல்லும், *the king's command runs every where* அரசன், for அரசனுடைய.
இவ்வழி பாளயங்கோட்டைக்குப்போகின்றது, *this road goes to Palamcottah.*

6. Apostrophe is likewise considered elegant in Tamul, thus:

Death is swallowed up in victory. O death! where is thy sting? O grave! where is thy victory, செயத்தினால் மரணம் விழுங்கப்பட்டது. ஓ, மரணமே உன் கூர்மையெங்கே. ஓ, பாதாளமே உன் செயமெங்கே.

O thou sword of the Lord! how long will it be ere thou be quiet? put thyself up into thy scabbard, rest and be still! How can it be quiet, seeing the Lord hath given it a charge against Ashkalon, and against the sea shore, ஓ, கருத்தாவினுடைய கட்கமே, நீ அமைதலடைகிறதற்கு எத்தனை காலஞ்செல்லும். உன் உறையிற் பிரவேசித்து இளைப்பாறிச்சும்மாவிரு : கருத்தர் அஸ்கலோனுக்குங் கடலோரத்திற்கும் விரோதமாக அதற்குக்கட்டளை கொடுத்தபடியினாலே எப்படியது அமைதலாயிருக்கும். This is as in English except the clause *put thyself up,* &c. The Tamulian does not say so, but simply, *go into thy scabbard.*

A few Tamil instances:

நீலமஞ்சேகேட்டி, *Hear! O thou dark blue cloud!* கேட்டி, is for கேளதி, the poetical form of the imperative second person.
வாராயமடநெஞ்சே, *O thou stuped mind! come away!* viz., a poet addresses his own mind to call it off from roving abroad. வாராய், is the same as வா, the imperative.

வருதிபெயர்திவருந்துதிதுஞ்சாய்,
பொருதிபுலம்புதிநீயும்,
கருதுங்கால்,
பண்டினையல்லையாற்பாழித்தோடகோதையைக்,
கண்டனையோவாழிகடல்.

In plain Tamul: ஓ, வாழ்வுடையகடலே, நீயும்வருகிறாய், போகிறாய், வருந்துகிறாய், தூங்காமலிருக்கிறாய், பொருதுகிறாய், புலம்புகிறாய், உன்னை நினைக்கிறபொழுது, நீ முன்னைப்போலல்லவே. பலத்த தோளையுடைய கோதையைக்கண்டாயோ, translated thus:

O prosperous Ocean! thou also (like myself) comest and goest, thou art troubled, thou dost not sleep; thou beatest (the shore) and roarest, when (I) consider (thee) thou art not as formerly. Hast thou (perhaps) seen the strong shouldered king of Maleyalam? In the above verse the form வருதி, பெயர்தி, &c. is the poetical form of the second person of the present tense; பொருதுகிறது, is மோதுகிறது; கருதுங்கால், is கருதுகிறபொழுது; பண்டினை, is the same as முன்னை, and அல்லை, is அல்ல. The affix ஆல், is merely expletive; பாழி, is பலத்த; தோட், is தோள், *the shoulder*; கோதை, is சேரன், *the King of Maleyalam*; கண்டனை is the second person of the past tense, the same as கண்டாய், வாழி, is வாழ்வுடைய; கடல் is here for கடலே, the vocative.

7. Antithesis. The Tamul well admits all the various modes of contrast or opposition of two objects, as in English, thus:

If you wish to enrich a person, study not to increase his stores, but to diminish his desires, நீர் ஒருவனை ஐசுவரியவானாக்க விரும்பினால்," அவனுடைய களஞ்சியத்தை நிரப்பவல்ல, அவனுடைய விருப்பத்தைக்குறைக்கப்பிரயாசப்படுவீராக.

If you regulate your desires according to the standard of nature, you will never be poor; if according to the standard of opinion, you will never be rich, நீங்கள் சுபாவப்படி உங்கள் ஆசைகளுக்கு இடங்கொடுத்தால் ஒருக்காலும் எளிமையுள்ளவர்களாகமாட்டீர்கள். உலகவழக்கத்தின்படி அவைகளுக்கு இடங்கொடுத்தால், ஒருக்காலும் ஐசுவரியவான்களாகமாட்டீர்கள்.

Howard has visited all Europe, not to survey the sumptuousness of palaces, or the stateliness of temples; not to make accurate measurements of the remains of ancient grandeur, nor to form a scale of the curiosity of modern art, not to collect medals, or collate manuscripts; but to dive into the depth of dungeons, to plunge into the infection of hospitals; to survey the mansions of sorrow and pain; to take the gauge and dimensions of misery, depression, and contempt; to remember the forgotten; to attend to the neglected; to visit the forsaken, and compare and collate the distresses of all men in all countries, ஒளவார்த்தென்பவர் இராசாக்களினுடைய அரண்களின் கோலத்தையுங் கோயில்களின் பெருமையையும் ஆராயவும் பூர்வீகத்தில் மகிமையாய்ச்செய்யப்பட்டுப் பாழாய்க் கிடக்கிற மாளிகைகளைத்திட்ட

மாய் அளக்கவும் இக்காலத்தில் வழங்குகிற விசித்திரமான தொழில்களுக்கு ஓரளவுகோலைச்செய்யவும் பூர்வீகக்காசுக்களைச்சேர்க்கவும் பூர்வீக கையெழுத்துக்களை ஒன்றோடொன்று ஒத்துப்பார்க்கவும் விரும்பாமற், குற்றவாளிகளை அடைக்கப்பட்ட குகைகளிற் பிரவேசிக்கவும் நோவாளிகளுடைய துற்கந்தமுள்ள வீடுகளுக்குட் புகவுஞ் சஞ்சலமும் நோவும் நிறைந்த குடில்களை நோக்கவும் நிற்பாக்கியம் ஒடுக்கம் நிர்ரைத யிவைகளின் அளவைப்பார்க்கவும் மறக்கப்பட்டவர்களை நினைக்கவும் ஒத்தாசையில்லாதவர்களுக்கு உதவிசெய்யவுங் கைவிடப்பட்டவர்களைச்சந்திக்கவுஞ் சகலதேசங்களிலுமுள்ள மனிதர் யாவருக்குமுள்ள உபத்திரவங்களை நிதானிக்கவுமே விரும்பி, ஐரோப்பாகண்டமெங்கும் பிரயாணமாய்ப்போனார்.

8. **Hyperbole is very common in India, thus:**

As swift as the wind, காற்றுப்போல விரைவாய்.
I told it him a thousand times, நான் ஆயிரந்தரம் அதையவனுக்குச்சொன்னேன்.

I saw their chief, tall as a rock, his spear, the blasted fir; his shield the rising moon; he sat on the shore like a cloud of mist on the hill, கல்மலைபோலப் பெரியவனாகிய அவர்களுடைய அதிபதியைக்கண்டேன் அவனுடைய ஈட்டி அடியற்றுவிழுந்த பிர்மரம்போலவும் அவனுடைய கேடகம் உதயமாகிற சந்திரனைப் போலவுமிருந்தன. மலையின்மேலுள்ள பனிமேகம்போலக்கரையில் உளுக்கார்ந்தான.

Tamil instances:

வாயுவேகமாய்ச்செல்லுகிறாய், *thou runnest as swift as the wind.*
அளவிறந்தபணஞ் செலவழித்தான், *he spent immense money.*

9. **Vision, when in animated and warm composition, instead of relating something that is past, we use the present tense, and describe it as actually passing before our eyes. The Tamulians use this likewise. Thus:**

I behold this city, the ornament of the earth, and the capital of all nations, suddenly involved in one conflagration. I see before me, the slaughtered heaps of citizens lying unburied in the midst of their ruined country. The furious countenance of Céthegus rises to my view, while with a savage joy, he is triumphing in your miseries, பூமியின் ஆபரணமுமாய்ச்சனக்கூட்டங்களெல்லாருடைய நகரமுமாயிருக்கிற இந்தப்பட்டினஞ் சடுதியில் ஒரேசுவாலையாய் எரிகிறதையும் வெட்டப்பட்டுக்குவியல் குவியலாகக்கிடக்கிற குடிகள் பாழாக்கப்பட்ட தங்கள் நிலங்களில் அடக்கம் பண்ணப்படாமற் கிடக்கிறதையும புலிமுகமுள்ள செத்தேகுசென்பவன் துஷ்டருக்குரிய சந்தோஷத்தோடே உங்கள் உபத்திரவங்களினாலே இறுமாப்பைப் பாராட்டிக்கொண்டிருக்கிறதையுங் காண்கிறேன்.

10. **Interrogation, when it is not a simple question, but an expression of the strongest confidence of the truth of our sentiment, and an**

appeal to our hearers for the impossibility of the contrary is likewise agreeable to the Tamil, thus:

> *Hath God said it? and shall he not do it?* பராபரன் சொல்லி யிருக்கச்செய்யாமலிருப்பாரா.
>
> *Is he a man that he should lie?* அவர் பொய்சொல்லுகிறதற்கு ஒரு மனுஷனா.
>
> *How long will you, Cataline, abuse our patience? Do you not perceive that your designs are discovered?* ஓ, கத்தலினா, எங்கள் பொறுமையை எதுவரைக்குஞ் சோதிப்பீர். உம்முடைய யோசனைகள் வெளிப்பட்டிருக்கிறதை யறியவில்லையா.

11. Exclamations are likewise in use. For instance:

> *Woe is me that I sojourn in Mesech, that I dwell in the tents of Kedar!* ஐயோ நான் மெசேக்கிற்சஞ்சரித்துக் கேதாரிலுள்ள கூடாரங்களில் வாசமாயிருக்கிறதினாலே யெனக்கு வேதனையுண்டு. Only the Tamulian would like to put the clause with வாசமாயிருக்கிறது before that of சஞ்சரிக்கிறது, as more natural.
>
> *O that my head were waters, and mine eyes a fountain of tears, that I might weep day and night for the slain of the daughters of my people!* என் சனங்களில் வெட்டப்பட்டவர்களுக்காக நான் இரவும் பகலும் அழுதுகொள்ளும்படிக்கு என் தலை குளமுமாய் என் கண்கள் நீரூற்றுமாயிருந்தால் நலமாயிருக்கும்.

12. Irony (குறிப்பு) is not uncommon in Tamul, thus:

> *You have taken great care indeed,* மெய்யாய் நீ நல்ல காவலைச் செய்தாய.
>
> *You are a very clever man!* நீ பலத்த கெட்டிக்காரனாயிருக்கிறாய்.
>
> *Cry aloud, for he is a god; either he is talking, or he is on a journey, or peradventure he sleepeth,* நன்றாய்ச் சத்தமிடுங்கள். அவர் தேவனல்லவா, ஒருவேளை சம்பாஷணை பண்ணுவார் அல்லது பிரயாணமாய்ப்போவார், அல்லது தூங்குவார்.

Here follow a few Tamul instances from poetry.

> நீயிர்பெரிதுமறிதிர i. e., நீர்மிகவும் அறிந்திருக்கிறீர், *you know a great deal;* meaning *you know nothing.* நீயிர், is நீர், அறிதிர், is a poetical form of the past tense; The same as அறிந்தீர்.
>
> கற்கறித்துநன்கட்டாய், i. e., having bitten a stone (in the rice) he addresses the cook: *thou hast boiled* (the rice) *well.* நன்கு, *good*, and அடுகிறது, *to boil, to cook.*

பல்சான்றீரோபல்சான்றீரே,
கயல்முள்ளன்ன நரைமுதிர் திரைகவுட்,
பயனில்மூப்பிற்பல்சான்றீரே.

In plain Tamul; ஓ, பல அறிவுகளையடைந்தவரே, பல அறிவுகளையடைந்தவரே, மீனுடைய முள்ளைப்போன்ற நரையையும் முதிர்ந்த திரையுள்ள கவுளையுமுடைய பலனில்லாத விருத்தாப்பியத்திலே பல அறிவுகளையடைந்தவரே, *O thou man of knowledge! Oh thou man of knowledge! wise in age which is fruitless, only with gray hair like the fins of fishes and with entirely wrinkled cheeks!* சான்று, is அறிவு, சான்றோர், is அறிவுடையவர்கள்; சான்றீரே, has the termination of the second person, with the sign of the vocative. See § XXXVII. கயல், is மீன் *a fish*; முள், *is a thorn, the fins of a fish*; அன்ன, is a comparing particle, like போன்ற; முதிர், is the root; for முதிர்ந்த, i. e., *full grown, entire*; திரை, *wrinkles*; கவுள், *the cheek*; பயனில், is for பயனில்லாத, பலனில்லாத; மூப்பு, *is old age*; மூப்பில், *in old age.*

உவர்க்கடலன்னசெல்வருமுளரே,
கிணற்றூற்றன்னநீயுமாருனையே,
செல்வர்தம்பெருந்திரு உறுக-பலபகல்,
நீ வாழியரோநெடிதே ஈயாச்
சிறுவிலைக்காலத்தாயினும்,
உறுபொருடந்தெஞ்சொற்கொள்வோயே.

In plain Tamil, உப்புக்கடலுக்கொப்பானசெல்வர் இருக்கிறார்களே கிணற்றின் ஊற்றுக்கொப்பான நீயும் இருக்கிறாய். அந்தச்செல்வருடைய மிகுந்தசெல்வம் இருக்கட்டும். கொடுக்கிறதற்கேதுவில்லாத சிறுவிலையுள்ள காலமாயிருந்தாலுந்தகுதியான பொருளைக் கொடுத்து எங்கள்கல்விகளைக்கொள்பவனே, நீ பலகாலங்குறையாது வாழக்கடவாய், i. e., *there are rich persons that are like the salt sea; thou art like the fountain of a well. Let the great riches of those rich men alone. Mayst thou for ever prosper without failing, thou, who even at this time of scarcity, when none can give any thing, hast received our instruction, and afforded the needful supply!* This is an address of a Poet to a liberal man whom he compares to the fountain of a well, and praises for his liberality; whilst he calls other rich persons, ironically, the large Ocean, which only yields salt water. உவர் is உப்பு, *salt*; அன்ன is போன்ற, *like*; செல்வர் is செல்வமுடையவர்கள், *the rich*; உளரே is உண்டு, or இருக்கிறார்களே, ஆருனையே is composed of ஆர் the root of ஆருகிறது *to be full*, and உனையே a peculiar appellative noun with a verbal signification in the second person. (See § XXXVII.) the meaning of ஆருனையே is the same as ஆர்ந்திருக்கிறாயே. தம் is தமமுடைய; பெரும் is பெரிய; திரு is மகிமை or செல்வம்; உறுக, is the optative of உறு the same as உறட்டும், i. e., இருக்கட்டும். நீவாழியர், i. e., நீ வாழக்கடவாய். The affix ஓ is merely expletive. நெடிதே, is குறையாதே, *not failing, not diminishing.* பலபகல், *many days, for ever.* ஈயா is the negative participle of ஈகிறது, *to give* and belongs to காலம், *the time in which none is able to give*; சிறுவிலை *is small sale*; and சிறுவிலைக்காலம், *is a time in which there is very little to be sold, a time of scarcity*, உறு is தகுதியான; பொருட்டந்தெஞ் *is* பொருள்தந்து எங்கள்; எஞ்சொல், *is* எங்கள்சொல், *our word* or *instruction*; கொள்வோய் is the poetical form for கொள்பவனே.

13. **Amplification or climax is well suited to the Tamil, thus:**

It is a crime to put a Roman citizen in bonds; it is the height of guilt to scourge him; little less than parricide to put him to death; what name then shall we give to the act of crucifying him? உரோமைபட்டினத்தானை விலங்கிற்போடல் குற்றம், அவனை வாரினால் அடித்தல் மிகுந்த குற்றம் அவனைக்கொலைசெய்தல் பிதாவைக்கொலைசெய்கிறபாதகத்திற்குச்சற்றேதாழ்வாயிருக்கும், அவனைச்சிலுவையில் அறைதலுக்கு எப்படிச்சொல்லலாம்.

After we have practiced good actions a while, they become easy; and when they are easy we begin to take pleasure in them; and when they please us, we do them frequently; and by frequency a thing grows into a habit; and confirmed habit is a kind of a second nature; and so far as any thing is natural, so far it is necessary, and we can hardly do otherwise; nay we do it many times when we do not think of it, சிலகாலம் நற்கிரியைகளைச்செய்துவந்தால் அப்படிச்செய்கிறது தாராளமாகும் தாராளமானபொழுது, அவைகளிற் பிரியமுண்டாகும், பிரியமுண்டானபொழுது, அவைகளை அடிக்கடிசெய்வோம், அடிக்கடிசெய்கிறதினாலே அவைகள் நமக்குவழக்கமாகும், அந்தவழக்கம்நமக்குச்சுபாவமாகும், அது நமக்கு எப்பொழுதும் வேண்டுவதாகும், பின்புநாம்வேறொன்றையும்விரும்பாமலிருப்போம் நாம் நினையாமலிருக்கும்பொழுதும் அப்படியேசெய்வோம்.

79. *Specimen of the Nannul, a part of the 4th rule of the*

சொல்லதிகாரம்.

மக்கடேவர் நாகருயர்திணைமற் றுயிருள்ளவு மில்லவுமஃறிணை, என்னின், நிறுத்தமுறையானேயிருதிணையாமாறுணர்த்திற்று இ-ள. மக்களுந்தேவருநரகருமுயர்திணையாமவையொழிந்த விலங்குமுதலியவுயிருள்ளனவும் நிலநீர்முதலியவுயிரில்லனவுமஃறிணையாமென்றவாறு. மக்கடேவர் நரகரெனப்படுதலவ்வயாக்கையு முயிருங்கூடிநின்றவழி யாதலினவைபிரிந்த வழியும் வேறுசுருதியவழியுமவருயிராயு முடம்பையு முயிரில்லனவாகிய வஃறிணையாக்கொள்ளப்படுமென்க. விலங்குமுதலியவற்றி னுயிருடம்புகளு மன்ன, மக்களாகப்பிறந்து புண்ணிய பாவமியற்றி, யப்புண்ணிய மிகுதியாற்றேவராயும் பாவமிகுதியானரகராயும் பிறத்தலின் மக்கடேவர்நரகரெனச்சாதனசாத்தியமுறையேவைத்தாரென்க. அன்றியுமாசிரியர்தொல்காப்பியர் உயர்திணை யென்மனார்மக்கட்சுட்டே யென்முன்னரக்கூறிப்பின்னரிவ்வெனவறியு மந்தந்தமக்கிலவாகிய தெய்வஞ்சுட்டிய பெயர் முதலியனவுமுயர்திணைமருங்கிற் பால்பிரிந்திசைக்கு மெனக்கூறலி னுயர்திணைப்பாற்படுத்து, மக்கடேவர்நாகருயர்திணை யெனமுறைதெரித்தோதினு ரெனக்கோடலுமாமென்க, திணைநிலங்குலனொழுக்காமென்பவர் கவிற்றிணையென் னும் பலபொரு ளொருசொல்லீண்டுக்குலத்தினை யுணர்த்திநின்றது. உயர்திணையல்லாத்திணை யஃறிணையெனப்பட்டது, இவ்விரண்டும் பண்புத்தொகை. உயர்வாய்குலம் அஃதன்மையவாய்குலமெனவிரியும், &c.

Explanation.

மக்கடேவர்நரகருயர்திணை, மற்றுயிருள்ளவுமில்லவுமஃறிணை என்னின, திறத்தகுமுறையானே யிருதிணையாமாறுணர்த்து.

Analysis: மக்கடேவர் is மக்கள்தேவர்; of which ள த are in the former contracted into ட by the rules of sundhi; மக்கள், means *men;* தேவர், *gods;* and நரகர் *demons* or *devils.* These are உயர்திணை, that is, of the high caste.—உயர் stands for உயர்ந்த, the relative participle, and திணை means *cast, sex.* மற்றுயிருள்ளவுமில்லவும் is மற்ற உயிருள்ளவைகளும் உயிரில்லாதவைகளும், i. e., *the other beings both animate and inanimate*, are அஃறிணை, that is, *not of high caste*, the word is composed of அல்திணை, where லத is changed into அஃறி, அல is the same as அல்லாத and means *not.*

Thus far the rule is in verse. The author then proceeds, and says: என்னின், this is a contraction of என்பது சூத்திரம் அதின்பொருளென்னவெனின்; and contains the beginning and the ending of this sentence, என்பது is a verbal noun introduceing the poetry, and means here as much as *this*, viz., this isthe சூத்திரம், i. e., *the rule; அதின்பொருளென்னவெனின்*, i. e., *if you ask nhat is the import of it?* என்னின், is the same as எனில், *it is this.* திறத்தகுமுறையானே, i. e., according to the above establsshed order, (viz. in the preceding rule) யிருதிணையாமாறு, *the way in which the two castes arise.* உணரத்து, this is a contraction of உணர்த்துதல்நுதலிற்று, containing the first and the last sylables, and means: *It (viz., the rule) declares* or *gives the information.* திறத்த, the infinitive, ought to be திறத்தின, the relative participle of திறத்துகிறது, *to establish;* or it is the relative participle of திறக்கிறது, *to weigh*, and then திறத்தமுறை, means the order which was before weighed or examined and stated. முறையானே is முறையாலே, the ablative of முறை, *order, series;* ஆம் is ஆகும், the relative participle of the future of ஆகிறது, and relates to the following noun, ஆறு, which means *a way* or *manner*, and stands here for the accusative case, governed by உணர்த்துதல், an active verb, signifying *to make to understand, to inform;* it is a verbal noun, and stands here likewise for the accusative case, because of நுதலிற்று, the 3d person singular of the past tense of நுதலுகிறது *to consider, to declare, to point out.* Its governing subject as சூத்திரம், a rule.

The translation of this sentence is thus: *This is (the fourth) rule. Its import is to point out the way in which the two casts arise, according to the order before stated.*

The author then proceeds, இன, which is a contraction of இதின் பொருள் of whioh it is the first and last letters, We must add ஆவது, viz. இதின்பொருளாவது, i. e., *its meaning is this.*

மக்களுந்தேவருநரகருமுயர்திணையாம், i. e., *men, gods and demons are of the high caste, viz.*, words signifying men, &c.

அவரை யொழிந்தவிலங்குமுதலிய வுயிருள்ளனவும்நிலநீர்முதலிய வுயிரில்லனவுமஃறிணையாமென்றவாறு, i. e., *excepting them, (viz.*

the men, gods, &c.,) the beasts and all other animate beings, and land, water, and all other inanimate beings are not of high caste. அவரை is for அவர்களை, referring to the preceding மக்கள், &c., ஒழித்த is the relative participle, belonging to உயிருள்ளன; this stands for உயிருள்ளவைகள், and உயிரில்லன, for உயிரில்லாதவைகள். என்றவாறு is என்றுசொல்லுகிற ஆறு.

மக்கடேவர் நரகரென்னப்படுத லவ்வவ்யாக்கையுமுயிருங்கூடிநின்ற வழியாதலி னவைபிரிந்தவழியும் வேறுகருதியவழியு மவருயிரையு முடம்பையுமுயிரில்லனவாகிய வஃறிணையாகக்கொள்ளப்படுமென்க. The Tamil here is rather obscure; and puzzles even the learned, மக்கடேவர் நரகரென்னப்படுதல், is the nominative case of the sentence, and literally means: *The saying (or calling of) men gods and demons (viz., to be of the high caste* உயர்திணை, *which must be understood.)* Its verb is ஆதலின் i. e., *because it is;* from ஆகிறது, ஆதலின் is the same as ஆகையால். வழி means here இடத்தில், which has the participles கூடிநின்ற, i. e., *in which are united;* அவ்வவ் is அந்தந்த, i. e., *their respective;* யாக்கை is தேகம், *body;* உயிர் *is life* or *the soul;* these nouns are nominatives, governing கூடிநின்ற; அவை *those,* refers to யாக்கை and உயிர், பிரிந்தவழியும் means பிரிந்த இடத்திலும் or பிரிந்த பொழுதும், *when they are separated,* i. e., *when the life or the soul departs from the body;* வேறுகருதியவழியும் means வேறாக்கருதும்பொழுதும், *when we consider them different,* even in life time, i. e., when we consider the body or the soul separately; அவர் is அவர்களுடைய, viz., of the men, gods, and demons; உயிரையும், *the soul,* உடம்பையும் *the body;* these accusative cases are governed by the following கொள்ள, i. e., *to take, to adopt, to accept;* உயிரில்லனவாகிய அஃறிணையாக, i. e., *as* அஃறிணை, or *no cast, which the inanimate beings are,* கொள்ளப்படும், is not the passive voice; but கொள்ள retains its active sense, and படும், is a mere expletive; or means as much as வேண்டும். என்க is the polite imperative, the same as என்பீர்களாக; and means here, as much as என்று அறிவீர்களாக, an address to the students. In plain Tamil, the sentence may be rendered thus; மக்கள் தேவர் நரகரானவர்களுடைய தேகமும் உயிரும்பொருந்தியிருக்கும்பொழுது அவர்கள் உயர்திணையென்று சொல்லப்பட்டிருக்கிறார்கள், அவர்களுடைய தேகமும் உயிரும் பிரிந்துபோகும்பொழுதும், நாம் அவைகளைவேறுவேறாக யோசிக்கும்பொழுதும், அந்தத்தேகமும் உயிரும் உயிரில்லாத அஃறிணையாகக்கொள்ளப்படுமென்று அறிவீர்களாக. *Know that men, gods, and demons are called* உயர்திணை, i. e., *of high caste, when their respective bodies and souls are united together; but when they (viz., the bodies and souls) are separated,* or *considered separately (whilst they are united) their bodies and souls must be taken as* அஃறிணை, i. e., *of no caste, like other inanimate beings.*

விலங்குமுதலியவற்றி னுயிருடம்புகளுமன்ன, analy. விலங்கு is *beast;*

முதலியவற்றின் is முதலானவைகளுடைய. உயிர் *soul,* உடம்பு *body;* the plural termination of the last noun, puts also the first into the same number; உம் means here *also,* or is here the completing conjunction, as there are but two subjects spoken of, the beasts, &c. அன்ன, means *are the same,* அத்தன்மையாயிருக்கின்றன. In plain Tamil, விலங்கு முதலானவைகளினுடைய உயிரும் உடம்பும் அத்தன்மையாகக்கொள்ளப்படும், translated: *the life (*or *soul) and body of beasts,* &c., *have the same character;* viz., have the same gender, (viz., அஃறிணை before mentioned.)

மக்களாகப்பிறந்து புண்ணியபாவமியற்றி யப்புண்ணிய மிகுதியாற்றேவராயும் பாவ மிகுதியானரகராயும் பிறத்தலின் மக்கடேவர் நரகரொனச்சாதன சாத்திய முறையே வைத்தாரொன்க. Anal. மக்களாகப்பிறந்து, *those born as men,* பிறந்து stands for பிறந்தவர்கள். புண்ணிய பாவமியற்றி; புண்ணியம் is *virtue,* பாவம் *sin,* இயற்றி is செய்து or நடப்பித்து *doing* or *performing,* which governs புண்ணியம் and பாவம் in the accusative, for which however the nominative stands; அப்புண்ணியமிகுதியாற்றேவராயும் the oblique case புண்ணிய stands for புண்ணியத்தினுடைய, *of virtue;* மிகுதியால் *by the multitude,* or rather, *the greater multitude;* தேவராயும் *as gods'* பாவமிகுதியானரகராயும்; பாவமிகுதியால் *by the greater multitude of sins;* நரகராயும் *as demons* or *devils;* பிறத்தலின் i. e., பிறத்தலானபடியால், or பிறக்கிறபடியால்; மக்கடேவர்நரகரொன, of which என் is என்று, the conjunction; சாதனசாத்தியமுறையே, of which சாதனம் means *the cause,* சாத்தியம் *the effect,* முறை, order, முறையே *in the order;* வைத்தார் *he* (viz. the author of the rule) *has put;* என்க is என்பீர்களாக, or என்று அறிவீர்களாக. In plain Tamil, மனிதர்களாகப்பிறந்தவர்கள் புண்ணியத்தையும் பாவத்தையும் நடப்பித்துப்புண்ணியத்தினுடைய மிகுதியினாலே தேவராயும் பாவத்தினுடையமிகுதியினால் நரகராயும்பிறக்கிறபடியினாலே, அவர்களை மக்கள் தேவர் நரகரொன்று சாதனசாத்தியத்தின் முறையே வைத்தாரொன்று அறிவீர்களாக. Translated, *beings born as men, perform virtuous and sinful actions; and by the abundance of virtuous actions are born as gods, and by the abundance of sinful actions are born as devils; know that for this cause, (the author of the rule) has placed men, gods, and devils in this manner, according to the natural order of cause and effect.*

அன்றியுமாசிரியர் தொல்காப்பியர் உயர்திணையென்மனார் மக்கட சுட்டேயென முன்னரக்கூறிப்பின்னரிவ்வெனவறியுமந்தந் தமக்கிலவாகிய செய்வஞ் சுட்டியபெயர் முதலியனவுமுயர் திணைமருங்கிற்பால் பிரிந்திசைக்குமெனக்கூறவினுயர் திணைப்பாற்படுத்துமக்கடேவர் நரகருயர்திணையென முறைதெரித்தோதினொனக்கோடலுமாமென்க. Anal: ஆசிரியர் தொல்காப்பியர், *The teacher* or *Professor Tolkapiyer,* முன்னர் *in the first plaee;* கூறி *has declared,* or *stated;* என for என்று *that;* என்மனார் i. e., என்று

சொல்லுவார்கள் ; the nominative to this verb is not expressed and must be understood, viv. முன்னோர்கள் *the ancients ;* for மக்கள் மக்களை, *men ;* உயர்திணை for உயர்திணையாக, *to be of the high caste ;* சுட்டே is the root of the verb சுட்டுகிறது, i. e., குறிக்கிறது, and stands here for சுட்டுகிறதை or சுட்டுகிறநாமங்களை ; ஏ is expletive. பின்னர், *afterwards,* கூறலின், i. e., கூறினபடியால், *because he declared,* என, for என்று *that,* இவ்வெனவறியுமந்தம், of which அந்தம் means *the end,* viz., the terminations of a word otherwise called விகுதி ; அறியும் the future participle, *by which (we) know,* இவ்வென for இன்னதென்று, *what (sex) it is,* தமக்கிலவாகியதெய்வஞ்சுட்டியபெயர்முதலியனவும், of which தமக்கிலவாகிய is for தமக்கில்லாததாகிய, *which* (viz., the termination or அந்தம்) *is not to them,* தமக்கு is the reciprocal pronoun referring to the following தெய்வஞ்சுட்டியபெயர்முதலியனவும், i. e., the names, &c. &c., of the gods, சுட்டிய is குறித்த, governing தெய்வம் in the accusative case ; முதலியனவும் is முதலியவைகளும், and becomes the nominative to இசைக்கும் which means காட்டும், i. e., *they show,* முதலியன however is here perfectly unnecessary, தெய்வஞ்சுட்டியபேர்கள் or நாமங்கள் is quite sufficient ; or தெய்வம்முதலான்பேர்கள் ; உயர்திணை மருங்கில், i. e., *at the high cast ;* or மருங்கில் *at,* stands for சார்ந்து, உயர்திணையைச்சார்ந்து, பால் for பாலை the gender, governed by இசைக்கும். பிரிந்து means here வெவ்வேறாக, i. e., *separately,* உயர்திணைபால் is உயர்திணையிடத்தில், படுத்து is சேர்த்து, மக்கடேவர் நரகருயர்திணையென் முறைதெரித்தோதினோர், of which முறை stands for முறையை, *the order* or *class,* தெரித்து is அறிவித்து, and ஓதினோர் is சொன்னோர் ; என is என்று, *that ;* கோடலுமாம், consists of கோடல், உம் and ஆம் ; கோடல் is a contraction of கொள்தல், i. e., கொள்ளுதல், the first short vowel being changed into a long one ; உம் is the conjunction, *also,* and ஆம் is ஆகும், and என்க is என்பீர்களாக or என்று அறிவீர்களாக. In plain Tamil: அன்றியும் முன்னோர்கள் மனிதரை உயர்திணையாகக்குறித்தார்களென்று ஆசிரியராகியதொல்காப்பியர் முன்னரக்கூறிப்பின்பு கூறினதெல்லாவென்றால், இன்னபாலென்று காட்டும் விகுதிகளில்லாத தேவர்களைக்குறிக்கிறநாமங்கள் உயர்திணையைச்சார்ந்து பாலை வெவ்வேறாகக்காட்டுமென்று கூறினபடியினாலே, அந்தத்தேவர்களுடைய பேரை உயர்திணையினிடத்திற் சேர்த்து, மக்களுந்தேவரும்நரகருமாகிய இவர்கள் உயர்திணையென்றுமுறையையறிவித்துச்சொன்னாரென்று கொள்ளவும் வேண்டுமென்று அறிவீர்களாக. Translated, *know further, that the teacher Tolkapiyer having first declared, that the ancients denoted* மக்கள் *(or men) to be of high caste, afterwards declared also, that the names of the gods, having no terminations showing, of what gender they are, belong to the high caste, and show the gender separately ; and therefore he (viz., the author) added the names of the gods to the high caste, and taught that men, gods, and demons are of high caste. This also must be adopted.*

திணை நிலங்குலமொழுக்கா மென்பவாகலிற்றிணை யென்னும் பலபொருளொருசொல்லீண்டுக்குலத்தினையுணர்த்தி நின்றது. Anal: திணை stands for திணையானது, i. e., *the word* திணை, ஆம் or ஆகும் means here *signifies*, நிலம் *land* or *place*; குலன் or குலம் *sex* or *class*; ஒழுக்கு *order*, என்ப is என்பர் or என்றுசொல்லுவார்கள், ஆகலில் is ஆகையால், which however is not necessary here, திணையென்னும் பலபொருளொருசொல், i. e., பலபொருளுள்ள திணையென்னுஞ்சொல், *the word* திணை *having various significations*, ஈண்டு is இவ்விடத்தில், here, குலத்தினை is குலத்தை *the sex* or *class*, உணர்த்தி i. e., காட்டி, நின்றது, is for நிற்கிறது or இருக்கிறது. In plain Tamil, திணையானது நிலத்தையுங்குலத்தையும் ஒழுக்கையுங்குறிக்கின்றதென்று போதகர் சொல்லுகிறபடியினாலே பலபொருளுள்ளதிணையென்னுஞ்சொல், இவ்விடத்தில் குலமென்பதைக்காட்டியிருக்கின்றது. Translated: *as the teachers declare that the word* திணை *signifies place, sex, and order, that word* திணை *having several significations, means here (or in this rule)* குலம், *that is, sex or class.*

உயர்திணையல்லாத்திணை யஃறிணை யென்னப்பட்டது. This is clear, Translated, *the* திணை, *which is not* உயர்திணை, *is called* அஃறிணை.

இவ்விரண்டும்பண்புத்தொகை. Anal. இவ்விரண்டும், *these two*, viz., உயர்திணை and அஃறிணை, பண்பு is குணம் or adjective, and stands here for பண்பின்உருபு, or the mark of an adjective, தொகை is *contraction*. In plain Tamil, இவ்விரண்டு சொற்களும் பண்பின் உருபமில்லாமற்சுருங்கிநிற்கின்றன. Translated: *These two words* (உயர்திணை *and* அஃறிணை) *have not the form of the adjective, expressed*, referring to the words உயர் and அஃ or அல்.

உயர்வாயகுலம் அஃதன்மையவாயகுலமென்றுவிரியும். Anal. உயர்வாய is உயர்வாகிய *that which is high;* அஃதன்மை is அல்லாதவைகள் *those which are not*, viz., *of the high cast*, ஆயகுலம் is ஆகியகுலம், என is என்று, விரியும் *it is explained*, viz., the தொகை. In plain Tamil: அந்தத்தொகையை விரித்தால், உயர்வாகிய குலமென்றும் அல்லாதவைகளாகிய குலமெனறும் வரும். Translated, *if those two words are explained, or written without contraction, it will be, the caste which is high, and the caste which is not of that high caste.*

FINIS.